RUNNING FOR FREEDOM

About the Author

Steven F. Lawson was professor of history at Rutgers University from 1998 to 2009 and is now professor emeritus. From 1992 to 1998 he was professor and head of the History Department at the University of North Carolina at Greensboro. Before then, he taught for 20 years at the University of South Florida in Tampa. He has received fellowships from the National Endowment for the Humanities, the American Council of Learned Societies, and the National Humanities Center. He has served as an adviser to the television documentary series *Eyes on the Prize* and has participated as a historical consultant on voting rights cases. His publications include *Black Ballots: Voting Rights in the South, 1944–1969* (1976), which was awarded the Phi Alpha Theta best first-book prize; *In Pursuit of Power: Southern Blacks and Electoral Politics, 1965–1982* (1985); *Civil Rights Crossroads: Nation, Community and the Black Freedom Struggle* (2003); *To Secure These Rights: The Report of President Harry S. Truman's Committee on Civil Rights* (2004), and numerous articles and essays on the civil rights movement and politics. Along with Nancy Hewitt he has published the documentary textbook *Exploring American Histories: A Brief Survey with Sources* (2013).

RUNNING FOR FREEDOM

Civil Rights and Black Politics in America since 1941

Fourth Edition

Steven F. Lawson

This fourth edition first published 2015
© 2015 John Wiley & Sons, Inc

Edition history: McGraw-Hill Publishers, Inc (1e, 1990 and 2e 1996),
John Wiley & Sons Inc (3e 2009)

Registered Office
John Wiley & Sons, Ltd, The Atrium, Southern Gate, Chichester, West Sussex, PO19 8SQ, UK

Editorial Offices
350 Main Street, Malden, MA 02148-5020, USA
9600 Garsington Road, Oxford, OX4 2DQ, UK
The Atrium, Southern Gate, Chichester, West Sussex, PO19 8SQ, UK

For details of our global editorial offices, for customer services, and for information about how
to apply for permission to reuse the copyright material in this book please see our website at
www.wiley.com/wiley-blackwell.

The right of Steven F. Lawson to be identified as the author of this work has been asserted in
accordance with the UK Copyright, Designs and Patents Act 1988.

Library of Congress Cataloging-in-Publication Data

Lawson, Steven F., 1945–
    Running for freedom : civil rights and black politics in America since 1941 / Steven F. Lawson. –
Fourth edition.
        pages   cm
    Includes bibliographical references and index.
    ISBN 978-1-118-83654-5 (pbk.)
    1. African Americans–Civil rights.   2. African Americans–Politics and government.
3. Civil rights movements–United States–History–20th century.   4. United States–Politics
and government–20th century.   I. Title.
    E185.61.L38 2015
    323.1196′073–dc23

                                        2014017308

A catalogue record for this book is available from the British Library.

Cover image: President Barack Obama and first lady Michelle Obama walk in the
Inaugural Parade during the 57th Presidential Inauguration in Washington, January 21, 2013.
Photo AP Photo/Charles Dharapak/Press Association

Set in 10.5/13pt Minion by SPi Publisher Services, Pondicherry, India
Printed and bound in Malaysia by Vivar Printing Sdn Bhd

1   2015

For Nancy and Scooter, best friends both

Contents

List of Images

Preface to the Fourth Edition

Winning is new people running.
Winning is also new voters.
Winning is more young voters.
Winning is providing hope. ...
We're not just running for an office.
We're running for freedom.

(Jesse Jackson, "On Winning," 1984)

In the more than five decades since the civil rights movement achieved some of the most momentous reforms of the twentieth century, scholars have produced a rich body of literature detailing the battle for racial and political equality. Initially, most of the works focused on the activities of major civil rights organizations and leaders and their efforts to enact national legislation, gain presidential support, and win litigation before the federal courts. In general, they concentrated on the responses of government institutions and officials to demands for social change. Subsequently, a second generation of scholarly studies shifted the emphasis away from powerful leaders, interest groups, and agencies to indigenous mass movements, seeking to discover their unique structures, ideologies, strategies, and tactics. From this perspective, black protest and politics are not viewed primarily as a struggle for obtaining civil rights laws in the national arena but for liberating black communities at the grassroots level.

As scholarly inquiry refocused the vision of this struggle "from the bottom up," it is appropriate to consider how efforts at the local level intersected with those on the national stage. Both national civil rights campaigns aimed at legislation and litigation and community organizing directed toward consciousness-raising were part of a larger process of empowerment. In an interconnected way, the civil rights movement altered local black institutions and shaped national goals; in turn, the actions of the federal government and established civil rights groups transformed local communities in the process of expanding freedom.

An interpretive synthesis, this book examines the freedom struggle and black political development since the beginning of World War II. Moving along two tracks, the national and the local, this study attempts to gauge the connections between the two. Pressure from below ultimately pushed the federal government to challenge disfranchisement. Northern blacks, whose votes swung the balance of power in close national elections, demanded that lawmakers remedy the plight of blacks deprived of their rights in the South. The urgency of a response became greater as southern blacks, prevented from registering their discontent at the polls, used nonviolent civil disobedience to spark crises, forcing the national government to come to their aid. In organizing against racism, the civil rights movement mobilized blacks for political action and prepared the way for extensive black participation in the electoral process following the passage of the 1965 Voting Rights Act.

The franchise figured prominently in the thinking of both white officials and black protesters, though in different ways. White leaders saw the ballot as a means of promoting orderly social change during a period when black protests and hostile white reactions to them threatened civic peace and the legitimacy of democratic institutions. Blacks considered the franchise less as an implement of social cohesion and more as a weapon for destroying racist institutions and encouraging liberation. In pursuit of group power, African Americans marshaled their forces to elect candidates of their own race, a preference that has highlighted the conflict between proportional representation and color-blind politics, between affirmative action and traditional notions of political equality.

Since 1941, the political system has been opened up, gradually though sometimes dramatically, to active minority participation, and black Americans are working through it to acquire the advantages long denied them. Consequently, they have come to rely much less on the tactics of agitation and confrontation employed so effectively during the civil rights struggle and to depend more on the process of bargaining and compromise associated with professional politics. As a result, increased electoral power at the local level and influence at the national level generally have come at the expense of mass-based activism. Many black leaders made the transition from the civil rights battlefield to the electoral arena, but they had to heed the realities of practical politics. Furthermore, despite considerable progress, the political system has only partially settled black grievances, especially those related to economic deprivation. Race has not disappeared as a divisive element, and polarization of the electorate often stands in the way of further resolution of critical problems.

Whatever these limitations, the quest for freedom over the past half-century released blacks from serving as passive objects of white domination and forged them into active agents striving to shape their own political destinies. Much of this story necessarily focuses on the South, where the civil rights movement originated and tested its most innovative political strategies. Yet the problems of racial inequality and political powerlessness were not confined to any one region, but were national in scope. Though they did not have to reacquire the ballot, as was the case in the South, northern blacks nonetheless had to struggle to mobilize their communities to compete successfully for electoral office and obtain political legitimacy. In doing so, they joined black southerners in trying to redefine the meaning of success and to infuse American politics with a greater dose of democratic participation.

For this fourth edition, I have provided some new material on the George W. Bush administration in Chapter 9, but more substantially I have added a new chapter (10) on the presidential election of Barack Obama, his first term in office, his reelection in 2012, and the first year of his second term. In addition to his two presidential elections, this chapter includes a discussion of the 2010 midterm elections, which produced a Republican majority in the House of Representatives and in statehouses across the nation; the impact of the killing of Trayvon Martin and the subsequent trial of George Zimmerman; the commemorations of the fiftieth anniversary of the March on Washington; and state voter suppression efforts and the Supreme Court's weakening of the Voting Rights Act. Indeed, I have tried to make this new concluding chapter up-to-date, though it necessarily remains a work in progress, as events continue to unfold even as these words are written.

Acknowledgments

I would like to acknowledge my debt to the many scholars of civil rights history and black politics whose fine works I have drawn on. The bibliographical essay at the end of the book is not only a guide for readers but also an expression of appreciation to the many authors from whom I have benefited.

Writing this edition constitutes something of an archaeological expedition into my career as a historian. The first edition coincided with my tenure at the University of South Florida; the second my years at the University of North Carolina-Greensboro; and the third my ten years at Rutgers. Although this fourth edition comes in my retirement from academic teaching and service, it evidences my continuing presence as a historian. For persuading me to undertake this latest edition, I thank Peter Coveney at Wiley-Blackwell, who has been a delight to work with over many years.

The silk thread weaving all four editions together is Nancy Hewitt. Without her generosity, sharp intellect and editorial skills, and her unflagging patience this book would have been impossible to write.

Steven F. Lawson
Metuchen, New Jersey

Abbreviations Used in the Text

ACA   Affordable Care Act
ACORN   Association for Community Organizations for Reform Now
ARRA   American Recovery and Reinvestment Act
BPP   Black Panther Party
CAP   Community Action Program
CBC   Congressional Black Caucus
CETA   Comprehensive Employment and Training Act
CIO   Congress of Industrial Organizations
COFO   Council of Federated Organizations
CORE   Congress of Racial Equality
DCVL   Dallas County Voters League
EEOC   Equal Employment Opportunity Commission
FEMA   Federal Emergency Management Agency
FEPC   Fair Employment Practice Committee
LCFO   Lowndes County Freedom Organization
MFDP   Mississippi Freedom Democratic Party
MIA   Montgomery Improvement Association
MOWM   March on Washington Movement
NAACP   National Association for the Advancement of Colored People
NACGN   National Association of Colored Graduate Nurses
NAG   Nonviolent Action Group
NCBCP   National Coalition on Black Civic Participation
NCLB   No Child Left Behind
NUL   National Urban League
PDP   Progressive Democratic Party
PLO   Palestine Liberation Organization
POWER   People Organized for Welfare and Employment Rights
PUSH   People United to Save Humanity

SCHW	Southern Conference for Human Welfare
SCLC	Southern Christian Leadership Conference
SNCC	Student Nonviolent Coordinating Committee
UFT	United Federation of Teachers
VA	Veterans Administration
VEP	Voter Education Project
VISTA	Volunteers in Service to America

1

World War II and the Origins of the Freedom Struggle

For African Americans, the ultimate aim of politics, either protest or electoral, has been liberation. Seeking emancipation from the bondage of white supremacy, disfranchised southern blacks challenged the political system for admission, even as they hoped to transform it by their participation. Civil rights proponents have long believed that blacks could not be free without obtaining the right to vote. At the turn of the century, W. E. B. Du Bois set the standard for rejecting racial solutions that excluded the exercise of the franchise. Attacking Booker T. Washington for his strategy of postponing black participation at the ballot box, Du Bois insisted that the right to vote was intimately connected to first-class citizenship. Without it blacks would never command respect, protect themselves, and feel pride in their own race. To Du Bois, a scholar of the freedom struggle after the Civil War, Reconstruction provided vivid evidence that black elected officials could transform the lives of their constituents. From this experience they derived the historical lesson, summarized by Eric Foner, that "it was in politics that blacks articulated a new vision of the American state, calling upon government, both national and local, to take upon itself new and unprecedented responsibilities for protecting the civil rights of individual citizens."

The long history to obtain the right to vote suggests that reenfranchisement was considered the decisive first step toward political equality. Civil rights proponents expected participation at the polls to yield the kinds of basic benefits that groups exercising the franchise customarily enjoyed. Yet, for black Americans, much more was at stake. With their systematic exclusion from the electoral process, the simple acquisition of the vote constituted an

Running for Freedom: Civil Rights and Black Politics in America since 1941,
Fourth Edition. Steven F. Lawson.
© 2015 John Wiley & Sons, Inc. Published 2015 by John Wiley & Sons, Inc.

essential element of liberation from enforced racial subordination. The political scientist Charles V. Hamilton, who studied the voting rights struggle both as a participant and as a scholar, found this passion for the ballot very understandable. "White America had spent so much effort denying the vote to blacks," he observed, "that there was good reason to believe that they must be protecting some tool of vast importance. Perhaps it was reasonable to put so much emphasis on the one fundamental process that clearly distinguished first-class from second-class citizens."

Victory at Home and Abroad

Going off to war in the months after Pearl Harbor, black GIs might very well have pondered the connection between politics and freedom. They had many reasons to wonder about the principles of the democratic creed and their promise of first-class citizenship for all. Like their white counterparts they remembered December 7, 1941, when Dorie Miller, a black sailor, performed heroic deeds that would win him the Navy Cross; but they also carried with them the memory of Sikeston, Missouri, where on January 25, 1942, a black prisoner named Cleo Wright was taken out of the local jail and cruelly burned and lynched by a white mob. Unlike Japan and its Axis partners, which were eventually defeated on the battlefield and forced to accept unconditional surrender, the killers of Cleo Wright were never brought to justice. Helping to combat fascism abroad, black fighting men and the families they left behind also demanded unconditional surrender from the forces of racism at home. Blacks failed to persuade the American government to wage total war in their behalf, but they did lay the groundwork for continuing the battle in the decades to come.

This determination to stand up for their rights, strengthened by World War II, grew out of both disillusionment and optimism. In response to Woodrow Wilson's pledge during World War I to make the world safe for democracy, blacks had followed the advice of Du Bois to "close ranks [and] while this war lasts, forget our special grievances." Rather than freedom, the end of the war produced bloody race riots and a continuation of Jim Crow practices. At the same time, African Americans refused to plunge into despair and experienced instead a heightening of racial consciousness. The Harlem Renaissance and the black nationalist movement spearheaded by Marcus Garvey explored the roots of black identity and helped forge renewed racial solidarity. A. Philip Randolph organized workers into the

Figure 1 Dorie Miller receiving the Navy Cross from Admiral Chester Nimitz. Miller was later killed in action. (Photo courtesy US National Archives)

Brotherhood of Sleeping Car Porters and not only fought for economic benefits from employers but also challenged racial discrimination within the trade union movement. In addition, the National Association for the Advancement of Colored People (NAACP), an interracial organization founded in 1909, kept alive the battle for equal rights by lobbying Congress to enact an antilynching bill and petitioning the Supreme Court to outlaw disfranchisement measures such as the white primary.

The Great Depression provided unexpected opportunities for black advancement. Franklin D. Roosevelt's New Deal extended economic relief to the one-third of the nation that was ill housed, ill clothed, and ill fed, which included blacks as well as poor whites. Blacks profited from these programs because of their poverty, not because of their race; in fact, many New Deal agencies, especially in the South, were administered to preserve prevailing racial practices that maintained blacks in a subordinate position. For example, programs for federal housing construction contained provisions guaranteeing segregation in the North as well as the South. Despite the perpetuation of racial discrimination and the unwillingness of President Roosevelt to fight for special civil rights measures, African Americans welcomed federal assistance. "Any time people are out of work, in poverty, have lost their savings," Du Bois remarked, "any kind of a 'deal' that helps them is going to be favored."

Blacks showed their appreciation by abandoning their traditional allegiance to the Republican Party of Abraham Lincoln and hopping aboard the Roosevelt bandwagon. This realignment was facilitated by the appointment of blacks to federal posts, a sufficient number to convene an informal "black kitchen cabinet" in Washington. Whites sensitive to racial concerns headed several New Deal agencies and worked to see that relief was distributed more fairly. Furthermore, Roosevelt's selections to the Supreme Court after 1937 paved the way for a constitutional revolution that augured well for NAACP attorneys preparing a legal assault upon racial discrimination. Most of all, the President's wife, Eleanor, nurtured the growing attachment African Americans felt toward the Roosevelt administration. Mrs. Roosevelt's commitment to civil rights was far greater than her husband's, and she served as an ally in the White House to see that complaints of black leaders received a hearing in the Oval Office. This combination of racial gestures and economic rewards led the majority of the black electorate to vote for Roosevelt beginning in 1936.

On the eve of World War II, blacks stood poised to consolidate their gains and press ahead for full equality. Their political agenda included an end to job discrimination, which helped keep black unemployment at a high 11 percent in 1940; legislation to empower the federal government to prosecute lynchers and to abolish the poll tax on voting imposed by eight southern states; the destruction of the lily-white Democratic primary; and the abandonment of the principle of "separate but equal" that actually produced segregated and unequal treatment in the armed forces, public education, and public accommodations. As the prospect of war increased, black aspirations collided with the reality of pervasive discrimination in a country where mobilization for war came first.

National defense took priority over racial equality in the armed services. As the nation inched closer to the side of the Allies and prepared to join them in war, the army maintained its customary policy of segregation, the navy recruited blacks only as messmates, and the marines and Army Air Corps generally excluded them. When pressed by black leaders for integration of the military in the fall of 1940, President Roosevelt refused to alter practices that had "been proved satisfactory over a long period of years." Instead, he directed the utilization of "the services of negroes ... on a fair and equitable basis." To do otherwise, he and his advisers believed, would risk upsetting white soldiers and would lower their morale, thereby jeopardizing the war effort.

The attempt to make the system of racial separation operate more equally failed to solve the problem. Black GIs assigned to military bases in the South encountered segregation both on and off the bases. Conforming to the law and customs of the surrounding communities, the military enforced segregation in recreation clubs, theaters, and post exchanges. In one camp, a sign on a chapel announced religious services for "Catholics Jews, Protestants, Negroes." When they received passes to travel into town, black soldiers rode on segregated buses and used Jim Crow facilities. With the population of many towns swollen with servicemen, an intolerable strain was placed on public transportation and accommodations. Crowded transit systems often led to pushing and shoving between black and white passengers, frequently ending in violence. In July 1942, a black army private in Beaumont, Texas, refused to vacate his seat in a section of a bus reserved for whites. After his arrest, he was shot by white patrolmen while in their custody. Racial incidents such as this were becoming increasingly commonplace throughout the South that year, culminating in a riot in Alexandria, Louisiana, in which 28 blacks were wounded and nearly 3,000 arrested.

Among the black soldiers encountering wartime discrimination was Jackie Robinson. Having attended the University of California at Los Angeles before entering the service, Robinson excelled in basketball, track, baseball, and football, a sport in which he was named as a college All-American. However, these accomplishments did not guarantee him an easy time in the army. When military officials attempted to keep him out of Officers' Candidate School at Fort Riley, Kansas, he successfully complained and gained admission to the program. Despite his athletic prowess, Robinson was barred because of his race from playing on the baseball team at the army training camp. In protest, he refused to join the football team, which was open to blacks. In 1944, Lieutenant Robinson again challenged unfair racial treatment. While stationed at Ford Hood, Texas, he steadfastly refused to follow a bus driver's order that he sit in the back of the vehicle with the other black passengers. Subjected to a military court martial for his defiance of local segregationist customs, the former All-American athlete was found innocent.

As a soldier, Robinson did not act alone in challenging racial discrimination in the armed forces. On the eve of America's entry into the war, civil rights groups such as the NAACP and National Urban League, along with the Negro press and black college officials, campaigned to break down the barriers that kept the Army Air Corps from accepting black pilots. The War Department believed blacks incapable of flying aircraft. One report claimed that the "colored race does not have the technical nor the flying background for the creation of a bombardment-type unit." Nevertheless, persistent pressure and the negative publicity tarnishing the nation's democratic war aims led the War Department in 1941 to agree to train African-American pilots. The black fighter squadron remained segregated from white pilots, prompting criticism from the NAACP and the black press, which favored the cessation of racial criteria in the military. The *Pittsburgh Courier* blasted the Jim Crow policy as "a citadel to the theory that there can be segregation without discrimination." Yet, by the end of the war, the exploits of the Tuskegee Airmen had made African Americans swell with pride. Stationed at Tuskegee army airfield in Alabama, on the grounds of an abandoned graveyard, black pilots eventually took to the skies over Europe and proved their skills in fighting the Nazis.

However, both overseas and at home, the Tuskegee Airmen battled racial discrimination. They fought against the military command's thinking that they could not make talented fighter pilots in combat, and they challenged segregated facilities on military posts in the United States. At the Tuskegee training center, the airmen conducted a successful sit-in protest to desegregate accommodations on the base. In response, Colonel Noel F. Parish discarded segregated signs, invited popular entertainers to lift the troop's morale, and desegregated the mess hall. At other military posts black pilots were segregated in the mess halls and movie theaters, while German prisoners of war who were quartered at the camps took seats in the "whites only" areas of these accommodations, an outrage black soldiers protested. Indeed, enemy prisoners of war could attend shows, movies, and dances, sponsored by the United Service Organizations (USO) and local chambers of commerce, which were barred to black soldiers. The situation was much the same once the soldiers left the military posts. In one highly charged incident, black airmen taking leave from Walterboro army airfield in South Carolina stopped to eat in a racially restricted café in nearby Fairfax, and were denied service. Brimming with anger, they told the white owner to "go to hell," brandished their service revolvers, and left the restaurant shouting the mock-salute, "Heil Hitler!" Slightly more successful, in November 1944, Walterboro airmen, spending a leave in Washington, DC, integrated the District of Columbia's airport cafeteria after having been first turned away. They may have received service out of deference to their military uniforms, because the airport resumed segregation in its accommodations once the war ended.

Protests also surfaced at Selfridge Field just outside of Detroit. On January 1, 1944, black officers teamed in groups of three at intervals throughout the day attempted to integrate the racially restricted officer's club. Although one group gained admission, the soldiers were soon ordered to leave by the base commander. The protest resumed the next day, but the club remained barred to blacks. One of the leaders of the challenge was Lieutenant Milton Henry from Philadelphia, who had had previous confrontations with segregation. In the spring of 1942, Henry had a run-in with a Montgomery, Alabama bus driver when he refused his order to sit in the rear of the vehicle. Henry demanded his nickel fare back and punched the driver in the mouth. The driver pulled out a gun, and the two began a struggle that spilled out onto the street. Henry managed to escape, but was sent to the military stockade for a brief period. A year later, he was stationed at Selfridge and helped plan the organized protests. The persistent Henry lodged a complaint with the War Department, which resulted in an investigation of racial discrimination at the airfield, under the direction of General Benjamin O. Davis, the military's highest ranking African-American officer. The report confirmed the protesters' charges, and the War Department ordered a reprimand for Selfridge's commander. However, Henry faced reprisals. In 1944, air force officials prosecuted him for insubordination in an incident unrelated to the officer's club demonstration. He was found guilty and discharged from the army on August 10.

An even more serious brouhaha occurred in April 1945, when Colonel Robert Selway ordered that the officers' club at Freeman Field in Seymour, Indiana, remain segregated. The policy sparked a challenge from members of the 477th Bombardment Group who were stationed there. Previously, black soldiers had staged a protest when Selway insisted on separating the races in the base's movie theater. Black airmen and their white sympathizers initiated "Operation Checkboard," and when the lights went down the soldiers switched seats so that they were sitting next to each other under cover of darkness. On April 5, 1945, several groups of black officers defied Selway's Jim Crow regulations and proceeded to enter the "whites-only" Club Number Two. In turn, the colonel had them arrested and proceeded to court-martial over one hundred African- American officers. The beleaguered airmen wired Secretary of War Henry Stimson that the continuation of segregation "can hardly be reconciled with the world wide struggle for freedom for which we are asked and are willing to lay down our lives." By this point in the war, the army high brass, under pressure from the NAACP and the black press, had grown less tolerant of overt racial discrimination, especially within its officers' corps, and set nearly all the accused airmen free. Nevertheless, General Frank O. Hunter, the commander of the First Air Force and a Georgia native who supported Jim Crow, convinced the War Department to approve the court martials of three of the protesters, Lieutenant Robert Terry, Lieutenant Shirley Clinton, and Lieutenant Marsden Thompson. The military panels acquitted Clinton and Marsden, but found Terry guilty; however, he received a light fine. At the same time, the army punished Colonel Selway and relieved him of the command of Freeman Field.

Meanwhile, African-American women endeavored to open up the military to women. Mabel Keaton Staupers, the director of the National Association of Colored Graduate Nurses (NACGN), tried to break down the rigid quota set by the military for employing African-American nurses. Despite a severe shortage of army nurses, the War Department refused to draft a large number of black nurses. By 1943, however, Staupers had managed to get the army to increase the number of military nurses from 56 to 160, chosen mainly to attend to black soldiers. Within the next two years, having recruited First Lady Eleanor Roosevelt to her side, Staupers succeeded in persuading the War Department to draft all qualified nurses, regardless or race, to serve in the army Nurse Corps. Mabel K. Staupers, Darlene Clark Hine wrote in summing up her accomplishments, "played the … active, highly visible role of 'interpreting the Negro nurse' to the general public and marshaling the mass support so essential to their short-run struggle for equal education, fair employment opportunities, and professional integration."

Black civilians also encountered blatant racial prejudice as they sought employment in wartime industries. Blacks had been especially hard hit by the Depression, and as the economy geared up for war production after 1940 they looked forward to taking their places in the booming factories. They had to wait in line, however, behind millions of unemployed white workers who were the first choice of employers. When African Americans showed up looking for work at aircraft plants, they were informed that "the Negro will be considered only as janitors and in other similar capacities." Of 100,000 aircraft workers in 1940, only 240 were black. In related electrical and rubber industries, black employees constituted a meager 1 percent and 3 percent of the workforce. The federal government, which let out war contracts and could have challenged discriminatory hiring practices, collaborated with employers in reinforcing them. According to the policy of the United States

Employment Service, "white-only" requests for defense labor would be filled in conformity with "the social pattern of the local community."

That whites did not intend the war to alter race relations was demonstrated in several other ways as well. Though the process of storing blood plasma was developed by a black scientist, Dr. Charles Drew, the Red Cross refused to mix donations of whites and blacks in their blood banks. In Tennessee, those blacks who wanted to fight for their country experienced difficulty in getting enlisted by all-white selective service centers. Refusing to appoint blacks to sit on draft boards, the governor of the state explained: "This is a white man's country. The Negro had nothing to do with the settling of America." In neighboring Mississippi, to avoid any suggestion that the war against totalitarianism overseas was meant to affect the status of blacks at home, the state legislature ordered the deletion of all references to voting, elections, and democracy in textbooks used in black schools.

Despite these racist setbacks, most blacks supported the war effort and responded to the global conflict, as did other patriotic Americans. One survey revealed that 66 percent of blacks considered that they had a great stake in the outcome of the war and 43 percent felt that they would be better off than before. Though daring victories of nonwhite Japanese over Caucasians early in the war inspired admiration in many blacks, the majority realized what would happen if the Axis powers emerged victorious. "If Hitler wins," the NAACP pointed out, "every right we now possess and for which we have struggled here in America for three centuries will be instantaneously wiped out." At least if the Allies triumphed black Americans would be free to continue fighting for their democratic rights. Desiring full participation as American citizens, they had no real difficulty choosing which side they were on.

Nevertheless, blacks remained sorely troubled by the discrimination they encountered at home. Their loyalty was not at issue, but as one knowledgeable observer declared, many blacks displayed a "lack of enthusiasm for a war which they did not believe is being fought for true democratic principles." Lloyd Brown, a black soldier stationed in Salina, Kansas, who was refused service at a restaurant that admitted German prisoners of war, poignantly expressed his disappointment: "If we were *untermenschen* [subhuman species] in Nazi Germany they would break our bones. As 'colored' men in Salina, they only break our hearts." That a fascist victory would exact a higher price than an Allied one was acknowledged by African Americans; yet this awareness did not bring contentment. No greater slogan of despair over the gap between the democratic creed and discriminatory practice existed than in the sardonic statement popular at the time: "Here lies a black man killed fighting a yellow man for the protection of a white man."

Cynical yet hopeful, African Americans used the war to pursue their own political aims. While blacks sought to defend their country on foreign battlefields alongside other American citizens, they also intended to open up a second front for freedom at home. Wartime ideology extolling the virtues of the "four freedoms" and denouncing the doctrines of Aryan racism was not lost upon blacks. On January 16, 1943, a black newspaper, the *Baltimore Afro-American*, published a "Draftee's Prayer," a poem that tersely summed up the twin goals black soldiers fought for:

> So while I fight
> Wrong over there
> See that my folks
> Are treated fair.

Black leaders agreed, and seized the opportunity to turn America's lofty pronouncements to their advantage. Shortly after Pearl Harbor, Walter White, the executive secretary of the NAACP, asserted that "declarations of war do not lessen the obligation to preserve and extend civil liberties here while the fight is being made to restore freedom from dictatorship abroad." These sentiments were echoed in the pages of the *Pittsburgh Courier*, a black newspaper that mounted a campaign for the "double V," victory at home and overseas. In this way, the black press not only reflected the increasing militancy of its readers but also reinforced black support for the war against the fascists. Not willing to postpone their egalitarian demands as they had during World War I, blacks planned to attack "the principle and practice of compulsory segregation in our American society."

This new assertiveness on behalf of full equality had its most powerful expression in the March on Washington Movement (MOWM). Organized by A. Philip Randolph, the militant trade union leader, the MOWM represented both the exclusiveness of racial pride and the integration of blacks into the mainstream of American life. The group barred whites from participation not out of prejudice but because, as Randolph explained, an all-black movement would promote "faith by Negroes in Negroes." The main goals of the movement were the desegregation of the armed forces and the elimination of discrimination in employment by government contractors. To gain these ends, Randolph proposed a mass march on Washington by some 75,000 to 100,000 blacks to take place in

June 1941. Though this proposal had the endorsement of established black groups such as the NAACP, the MOWM derived its power from the black masses rather than middle-class reformers, who generally worked for change through the courts and legislatures. In this way, the MOWM fore-shadowed the successful protest tactics of the later civil rights movement.

The MOWM timed its efforts well. The prospect of tens of thousands of blacks descending on the nation's capital as the United States prepared for war disturbed the President. Concerned about tarnishing the nation's image as well as about hampering attempts to rally support for the Allies, Roosevelt tried to get Randolph to halt the demonstration. Unsuccessful, the chief executive agreed partially to meet the movement's demands. Issuing Executive Order 8802, the President created the Fair Employment Practice Committee (FEPC) to investigate and publicize cases of employment discrimination. However, he left the policy of segregation in the military basically unchanged. Not getting all that he wanted, Randolph nevertheless called off the march, convinced that he had won an important political victory and confident that the movement would continue to apply pressure for social change. The MOWM did function throughout the war, but it never reached the same level of influence as it had during this first confrontation with the President.

Rising black militancy stimulated the growth of existing civil rights organizations. Foremost among them, the NAACP kept up the pressure to lower racial barriers along the color line. Although this oldest of civil rights groups had thrown its weight behind the MOWM, it preferred to operate in the traditional arenas of litigation, legislation, and lobbying. The national association's staff of dedicated attorneys prepared suits against white Democratic primaries in the South, segregation of passengers on interstate buses, and unequal educational facilities and teacher salaries. The NAACP functioned as a clearinghouse for complaints from black soldiers and civilians experiencing discriminatory treatment and directed them to the attention of officials in Washington. It prodded the Justice Department to investigate and prosecute perpetrators of lynching and other forms of violence and joined with white liberals and labor unions in petitioning Congress and state legislatures to lift poll-tax restrictions on the ballot. As a reflection of both its increased activism and the rising expectations of blacks, NAACP membership soared from 50,000 in 1940 to over 450,000 in 1946. Of these new recruits an estimated 15,000 black GIs signed up while they were still in uniform.

In addition, black activism spawned the formation of new protest groups. Most important for the future was the creation of the Congress of Racial

Equality (CORE) in 1942. Like Randolph's March on Washington Movement, CORE believed in the tactic of direct action to spotlight racist problems and bring them to an immediate resolution; in contrast to MOWM, however, the group welcomed white participation. Founded in Chicago by pacifists committed to the principle of nonviolence, its interracial membership initiated sit-in and picketing campaigns to desegregate public accommodations in northern cities. These innovative techniques led to the desegregation of restaurants and movie theaters in Detroit, Los Angeles, Denver, and Chicago.

CORE partisans were not the only ones to devise innovative tactics for protest. In Washington, DC, students at Howard University conducted their own sit-ins against racial discrimination in restaurants. In January 1943, shortly before the CORE protests in Chicago, three undergraduate women, Ruth Powell, Marianne Musgrave, and Juanita Morrow, were refused service at the counter of a United Cigar store. After the police instructed the waitress to serve the trio, she overcharged them for cups of hot chocolate. They insisted on paying only the regular amount, which then led the police to make a turnabout and arrest them for refusing to pay the specified bill. Sparked by this action, Howard students formed a Civil Rights Committee under the auspices of the college chapter of the NAACP. It zeroed in on restaurants in the area that surrounded the campus. Pauli Murray, a student from North Carolina attending Howard Law School, served as adviser to the group, and on April 17 student volunteers marched to the Little Palace Cafeteria on Fourteenth and U Streets, NW. Teams of three entered the facility and were rebuffed. While they sat at the tables and read their textbooks, others picketed outside hoisting posters with slogans such as "We Die Together – Why Can't We Eat Together?" The owner closed the cafeteria after the police refused to arrest the peaceful demonstrators. After two more days of protest, the restaurant capitulated, and African Americans could eat a meal alongside whites.

The following year, again led by Murray and Powell, Howard students resumed their desegregation drive against a major Washington, DC, cafeteria chain – John R. Thompson. They chose the restaurant at Eleventh Street and Pennsylvania Avenue, NW., because it was moderately priced, opened 24 hours a day, and was conveniently located for black government workers who were employed nearby. On Saturday, April 22, 1944, groups of black and white students entered the cafeteria and remained seated at tables after they were denied service. Outside, students walked a picket line. The demonstration received a big boost when six black soldiers came into the cafeteria and joined the students seated in protest. Following a four-hour standoff and a sharp drop in business, the manager of Thompson's, after consulting with corporate headquarters in Chicago, instructed his staff to wait on the black customers. However, the students' joy proved short lived. A few days after this initial victory, Thompson's barred a Howard student from eating. Before the civil rights forces could spring into action, Howard's president, Mordecai Johnson, issued a directive to the NAACP chapter members "to desist from its program of direct action in the City of Washington." Funded by Congress, Howard administrators feared that hostile lawmakers, especially from the South, would retaliate and cut the university's appropriations if the demonstrations persisted.

The students' campaign, however, eventually bore fruit. At the time of the sit-ins, Pauli Murray discovered an old District of Columbia statute from 1872 that prohibited racial discrimination by restaurants, ice-cream parlors, soda fountains, hotels, barbershops, and bathing establishments. In subsequent codifications of local statutes this antidiscrimination law had been omitted but not repealed. Murray suggested bringing a court case based on this long-forgotten, Reconstruction-era provision, but she did not find any backing at the time. Nevertheless, nine years later in 1953, the Supreme Court ruled that the 1872 law was still in effect to protect the rights of African Americans to obtain equal access to public accommodations. The suit had been initiated by Mary Church Terrell, the nonagenarian founder of the National Association of Colored Women, against Thompson's cafeteria for its ongoing policy of excluding blacks from dining.

African Americans also encountered racial difficulties in the West, where they had traveled outside of the South in search of wartime jobs in aircraft factories and shipyards. Furthermore, many blacks were stationed there in military camps. The black population of the region swelled during the 1940s by 33 percent, or some 443,000 people. Most of the migrants congregated in California, which absorbed about 75 percent of the increased number of minority residents. The San Francisco Bay area alone saw the size of its black population leap 798 percent; Los Angeles followed with 168 percent. Seattle, Washington, and Portland, Oregon, experienced huge growth as well. Throughout the West Coast blacks encountered employment discrimination and segregated housing. Ironically, African Americans took up residence in the homes of Japanese Americans, who had been relocated during the war, and remained in them once peace returned. Blacks and Latinos managed generally to coexist peacefully, but violence in crowded cities did erupt between African Americans and whites. Fights broke out between black and white soldiers in Seattle and San Luis Obispo, California. In 1943 interracial confrontations occurred in Portland and Los Angeles shipyards, and in the following year black civilians and white sailors brawled in Oakland.

Within these surroundings, African Americans encountered discrimination in public accommodations. Although buses and theaters were not segregated, restaurants and other establishments did exclude blacks, sometimes in subtle ways. A woman who migrated from Pine Bluff, Arkansas, to Oakland remembered: "They didn't have 'No Colored' signs or anything like that, but they had ways of telling you they didn't want you." Her memory may have been a bit faulty, because in 1946 the Oakland Institute on Human Relations reported that many businesses in the city displayed signs reading "We Refuse Service to Negroes" and documented instances of black patrons unable to obtain service in East Bay hotels, bars, and restaurants. The Alameda branch of the NAACP, which included Oakland and Berkeley, brought litigation against businesses that denied access to black customers. Even those African Americans who managed to have a meal in a restaurant found themselves subject to rude treatment by the staff. Despite these frustrations, the greatest problems black migrants along the West Coast faced concerned jobs, housing, and treatment by the police more than public accommodations.

As blacks actively confronted Jim Crow and pushed for their rights they often came into sharp conflict with hostile whites. The friction did not result as much from legal battles in the courts and in legislatures and along picket lines as from the increasing daily contact between blacks and whites in the overcrowded communities the war had produced. The influx of blacks into urban areas in search of jobs brought them into direct competition with older white residents and newer white migrants for employment, housing, and recreational facilities. By 1943, 50,000 southern blacks and 500,000 whites had swarmed into Detroit to find work. Instead, many of them found substandard housing and high rates of tuberculosis and infant mortality. These deplorable conditions fell hardest upon blacks, and when attempts were made to provide some measure of relief whites resisted them. On June 20, 1943, this explosive situation finally erupted in a bloody race riot over a fracas at an amusement park, and after the smoke cleared 34 people had been killed, 700 injured, and $2 million in property destroyed. Only the intervention of federal troops restored peace to the "Motor City." By the end of the year, another 241 racial disturbances in 47 cities had broken out, though none as severe as in Detroit.

With violence spreading throughout American cities, civil rights leaders became alarmed. Following a riot in Harlem, New York City's black newspaper, the *Amsterdam News,* warned that only by making blacks "feel that they are part of this country" would the violence cease. The way to achieve that, most black leaders believed, was to continue to press for the "double V" through peaceful channels. The NAACP called upon its chapters to step up the campaign for racial equality in the courts, legislatures, and ballot boxes, thereby removing potentially incendiary conflicts from the streets. This preference for seeking social change in a deliberate and orderly fashion diminished support for the tactics of direct mass action. After 1943, the once popular MOWM received criticism from the black press as "just Ku Kluxism in reverse" for its all-black policy, and a poll of black newspaper readers showed that 70.6 percent opposed the March on Washington Movement. Established civil rights leaders and their organizations did not retreat from the goal of securing full equality, but their strategy of measured militancy helped defuse the appeal of more confrontational approaches toward achieving that end.

To combat racial discrimination, they increasingly put a premium on attracting sympathetic whites. Before the war, white liberals thought primarily in economic rather than racial terms. They figured that the New Deal's recovery programs would lift blacks out of poverty along with whites and improve black chances of gaining acceptance for civil and political equality. However, the end of the Depression had not significantly extended first-class citizenship. Wartime ideals and the persistence of racism exposed by the 1943 riots persuaded liberal whites to assign a higher priority to civil rights. Fighting Hitler's atrocities abroad shifted the focus of racism at home from an economic to a moral issue, prompting liberals to try to prove that their society did not behave like Nazi Germany. Accordingly, they joined with blacks to set up interracial committees in scores of communities to open up better lines of communication and avoid the type of situation that engendered racial violence. The increasing presence of whites in the civil rights movement after 1943 had a further moderating effect on black militancy and reinforced those who favored the tactics of cooperation over confrontation, legalism over disruption, the ballot over direct action. The most prominent of all white liberals, Eleanor Roosevelt, endorsed this approach in contending that blacks should strive for complete equality but should "not do too much demanding [or] try to bring those advances about any more quickly than they were offered."

Mrs. Roosevelt's husband had the power to influence the pace of racial change, and he chose to act cautiously. According to the historian Harvard Sitkoff, President Roosevelt held a paternalistic view toward racial affairs, believing that the "Negro" was "an unfortunate ward of the nation to be treated kindly and with charity as a reward for good behavior." Ordinarily preferring gradualism and education to promote racial toleration, FDR felt even more inclined toward those methods at a time when winning the war was his chief concern. Though he disapproved of any racial prejudice that lowered black morale, he also took into account the position of southern white politicians who opposed any change in the racial status quo and whose legislative support for war appropriations he greatly needed. Black voters had joined the New Deal Democratic coalition, but their political clout remained weaker than that of Dixie politicos. In offering encouraging words to African Americans, "Dr. Win-the-War" Roosevelt never forgot that, while the overseas conflict lasted, "the long-range problems of racial and minority-majority antagonism cannot be settled.... the war must be won first."

The experience of the Fair Employment Practice Committee demonstrated this point. Created by Roosevelt to head off the proposed June 1941 march on Washington, the FEPC was authorized to investigate discrimination in defense-related employment but lacked the power of enforcement. Instead of coercion it relied on publicity and persuasion to expose and alter biased practices. Reflecting the President's philosophy, committee members believed that winning the war should take precedence over the pursuit of racial equality. One commentator summed up their thinking: "For the government to terminate an important war contract by reason of the contractor's indulgence in discriminatory employment would be highly impractical."

Unable to compel compliance and unwilling to alienate powerful employers, the FEPC achieved mixed success. Of 8,000 complaints submitted to the committee, two-thirds were dismissed as without merit and only one-fifth were settled in the South. Employers and unions, which were also covered under the executive order, ignored 35 of 45 compliance decrees. For example, the railroad brotherhoods and southern railway lines signed an agreement restricting employment opportunities for blacks and then disregarded an FEPC order against it. The government did not dare take action that might provoke a crippling strike by a powerful union and also antagonize the white South. In contrast, the President sometimes backed the committee when the political risks were not so great. In

Philadelphia, a strike by a dissident union faction in protest at an FEPC ruling upgrading black jobs on streetcars triggered President Roosevelt's decision to send in federal troops to resume normal operation of the transit system. In this instance, a stronger rival union supported the black position, and the residents of the "City of Brotherly Love" did not threaten a political revolt over the settlement. Even the lukewarm record of the FEPC proved too much for southern members of Congress, who succeeded in 1944 in enacting a provision that paved the way for the committee's legislative funding to be cut off two years later.

Although blacks did obtain some benefits from the FEPC, their main economic gains resulted from labor shortages during the war. As millions of whites marched off to battle and industrial production expanded, blacks helped plug the job holes on the home front. Black employment rose by over 1 million; the number of unemployed dropped from 937,000 to 151,000; union membership doubled; and the percentage of blacks in defense work climbed from 4.6 to 8.3. African Americans found jobs in factories where employers had initially resisted hiring them. Under the strain of war, the number of black employees increased from 6,000 to 14,000 in shipyards and from zero to 5,000 in aircraft plants. The federal government itself gave black employment a big boost, increasing its rolls from 60,000 to 200,000 African-American workers. On the down side, most of the blacks entering the labor force took jobs at low levels as janitors and custodians. Consequently, blacks made up only 3.6 percent of craftsmen and foremen, 2.8 percent of clerical and sales personnel, and 3.3 percent of professional and technical staff. Concentrated in low-paying jobs, black families on the average earned about half the income of whites. Nevertheless, the improvements in their economic condition whetted black appetites for more and raised expectations that opportunities would continue to grow once the war ended.

African Americans also beefed up their political muscle as a force for freedom. In the North, where voting booths were open to blacks, both the Democratic and Republican parties courted them. In 1940 the GOP presidential candidate, Wendell Wilkie, campaigned hard for the black vote and made slight inroads in a losing effort. In lining up behind Roosevelt's third-term bid, the black electorate moved the victorious President to grant them concessions. Black support spurred FDR to add an antidiscrimination clause to the Selective Service Act, appoint Colonel Benjamin O. Davis as the first black (brigadier) general, select blacks as civilian aides in the War Department and Selective Service, and establish an Army Air Corps training school at Tuskegee Institute. Four years later, though the Democrats did not draft a strong civil rights plank for their platform, FDR personally called for a permanent FEPC and elimination of restrictions on the ballot. Again, the black electorate responded enthusiastically.

Because black support for the President was much stronger than for the Democratic Party as a whole, the minority vote seemed very much up for grabs once the popular chief executive was no longer a candidate. In 1940, 67 percent of African-American voters had backed the President, though only 42 percent considered themselves Democrats. After the election in 1944, both Democrats and Republicans took note that a shift in the black vote in eight states would have defeated Roosevelt's reelection for a fourth term. Given their strategic location in major urban centers in northern states rich in Electoral College votes, blacks looked forward to wielding the balance of power in close presidential races in the future.

Meanwhile, in the South, where blacks remained largely disfranchised, wartime developments lifted hopes for change. In 1944 the Supreme Court's *Smith v. Allwright* decision struck down the Democratic white primary. Victory in these preliminary contests ordinarily determined the winners in subsequent general elections in the one-party South, and hence the destruction of the white primary would remove a major obstacle to black participation in the region. The assault on the primary had begun two decades earlier. In 1923, after the Texas legislature officially barred blacks from participating in Democratic primaries, the NAACP mounted a legal challenge that had great significance for blacks in the Lone Star State as well as for those in the rest of the South where the exclusionary practice also flourished.

Initially, the NAACP convinced the judiciary of its argument, but these triumphs neither settled the issue nor did they gain for blacks the right to vote. In 1927, and again in 1932, the Supreme Court ruled that a state could not officially authorize racial discrimination in the fashion of Texas without violating the Fourteenth Amendment of the Constitution. However, in a pattern that would become increasingly common in the face of rising black protest, southern officials resisted attempts to dismantle segregation and disfranchisement by countering with measures purporting to conform with the law while at the same time managing to evade it. In this instance, the Texas legislature obeyed the court's pronouncement by repealing its white primary regulation, thereby leaving the state Democratic Party free to adopt rules denying blacks access to its internal affairs. Previously the high tribunal had struck down the white primary because the state had deliberately created and maintained it, but the court had left open the question of whether a political party, operating as a private association, could deny blacks participation in its activities. Presented with another case in 1935, the Supreme Court decided that a political party had the constitutional right to fix its own qualifications for membership and therefore could legally exclude blacks if it so desired. In *Grovey v. Townsend* the justices argued that the conduct of a primary was strictly a private party matter and was immune from the guarantees of the Fifteenth Amendment, which forbade interference with the right of blacks to vote in general elections open to the public.

Before they could overcome this judicial blow to reenfranchisement, blacks first had to settle some differences that had hampered their legal battle. The main problem concerned the conflict for control of the case between local blacks and the NAACP, headquartered in New York City. Run in a hierarchical manner, the national association insisted on maintaining tight supervision of its programs from the top down. This style irritated some black attorneys and other leaders in Texas, who believed they should play a greater role in shaping policies and legal strategies directly affecting their community. They also wanted the NAACP to make a greater effort in recruiting black lawyers whenever possible to try suits and to rely less heavily on whites. These tensions had produced unfortunate results. Against the wishes of the NAACP, which considered the attempt premature, a group of black Texans had initiated the *Grovey* case and the cause of black voting rights had suffered a severe setback as a consequence.

Following this debacle, the NAACP sought to remedy the difficulties. Under the leadership of Charles Houston, the dean of Howard Law School, and his protégé, Thurgood Marshall, the national association assembled a talented staff of black attorneys and labored to work more closely and harmoniously with blacks in the local areas from which the legal challenges arose. This interaction between national and grassroots forces became the hallmark of the burgeoning civil rights struggle. In the wake of *Grovey*, the NAACP organized black Texans into a mass movement for first-class citizenship. Its state convention created a Democratic Primary Defense Fund, which galvanized black churches, civic leagues, fraternities, and business groups behind a fundraising campaign to finance a new court suit. "Brother, have you spared that dime for your liberation and freedom?" asked a black newspaper, and the response was generous. As Darlene Clark Hine has observed: "The white primary became a rallying cry for black Texans and assisted them in developing black solidarity." In addition to contributing money and generating publicity, local blacks furnished the plaintiff to contest the white primary. Represented by Marshall, a Houston dentist and NAACP member named Lonnie Smith filed litigation against S. E. Allwright, a state election official who had refused to allow him to cast a ballot in the 1940 Democratic primary.

On this fourth attempt to wipe out the offensive and highly resilient discriminatory electoral procedure, African Americans finally triumphed. Drawing upon a recent opinion in a case brought by the federal government against voting fraud in a Louisiana primary, on April 3, 1944, the Supreme Court reversed *Grovey*. The justices held that where a primary was an integral part of the electoral process, as was the circumstance in Texas, blacks were entitled to the protection of the Fifteenth Amendment, which sheltered their right to vote from racial discrimination. Smith not only won for himself the right to participate in the crucial Democratic primary, but he greeted his victory as a second emancipation for blacks throughout the South. The Houston dentist gleefully commented that this ruling would affect the political history of the country more than any case since the infamous *Dred Scott* decision before the Civil War. If the joy of victory caused this happy plaintiff to exaggerate somewhat, many could still agree with the assessment of an NAACP attorney that the "Supreme Court released and galvanized democratic forces" which one day would transform the political life of the South and the nation.

Toward this end, suffragists had also aimed their attack at another troublesome obstacle to black voting: the poll tax. Confined to the South, this financial requirement differed from state to state but generally discouraged the poor of both races from going to the polls. In fact, it worked a greater hardship on whites than on blacks, as long as the white primary and the racially biased administration of literacy tests operated to chase southern blacks away from the ballot box. Encouraged by Roosevelt's New Deal, progressive southerners tried to find ways of extending economic and political democracy to the region. Consequently, in 1941 they formed the National Committee to Abolish the Poll Tax, composed of labor, liberal, and civil rights groups. Actively cooperating with the NAACP and the Congress of Industrial Organizations (CIO), the anti-poll-tax alliance lobbied national lawmakers to enact a measure repealing the restrictive levy in federal elections.

America's entry into World War II provided proponents of abolition with fresh ammunition for their attack. Reformers claimed that the disfranchising effects of the tax hurt public morale, and they compared the decline of free elections in fascist-dominated Europe with the shrinking of the electorate in the poll-tax South. Twice during the war, the repeal advocates convinced the House of Representatives to support their proposal, only to suffer defeat in the Senate. Though whites stood to gain more than did blacks from elimination of the tax, southern foes warned their constituents of the dangerous racial consequences of legislative repeal. "If the [anti] poll tax bill passes," Senator Theodore Bilbo of Mississippi contended, "the next step will be an effort to remove the registration qualification, the educational qualification of the negroes. If that is done we will have no way of preventing negroes from voting."

Despite such fears, pressure from the progressive, interracial coalition encouraged Congress to take some limited but positive action to soften the burden of the poll tax. In 1942, lawmakers exempted soldiers from having to meet poll-tax requirements to vote in national elections. Reformers also made some progress at the local level. In 1945, Georgia abolished its franchise tax entirely, and at the war's end most of its neighbors in the region released their returning veterans from having to pay for casting a vote. Even with these wartime changes, most blacks remained disfranchised. Southern officials discriminated against black soldiers seeking to claim their poll-tax exemption, and the majority of blacks continued to encounter insurmountable suffrage barriers, such as literacy tests. Yet the easing of poll-tax restrictions, together with the Texas white primary ruling, had a liberating impact. Between 1940 and 1947, the proportion of southern blacks enrolled to vote climbed from 3 percent to 12 percent.

Taking advantage of these opportunities, blacks marshaled their forces at the local level to convert votes into power. To stimulate both greater registration and political involvement, grassroots organizations offered citizenship classes, conducted poll-tax payment drives, and initiated challenges to discrimination within state Democratic parties. In one imaginative move, black activists in South Carolina, in cooperation with the NAACP, formed a statewide Progressive Democratic Party (PDP), which attempted to unseat the regular Democrats at the 1944 national convention. Though unsuccessful, the PDP still managed to stimulate political activity, and by 1948 more than 35,000 blacks voted in the regular Democratic Party primary, a figure ten times greater than the turnout four years earlier.

The South Carolina campaigns received the enlightened guidance of three members of the state's black middle class. Segregation had produced unequal treatment and inferior public facilities for nonwhites, but it had also provided blacks with opportunities to develop separate religious, economic, and civic institutions under their exclusive control. Having achieved a measure of independence within their business and professional spheres, some of them attempted to gain for the majority of blacks the right to participate in governing their own communities. The Reverend James Hinton held a managerial position with Pilgrim Life Insurance Company, a black-owned enterprise, and headed the Palmetto State's NAACP Conference. He was joined by Osceola McKaine, a native of Sumter and a World War I veteran who had established a successful restaurant business in Belgium before returning home shortly after the onslaught of Hitler's army. Rounding out the trio, John McCray provided valuable leadership as editor of the *Lighthouse and Informer*, a black newspaper in Columbia that editorialized against racial injustice and for first-class citizenship. As Hinton, McKaine, and McCray showed, middle-class blacks did not have to confine their egalitarian impulses to seeking change exclusively through the courts. They worked tirelessly to organize South Carolina blacks behind a variety of grassroots activities to regain the precious ballot snatched away in the late nineteenth century. McKaine, also an editor of the *Lighthouse and Informer*, saw the black masses aroused by the war against fascism and responsive to the renewed efforts to advance their political fortunes. In his view, the creation of the PDP marked a revolutionary beginning "to give the disinherited men and women of both races in South Carolina some voice in their government, [and] some control over their destinies."

To reinforce their local drives, black leaders requested federal assistance. They usually met with disappointment. An organizer of the South Carolina PDP held the national Democratic Party "as responsible as the state party for the denial of membership to Negroes in that it tolerates discrimination in the South." This policy would not change so long as white voters constituted the foundation of the Democratic Party in the South and their elected representatives played a key role in determining the outcome of legislation desired by the President. Based on this political calculation, Roosevelt's Justice Department refused to follow up *Smith v. Allwright* with criminal prosecutions against suffrage violators. When Senator Lister Hill of Alabama, a legislative ally of President Roosevelt, heard that such legal action was contemplated in his home state, he warned the White House that it would be "a very dangerous mistake." Worried about a political revolt at the polls in Dixie and concerned about getting along with the southern-influenced Senate Judiciary Committee, the Justice Department backed off with the President's blessing. For similar reasons the chief executive declined to give more than lip service in favor of congressional measures designed to repeal the remaining poll-tax requirements in the South.

While Roosevelt attempted delicately to balance the political wishes of southern whites and blacks, demographic forces were in motion that would eventually upset that equilibrium. During the war southern blacks voted with their feet and migrated northward, more than doubling the number of their race living above the Mason–Dixon line. Increased urbanization was propelled by changing labor patterns on the farm. The extension of mechanized agriculture, especially the use of the tractor, during the 1940s pushed blacks off the farm and sent them to northern cities in search of jobs. Remembering the plight of friends and relatives left behind, they intended to use their unfettered ballots to select candidates favoring civil rights measures. Some 750,000 blacks journeyed from rural areas to cities within the South, and there they usually encountered a less restrictive application of suffrage requirements. Moreover, the urban environment afforded wider social space to develop racial solidarity and community organizations for political and economic emancipation. Away from the tight regulations exacted by the plantation economy, they were more readily exposed to the wartime promises of democracy and became more determined to challenge enduring forms of racial discrimination. These demographic changes were a precondition for the building of a movement to transform race relations in the postwar South.

The tempo and direction of that change would be determined by the interconnected efforts of federal officials and local black communities across the South. Civil rights groups, including national associations and their local chapters, as well as civic, fraternal, and religious organizations, initiated the struggle to eradicate racial barriers, mobilize the black masses to confront these obstacles, and apply ongoing pressure on white officials to demolish them. In cities and towns throughout the region, blacks were joining together to transform their own lives economically, politically, and psychologically, seeking to liberate themselves totally from the bonds of oppression. The process of struggle could free blacks spiritually and forge racial pride and solidarity, but their liberation would not be completed without allies in Washington helping them crack potent southern white opposition and enacting their goals into law.

World War II was the seedtime of the racial and legal metamorphosis that was to sweep over the South. The war propelled a growth of racial consciousness and a burst of militancy that foreshadowed the assault on Jim Crow. It provided new economic and political opportunities and at the same time underscored the failure of the nation to allow African Americans to take full advantage of them. Having caught a glimpse of a better life and frustrated by the resistance to achieving it, blacks did not intend to retreat. They had already seen some of the old hurdles tumble in the courts, and their nascent political influence had pressured the President into supporting limited reforms. By VJ Day, black troops had fought together with whites on an emergency basis in the European theater of war, and planning for integration had begun in the navy. Surveys showed that the more contact whites had with blacks in the military and in the workplace the more likely they were to oppose segregation. Buoyed by these initial advances and imbued with egalitarian wartime ideology, African Americans looked ahead with great expectations for the future.

Yet the war alone would not solve the manifold problem of racial inequality. One of the great rewards for veterans was congressional passage in 1944 of the Servicemen's Readjustment Act, commonly known as the GI Bill of Rights. Under this program the government provided educational benefits for returning soldiers as well as a year's unemployment compensation and loans to purchase homes and start businesses. However, in the South most black veterans encountered discrimination that deprived them from receiving the benefits due them. As one historian of this program noted, in April 1947, the Veterans Administration (VA) "found only 5 percent of all black veterans enrolled in courses and programs under the education benefit. This occurred at the same time that the total veteran enrollment at colleges throughout the country reached its peak during the postwar era." Housing also proved difficult for black veterans to obtain in integrated areas in the cities or suburbs. In places like Chicago and Detroit, biased real-estate brokers and bankers engaged in a variety of practices that steered African Americans away from homes in white neighborhoods. Taken together, the shortcomings in administration of the GI Bill of Rights along with housing, lending, and employment discrimination excluded most blacks from the postwar expansion of the middle class and widened the economic gap between blacks and whites.

A Troubled Peace

Black veterans marched at the forefront of those demanding unconditional surrender from the forces of fascism at home. Having fought for their country and demonstrated their worth on the battlefield, they returned to their communities intent on challenging the racist practices they had temporarily escaped from. On May 19, 1945, before shipping out of Okinawa,

Private Herbert W. Seward expressed the view of many of his black buddies in a letter to the *Pittsburgh Courier*:

> Our people are not coming back with the idea of just taking up where they left off. We are going to have the things that are rightfully due us or else, which is a very large order, but we have proven beyond all things that we are people and not just the servants of the whiteman.

By reading black newspapers and letters from home they had kept track of the many incidents of racial discrimination and abuse that blacks experienced during the war. The "majority will return home," Walter White of the NAACP predicted, "convinced that whatever betterment of their lot is achieved must come from their own efforts."

One such veteran was Jackie Robinson. Having played on an integrated baseball squad in college, Robinson was determined to crack the color line

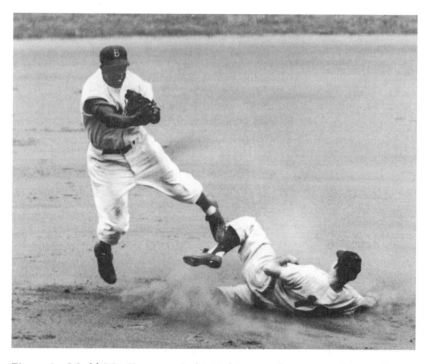

Figure 2 World War II veteran Jackie Robinson, who integrated major league baseball and became a star with the Brooklyn Dodgers. (Photo © B. Bennett / Getty Images)

that barred blacks from the major leagues. While playing professional ball with the Kansas City Monarchs in the Negro Leagues in 1945, he was spotted by the Brooklyn Dodgers' owner, Branch Rickey, who wanted to integrate the country's national pastime. Displaying the same fierce pride that pushed him to protest wartime discrimination, Robinson readily accepted the challenge. "I'm ready to take the chance," he declared, in anticipation of his task. "Maybe I'm doing something for my race." After playing a season in the minor leagues, in 1947 Robinson joined the Dodgers and succeeded in opening up one of America's most cherished institutions to blacks. Indeed, Robinson served as an enormous source of pride for all African Americans looking for expanded opportunities and equal rights in the postwar years.

At the same time, black southerners directed much of their energy toward extending the right to vote, which they considered the essential weapon in gaining and protecting the rest of their civil rights. Many black GIs had barely taken time to remove their uniforms before they marched to local courthouses to register to vote. In Birmingham, Alabama, about a hundred ex-soldiers paraded in double file through the main street of the city, ending up at the registrars' office. Veterans like these reasoned that as long as blacks did not determine who governed them they would continue to be victimized by racial discrimination. One discharged soldier from Georgia thought that conditions would be better in the future. "Now that the war has been won," he wrote, "the most difficult job ahead of us is to win the peace at home. 'Peace is not the absence of war, but the presence of justice' which may be obtained, first, by becoming a citizen and registered voter. If you become a registered voter we may be able to win the peace." Black leaders concurred. The *Pittsburgh Courier* predicted that "once Negroes start voting in large numbers … the jim crow laws will be endangered and the whole elaborate pattern of segregation threatened and finally destroyed."

Southern officials tried to block this chain of events at the first step, resorting to a variety of racist subterfuges to perpetuate black disfranchisement. Even after the destruction of the white primary, registrars were able to exclude blacks from the suffrage by administering literacy tests for prospective voters. In the hands of bigoted clerks these examinations were manipulated to prevent qualified black applicants from enrolling and were interpreted to allow illiterate whites to pass. White registrars accomplished this biased feat by asking only blacks the meaning of highly technical clauses in state and federal constitutions or by asking them such absurd questions as "How many bubbles are there in a bar of soap?" One Mississippi official frankly admitted that he "didn't care which way the [Negroes] answered those questions, it wouldn't come up to his satisfaction."

Mississippi had long been a leader in reducing blacks to second- class citizenship. Combining the white primary, literacy tests, and the poll tax, with terror and coercion thrown in for good measure, the Magnolia State had created a "closed society." Blacks lived at the bottom of a rigid caste structure, held down by a separate and unequal educational system, dependent upon white-controlled economic institutions for survival, and disciplined to remain in place by official and private acts of violence. Generations of white supremacists had sternly taught Mississippi blacks that participation in civic life was folly. Not surprisingly, in 1944, out of 350,000 adult black Mississippians only 2,500 had managed to register to vote.

However, for several years after World War II the idea that "politics is white folks' business" was challenged by a small but determined group in the Magnolia State. In 1944, a small circle of middle-class blacks from Jackson, led by T. B. Wilson, the secretary of the local NAACP chapter, formed the Mississippi Progressive Voters League. Designed to stimulate black enrollment, the league attempted to educate black citizens to recognize the importance of the suffrage. This task was made a bit easier after *Smith v. Allwright*. Until that ruling, Wilson explained, blacks "were indifferent, disinterested, but when we worked up this case of registering and voting them because the Supreme Court decision gave us to understand that we could vote, then they began to register." In addition, like most other southern states, Mississippi exempted veterans from payment of the poll tax for voting. Their racial and political consciousness heightened by the war, black veterans in Mississippi attempted to exercise their franchise rights.

In doing so, they ran up against Senator Theodore "The Man" Bilbo. An outspoken bigot whose storehouse of invectives was plentiful enough to smear racial, religious, and ethnic minorities alike, Bilbo had few peers to match the virulence of his antiblack tirades. In the midst of his reelection campaign in 1946 he encouraged white Mississippians to keep the ballot boxes shut to the growing number of blacks who were seeking to register. "The Man" unabashedly suggested to the registrars that if "there is a single man or woman serving ... who cannot think up questions enough to dis- qualify undesirables then write Bilbo or any good lawyer, and there are a hundred good questions which can be furnished." Bilbo was confident that the Magnolia State's brand of racial justice would not pose a hazard to these biased attempts. "How many registrars do you think can be convicted here in the state of Mississippi?" he asked rhetorically. If such chicanery did not do the trick, the senator informed his audiences, "You and I know what's the best way to keep the nigger from voting. You do it the night before the election. I don't have to tell you more than that." Apparently getting his not too subtle message, one county clerk refused to register a black veteran because "niggers don't vote in this county." To add injury to insult, the rejected ex-GI was abducted and flogged by white vigilantes as he left the courthouse. Given these potent lessons in repression, fewer than 1 percent of adult blacks registered to vote, and a majority of white electors cast their ballots to return Bilbo to the Senate.

Meanwhile, Bilboism did not go unchallenged. Aided by the NAACP and sympathetic whites in the North, the Progressive Voters League compiled affidavits documenting the racist nature of the senator's demagoguery. Sufficient evidence was accumulated to convince the Senate to send a special committee to conduct public hearings in Jackson on the charge that Bilbo's election was tainted with fraud and corruption. Because the five-member investigation team contained a Democratic majority including three southerners, and because it was chaired by Allen Ellender, an avid defender of white supremacy in Louisiana, blacks did not expect a favorable report. Instead, they hoped to expose how disfranchisement operated in Mississippi and to arouse northern senators to block Bilbo from taking his seat.

On December 2, 1946, blacks journeyed from all over the state to puncture the myth of their contentment with race relations in Mississippi. They jammed the hearing room to testify before a mixed gallery of friends, hostile whites, and the national press. With veterans in the forefront, they braved the danger of possible retaliation from angry whites resentful of the unfavorable publicity the proceedings trumpeted throughout the country. An observer compared the plight of the black witnesses to that of a "pedestrian in any typical American city or community, attempting to cross the street with a green light and the law in his favor but who, nevertheless, is seriously injured or killed in the process."

For three days courageous black veterans recounted their frustrated attempts to enroll and vote. They detailed stories of threats, beatings, and police brutality. The testimony revealed that the registrars misused the literacy exam to prevent them from qualifying to vote. Amazingly the registrars themselves corroborated the damaging testimony. One official admitted that he had told a black not to cast his ballot, because "in the southern states it has always been a white primary, and I just couldn't conceive of this darkey going up there to vote." The candor of this testimony prompted an NAACP representative on the scene to remark: "Sometimes I think Jesus Christ must be ill at ease in Mississippi."

Although these revelations proved that blacks were disfranchised on racial grounds, the Ellender committee voted to exonerate Bilbo of any personal guilt. Instead, the Democratic majority blamed the blacks' failure to vote on the white primary tradition and on lethargy. However, the challenge was not over. As the NAACP had hoped, when the matter reached the Senate floor, in early January 1947, a bipartisan coalition of Republicans and northern Democrats succeeded in postponing consideration of Bilbo's credentials. Suffering from jaw cancer, the Mississippi senator agreed temporarily to withdraw his claim to his seat while he sought treatment for his ailment. This solution turned out to be permanent: on August 21 "The Man" died.

Incipient black militancy in Mississippi yielded limited short-run returns, but it raised promising expectations for the long run. Although Bilbo had departed, the white supremacist system lived on. When John Stennis replaced Bilbo, only the cruel rhetoric and not the underlying policy of disfranchisement changed. Behind the Magnolia Curtain, blacks continued to encounter most of the old difficulties and a few new ones in trying to vote. Yet they benefited from having stood up to Bilboism. The public hearings demonstrated rising political awareness, especially among younger blacks. Despite persistent obstacles in front of ballot boxes, nearly 20,000 blacks added their names to registration lists in the decade after the war's end. This modest increase revealed the development of tiny chinks in the armor of the closed society. White politicians who justified their racial policy on the basis that African Americans were content with their lot had that explanation graphically disputed by black veterans and their friends who defied white hostility to appear in Jackson. As a matter of fact, the Senate investigation documented only part of the rising tide of black protest. A former soldier not called to testify about his own encounter with Bilboism, Medgar Evers later became state field secretary of the NAACP and worked tirelessly to organize blacks against racial discrimination and disfranchisement. In that capacity, working alongside a new breed of blacks, he helped breathe life into the civil rights movement in Mississippi until additional recruits and allies were mobilized.

Black Mississippians were not alone in their struggle to obtain the franchise. Throughout the postwar South, blacks campaigned to break down suffrage barriers. The NAACP, while concentrating its energies in the courts, was among the groups promoting the use of the ballot. After *Smith v. Allwright*, many of its branches created citizenship schools to teach blacks how to fill out registration forms properly and to answer typical questions that the clerks posed. The national association made cash awards to those who took up this work; in 1947, for example, the organization presented a prize to its chapter in Monroe, Louisiana, for having conducted a drive that added over 600 names to the voter lists. Assistant secretary Roy Wilkins expressed the value to blacks in creating these voter education classes: "The issue of civil rights is politics. If we are to win the fight for civil rights we must use our political strength."

African Americans also organized voter leagues to supplement the efforts of the NAACP. These groups solicited support from various organizations in the black community – civic, fraternal, religious – and thus they recruited many individuals outside of the national association's orbit of influence. In 1946, an Atlanta All Citizens Registration Committee was formed because "previously NAACP registration drives had failed to reach the masses." Within four months, this committee assisted in bringing out some 17,000 blacks to sign up to vote. C. A. Bacote, a historian at Atlanta University, chaired the committee, and Grace Towns Hamilton, the executive director of the Urban League, coordinated the day-to-day activities, which included mass distribution of flyers and door-to-door canvassing. Hamilton came from a civic-minded family and she had attended Atlanta University. She worked for the YWCA for several years before taking over leadership of the Urban League in 1943. The league stressed community self-development and worked on improving housing and employment conditions for Atlanta blacks.

While male faculty members from Atlanta University and ministers such as the Reverend Martin Luther King, Sr., played an important role, the presence of Hamilton shows that women were as critical to the success of the drive as were men. Women's groups lent their expertise and personnel to the effort. For example, a group called the MRS Club, comprised mainly of young teachers, succeeded in registering all of its members. One of them, Narvie J. Harris, believed that citizenship education had to extend beyond the classroom to the larger community, and she established a PTA Council to promote adult education. Her extensive involvement in the social networks of her community proved invaluable in reaching potential voters throughout Atlanta's black neighborhoods. The drive also benefited from the participation of Ruby Blackburn. From a more humble background than Hamilton and Harris, Blackburn had worked as a maid at a black school and later became the owner of Ruby's Beauty Shoppe. Beauty parlors were an important meeting place for black women during the era of segregation and provided an independent space for discussion and dissemination of information. When the operators were as political as Blackburn, who also was active in the NAACP, the shops furnished a way to reach many women outside the middle-class social orbit of professionals like Hamilton and Harris.

In Winston-Salem, North Carolina, an alliance of blacks and organized labor succeeded in electing a black to the city council. In Richmond, Virginia, a similar coalition supporting the election of a black veteran to the state legislature only narrowly failed. Elsewhere, in union halls, business establishments, farm groups, and small county associations, men and women gathered to plan suffrage crusades. Joining them, representatives of the Southern Conference for Human Welfare (SCHW), an interracial group of New Deal liberals formed in 1938, carried on voter registration drives throughout Dixie. In addition, from church pulpits ministers urged their congregants to go to the polls. During the Atlanta registration drive the Reverend Martin Luther King, Sr., preached for the cause of enfranchisement, thereby providing a role model for his son to follow.

The situation in Winston-Salem especially illustrated new possibilities for black political advancement stirred by the war. A drive by Local 22 of the Food, Tobacco, Agricultural and Allied Workers, a CIO affiliate, to gain a collective bargaining agreement with R. J. Reynolds Company boosted union membership among blacks and stimulated efforts to challenge racial discrimination within their community. This interracial union chapter, with Communists actively in the lead, mobilized working-class blacks to take part in the freedom struggle that had been waged haltingly in the past by a small middle- class segment of blacks associated with the NAACP. By 1947, CIO and NAACP voter registration campaigns had succeeded in enrolling ten times the number of blacks eligible to vote three years before. "I didn't take registration seriously until the union came in and we began to talk about … the importance of voting," one newly signed-up registrant commented. In 1947, Kenneth Williams, a black minister, won election to the Winston-Salem Board of Aldermen largely on the strength of this emergent African-American electorate. The efforts of Local 22 and its allies in heightening racial and political consciousness greatly impressed a visiting black journalist, who reported: "I was aware of a growing solidarity and intelligent mass action that will mean the dawn of a New Day in the South. If there is a 'New Negro', he is to be found in the ranks of the labor movement." Ultimately, however, much of the hope for this trade union path toward racial equality was dashed by the rising anti-Communist reaction that gripped the United States during the Cold War era (see Chapter 2).

Attempts to increase black political involvement throughout the South produced substantial dividends. Within a decade after *Smith v. Allwright*, over 1 million blacks, about four times the number in 1944, had qualified to vote. As Everett C. Ladd, Jr., noted, blacks were transformed "from 'blanks' to participants to city politics." Black voters sometimes held the balance of power in close elections and increasingly helped defeat the most racist of candidates. Commentators noted that where blacks voted in sizable numbers treatment by police improved, black patrolmen were hired, and health, education, and recreational facilities were constructed. Streets in black neighborhoods in those areas were paved. Osceola McKaine, who after the war served as a field representative of the SCHW, reported from his travels: "The Negro masses are becoming keenly aware that the questions of jobs and schools are essentially political questions and these are the things that interest them most." The greater turnout at the polls also encouraged blacks to seek political office in the South, and for the first time in the twentieth century nearly a dozen blacks in the South were elected to posts as aldermen, county supervisors, and members of city councils.

Women and the Civil Rights Movement

With the emphasis usually on returning veterans, namely men, it should not be forgotten that World War II also encouraged women to participate in the struggle for first-class citizenship. Inspired by the wartime rhetoric of equality, some 4,000 black women managed to gain admission into the Women's Army Corps and other branches of the military. Moreover, the war whetted the appetite of black women for continued progress. Having profited from the greater availability of jobs during the war, many African-American women desired to hold on to them in peacetime. As Paula Giddings noted, the postwar period witnessed a rising percentage of black women college graduates and professionals and their entry into the middle class. As their educational and economic achievements grew, African-American women heightened their expectations of attaining the political and constitutional rights that marked full citizenship. As already discussed in this chapter, women such as Pauli Murray, Mabel K. Stauper, and Grace Towns Hamilton were instrumental in leading the charge against segregation and disfranchisement.

Furthermore, black women – married and single – more of whom worked outside the home than white women, experienced other frustrations of racial discrimination. From early in the century they constituted a large share of the passengers on public transportation and encountered rude treatment and arbitrarily enforced segregation rules. As Giddings pointed out, "there had always been a tinderbox quality to the ill treatment of Black women on public conveyances." It was not only women who worked in menial jobs in white sections of their communities who experienced the harshness of racism, but also more prominent black women such as the turn-of-the-century journalist Ida B. Wells and the North Carolina educator Charlotte Hawkins Brown. With expectations rising for racial equality after World War II, it was only a matter of time before women trained their sights on public transportation to express their grievances. Not surprisingly, as we shall see in the next chapter, if there has been one woman identified with the civil rights movement among the crowd of prominent men it is Rosa Parks, the catalyst for the 1955 Montgomery bus boycott.

Overall, women not only sustained African-American communities in the South through religious and social activities, they also nurtured the civil rights struggle in their familial roles as wives and mothers. Without the sources of support they provided, the movement would never have gotten off the ground. Because the struggle would rely on young people as plaintiffs in education cases and as marchers in demonstrations, women had enormous influence in shaping their children's decision to join the cause. It took great courage and faith to put their daughters' and sons' lives in jeopardy in the face of often brutal white resistance. Both inside and outside the home, women played an essential part in building the foundation for the movement to flourish. Depicting women as organizers, however, does not do justice to the leadership they exhibited. They did not usually hold official titles or follow formal job descriptions, but, operating behind the scenes in routine, often gendered ways, women functioned as "bridge leaders." According to Belinda Robnett, who coined this term, women in the civil rights movement served as intermediaries between local communities, where their power was greatest, and regional and national civil rights agencies, where their access was much more limited.

Seedtime of Reform

The struggle to expand the vote following World War II was a prelude to the civil rights struggle that mushroomed in the years after the landmark *Brown v. Board of Education* school desegregation case. The blatant discrimination in registration procedures that had been shockingly revealed to the public and a virtual reign of terror to preserve disfranchisement underscored the need for a second reconstruction in which the national government intervened in the South. As one black journalist explained: "Each time the United States Supreme Court outlaws one of these 'Negro stoppers' a new one is invented. It is clear that sooner or later the federal government will have to step in." It would not be too long before politics combined with principle. In a little more than a decade Washington lawmakers would enact four civil rights measures to extend the suffrage to southern blacks.

Just as vital as federal intervention was local assertiveness. Voter registration activities at the grassroots level paralleled the development of the "new Negro," the African American unafraid to stand up for his or her rights in the face of grave danger. The million-plus blacks who registered to vote demonstrated that politics was no longer for whites only. Enrollment drives often brought suffrage reformers into direct confrontation with

Figure 3   Blacks in Charleston lining up to vote in the 1948 Democratic Party primary. (Photo © Bettmann/Corbis)

representatives of the racist system in the South and sustained a protest tradition upon which more militant action would be built in the future. It required courage, pride, and emotional strength for blacks living in Dixie to enter courthouses and run the gauntlet of registrars likely to reject their applications and sheriffs anxious to punish them for having made the attempt in the first place. The lessons learned by the civil rights workers of the late 1940s and early 1950s proved valuable to the "new abolitionists" of the 1960s. They taught that the right to vote could be obtained if the federal government intervened to destroy the white stranglehold over the registration process and civil rights groups rallied the mass of blacks behind the ballot. By virtue of this interdependent relationship, the national government changed the law while the civil rights movement erected a support network emboldening blacks to transform their local communities. Although suffragists were only slightly successful in the 1940s, most of them were still around to see a majority of southern blacks enfranchised within a generation.

The World War II era furnished the staging ground for the black revolution. It revitalized black solidarity, tested innovative protest tactics, and moved the federal government closer to the side of racial equality. Wartime urban migration and improved economic opportunities laid the basis for later social and political changes. The war loosened some of the old chains of subservience imposed by the southern caste system and freed blacks in hundreds of locales throughout Dixie to join together to overthrow Jim Crow. What the historian Nancy J. Weiss concluded about Franklin D. Roosevelt and the New Deal should be extended to the years that followed: "The growing interest of blacks in politics, their involvement in the Democratic party, and their new sense that the political process could be responsive to their needs became essential underpinnings of the drive for civil rights." Along two fronts, black soldiers and veterans and their families and friends steered the United States toward living up to its democratic political principles.

2

Ballots, Boycotts, and the Building of a National Agenda

While black southerners struggled to clear racial obstacles in the path of the right to vote, their allies in the North applied increasing pressure to move the federal government behind the cause of civil rights. The Supreme Court had taken the lead in beginning to dismantle barriers blocking equal access to public education, housing, and the ballot box, but neither the President nor Congress had taken very firm steps in that direction. Roosevelt's Fair Employment Practice Committee lacked the necessary administrative authority to combat discrimination in employment, and during World War II the chief executive generally refrained from engaging in controversies over racial issues that would offend white segregationists and threaten national unity. Similarly, southern lawmakers succeeded in strangling congressional attempts to punish lynchers, repeal the repressive poll-tax requirement for voting, and preserve the FEPC. The antifascist rhetoric of wartime notwithstanding, in the absence of sufficient political leverage appeals to moral conscience were not enough to guarantee first-class citizenship for African Americans.

The proponents of civil rights did not lack political resources. Though a majority of black southerners remained disfranchised in the decade following *Smith v. Allwright*, northern blacks could exercise the franchise as a strategic weapon to combat racial discrimination. Precipitated by World War II, the migration of blacks to the urban centers of the North and Far West in search of defense jobs placed them in a favorable position to tip the balance of power in tight elections. Where this critical mass of voters existed, even blacks themselves managed to win election. This incipient

Running for Freedom: Civil Rights and Black Politics in America since 1941,
Fourth Edition. Steven F. Lawson.
© 2015 John Wiley & Sons, Inc. Published 2015 by John Wiley & Sons, Inc.

strength placed two blacks in the House of Representatives – Adam Clayton Powell of New York City and William Dawson of Chicago – as well as a sprinkling of officials in local positions. Yet black influence derived from something more than actual minority-group representation, which was meager. Rather it rested in its potential to sway white politicians – to reward friends and punish enemies, the most basic axiom in politics.

The Truman Administration and Civil Rights

President Harry S. Truman had to factor in such political calculations in finding the right political equation for dealing with African Americans. The successor to FDR, Truman inherited the New Deal's black converts to the Democratic Party. However, in 1945 it was not clear whether this new-found partisan allegiance of blacks was a personal or an institutional one. Would it survive Roosevelt's death or would the black electorate return to its historical Republican mooring? Though the majority of blacks remained faithful to the party of Roosevelt in the November 1946 midterm legislative elections, the GOP recaptured some of FDR's black followers on its way toward securing control of the Eightieth Congress. Charles Houston, the noted attorney and legal adviser to the NAACP, expressed the disaffection of many blacks several months before the elections: "The president may do this and he may do that as leader, but if he cannot produce, well, there is no such thing as gratitude in politics." In December 1945, Houston had evidenced his own frustration with the lack of presidential leadership in civil rights by resigning as a member of the increasingly ineffective FEPC.

A practical politician, President Truman was prepared to heed these warning signals. Many of his early attitudes toward race were grounded in political considerations. As a border-state senator from Missouri during the late 1930s and early 1940s, Truman had supported, without much enthusiasm, abolition of the poll tax and passage of an antilynching bill. About the latter, he admitted to a southern colleague and opponent of the measure: "All my sympathies are with you, but the Negro vote in Kansas City and St. Louis is too important." At the same time, Truman backed legislation to fund the FEPC and spoke out for giving "the Negroes the rights that are theirs." His moderate positions on race made him acceptable to both southern and northern Democrats as the compromise candidate to replace the more controversial Henry A. Wallace as Roosevelt's running mate in 1944.

As President, he quickly received an education about racial injustice that deeply affected his thinking. In 1946, vicious attacks on returning black servicemen in the South generated widespread notoriety. "My God! I had no idea that it was as terrible as that!" the chief executive exclaimed after learning that Isaac Woodard, still in uniform, had been severely beaten and blinded while passing through South Carolina en route home. Together with a bloody race riot in Columbia, Tennessee, and mounting violence and threats of attack against blacks who sought to exercise their newly won suffrage rights, these events shocked Truman.

He responded by appointing a special committee to investigate the deteriorating condition of civil rights and devise remedies for its improvement. The moral concerns that prompted the formation of this group were reinforced by sound political considerations. The defeat of the Democrats at the polls in the 1946 congressional election charted the President's declining political health and brought a prognosis of doom for the party's presidential nominee two years hence. The once robust Roosevelt coalition appeared to be dying in the wake of Truman's inability to solve the postwar reconversion problems of inflation, shortages, and labor conflict as well as growing racial tensions. The establishment of the President's Committee on Civil Rights provided one way for Truman to resuscitate the ailing Democratic alliance in time to achieve a reelection victory.

This strategy was put to a stiff test after the committee issued its report in October 1947. *To Secure These Rights* urged greater federal involvement in promoting racial equality. It endorsed removal of the poll tax and other discriminatory obstacles to voting, creation of a Civil Rights Division in the Department of Justice, and desegregation of the armed forces, interstate transportation, and government employment. These suggestions broke new ground in establishing a reform agenda, and alarmed southern white politicians. Already troubled by their perception that Roosevelt's New Deal had tilted the axis of Democratic power away from the rural South to an urban North teeming with ethnic and racial minorities, many southerners resented the Truman committee's assault upon the racial status quo.

Their complaints forced the President to move circumspectly. Despite delivering an unprecedented special message on civil rights to a joint session of Congress in February 1948, Truman failed to press lawmakers to consider particular measures based on the committee's recommendations. He did not want to provoke a southern revolt in the upcoming presidential election, and the prospect of a southern filibuster against any civil rights legislation would prove even more divisive to party unity. Furthermore, southern legislative support for his Cold War economic and military policies toward the Soviet Union commanded a higher priority than did passage of civil rights bills, however worthy they might be.

Yet the Cold War offered a double-edged sword for racial advancement. Having recognized the difficulties in challenging the white South, Truman could not afford to risk the political consequences of ignoring rising black militancy. Since World War II, blacks in and out of the South had begun mobilizing for first-class citizenship, prepared to force the United States to live up to its democratic ideals. This also came at a time when the country was venturing into a fierce propaganda battle with the Soviet Union for allies in global struggle. Committed to the United Nations, President Truman did not want domestic racial conflicts to diminish his diplomatic efforts in the international arena. In this context, the attempt by Mississippi blacks to unseat the racist Senator Theodore Bilbo not only demonstrated a growing collective consciousness against oppression at the local level, but also focused national and world attention on the gap between democratic pronouncements and the reality of bigotry. Recognizing such predicaments, the President's Committee on Civil Rights declared in 1947: "An American diplomat cannot argue for free elections in foreign lands without meeting the challenge that in sections of America qualified voters do not have access to the polls."

Black protest leaders sought to exploit Truman's vulnerability on this point. In its traditional, legalistic manner, the NAACP petitioned the United Nations to consider a list of grievances against American racial practices. In a less conventional way that prefigured future campaigns against racial discrimination, A. Philip Randolph called upon blacks to apply pressure through civil disobedience. In early 1948, the "father" of the March on Washington tangled with Truman over an issue he had first brought up with Roosevelt seven years earlier and had failed to resolve: desegregation of the military. During a period when Truman sought increased military measures to combat Soviet aggression, Randolph urged the President to promulgate an executive order abolishing segregation in the armed forces or he would counsel black youth "to resist a [Selective Service] law, the inevitable consequences of which would be to expose them to un-American brutality so familiar during the last war." Although black leaders divided over Randolph's threatened action, a survey revealed that 71 percent of draft-age blacks supported the proposed boycott.

The danger of black insurgency was not confined to Truman's defense program; it menaced the political fortunes of the President. The black electorate gave some indication of rallying around the candidacy of Henry Wallace, who criticized Truman for responding too aggressively in seeking to contain the Soviet Union in foreign affairs and for not acting forcefully enough to repel racial discrimination at home. As early as May 1946, a poll showed that 91 percent of black voters favored Wallace as the Democratic nominee in 1948. Since then the President had appointed a pioneering civil rights committee and presented Congress with a pathbreaking legislative reform agenda. Nevertheless, Wallace carried a strong appeal for black voters. In late 1947, he campaigned throughout the South, audaciously addressed integrated audiences that included many of the region's newly enfranchised blacks, and spoke out in favor of racial equality. Up North, a special congressional election in a Bronx district in New York City with a large black population resulted in the victory of a pro-Wallace candidate.

These political rumblings did not exactly catch Truman by surprise. In November 1947, one of his key advisers, Clark Clifford, had counseled the President to concentrate on appealing to the liberal elements of the Democratic coalition, particularly blacks and labor union members, to ensure his reelection the following year. "Unless there are new and real efforts," Clifford predicted, "the Negro bloc ... will go Republican." A strong civil rights stand might disturb the Democratic South, but Clifford suggested that the former Confederate states would not bolt the party of their forebears.

Initially, however, Truman responded cautiously to this advice. Unwilling to confront the southern wing of his party any further, the President backed away from pressing his bold civil rights initiatives in Congress. True, the chief executive had some very good tactical reasons for backing off, given the likelihood that a southern filibuster would kill reform bills as well as stall passage of those pertaining to Cold War remilitarization. But Truman did not face the same legislative hurdle with respect to desegregation of the armed forces. In that case, he could have dealt with the matter by executive decree; this he refused to do. Moreover, he displayed excessive timidity in failing to endorse his own committee's civil rights recommendations as part of the Democratic Party's platform. Instead, he planned to run on the Democrats' mild 1944 plank vaguely worded in support of granting minorities equal rights under the Constitution.

Once again, strong political forces knocked the President off dead center and moved him to the left. At the Democratic National Convention in July 1948, party liberals engineered an end run around the Truman-controlled

Platform Committee and won a floor fight for a stronger resolution on civil rights. Though stopping short of pledging an end to segregation in the military, it did promise "equal treatment in the service and defense of our nation" as well as the "right to equal opportunity of employment." Hubert H. Humphrey of Minnesota, a leader of the liberal upstarts, eloquently captured the spirit behind the proposals: "The time has arrived for the Democratic Party to get out of the shadow of states' rights and walk forthrightly into the bright sunshine of human rights."

Embracing the revised platform rhetoric was not sufficient. With Randolph still intending to lead a mass draft-evasion movement and with Henry Wallace running on an independent Progressive Party ticket, Truman took the kind of concrete action on civil rights he had hesitated to implement previously. Shortly after the Democratic Convention adjourned, the President signed two executive orders establishing a nondiscriminatory fair employment policy for the federal government and creating a committee to promote equal opportunity in the armed forces, with the ultimate aim of eliminating segregation. He also convened a special session of Congress to act on his party's civil rights proposals, but southern lawmakers succeeded in blocking them.

These assorted efforts precipitated a revolt by white southerners, contrary to Clifford's predictions. After staging a walkout from the Democratic National Convention, a band of southern dissidents formed the States' Rights Party (Dixiecrats) and nominated Governor Strom Thurmond of South Carolina for President. These Democrats condemned federal tyranny and reaffirmed their allegiance to the principle of racial segregation. Rather than pushing Truman to mend his political fences in the South, this uprising produced the opposite effect. It reinforced the President's determination to secure minority backing in the North. According to this line of thinking, the "Negro votes in the crucial states will more than cancel out any votes he may lose in the South."

Not only might this strategy neutralize southern losses, but it could also undermine black support for Truman's main rivals in the North. The Republican nominee, Governor Thomas E. Dewey of New York, ran on a platform that declared its opposition to racial segregation in the military, a declaration omitted from the Democratic manifesto. Furthermore, Henry Wallace's Progressive Party denounced all forms of segregation and gained the endorsement of such prominent blacks as Charles Houston, W. E. B. Du Bois, and Paul Robeson. To secure black votes against his opponents, Truman emphasized his civil rights accomplishments during

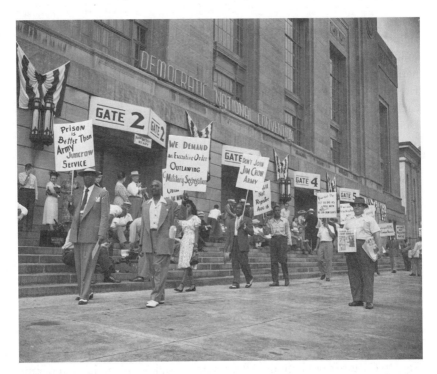

Figure 4   Protesting discrimination in the military, A. Philip Randolph heads a picket line at the 1948 Democratic National Convention. (Photo © Bettmann/ Corbis)

his first term and, in a symbolic gesture, swung his campaign through Harlem, the first President to do so. He hammered away at the Republican-controlled Eightieth Congress for doing nothing to pass his civil rights proposals. At the same time, he attacked Wallace for permitting Communists to collaborate with his Progressive Party, a charge designed to appeal to black civil rights leaders wary of Communist infiltration of their own organizations.

Truman's maneuvering paid off in his reelection. As his counselors had forecast, the loss of five Deep South states to the Democrats was more than offset by the huge margins Truman piled up among black voters in the urban North. He captured 69 percent of the black ballots cast in 27 major cities, and in California, Illinois, and Ohio black votes made the critical difference in his victory. Indeed, his share of the black electorate exceeded that of FDR, and as Nancy Weiss has pointed out, Truman managed to use the civil rights issue "as a means to transform black Roosevelt supporters into black Democrats." The incumbent's pro-civil rights record along with Dewey's lackluster campaign and the unwillingness of most blacks to "waste" their votes on a Wallacite third-party bid, especially one tainted with the stigma of Red radicalism, solidified black fidelity to the New Deal coalition.

The cementing of black loyalty to the Democratic Party as an institution, rather than to a single leader, depended on more than the attraction to civil rights. Though the vote of the cohesive black bloc grew out of racial concerns, class issues also shaped it. In casting a ballot for the Democratic presidential nominee, blacks were endorsing the party that brought economic relief from the Depression, sponsored measures to increase employment, and defended labor unions from restrictive assaults. The scant evidence that exists for the New Deal era suggests that lower-income blacks, like their white counterparts, were more inclined to back the Democrats than were those higher on the economic scale. This pattern persisted during the Truman years. Donald R. McCoy and Richard T. Reutten have noted that, whereas nearly all black newspapers supported Dewey in 1948, reflecting the higher socioeconomic status of their publishers, the lower-income readers of these publications sided overwhelmingly with Truman. For most African Americans, who were still not afforded equal economic and citizenship rights, race and class interests coincided.

The election of 1948 established civil rights as a key issue on the agenda of presidential politics. Three out of the four political parties had endorsed the extension of racial equality. Black delegates attended the Democratic Convention in comparatively small but record numbers and contributed to passing the minority civil rights plank. Blacks were also represented in prominent ways in the Progressive Party campaign, and the GOP, the former home of the majority of the black electorate, created a National Council of Negro Republicans to lure them back.

Yet the growing visibility of the civil rights issue did not mean that black Americans, especially those residing in the South, were about to achieve their goal of first-class citizenship through electoral politics. Southern seg-regationists continued to retain key positions within the Democratic Party and in Congress, ready to shred any legislative proposal on civil rights that appeared. Though the chief executive owed blacks a big debt for his reelec-tion, he lacked the substantial commitment necessary to tackle powerful conservative congressional forces against civil rights. For Truman, the Cold War and national security took precedence over domestic reform, and he hesitated to antagonize the southern lawmakers whose support he needed. Besides, Truman's policy of global containment fueled excessive anti-Communist sentiment in the United States. Zealous "Red baiters" equated any challenge to the status quo with un-Americanism. Even liberal and labor organizations such as the NAACP and the CIO hunted for suspected Communists in their ranks. No matter how hard they tried to achieve the requisite purity, civil rights groups still came under attack from segregationists who considered advocates of racial equality soft on Communism. This fear of social change and the attempts of politicians to capitalize on it created an inhospitable environment for civil rights activism.

To crack the entrenched opposition to racial equality required a public zeal that did not yet exist. In fact, the majority of whites did not embrace the cause of civil rights. In March 1948, a Gallup poll that asked whether Americans favored Truman's moderate civil rights program found out that 56 percent did not. Northerners were more likely than southerners to express sympathy, but most of them remained poorly informed about the issue.

The Election of Dwight D. Eisenhower

The election of Dwight D. Eisenhower in 1952 did not place a forceful advocate of civil rights in the White House, yet neither did it bring in someone totally unsympathetic to the principle of desegregation. The Republican President did not intend to turn back the civil rights clock to the days before the Truman administration. However, events were pushing ahead the timetable for racial equality and creating new standards of measurement to gauge presidential performance. Faced with this accelerated schedule, Eisenhower moved forward, but did so too cautiously to keep in step with the quickened rate of black expectations.

President Eisenhower began his first term in office without having accumulated any political debt to blacks. The overwhelming share of the black vote, 73 percent, had gone to Eisenhower's Democratic rival, Adlai E. Stevenson. The former Illinois governor exceeded Truman's ratio of the minority vote by recovering the backing of black Wallacites. The newly expanded southern black electorate in Louisiana, South Carolina, Kentucky, and Arkansas provided the margin of victory for Stevenson in those states. The majority of blacks stuck with the Democratic Party even though its platform did not retain the strong language of 1948 and its vice-presidential nominee was Senator John Sparkman of Alabama, who had opposed Truman's civil rights program.

Unlike in 1948, the black vote did not save the Democrats from defeat. The popularity of General Eisenhower among whites throughout the nation more than canceled out the impact of the black vote. The black electorate could play a decisive role in swinging the outcome of elections only when, as the *Pittsburgh Courier* noted, "the balance between the two major political parties is so even." Such was not the case in 1952. Eisenhower captured 55.2 percent of the popular vote and 442 electoral votes. His winning electoral column included 57 votes from the South, 18 more than the Dixiecrats had gathered four years earlier.

Despite the fact that Eisenhower had made inroads into Dixie and gained endorsements from popular figures such as Governor James F. Byrnes of South Carolina, he entered the White House with a civil rights agenda in mind. The Republican platform had differed from the Democrats' chiefly in its unwillingness to propose federal measures to combat employment discrimination, preferring instead to rely on state authority, Otherwise, the GOP advocated federal action to eliminate lynching, poll taxes, and segregation in Washington, DC. Eisenhower had also assured black leaders that he would strive to end discrimination in federal employment under his direct control, continue desegregation of the armed forces, and in a campaign address in Harlem he invited blacks to join his crusade "based upon merit and without respect to color or creed."

However, there were definite limits to Eisenhower's plans for obtaining racial equality. Committed to a view of government that emphasized persuasion over coercion in shaping social and economic relations, Eisenhower wanted to give state, local, and private sectors broad discretion in resolving conflicts in public policy. He believed that problems of race were deeply embedded in the fabric of southern society and could not be easily removed. Still, he considered white southern politicians as law-abiding and responsible, and he had faith in their willingness over time to abandon discriminatory racial practices. Consequently, the chief executive would not compel white southerners hastily to change their longstanding racial customs. Gradualism rather than speed characterized his approach. Eisenhower consistently declared in public what he confided to his personal diary at the beginning of his term: "I believe that Federal law imposed upon our states in such a way as to bring about a conflict of the police power of the states and the nation, would set back the cause of progress in race relations for a long, long time."

Community Mobilization and the Montgomery Bus Boycott

While the cause of civil rights inched along slowly under Truman and Eisenhower in the national arena, southern blacks and a handful of sympathetic whites in their home communities struggled to set themselves free. Civil rights leaders viewed electoral politics as a prime instrument for achieving racial gains. Political exclusion had pinned a twentieth-century badge of subordination on black southerners which enfranchisement promised to remove. Without a free and unfettered right to vote, the constitutional guarantee of full citizenship would remain elusive. Given the history of their official exclusion from the governing process, indeed their legitimacy as participants in government denied, blacks sought to enter politics as a fundamental act of liberation. The vote could be wielded as a tool of protest, a means of asserting dignity and pride, a source of personal and group autonomy. "There's one thing the Negro has that the white man wants but can't get unless you give it to him," a black Floridian remarked. "That's your vote. He can offer you a million dollars for your vote, but he can't get it unless you give it to him."

These symbolic qualities were not the only rewards attributed to the suffrage. The ballot had a practical side that offered a way to improve the daily living conditions of those deprived of basic public services most white Americans took for granted: paved streets, regular sanitation disposal, adequate police and fire protection, and access to recreational facilities. The vote would convert blacks into constituents, providing them with an opportunity to elect representatives whom they could hold directly accountable at the polls for delivering material benefits. This classic view of civic democracy did not take into account the pervasiveness of race and class as features that would retard black political influence, but it did conform to the conventional American creed of self-help and equal opportunity for advancement. In sharing and promoting this ideal, black suffragists attached their cause to republican principles and portrayed their foes as undemocratic and un-American.

Whatever the merits of their argument, black southerners still had to overcome numerous barriers to their entry into politics. Federal law had eliminated the white primary, but poll taxes, literacy tests, intimidation, and fear induced by centuries of discrimination kept most blacks disfranchised. With federal involvement growing but unreliable and southern resistance firm, blacks assumed increased responsibility for marshaling their resources against discrimination. According to Henry Lee Moon, an NAACP official who closely monitored this heightened political activity, "the real drive to register and get out the vote is essentially a grassroots movement with local Negro leadership."

The postwar voter and citizenship education campaigns, discussed in Chapter 1, demonstrated the need for collective action. Civil rights groups, in concert with voter leagues and sympathetic labor union locals, especially those in the CIO, waged intensive efforts to sign up black registrants and bring them out to the polls on election day. These organizations were necessary to arouse black consciousness to the efficacy of voting, counsel blacks on how to meet the suffrage requirements they faced, and sustain encouragement and support for those willing to break from the past when politics was the exclusive domain of whites.

These endeavors initially worked best in urban areas of the South. In the cities blacks had greater access to education, economic opportunities, and cultural institutions, all of which encouraged civic participation or preparation for it. Even those barriers that still existed there were not erected as high as in the rural black belt where African Americans were isolated, economically dependent on whites, and vulnerable to reprisals. In 1947, when Richmond, Virginia, blacks mounted a successful voter registration drive, the city's leading newspaper acknowledged: "We do have a democratic tradition which holds that American citizens are entitled to vote and to hold office. So we may as well accustom ourselves to [it]." In Atlanta, Georgia, blacks extended their political influence by forming a coalition with wealthy businesspeople to elect a white mayor, William B. Hartsfield, in 1949. Four years later, this biracial alliance, which cut across class lines, succeeded in electing Dr. Rufus E. Clement, the black president of Atlanta University, to the board of education, turning aside his white opponent.

However, other attempts at forging interracial coalitions based on shared economic experiences ran into trouble. Issues of political ideology divided people with common class grievances, as the situation of tobacco workers in Winston-Salem revealed. Following World War II the R. J. Reynolds Company undertook to roll back the gains that Local 22 of the CIO had made in unionizing black and white workers. A majority of the city's employed black women worked in tobacco factories. One of these women, Geneva McClendon, explained why she joined the Tobacco Workers Organizing Committee: "Everybody would almost cry every day the way they would work you and talk to you. Working conditions was so bad you needed God and a union." It is not an exaggeration to conclude, as does

Robert Korstad, the foremost historian of this local movement, that black women and men "whose names ... have been largely lost to history" provided the leadership for this labor and political struggle.

In 1947, after management refused to agree to demands for a wage increase, the union went out on strike. The company, supported by the local newspaper, attempted to undermine the walkout by shifting the focus from collective bargaining to Communist infiltration of the union. Indeed, Communists did occupy top positions in Local 22, which left the organization susceptible to charges that it was operating as an agent of a foreign power and using blacks to foster subversive aims. In the highly charged Cold War climate, the company succeeded in attacking the union for its Communist affiliations, but it could not triumph without assistance from the national CIO, which was also engaged in eliminating Communists from its ranks. Whereas the company was attempting to squelch unionization, the CIO merely wanted to establish a non-Communist affiliate. However, "if purging communist leadership also led to a destruction of the legitimate battle to organize the unorganized and achieve social justice," William H. Chafe has argued, "any victory would be hollow." Arrayed against the combined forces of union and management, Local 22 collapsed.

Its defeat under this anti-Communist assault seriously affected the shape of the black freedom struggle in Winston-Salem and in other areas to which progressive unions might have expanded. Blacks continued to play a role in the political life of the North Carolina city, but they lost the kind of civil rights militancy that the union had energized during its heyday in the 1940s. As Robert Korstad and Nelson Lichtenstein have shown, Winston-Salem became a "model of racial moderation." Politics consisted mainly of registering to vote and turning out at the ballot box on election day, with a de-emphasis on protest activities and community organizing. Even the NAACP felt the negative effects, as its membership dwindled during the 1950s to less than 500. Political affairs were run by a select group of white and black leaders, with the mass of black residents increasingly relegated to the background in vital decision-making.

Nevertheless, civil rights activism did not disappear from the South. As a matter of fact, in cities such as Montgomery, Alabama, the expanding political clout of the black electorate raised expectations for the possibilities of social change. In the "cradle of the Confederacy" blacks counted for between 7 and 8 percent of the registered voters by 1955, a figure slightly above the statewide average. Even with this relatively small ratio of voters, in 1953 blacks had helped ensure the election of a white city commissioner running against the political establishment. This victory encouraged blacks to make demands on local officials, and several individuals who had actively engaged in political organizing following the demise of the white primary led the way. Edgar D. Nixon, a representative of the International Brotherhood of Sleeping Car Porters and a driving force in the NAACP, obtained a noteworthy 42 percent of the vote in a losing contest for a seat on the county Democratic Executive Committee. Jo Ann Robinson, an English instructor at Alabama State College, headed the Women's Political Council, which served not only to get out the black vote but also to petition the city commission to redress black complaints. Nixon and Robinson were often joined by Rufus A. Lewis, a businessman who chaired the Citizens' Steering Committee.

Buoyed by their growing political confidence, black leaders met with modest success. With the lone commissioner blacks had helped to elect in their corner, they persuaded white officials to increase the number of black police officers and improve bus services in black neighborhoods. Civil rights proponents also pressed demands for the appointment of a black to the Parks and Recreation Board and for the elimination of certain humiliating policies related to bus transportation. Particularly irksome were the requirements that black passengers first pay their fares at the front door and board through the back door, and that they remain standing when seats were available in the white but not the colored area. The limits of their political strength became manifest when the city rejected their requests for change, and in 1955 their white ally on the commission went down to defeat for reelection, beaten by an opponent who injected explicit racial appeals into the campaign.

Thus, black progress remained at a standstill and black political influence appeared to be on the decline when Rosa Parks was arrested on December 1, 1955. A seamstress, former secretary of the local NAACP branch, and recent participant in interracial workshops at the Highlander Folk School in Tennessee, Mrs. Parks refused to vacate her seat for a white passenger on a crowded bus. A spontaneous action only in the sense that the exact details were not planned in advance, her defiance reflected longstanding personal involvement in civil rights activities as well as the natural extension of political efforts by fellow blacks to challenge racism in Montgomery. Parks had long participated in efforts to defend women from sexual abuse, whether it was verbal abuse from bus drivers or to seek justice against predatory white men who raped black women without paying the legal consequences. Consequently, Parks turned to E. D. Nixon for assistance in bailing her out of jail, and he, along with Jo Ann Robinson, hatched plans for a boycott of the buses. The Women's Political Council took the lead in spreading word of the proposed strike by cranking out some 40,000 hand-bills on a mimeograph machine borrowed by Robinson.

Once plans for the boycott were set in motion, black ministers, including Dr. Martin Luther King, Jr., were tapped to assume direction of the protest activities. The recruitment of the clergy brought an important dimension to the struggle. A network of independent churches provided a base from which to mobilize the black masses in a way that middle-class-oriented civil rights groups, civic leagues, and political clubs had failed to accomplish. Though ministers like Dr. King's father in Atlanta had used their pulpits on behalf of voter registration drives, they had rarely before undertaken a project that rallied blacks on such a large, community-wide scale against racial discrimination.[1] The boycott drew support from all segments of the African-American community. Middle-class women like Jo Ann Robinson stood alongside working-class black maids and cooks, the majority of the bus riders. Without their participation, the boycott would have collapsed. So long as most black Montgomerians were barred from participating in the electoral process as voters, they resorted to mass protest to achieve their political aims.

Blacks who participated in the year-long boycott were transformed by the struggle. Reverend King and the Montgomery Improvement Association (MIA), which he directed, came to realize the intransigence of the segregationist forces opposing them and modified their demands accordingly. Originally they had accepted the concept of segregation on the buses and merely sought more courteous treatment and a system that did not force them to relinquish their seats to whites when the black section was filled. But then the city refused to negotiate, black leaders were arrested, and King's home was dynamited. These acts of resistance stiffened the MIA's resolve, and the organization decided to settle for nothing less than complete desegregation of the buses. Mass meetings sustained the minister/leaders and their congregants behind this evolving goal. The inspiring sermons of the charismatic Dr. King and the singing of gospel songs filled with messages of freedom reinforced group solidarity and the determination to persevere. Nevertheless, collective action alone was not enough to destroy Jim Crow, and victory came only after the Supreme Court, on November 13, 1956, voided segregation on public buses.

The lessons that emerged from the Montgomery bus boycott had profound significance for the battle to obtain civil and political rights. Indeed,

---

[1] In 1953 the Reverend T. J. Jemison led a seven-day bus boycott in Baton Rouge, Louisiana, which ended in a compromise. A small number of seats were reserved for whites in the front and for blacks in the rear of the buses, but those in between were open to all.

Figure 5   The Montgomery police fingerprint Rosa Parks after her arrest for failing to vacate her seat on a segregated bus. (AP Photo/Gene Herrick/Press Association)

it showed that the two were inextricably linked. Acquisition of the ballot by itself did not bring power, nor did the piecemeal dismantling of the limbs of Jim Crow. Even after the buses were desegregated blacks in Montgomery faced sporadic violence against their enjoying this right, and most continued to meet obstacles in enrolling as voters. Unless black southerners devised new techniques in mounting grassroots protest, thereby dramatically exposing their plight to the rest of the country, the white South would not voluntarily yield. As J. Mills Thornton has observed: "In the end, the bus boycott teaches that segregation could have been disestablished only in the way in which it was disestablished: by internal pressure sufficient to compel intervention from outside the South." The Supreme Court set the lead in this direction; it remained for the President and Congress to follow.

Massive Resistance and Eisenhower Moderation

The high tribunal's monumental decision in *Brown v. Board of Education* (1954) presented new opportunities for and challenges to the quest for black political equality. Though the ruling applied to the desegregation of public schools, it carried far-ranging implications. Richard Kluger has written that the opinion "represented nothing short of a reconsecration of American ideals." The court removed the legal sanction a prior bench of justices had conferred on the doctrine of white supremacy in *Plessy v. Ferguson* nearly 60 years before. "Separate but equal" no longer bore legitimacy, and blacks could pursue their full rights of citizenship armed not only with morality but with the law. Yet racial justice did not arrive so simply. The Supreme Court left implementation of *Brown* in the hands of southern federal judges and instructed them to proceed with "all deliberate speed." Whatever that phrase signified, it did not mean "soon." Given some leeway, the southern states attempted to push compliance back for as many tomorrows as possible.

The South embarked on massive resistance to preserve segregation in the schools and black subordination in political affairs. State legislatures passed interposition resolutions "nullifying" *Brown*, and enacted pupil placement laws assigning students and teachers to segregated schools according to nonracial criteria. Members of Congress from Dixie issued manifestos denouncing the landmark judicial opinion as unconstitutional and pledging to seek to reverse it. Organizations calling themselves "White Citizens' Councils" arose to buttress the efforts of politicians to concoct supposedly legal means to preserve the status quo. However, this middle-class group of solid citizens – the "uptown Ku Klux Klan" – frequently resorted to illegal or extralegal methods of keeping blacks in their place. As employers they fired "uppity" blacks; as creditors they denied loans to blacks or foreclosed their property; and if all else failed the "uptown Ku Klux Klan" retaliated physically.

White supremacists also waged a fierce battle to destroy the NAACP, the organization that had successfully litigated the *Brown* case. Charging it with subverting the established system of segregation, southern lawmakers tried to drive it from the region. In 1956, Alabama demanded that the NAACP register with the state as an outside corporation and turn over its membership lists. When the association refused to do so for fear of subjecting its members to racial intimidation, Alabama prohibited the NAACP from operating and tied it up in the courts for nearly a decade before it could legally function again. The South hatched a variety of additional schemes to put the organization out of business. Virginia passed anti-barratry legislation aimed at hindering the NAACP from initiating or sponsoring lawsuits against segregation. Louisiana barred teachers from advocating integration of the schools, and South Carolina banished NAACP members from public employment. States such as Florida wielded the weapon of anti-Communism against the association, targeting the NAACP as a subversive organization and establishing a legislative committee to investigate its activities. Although managing to survive, the group suffered considerable damage. In order to defend itself from attack, the NAACP had to divert precious resources away from the main battle against Jim Crow and disfranchisement.

Under this counterassault the drive toward racial equality sputtered. School desegregation moved ahead at a trickling pace and was mainly confined to a handful of cities around the southern periphery; the Deep South shouted "Never!" White opposition had a similarly chilling effect on the advancement of blacks into electoral politics. Though the rate of black voter registration had begun to slow before *Brown*, new recruits were harder to sign up as tensions escalated over the segregation issue. The White Citizens' Councils in Mississippi and Louisiana did their best to keep black applicants off the voter rolls and connived to purge many of those who had managed to get on. In Ouachita Parish, Louisiana, of the 4,000 blacks who had registered through September 1956, only 1,000 remained after Council-inspired challenges. The head of the Mississippi Council facetiously explained the thinking of the disfranchisers: "Why, it'd be like giving the vote to these children of mine, you give the vote to my children and you know who they'd elect for President? Elvis Presley!" Not surprisingly, between 1952 and 1956 only 215,000 additional blacks succeeded in enrolling to vote in the South, leaving 75 percent without the ballot.

Southern blacks had fallen short of reaching their registration potential for several reasons. The voter leagues and the NAACP had merely skimmed the surface. Blacks located in the urban areas of the upper South and in the largest cities in the heart of Dixie made up the biggest proportion of the new voters. However, in rural sections of the black belt, African Americans with little schooling and money were unable and unwilling to register. In these areas they had trouble developing independent leadership because the tiny group of professionals remained tied to white purse strings. School boards threatened to fire teachers who exhibited signs of militancy, and banks refused to extend credit to businesspeople and farmers who tried to organize suffrage drives. If economic pressure did not work, registrars managed to apply literacy tests in such a biased manner that hardly any blacks could pass. And whites were not hesitant to use old-fashioned brute force.

Although the issue of school desegregation became the storm-center of political controversy between white and black southerners following *Brown*, the acquisition of the suffrage continued to loom large as a source of contention between the races. Each side saw much at stake in the outcome. White extremists raised the bugaboo of racial amalgamation that supposedly would follow black political participation. Blacks "desire a much shorter detour, via the political tunnel," Judge Tom Brady, the founder of the White Citizens' Councils, claimed, "to get on the intermarriage turnpikes." Whether or not most white southerners actually feared racial politics entering their bedrooms, they were concerned that black ballots would lead to a basic rearrangement of power and prestige in society. This view received support from blacks themselves. One commentator declared: "desegregation would be much further along if Negroes in the South could vote more nearly in proportion to their potential voting population." In effect, both groups exaggerated the importance of the suffrage as a springboard to equality, but each correctly understood that without the extension of the franchise blacks remained vulnerable to rulers not of their own choosing and whites could not be held strictly accountable for the racist policies they imposed.

The key question was how to achieve enfranchisement. As black southerners struggled against resistance from below, they looked to the federal government for support. Once before – during the Reconstruction period following the Civil War – the national government had provided protection for the right to vote from racial discrimination, but ultimately retreated in the face of southern obstructionism. This time African Americans called for a Second Reconstruction with staying power. During the 1950s they had to rely on a President whose views on race were paternalistic and who preferred to keep Washington out of the internal affairs of the states. This left the job to Congress, a body dominated by a conservative coalition in which southerners routinely pounced on reform measures. Thus, the prospects for assistance from above appeared dim, but they were not hopeless.

Most civil rights leaders and scholars have disapproved of President Eisenhower's handling of racial affairs. Roy Wilkins, the executive director of the NAACP during the Eisenhower years, summed up the perspective of his colleagues: "President Eisenhower was a fine general and a good, decent man, but if he had fought World War II the way he fought for civil rights, we would all be speaking German today." This judgment has been echoed by nearly every historian who has studied this period: "Eisenhower and his subordinates," Robert F. Burk concluded, "had displayed a consistent pattern of hesitancy and extreme political caution in defending black legal rights."

The strength of this criticism lies primarily in the failure of the President to take a firm moral stand in support of *Brown*. When asked whether he endorsed or merely accepted the desegregation ruling, Eisenhower replied: "I think it makes no difference whether or not I endorse it," though he added that he would "do my very best to see that it is carried out in this country." Yet for southern black children it made a critical difference whether the President, especially one as popular as Eisenhower, affirmed their moral, as well as legal, right to attend desegregated schools. The chief executive delayed that possibility by refusing to throw his considerable weight behind the integration process, which, in turn, allowed the momentum to pass to those advocating massive resistance in the South. Ironically, he repeatedly preached the value of education in changing the hearts and minds of individuals, but he distinctly failed to use his presidential pulpit to instruct white southerners about their moral duty to obey the law. Furthermore, he offered scant encouragement to blacks who struggled peacefully to persuade white segregationists to abandon Jim Crow according to the voluntaristic principles Eisenhower espoused. Thus, despite the urging of Martin Luther King, Jr., the President remained silent during the year-long Montgomery bus boycott.

Even with these failings, Eisenhower's record was not without significant accomplishments. He fulfilled his campaign pledge to work for desegregation of the nation's capital in a variety of ways. Without much fanfare, the White House facilitated the desegregation of local movie theaters, hotels, and municipal agencies. The chief executive placed Vice-President Richard M. Nixon in charge of the President's Committee on Government Contract Compliance, and although this agency, like the FEPC before it, lacked enforcement power, it persuaded the transportation company serving the District of Columbia to hire more black bus drivers and streetcar operators and convinced the local telephone company to end segregation in its offices. Moreover, following *Brown*, Eisenhower pressed the District of Columbia to desegregate its schools and likewise ordered several southern military bases to desegregate their educational and service facilities.

These deeds reflected a growing working relationship between the White House and one of black America's premier politicians, Adam Clayton Powell. Along with William L. Dawson of Chicago, Powell sat in the House of Representatives, occupying the highest national elected office held by blacks since Reconstruction. Whereas both belonged to the Democratic Party, they displayed very different styles. A product of Chicago's political machine, Dawson usually placed organizational interests above racial goals. For example, in 1952 he assumed a major role in working out a compromise on the civil rights plank of the party platform that represented a weaker version than that of 1948. In contrast, Powell had been an active protest leader in New York City, had a well-deserved reputation as a political maverick, and had voiced sharp criticism of party leaders, particularly Adlai Stevenson, for hedging on civil rights during the 1952 campaign.

With Eisenhower installed in the Oval Office, Powell aimed his sights at the Republicans, and found a receptive target. The New York congressman brought the issue of segregated military installations to public attention, and he met with presidential counselors to arrange a satisfactory settlement. Powell added to his influence within GOP circles by the publication in *Reader's Digest* of his highly complimentary article about the President's civil rights achievements. Writing in 1954, he lavishly praised Eisenhower for quietly launching a "revolution" that would mean "an era of greater promise for Negro citizens." Nor did Powell's flattery diminish because the chief executive refused to support the congressman's periodic attempts to attach desegregation riders to school construction bills. This rejection did not smart so much, for Powell did not find any stronger support for his amendment among Democratic leaders.

Powell further manifested his independence by bolting to Eisenhower for President in 1956, opening the possibility of large numbers of blacks following him. Some of Eisenhower's advisers recognized the political dividends to be earned from closer administration identification with Powell and the cause of civil rights. They rewarded the congressman with donations to defray the costs of his campaign for reelection. In a less pecuniary vein, Republican officials believed that their party had a "wonderful story to tell," and recommended publicizing more extensively to black audiences the President's favorable record on civil rights.

The possible payoff from doing so was high. In 61 legislative districts outside the South, blacks held the balance of power in the 1954 congressional elections that produced 32 Democratic and 29 Republican victories. In 25 of these constituencies, GOP candidates won with a ratio of less than 55 percent of the vote, while in 14 of those districts the Democrats triumphed in similar fashion. An exchange of 15 seats from the Democratic to the Republican side would furnish the GOP with a majority in the House. A shift of two seats in the Senate would achieve Republican dominance of that body. With the political importance of this in mind, in 1956 Vice-President Nixon told a campaign audience that he awaited the day "when American boys and girls shall sit side by side, at any school ... with no regard paid to the color of their skin."

Eisenhower weighed these considerations against the potential for boosting Republican votes in the South. He hoped to build upon the four southern

Figure 6 Congressional representatives William L. Dawson, on the left, and Adam Clayton Powell, standing in front of the nation's Capitol, were known for contrasting styles of political leadership. (Photo © Bettmann/Corbis)

states he had garnered in 1952. The *Brown* decision, identified with Chief Justice Earl Warren, an Eisenhower appointee, posed a dilemma for a GOP southern strategy, but the President had reduced this liability by persistently declining to speak out forcefully for school integration. Furthermore, he refused to permit his party's 1956 platform to state more than an acceptance of the court's desegregation ruling. At the same time, Ike set out actively to court white southern ballots, especially in the states of the upper South, where Democratic attachments were less solid.

These overtures certainly dismayed black voters, but they also had reason to question the Democrats' commitment to civil rights. Concerned with recovering their earlier presidential losses among whites in the South, the Democrats attempted to soft-pedal the civil rights issue. Their nominee, Adlai Stevenson, sounded very much like Eisenhower in offering his opinion that "only 'gradual' means would satisfactorily settle the school crisis and other problems affecting equal rights for all Americans." In fact, Roy Wilkins found little to choose between the Democratic and Republican platforms. Expressing displeasure with both, he sarcastically observed: "The Democratic plank smelled to heaven; the Republican plank just smelled." In addition, the prominence of obstructionist southern lawmakers in the Democratic Party annoyed blacks. Referring to James Eastland, the powerful chairman of the Senate Judiciary Committee, Clarence Mitchell, the NAACP's Washington lobbyist, called the segregationist senator from Mississippi a "stinking albatross around the neck of the Democratic Party." This appraisal was reinforced by Congressman Powell, who urged black voters to repudiate "Eastlandism."

Bombarded by mixed signals emitted by both partisan camps, the black electorate stuck with the Democrats while displaying some movement toward the Republicans. Though Stevenson received between 60 and 65 percent of the black vote, Eisenhower's portion rose more than 5 percent from its 1952 level. In Harlem, his share climbed by 16.5 percent, and in Chicago it jumped 11 percent. In the South, where the Democratic Party stood most strongly for white supremacy, blacks exhibited the sharpest reversal from past form. Eisenhower increased his share of the black vote by 25 percent, thereby allowing him to win Tennessee and Kentucky. In the urban South, where most enfranchised blacks resided, the GOP incumbent won a majority of nonwhite votes in Atlanta, New Orleans, Memphis, and Richmond. Whereas blacks might cast a mild civil rights protest vote by favoring Eisenhower, most stayed with the Democratic Party, probably in recognition of the New Deal and Fair Deal economic programs from which they benefited. Nevertheless, Roy Wilkins conjectured that the "Republicans could have wrapped up at least 65 percent of the Negro vote … if they had early and emphatically backed the [*Brown*] decision."

Although Eisenhower succeeded once again without the majority of the black electorate behind him, his improved showing encouraged the Republican administration to proceed with pushing ahead its civil rights agenda. As usual, Eisenhower moved cautiously for both philosophical and political reasons – five southern states, one more than in 1952, had supported his reelection bid. But he intended to obtain legislation from Congress, something neither Roosevelt nor Truman had been able to do.

His legislative program centered on expanding the suffrage and drawing blacks into the political mainstream. The chief of the Justice Department's Civil Rights Section, Arthur Caldwell, aptly reflected the President's viewpoint. "The heart of the whole problem of racial discrimination," he asserted, "lies in determined efforts to prevent the Southern Negroes from participation in local government through the use of the vote." In contrast with his attitude toward school desegregation, Eisenhower embraced the franchise as a proper sphere of federal intervention. He considered the right to vote as the foundation of constitutional republicanism, with specific guarantees for its protection from racial bias spelled out in the Fifteenth Amendment. Besides, the chief executive emphasized the suffrage because it suited his gradualistic approach toward racial equality. As blacks gained access to the ballot box, he reasoned, they could quietly and methodically remove the barriers that confronted them. Accordingly, this deliberate process would reduce tensions by allowing time for white southerners to change their hearts and minds slowly but surely. Furthermore, especially in light of the inroads the Republicans had made among the black electorate in 1956, the President and his political aides looked forward to bringing newly enfranchised blacks into GOP ranks.

The vehicle for the Eisenhower administration's designs became the Civil Rights Act of 1957. This measure had originated two years earlier after the attorney general, Herbert Brownell, became alarmed by rising violence against southern blacks. In 1955, two black Mississippians had been murdered while engaging in voter registration activities, and a 14-year-old youth, Emmett Till, was kidnapped and killed by two Mississippi whites for allegedly making an improper remark to a white woman. Along with Brownell, sympathetic White House aides worried about a "dangerous racial conflagration" brewing in the South. At the same time, the Montgomery bus boycott indicated the determination of black southerners to wage, albeit nonviolently, a prolonged struggle against Jim Crow. In April 1956, Brownell responded to the potential for disruption caused by black protest and white resistance by proposing to Congress a four-part civil rights measure. This omnibus bill created a Commission on Civil Rights, upgraded the Civil Rights Section into a division within the Justice Department, and empowered the attorney general to initiate civil proceedings to enforce school desegregation and voting rights suits.

The President hesitated to embrace his attorney general's broad proposal. His cabinet divided over the matter, FBI director J. Edgar Hoover warned about Communist influence in the civil rights movement, and the chief executive appeared reluctant to offend his white southern allies. At first, he agreed to approve only the two least controversial provisions, those establishing a Civil Rights Commission and a Civil Rights Division. However, in the heat of his campaign battle for reelection in 1956, he adopted the entire package as his own. Passed by the House, the bill died in the Senate in the clutches of Senator Eastland's Judiciary Committee.

Following Eisenhower's presidential victory, the administration revived the civil rights measure with all four sections intact. That did not last for long. A combination of presidential moderation and Democratic Party factionalism shaped the final version of the bill. Never enthusiastic about the item authorizing the Justice Department to seek court orders for school desegregation, the chief executive virtually withdrew his support for it. In one memorable instance, he publicly confessed that he "didn't completely understand" the proposal. In contrast, he did not waver in his support for the suffrage recommendation. "This was the overriding provision of the bill I wanted set down in law," he told a prominent southern senator, and added: "With his right to vote assured, the Negro could use it to help secure his other rights."

The President found a powerful ally on the Democratic side of the congressional aisle. Majority leader Lyndon B. Johnson of Texas also wanted a measure restricted to the suffrage that avoided the pitfalls of the more emotionally charged issue of school desegregation. The Texas senator was at the stage of his career when he was trying to shape a national reputation to distinguish himself from his segregationist southern colleagues. Although opposed to civil rights legislation earlier in his tenure as a lawmaker, he was never a diehard segregationist and most recently had refused to sign the Southern Manifesto condemning the *Brown* decision. With presidential ambitions possibly in his mind, he was now ready to advance a step further.

The majority leader sought to fashion a bill that would be acceptable to both liberal and conservative wings of his party, one which northern Democrats could claim as a victory for civil rights and southerners could accept as least objectionable. This last concern was particularly important. Though Johnson hoped to enhance his image in the North, he retained strong roots in and affection for the South. In fact, he wished to save the region from its worst instincts, as his legislative aide explained: "The South is now completely without allies. In this situation, the South can stave off disaster only by appealing to those men who wish to see a civil rights bill enacted but who are willing to listen to reason." In serving as a broker between the two opposing camps of congressional Democrats, Johnson would improve his own chances for higher office, build party unity, and strengthen the Democrats for competing in upcoming national elections.

Driven by Johnson's skillful parliamentary maneuvering, Congress produced a moderate civil rights law. After the House passed the original four-part version of the bill, the Johnson-led Senate sliced the school desegregation feature, leaving the sections on the Civil Rights Commission, Civil Rights Division, and voting rights litigation. With these features intact, Johnson made a gesture to keep his fellow southerners from waging a filibuster against them. He engineered passage of a proviso that required voting rights infractions in certain cases to be tried before a jury. Until this point, Eisenhower had approved of Johnson's handiwork, but he balked at adding the jury trial proviso. In this instance he joined liberals in both parties who believed that reliance upon southern white juries for enforcement would severely weaken the bill. In the end, Johnson forged an alliance of southerners, Democratic moderates from the North and West, and conservative Republicans to approve the disputed item. After adopting some modifications acceptable to the President, Congress passed the bill and Eisenhower signed it into law.

The first Civil Rights Act in 82 years owed its passage to a variety of sources. The Eisenhower administration sponsored the original measure and then cooperated with Johnsonian Democrats to mold it into a right-to-vote law. Southerners refrained from sabotaging the proposal through a filibuster because they could live with a bill restricted to the franchise. Though liberal lawmakers and civil rights advocates expressed great disappointment in the final outcome for its omission of school desegregation, they still took some satisfaction in securing this "half-loaf." Senator Hubert Humphrey of Minnesota remarked to Roy Wilkins: "Roy, if there's one thing I have learned in politics, it's never to turn your back on a crumb." At the very least, the NAACP and its allies had a bill aimed at expanding black voter registration, which they regarded as a significant advance. Moreover, they had a legislative precedent to build upon for the future.

The Tuskegee Struggle

Ultimately the success or failure of the act would be judged by its performance at the local level. The struggle for enfranchisement in Macon County, Alabama, offers a look at the interrelationship between federal policy and grassroots social change. With a unique history and social structure of its own, the county nevertheless shared many of the same experiences as hundreds of localities throughout the black belt of the South.

Located in the southeastern portion of the state, about 45 miles from Montgomery, the county had a black population exceeding 80 percent. Its county seat of Tuskegee also had a substantial black majority, many of whom came to teach or study at the famous institute founded by Booker T. Washington in the 1880s. Many of the town's residents were employed at the Veterans Administration hospital built in 1923, and some had arrived as soldiers for training at the army airfield during World War II. In the postwar era, the size of the black middle class in Tuskegee swelled, and blacks held a majority of the white-collar jobs in the town. The presence of a rising black bourgeoisie centered in Tuskegee, however, could not obscure the existence of widespread poverty, especially in the rural areas of the county. In 1960, 15 percent of Macon County blacks earned $6,000 or more, a stark contrast to the 64 percent with incomes of less than $3,000.

Since the days of Booker T. Washington, when whites had cooperated in establishing Tuskegee Institute, relations between the races had been paternalistic. Whites and blacks took pride in the school as a model for racial advancement as long as it developed within a rigidly segregated environment. Early in the twentieth century a leading white politician explained how things worked: "The very best representatives of the white race, from its beginnings until now, have controlled the destinies of the town ... and by the grace of God, will continue that control to the end." This "model community" depended on accommodation on the part of blacks in return for civility from whites in order to maintain this customary power relationship. Yet the pattern of interaction inherited from Washington's era contained the seeds of its own destruction. Given the space to develop their own educational and economic institutions, to lift themselves up by their bootstraps as Washington had prescribed, black Tuskegeeans demanded the full citizenship rights to which their advancement into the middle class entitled them.

To leaders of this upwardly mobile group no badge of inferiority seemed more irksome than their exclusion from the ballot. No one had worked harder to achieve the goal of black political enfranchisement than Charles G. Gomillion. A sociologist at the institute, he was one of fewer than a hundred blacks in Macon County to have registered to vote by 1939. Two years later, he converted the Tuskegee Men's Club into the Tuskegee Civic Association, admitted women, and embarked on a concerted campaign to rally blacks to challenge their treatment as second-class citizens. Gomillion based his approach on the concept of "civic democracy," by which he meant that all citizens, regardless of color, had "the opportunity to participate in societal affairs, and benefit from or enjoy public services, in keeping with their interests, abilities, and needs." Without the chance for color-blind political participation, Gomillion reasoned, blacks would continue to suffer from discrimination in the allocation of resources for essential municipal services, such as health and education. Until black Tuskegeans exercised the power of the ballot, white officials could afford to ignore their requests for equal treatment.

However cordially white rulers behaved out of a sense of paternalism toward blacks, the whites did not intend to be held politically accountable to blacks. Instead, the whites had devised a series of hurdles to prevent blacks from registering to vote. In addition to the standard poll-tax restriction, the three-person county election board administered a harsh literacy test to black applicants that whites did not have to endure. The panel used its discretion to fail blacks, no matter how educated they were. If blacks pressed on and refused to give up, they often could not find the board in session to risk another try. When in operation, the registrars processed black applications at a snail's pace and confined waiting blacks to cramped quarters, making it uncomfortable for them to show up at the courthouse. According to Alabama law, registrars could require applicants to bring a voucher to identify them as a proper resident of the area, and in Macon County the board insisted that a black could not vouch for more than two registrants per year.

In 1945, the Tuskegee Civic Association, in cooperation with the NAACP, decided to bring the election board to court. William P. Mitchell served as the plaintiff. An employee of the VA hospital and executive secretary of the Civic Association, Mitchell had been doggedly and unsuccessfully trying to register for years. The case dragged on for two years and became moot when local officials belatedly "discovered" that Mitchell had been registered in 1943, though he had never been informed of that fact. The situation improved for a stretch of time in the late 1940s after Herman Bentley, a newly appointed member of the registration board who held a populistic commitment to political democracy, broke from tradition and agreed to sign up nonwhites. After more than 400 blacks added their names to the rolls, the other two members of the board put a halt to further progress by boycotting meetings, thereby hamstringing the panel from functioning.

This upsurge in black political participation frightened white officials. In 1950, blacks, now 30 percent of the electorate, wielded their balance of power to defeat the incumbent sheriff and replace him with a more sympathetic white candidate. The landmark *Brown* decision in 1954 and the bus boycott in nearby Montgomery the following year highlighted the threat that rising black activism posed for white supremacy. In response, Macon County officials fought back. Led by State Senator Samuel M. Engelhardt, Jr., they slowed down black registration by removing Bentley from the board and, in 1957, devised a scheme to eliminate nearly all black voters from Tuskegee. Through an imaginative redrawing of the town's boundary lines, the state legislature carved black neighborhoods out of the city, leaving the black electorate disfranchised in municipal elections and not plentiful enough to exert much influence in the county.

Whatever illusions middle-class blacks in Tuskegee may have retained about the fairness of paternalistic whites operating within a segregated system were shattered by the flagrant gerrymander. In response, the Civic Association organized a boycott – a selective buying campaign – against local white merchants. Though lay political leaders like Gomillion led the protest, ministers played an important role in mobilizing masses of blacks who regularly attended church but remained outside the sphere of Civic Association influence. The protest against the gerrymander succeeded in connecting middle-class blacks in the town with impoverished rural blacks in the surrounding county. Paralleling the situation in Montgomery, the Tuskegee boycott welded a community into a palpable force for political change. Years of voter education and litigation by the Civic Association had paved the way, but the experience of collective action rallied ordinary individuals as well as college teachers and professionals into agents of political participation. Gomillion's civic democracy came alive, as mass meetings provided an inspirational forum to build morale, share information, and maintain discipline.

Also like its Montgomery counterpart, the boycott did not force whites to capitulate to black demands; the federal government did. In 1960, the Supreme Court finally declared the gerrymander unconstitutional and restored black voters to the city's political boundaries. In *Gomillion v. Lightfoot*, Justice Felix Frankfurter denounced Alabama's peculiar "essay in geometry and geography" that impaired black voting rights under the guise of "the realignment of political subdivisions."

Macon County blacks had learned at first hand that protest had to be reinforced by federal intervention in order to achieve equal citizenship rights. Besides the gerrymander battle, the Tuskegee Civic Association was directly involved with obtaining national legislation to erase suffrage discrimination. During the debate over the 1957 Civil Rights Act, Charles Gomillion and William Mitchell traveled to Washington to tell their stories of voter discrimination by county registrars. New York City's *Amsterdam News*, a black newspaper, declared that "nothing could throw the spotlight so brilliantly on the shame and hypocrisy of southern legislators than the fight the Negroes are now waging in Macon County ... for constitutional rights to register and vote." Following passage of the 1957 law, Senator Paul Douglas, a liberal Democrat from Illinois, advised Mitchell to "continue to assemble the facts that will help to make the case for the next forward steps."

This Mitchell did by turning over to the Justice Department the voluminous records of suffrage bias he had carefully compiled over the years. As a result, one of the first suits the federal government initiated under the 1957 law pertained to Macon County. However, the Civic Association suffered a setback in 1959, when a federal judge ruled that the statute did not apply to the situation at hand. Because the members of the registration board had resigned, the government had no party to sue.

In the meantime, county residents themselves provided dramatic testimony of the trouble they experienced in attempting to exercise their political rights. In December 1958, the United States Commission on Civil Rights convened public hearings in Montgomery to investigate franchise abuses. The testimony it heard, which was recorded for broadcast on national television news programs, came across as a vivid morality play. Blacks stepped forward to testify, with both passion and dignity, to the affronts they had suffered in trying to accomplish what should have been a simple act of signing up to vote. Instead, property owners, taxpayers, veterans, college graduates, and VA hospital employees explained how the members of the registration board frequently went into hiding, how they engaged in work slowdowns, and how they failed applicants on the literacy tests without ever notifying them of the reason. "I have come up to the other requirements to make myself a citizen," a black Macon County farmer declared. "I would like to be a registered voter; they ought to give that to me. It's like I want to become a part of the government activity."

In contrast, the civil rights commissioners and television viewers saw local officials refuse either to testify under oath about their behavior or to furnish suffrage files that had been subpoenaed. One of Macon County's registrars, Grady Rogers, invoked his constitutional right against self-incrimination and further denied that the commission had the authority to probe into his activities. Faced with this lack of cooperation, the panel obtained the vital information through a court order. The records its investigators subsequently examined convinced the commissioners that the federal government would once again have to intervene to correct widespread voting discrimination. Released in 1959, the agency's report catalogued the obstructionist practices manipulated by Alabama registrars against black applicants and recommended that Congress empower the President to dispatch federal registrars to enroll qualified black voters in the South.

Though civil rights advocates like William Mitchell wholeheartedly endorsed such a proposal, national lawmakers refrained from going so far. The alliance between the Eisenhower administration and Johnson Democrats that had succeeded in 1957 triumphed again three years later. Despite objections from liberals in both parties and from civil rights lobbyists, in 1960 Congress passed a voting rights law that retained judicial supervision over the suffrage process. Instead of federal registrars, legislators authorized court-appointed referees to resolve difficult franchise cases. This procedure was substantially weaker than the one proposed by the Civil Rights Commission because it continued to rely on litigation that had proven to be slow and cumbersome in furnishing a cure for chronic discrimination.

Nevertheless, a provision of the new law immediately benefited Macon County blacks. Allowed to sue state officials when a county registration board ceased functioning, the Justice Department succeeded in obtaining a federal court injunction against prevailing voter bias in the county. In 1961, Judge Frank M. Johnson of Alabama, whose rulings on race made him one of the most liberal federal judges in the South, reviewed the copious documents gathered by the Justice Department in cooperation with the Tuskegee Civic Association and had no trouble finding ample evidence of bias. Consequently, he ordered the registration board to cease its discriminatory practices and to take positive action to speed up its work schedule, enroll qualified applicants, and report back to him on a regular basis. Within a short period, black registration more than doubled to nearly 2,500. After so many years of determination and frustration, William Mitchell was elated. "We had not even thought of such an all-inclusive decree," he jubilantly remarked.

Fayette County, Tennessee

While African Americans in Tuskegee squared off against white officials who sought to deter them from voting, a band of courageous blacks began a voting campaign in Fayette County, Tennessee, whose county seat of

Somerville is located 50 miles from Memphis in the southwestern portion of the state. Before it was over, the suffrage campaign led to the eviction of black sharecroppers, the erection of a tent city for the dislocated, and the intervention of the federal government in support of black voting rights. This voting struggle lasted for some three years, reinforcing the importance of indigenous movements in pushing the civil rights struggle forward and persuading the federal government to come to their side.

The catalyst for the massive voter registration drive that led to the eviction of hundreds of sharecroppers and their families from 1959 to 1960 was the trial of Burton Dodson. In 1941, Dodson fled his farmhouse in Fayette County after a shoot-out with white night-riders left one white man dead. Earlier that day he had gotten into an argument with a white man over a black woman and eventually the two of them "came to blows." The white man, having been offended by Dodson's actions, gathered a mob and went to his farmhouse in the middle of the night. "They were shootin' from the smokehouse and outa the top of trees and all out from around the house," remembered Harpman Jameson. Dodson was able to escape by running out the back of his house "running west, shootin' back, and that mob chased him into the woods." Dodson moved to East St. Louis, Illinois, where he stayed for 18 years. In March 1959, word got out that he was still alive (he was in his seventies by then), and he was brought back to Fayette County to face murder charges.

The trial in April 1959 mobilized local blacks because Dodson was defended by a black lawyer named J. F. Estes. Estes drove from Memphis for the trial and African Americans in Fayette County flocked to the courthouse to watch him work, since "a black lawyer appearing to defend a black man was unheard of [and] people put aside their farm work and flocked to the courthouse to see it for themselves." John McFerren and Harpman Jameson, African-American farmers in the area, wanted to serve on the grand jury. When "we found out you had to be registered before you could serve on the grand jury," Jameson remembered, "... we got interested in registerin' and getting our people registered." After Dodson received a 20-year sentence for a murder he did not commit, Jameson and McFerren "began to register to vote."

At the time of the trial, 16,927 African Americans lived in Fayette County, Tennessee, making up the majority (68.9 percent) of the population, yet only 58 blacks had managed to sign up to vote between 1952 and 1959. One month after the trial, McFerren and Jameson organized the Fayette County Civic and Welfare League and held their first voter registration rally at the

Fayette County courthouse in Somerville. (They also helped form a sister organization in neighboring Haywood County.) That day they registered 300 African Americans. In July, they registered another 380. After that, however, the registrar began to make things difficult. "And we began to get a whole lotta junk then," Jameson recalled. "There was one day somebody got up on the courthouse and sprinkled pepper down on the people. And they got up there paintin' one day and they were throwin' paint down on the people in line. And we have had a tough time getting registered all the way on up until now."

These problems were a prelude of things to come. When Fayette blacks went to vote for the first time that August, they were turned away and told that the primary election was for whites only, despite the fact the Supreme Court had declared the white primary unconstitutional in 1944. McFerren sought the help of J. F. Estes, the attorney who had defended Burton Dodson earlier that year, and asked him if they could file a legal complaint with the federal government. Estes thought they could, under the Civil Rights Act of 1957, and so in November 1959 they drove to Washington, DC, to meet with John Doar, a lawyer in the newly created Civil Rights Division of the Justice Department. McFerren, Jameson, Estes, and two others returned to Fayette County with word from the Justice Department that it planned to bring an indictment against the landowners who denied them the right to vote. The lawsuit filed by the Justice Department charged the Fayette County Democratic Executive Committee and its members with failing to let African Americans vote in the August 1 Democratic primary. In response, members of the Fayette County Election Commission resigned in hope of creating a county-wide shutdown of voter registration and evading the lawsuit.

Nevertheless, on April 25, 1960, the Justice Department and the county settled the dispute, which led to the appointment of new election commissioners and an agreement to end voting discrimination. As a result, nearly 1,000 African Americans added their names to the electoral lists. Spurred on by the federal decree, blacks held mass meetings in the spring of 1960. They met at Mount Olive Baptist Church – the only church in the area that would allow the Fayette County Civic and Welfare League to meet regularly.

This upsurge in black suffrage spurred white reprisals. By the fall of 1960 the White Citizens' Council had created a "blacklist" that contained the names of every registered African American. White business owners passed the list around – even to businesses outside Fayette County – and used it to target blacks for economic retaliation. White grocers refused to sell milk and other necessary foodstuffs; banks refused to give loans; and white farmers deliberately began to mechanize their farms to eliminate the need for black labor. Additionally, Gulf, Esso, Texaco, and Amoco oil outlets refused to sell their products. Only in August 1960, after the national NAACP, with its 350,000 members, threatened to boycott the oil companies, was the embargo called off.

Worst of all, sharecroppers who registered to vote were evicted from their homes and kicked off the land they had worked for decades. Black farmers who were already mired in poverty struggled to simply stay alive. James Forman, the executive secretary of the Student Nonviolent Coordinating Committee (see Chapter 3), who worked as a volunteer and citizenship teacher in Fayette County, estimated that over 700 sharecropping families were evicted that year. Other estimates put the number between 257 and 400, but regardless of the exact figures most of those ejected had no money and could not find work. They could not get credit at grocery stores and could not access medical care.

Georgia Mae Turner registered in late 1960 – timed to make sure she received her last paycheck – and shortly thereafter her employer for 38 years told her she had to pack her stuff and leave before the start of the New Year. "She made me get out of her house in the snow," Turner recalled. "I had to get out before winter was even over." Despite her situation, Turner tried to maintain a sense of humor: "They say if you register, you going to have a hard time. Well, I had a hard time before I registered. Hard times, you could have named me that – Georgia Mae Hard Times." Besides always living in "hard times," Turner said she went to register "because I want to be a citizen … I registered so that my children could get their freedom. I don't figure it would do me no good."

Evicted sharecroppers like Georgia Mae Turner moved to "Tent City" – a stretch of land owned by Shepard Towles, an independent black farmer. Towles allowed the sharecroppers to pitch tents on his land and live there while they protested their evictions and demanded their right to vote. A second camp was set up near Moscow, Tennessee, on land owned by Gertrude Beasley, an African-American woman. While Tent City was "the scene of severe hardship" it was also "a symbol of defiance and fierce pride." Tent City also became the site of several shoot-outs between members of the White Citizens' Councils and the African Americans who lived there. Forman described the armed guards that kept watch over the tents each night: "black men with guns, guns, and more guns were deployed around the tents, on the side of the road, behind bushes, and in the fields." Early B. Williams, a resident of Tent City, was hit by a stray bullet one night and had to be driven all the way to Memphis to receive medical care. The bullet just barely missed his sleeping toddler.

Tent City received national attention in the *New York Post, Ebony*, and the *New York Times*, which helped launch food and clothing drives all around the country. According to the historian Robert Hamburger, a "convoy of seven forty-foot trucks carried 50 tons of food and clothing from New York to Tent City." The federal government did not authorize shipments of surplus food until July 1961, but in the meantime, on December 14, 1960, the Justice Department filed another lawsuit against 45 landowners, 24 merchants, and a bank, accusing all parties "of violating the civil rights of black citizens of Fayette County." Not until June 26, 1962, did a consent decree in federal district court in Memphis end all pending lawsuits against the 74 defendants, landowners, and merchants. The agreement permanently "enjoined the defendants from engaging in any acts for the purpose of interfering with the right of any person to vote." The ruling proved something of an empty victory; reprisals against African Americans continued, and many found it difficult to gain suffrage rights without risking their lives or livelihoods thereafter. Still, the struggles of the black people of Fayette County yielded tangible results. In 1966 the first African-American men and women won election to the Fayette County Quarterly Court.

A Measure of Progress

The struggle to obtain the ballot, the prerequisite for blacks to compete in the electoral system, moved forward with some success during the 1950s. Compared with the more emotional issue of school desegregation, reenfranchisement drew greater support from northern politicians and less opposition from southern officials. By lining up behind two voting rights measures in 1957 and 1960, the Eisenhower administration preferred bipartisan legitimacy to the civil rights agenda initiated by President Truman. Clearly on the defensive, white southerners, particularly in the rural black belt and in some major cities, continued to probe how they could keep black political participation to a minimum. In fact the laws were too weak to overcome all the difficulties that remained, but they did establish a crucial precedent for renewed federal intervention against racial discrimination in the South. Eisenhower also set a pattern that would guide his successors: federal intrusion into state control over racial matters would proceed cautiously, with cooperation rather than coercion the standard. Intervention did not necessarily mean invasion, and only as a last resort, as Eisenhower did in Little Rock in 1957, would a president send troops into the South to enforce federal court rulings.[2] Voluntarism, backed up by litigation and administrative pressure, was the preferred technique.

For civil rights activists this approach dictated a strategy that increasingly emphasized confrontation. Only by challenging racism directly could they produce the kind of disorder and crisis that would bring federal intervention on their side. Events had already demonstrated that the civil rights movement needed to operate along two tracks – the national and the local. Without pressure from below, neither the stimulus for change nor the group solidarity to propel the struggle would exist. Without assistance from above, the weapons to shatter entrenched local resistance would be missing. Blacks in Montgomery and Macon County, Alabama, and Fayette, Tennessee, had shown the truth of this proposition. Combining mass action, litigation, and lobbying, African Americans were defining their goals, mobilizing their communities around them, and drawing in national allies on their side.

[2] After a federal court decreed the desegregation of Little Rock's Central High School, Governor Orval Faubus blocked the order by deploying the Arkansas National Guard to keep out nine black students. Having initially remarked that he could foresee no circumstances that would compel him to send military forces into the South, President Eisenhower changed his mind in order to uphold the primacy of national authority. Consequently, he federalized the National Guard and dispatched paratroopers from the 101st Airborne Division to implement the law and preserve order while the students attended the school.

3

Surging Protest, Shifting Politics

The initial ferment of black discontent in the 1950s left white supremacy challenged but unbroken. Although innovative boycotts succeeded in rallying black communities against segregation and disfranchisement, they failed to crack Jim Crow or destroy the virtual white monopoly over public affairs. Along with litigation and lobbying, sustained protests in Montgomery, Tuskegee, and scattered cities throughout the South managed to engage the federal government against racial discrimination. However, the combination of local black activism and national involvement had not yet created sufficient force to overcome massive white resistance to extending political power to blacks. Despite passage of the 1957 Civil Rights Act, by the end of the decade slightly fewer than three in ten adult black southerners had qualified to participate in the electoral process.

Crusaders for Citizenship

The bus boycott struggle had produced a new and potentially powerful institutional weapon to gain first-class citizenship. In 1957, the Southern Christian Leadership Conference (SCLC) was formed to coordinate local black protest movements that emerged to challenge racial bias in the South. Black ministers directed the organization. In the past the clergy had often provided conservative racial leadership, stressing otherworldly rewards for those who patiently suffered their fate in the here and now. Following World War II, a new breed of preacher arose, emphasizing the Christian virtues of

Running for Freedom: Civil Rights and Black Politics in America since 1941,
Fourth Edition. Steven F. Lawson.
© 2015 John Wiley & Sons, Inc. Published 2015 by John Wiley & Sons, Inc.

brotherhood, equality, and justice as ideals to be attained on earth as well as in heaven. From pulpits in Montgomery, Birmingham, and Mobile, Alabama; Baton Rouge, Louisiana; Atlanta, Georgia; Nashville, Tennessee; and Tallahassee, Florida, these ministers activated the machinery of the black church and the language and symbols of the Bible to lead their congregants in battles against racism.

In effect, the SCLC functioned as "the political arm of the black church." It attempted to supplement the traditional civil rights work of the NAACP with its own brand of activism. Unlike the older group, which preferred to achieve political change through legislation and the courts, the SCLC focused on direct-action techniques to obtain that goal. Drawing upon their recent experiences in attacking Jim Crow, the founders of the Conference chose nonviolent resistance as their primary means of combating white supremacy. This meant that the black masses would be mobilized in their local communities to confront directly the sources of their oppression. More than any other institution, the black church could provide an independent base from which to stage demonstrations and furnish the moral and social support necessary to nurture collective action. Thus, the SCLC fused religious traditionalism – the cultural heritage of the church – with political progressivism.

Though many strong-willed and independent-minded ministers created the SCLC, Martin Luther King, Jr., stood out to lead it. His compelling oratory and his courage in the face of violence during the Montgomery bus boycott thrust him into the national limelight. He had a special ability to give voice to the immediate concerns of ordinary black folks and to place their goals and aspirations within a larger national and international movement for freedom. As one of those people who sat in the mass meetings in Montgomery and heard him preach later recalled: "I mean, he was talking about what we oughta have, and what we oughta be, and what the situation oughta be in the South, and what kind of country we oughta live in." Along with many others, that listener found inspiration in King's powerful message to his audience: "If you will protest courageously, and yet with dignity and Christian love, when the history books are written in future generations, the historians will have to pause and say, 'There lived a great people – a black people – who injected new meaning and dignity into the veins of civilization.' "

King's political strategy developed from both secular and religious influences. An intellectual with a doctorate in theology from Boston University, King studied the philosophical tracts of Henry David Thoreau, Karl Marx, G. W. F. Hegel, and Reinhold Niebuhr, among others, which provided him with a framework for action in which struggle was necessary to liberate oppressed people everywhere. From Mahatma Gandhi, whose ideas he became better acquainted with through advisers such as Bayard Rustin, Dr. King adopted the philosophy of nonviolent resistance to evil. But, perhaps above all, he owed his personal resolve to challenge racism, actively yet peacefully, to Jesus of Nazareth. In his darkest moments of despair, King turned to Christ for strength in confronting the hardships of racial tyranny. In late January 1956, his arrest and the receipt of numerous threats against his life left him sorely troubled. One evening, in the quiet of the midnight hour in the kitchen of his home, he heard the voice of Jesus consoling him: "Martin Luther, stand up for righteousness. Stand up for justice. Stand up for truth. And lo I will be with you, even unto the end of the world."

This total commitment to nonviolence as a religious and ethical principle did not make King politically soft-minded. Though often speaking about converting the hearts and minds of white supremacists through the example of Christian love, suffering, and forgiveness on the part of blacks, he always understood that this transformation would not occur merely by persuading whites voluntarily to abandon discriminatory practices. Instead, he backed up his moralistic appeals with practical acts of coercion. Ecumenical arguments alone would never lead blacks to freedom; the application of power was essential to changing racist behavior and the underlying institutions that supported it. "When King spoke of 'converting' the oppressor," Adam Fairclough has argued, "he was thinking of a long-term historical process rather than an immediate personal response."

King and the SCLC aimed one of their first efforts at exerting political pressure on the Eisenhower administration and Congress to pass the Civil Rights Act of 1957. Joined by A. Philip Randolph, the architect of the 1941 March on Washington Movement, and Roy Wilkins of the NAACP, King convened a "Prayer Pilgrimage" in the nation's capital "to give thanks for progress to date, and pray for wiping out the evils that still beset us." For months the SCLC chief had pressed Eisenhower to condemn racist violence against blacks in a major address delivered in a southern city. Repeatedly rebuffed, King informed him that: "[if] you, our President, cannot come South, we shall have to lead our people to you." On May 17, 1957, in commemoration of the third anniversary of the *Brown* decision, nearly 30,000 people gathered to hear King call for the passage of legislation guaranteeing the ballot, which, he declared, would clear the way for the attainment of the other basic rights blacks sought.

Though the convocation came off smoothly, it took final shape in a manner different from that originally conceived. While King prepared to practice the new politics of mass mobilization, Adam Clayton Powell and leaders of the NAACP implemented the old-fashioned politics of power brokerage. The close relationship between the New York City congressman and the Eisenhower administration paid off for the President. Powell, as well as Roy Wilkins, opposed the march as a means of applying pressure on the chief executive. Rather, they favored the protesters directing their full force at Congress, urging it to pass civil rights legislation. Along with NAACP representatives, Powell succeeded in steering attention away from the President as a target of the demonstration. Administration officials breathed a sigh of relief that they had avoided "the damaging effects of a spectacular effort designed to criticize the president." Consequently, in his address Dr. King denounced the lawmakers of both parties who "so often have a high blood pressure of words and an anemia of deeds."

At this early stage in his career King had limited effectiveness as a national political leader. However significant the Washington demonstration may have been in rallying tens of thousands of blacks in protest against racial discrimination, it had little impact on the eventual enactment of the civil rights bill. Furthermore, it had no immediate impact in persuading the President to make even a symbolic gesture that would recognize the legitimate concerns of civil rights advocates. In June 1957, the Reverend King managed to meet with Vice-President Richard Nixon, who affirmed his personal support for civil rights; nevertheless, the President himself refused to confer with black leaders despite their repeated requests for an appointment. Not until June 1958 did the chief executive hold his first and only conference with a delegation of black leaders. On this occasion they discussed voting rights enforcement, but reached no agreement on the need for stronger implementation by the federal government of the 1957 statute.

By then, King and the SCLC had launched their own project within the South designed to register the majority of disfranchised blacks. They hoped to build upon the momentum of the bus boycotts and galvanize the black electorate as an active force in regional and national politics. "The time has come to broaden the struggle for Negroes to register and vote," the SCLC declared, "for the simple reason that until this happens, we cannot really influence the legislative branch of government." In the past the NAACP, civic leagues, unions, and the churches had conducted voter registration drives. The SCLC sought to link these traditional efforts with its emerging direct action program. The passage of the 1957 Civil Rights Act offered the prospect of federal judicial support for the suffrage, but King believed the effectiveness of the remedy would "depend in large degree upon programs of sustained mass movement on the part of Negroes." According to the SCLC's president, "History has demonstrated that inadequate legislation supported by mass action can accomplish more than adequate legislation which remains unenforced for lack of a determined mass movement."

On February 12, 1958, the birthday of Abraham Lincoln, the SCLC embarked on a project to help emancipate blacks from the "strong fear and deep antipathy toward having anything to do with politics." The Crusade for Citizenship hoped by 1960 to enroll an additional 3 million black southern-ers as voters, doubling the number already on the books. Toward that goal, it planned to coordinate mass registration campaigns through community-based civic organizations and churches. Workshops, clinics, and rallies were conducted in cities throughout the South – Montgomery, Birmingham, Memphis, Atlanta – where SCLC had strong affiliates. Not only would pro-spective registrants learn how to satisfy suffrage requirements, but they also would learn about the strategy of direct action that SCLC espoused. At the very least, the Crusade intended to gather specific complaints of voter discrimination and turn them over to the federal government.

These ambitious designs went largely unrealized. As a fledgling organiza-tion the SCLC lacked the funds and experience to implement such a massive enterprise. Budgeted for $200,000, the Crusade failed to raise more than a quarter of that amount. Inadequate finances placed an economic burden on the Crusade's overworked staff. Ella Baker, who nearly single-handedly managed the operation, received little support from the agency's ministerial leaders. Baker did not lack the talent or experience to perform the job, for she had served as field secretary and director of branches for the NAACP. However, she was the lone female on the SCLC's administrative staff, and she suffered from the slights of paternalistic male preachers, who did not view women as equal partners and whose powerful egos made it difficult to impose strict organizational discipline upon them.

Even without these internal problems, the SCLC encountered a nearly insurmountable task. The rise of massive white resistance following the *Brown* ruling, though directed mainly at halting school desegregation, thwarted civil rights activities of any kind. Southern officials employed literacy tests and other restrictive registration methods to retard black electoral participation. In the face of suffrage discrimination and in a hos-tile environment that punitively discouraged minority voting, the SCLC had little chance of reaching most disfranchised southern blacks. Instead of the 3 million new voters that the SCLC targeted, only 160,000 blacks signed up to vote between 1958 and 1960. Still, the group did compile a list of suffrage grievances and presented them for investigation to the United States Civil Rights Commission and the Justice Department.

In addition, the SCLC received scant help from the NAACP. Under assault by southern state governments, the association's activities were suspended or severely limited in several areas. Besides, the NAACP viewed the formation of the SCLC with misgivings, fearful of the competition it would provide for funds and publicity. During this same period the NAACP, despite its hardships, inaugurated a campaign to register 3 million southern blacks. It, too, fell far short of the mark. Neither conventional registration drives nor those linked to direct action worked against the firm obstacles erected by the white South. Beset by serious internal and external difficulties, by 1960 King and the SCLC had failed to rally the black masses behind the ballot.

With the efforts of the SCLC and the NAACP stymied, the movement for first-class citizenship needed a boost. Blacks had barely penetrated the wall of white supremacy, and fresh troops and ideas were needed to scale it. The federal government had provided some welcome judicial and legislative relief, but Washington expected southern blacks and whites to resolve their problems largely at the local level.

Civil rights leaders recognized that they did not have sufficient power to win by themselves; yet, at the same time, they understood the importance of blacks joining together to fight for their own freedom. The adoption of boycotts as a response to discrimination had evidenced this. A useful means of forging collective action, they nevertheless possessed limited political advantages. A boycott had the effect of withdrawing blacks from participation in economic and civic life until white businesses or local officials capitulated. Civil rights proponents needed additional techniques that would actively engage blacks in directly confronting white racist practices, particularly those from which they were excluded. Through such encounters they would dramatically expose the source of their oppression, bring the evil to the surface, and exert moral pressure to eradicate it. In the process, people would have to break laws they considered unjust and go to jail for their convictions. By doing so they would ultimately transform themselves, their communities, and their nation.

On February 1, 1960, southern blacks took a critical step in forging those new tactics. Students in Greensboro, North Carolina, shook up the freedom struggle, provided a powerful nonviolent weapon, and furnished fresh, youthful people to deploy it. By sitting down at a segregated Woolworth's lunch counter that would not accommodate them and demanding equal service, four black undergraduates at North Carolina Agricultural and Technical State University energized a sagging protest movement. Within two months their action sparked similar demonstrations in some 60 cities throughout the South, involving thousands of high-school and college students, and by year's end protests had sprouted in over 200 cities. What King's Crusade for Citizenship had failed to do for direct action over a span of two years was achieved virtually overnight. These sit-ins spawned wade-ins, kneel-ins, stand-ins, and freedom rides, all designed to bring together ordinary folks to challenge racial oppression head on. The result of these dynamic efforts did not always lead immediately to integration or equality; however, they did help liberate those who participated in them. "I felt as though I had gained my manhood," Franklin McCain, one of the original Greensboro four, declared, "not only gained it, but had developed quite a respect for it."

Many cities throughout the South proved ready to be ignited by these young activists. In Greensboro, for example, the roots of protest were sunk deep. The NAACP had maintained an active chapter since the 1930s, and in 1943 Ella Baker had established an NAACP youth group in the city, an organization that two of the original sit-in demonstrators subsequently joined. The local black high school also served as a training ground for black insurgency. Several teachers inspired their students to think about the history and culture of African Americans as a struggle for freedom and to relate their own lives to that quest. "I had to tell youngsters," one instructor remarked, "that the way you find things need not happen.... I don't care if they push and shove you, you must not accept [discrimination]." This lesson received positive reinforcement from the pastor of the Shiloh Baptist Church, which some of the students attended. During the 1950s, their minister had been active in civil rights affairs and had only recently succeeded in leading a drive to double the membership of the NAACP chapter.

Furthermore, the young protesters lived in a city in which blacks had gained a measure of access to the electoral process. The heightened political assertiveness that blacks displayed after World War II surfaced early in Greensboro. In 1949, two black candidates for the city council made it through the primary, only to lose in the general election. Following this contest the Greensboro Citizens Association, a black civic league interested in improving municipal services in their community, mounted a voter registration drive that led to the election of its president, Dr. William

Hampton, to the council in 1951. Although Hampton ran reasonably well in white precincts, he scored much more impressively in black districts. In unprecedented fashion, black voters united as a solid bloc behind a candidate of their own race. In previous years they had split their votes among various white contestants, but, as one black politician later explained, "You don't help a black by putting his name on the ticket and then voting for six white candidates because you are scattering your vote."

This modest electoral success did not fulfill rising black expectations. During the 1950s the single council seat occupied by a black, as well as the selection of a black to the school board, did not alter traditional patterns of racial inequality. Instead, what William H. Chafe has termed "sophisticated American racism" prevailed in Greensboro. Following the *Brown* decision, white leaders permitted only token desegregation of the schools, closed recreational facilities rather than integrating them, and steered black college graduates away from white-collar employment. They did so with civility, not brutality, thereby projecting an image of progress. Outnumbered by whites, the lone blacks on the council and the school board had no leverage to reverse this course. Ironically, their very presence on these panels served to legitimize the discriminatory policies the majority adopted. Thus, the Woolworth sit-in represented both continuity with the black community's past and a significant departure from the electoral and judicial strategies that had stalled in obtaining racial justice.

The creative energy of the sit-ins flowed into the formation of the Student Nonviolent Coordinating Committee (SNCC). Convening in Raleigh, North Carolina, in April 1960, recent protest veterans sought to establish an organization that offered new political leadership. James Lawson, who had been active in the development of the Nashville sit-in movement, expressed the participants' disdain for "middle-class conventional, half-way efforts to deal with radical social evil." They wanted to replace the NAACP's emphasis on litigation with the nonviolent power of "a people no longer the victims of racial evil who can act in a disciplined manner to implement the Constitution." Toward this end, SNCC founders shared the vision of an interracial beloved community preached by Dr. King and SCLC. Indeed, Lawson and others had been inspired by the Montgomery bus boycott and the exercise of grassroots direct action.

Yet if the iconoclastic committee rejected the tactics of the NAACP it also eschewed any formal affiliation with the SCLC. Part of this independence resulted from a need for self-preservation, a desire not to become absorbed within another organization, and a preference for retaining maximum flexibility of action. But the choice of autonomy reflected an even deeper wish to break with the style of leadership exhibited by Dr. King. Though SNCC's philosophy of nonviolent civil disobedience dovetailed with that of the SCLC, the student group had doubts about organizing a mass movement around a single charismatic personality. It adopted instead a decentralized organizational structure, stressed group decision-making, and encouraged the emergence of leadership from indigenous black communities. In effect, SNCC echoed the criticism of Ella Baker, who had become disenchanted with the SCLC. Miss Baker, as she was affectionately called, argued that a "prophetic leader" like Dr. King ultimately stifled the opportunity for people to tailor unique programs to suit their own particular needs.

The perspectives that separated the two groups did not deter the students from cooperating with Dr. King. The SCLC president had earned a national reputation for his civil rights activities, which gave him contacts with important political figures that they did not have. By the autumn of 1960 King had moved from Montgomery to his birthplace of Atlanta, where he co-pastored the Ebenezer Baptist Church with his father. In the "City Too Busy to Hate," as the mayor referred to it, black students from Morehouse College, King's alma mater, initiated sit-in demonstrations to desegregate downtown eating establishments. Moderate white and black leaders, including "Daddy" King, disapproved of the continuing protests, but the demonstrators persuaded a reluctant Martin Luther King, Jr., to join them. In doing so not only did they receive prominent help for their local struggle, but they also set off a chain of events that reverberated nationally and connected black politics with the White House.

On October 19, 1960, Dr. King joined some 75 demonstrators in seeking to integrate the cafeteria at Rich's Department Store, where blacks were welcome to spend their money but not to eat. The protest ended in the arrest of King and the others for trespassing. Detained for several days, all but Dr. King were finally released. Earlier in the year, the Atlanta minister had been arrested for driving without a valid Georgia license, issued a fine, and placed on one year's probation. As a result of his current arrest, a county judge ruled that King had violated his probation and sentenced him to four months of hard labor at the state prison.

Although the harsh sentence was not anticipated, the arrest fitted in with a larger plan the student demonstrators had formulated. The incident came in the midst of the presidential contest between John F. Kennedy and Richard M. Nixon, an opportunity the civil rights forces hoped to exploit. One of the organizers of the protest at Rich's recalled that it was deliberately timed "so as to influence the election." The student activists expected that King's arrest "would create enough of a national uproar in the black community," and they intended to put the candidates on the spot concerning their positions on civil rights. "I did not have a preference, believe it or not, between Nixon or Kennedy," recalled Lonnie King, a student activist who was not related to the imprisoned minister.

This neutral stand was hardly surprising. As a Republican member of Congress, senator, and vice-president, Richard Nixon had antagonized liberals on the issue of anti-Communism, but on racial matters he backed reform. One of the few top-level officials in the Eisenhower administration to endorse the *Brown* ruling, the vice-president strongly supported the 1957 civil rights legislation and used his position as presiding officer of the Senate to assist in passage of the measure. Nixon also chaired the President's Committee on Government Contracts, which investigated charges of racial discrimination in federally related employment and sponsored education campaigns to further equal opportunity. He had conferred with Martin Luther King on a couple of occasions during the 1950s and earned praise from the civil rights leader for making "a real impression on the Negro."

As might be expected of a Democratic senator from Massachusetts, John F. Kennedy had routinely supported proposals to relieve the plight of blacks in the South. He voted for civil rights legislation in 1957 and 1960, and spoke out firmly for acceptance of the *Brown* verdict. Yet, Carl Brauer has noted, Senator Kennedy approached civil rights issues as "a moderate by conviction and design." Unwilling to address racial matters as a category of special concern, he considered them an expression of larger social and economic problems. The senator acted more for political reasons than out of any moral obligation, and did just enough to court the black electorate in his home state. At the same time, he spent much effort in wooing the white South. In 1957 Kennedy voted for Lyndon Johnson's jury trial amendment to the civil rights bill, a deed that angered liberals and delighted southern conservatives. His pragmatic approach to civil rights questions won for his presidential bid the early endorsement of Governor John Patterson of Alabama, who thought Kennedy "would probably be more understanding of our situation down here" than any other possible Democratic candidate.

That same practical outlook guided Kennedy in his pursuit of the presidency. As the Democratic nominee he selected Harris Wofford, a white attorney with the US Commission on Civil Rights, and several prominent blacks for his campaign staff. One of them, Louis Martin, the editor of the *Chicago Defender*, convinced the opportunistic congressman Adam Clayton

Powell, who had flirted with the Eisenhower administration for the preceding half-dozen years, to join the Kennedy bandwagon. Along with the perennial Democratic stalwart, Congressman William Dawson of Chicago, Powell very effectively spoke in northern black ghettoes on Kennedy's behalf. Wofford also introduced Kennedy to Dr. King, who came away from the meeting with a favorable impression of the Democratic aspirant. Still, King considered Nixon a loyal supporter of civil rights, and he declined to endorse either candidate.

The influential black presence in the Democratic camp partially offset Kennedy's choice for vice-president, Senator Lyndon B. Johnson of Texas. Apparently chosen to appeal to Democratic voters in the South, this grandson of a former Civil War Confederate received a low rating among party liberals and blacks for weakening civil rights legislation. Nevertheless, while Johnson soothed southern audiences with his down-home stories, he also reassured blacks "that I have done my dead best to make progress in the field of civil rights."

Nixon followed a similar route. Like Kennedy he ran on a strong civil rights platform that pledged firm executive leadership, promised new legislation to combat suffrage and employment discrimination, backed legal and technical assistance for school desegregation, and upheld the right of sit-in demonstrators to assemble peacefully. Also, like his Democratic rival, Nixon labored to improve his standing with southern whites. The GOP nominee campaigned vigorously in the deep South, where he counseled gradualism and urged justice for blacks not as a moral imperative but as a means of undermining Communist exploitation of racial tensions for propaganda purposes. Furthermore, by not appearing in Harlem, as Eisenhower had done, and by appointing few blacks to important and visible roles in his campaign, Nixon avoided offending the white South. One prominent black who joined Nixon's staff, E. Frederic Morrow, an assistant in the Eisenhower White House, bitterly complained that he did not receive any specific assignment or support.

The political balancing acts of both candidates suffered a severe jolt from the arrest of Dr. King in October, just as the student activists had hoped. The nominees reacted very differently, however. Treading lightly at first, Senator Kennedy decided to work for King's release on bail through Georgia's Democratic governor, Ernest Vandiver, and his state campaign director, Griffin Bell. When negotiations stalled, Harris Wofford and Louis Martin came up with the idea of having Kennedy telephone a worried Mrs. Coretta King to express his concern for her husband's safety. This sympathetic gesture did not free the celebrated prisoner, and the candidate's brother and closest adviser, Robert Kennedy, wrestled with the thorny question of whether to take additional action. Initially he had been angry with Wofford for his attempt to involve the senator directly in the King affair, fearing an adverse southern white response. Also concerned with black ballots, he quickly changed his mind, interceded with the Democratic county judge presiding over the case, and obtained King's release on bail. "I called him," Robert Kennedy told Wofford, "because it made me so damned angry to think of that bastard sentencing a citizen to … hard labor for a minor traffic offense and screwing up my brother's campaign."

In contrast, Nixon remained publicly silent during this episode. Privately he believed that King had received a "bum rap," but that it would be improper for him as a lawyer to communicate with the judge. Perhaps he was more interested in political calculations. Nixon refused to heed the plea of a prominent black Republican in Atlanta to make a statement in support of King, telling him "He [Nixon] would lose some black votes, but he'd gain white votes." Still, seeking to walk a fine tightrope, he had the Justice Department draft a statement for President Eisenhower's release, calling the sentencing of King "fundamentally unjust" and directing the attorney general "to take all proper steps" to free him. When Eisenhower declined to authorize such a statement, Nixon lost the opportunity to neutralize Kennedy's efforts on King's behalf.

The Democrats turned the King incident to their advantage. The civil rights leader commended Senator Kennedy for his courage, and remarked: "There are moments when the politically expedient can be morally wise." With less than two weeks before the election, the Kennedy campaign distributed nearly 2 million pamphlets, entitled *The Case of Martin Luther King*, in black communities throughout the nation, publicizing the matter. One of the endorsements Kennedy obtained came from Dr. King's father, a Baptist minister who originally had intended to vote against the Democrat because of his Catholic religion. "I've got all my votes and I've got a suitcase and I'm going to take them up there and dump them in his lap," the Reverend King, Sr., declared. Likewise, the younger King's closest friend and colleague in the SCLC, Ralph David Abernathy, remarked: "I earnestly and sincerely feel it is time for all of us to take off our Nixon buttons."

Approximately 68 percent of the black electorate agreed by casting their votes for Kennedy. The Democrats won by fewer than 120,000 popular votes, three-tenths of 1 percent of the total, and by 84 electoral votes. This razor-thin victory highlighted the significant role played by African

Americans in determining the outcome. In several key northern states rich with electoral votes – Illinois, Michigan, New Jersey, and Pennsylvania – black votes made the difference. In the South, blacks helped put the Kennedy–Johnson ticket over the top in South Carolina and Texas. Nixon carried only three states in the region – Florida, Tennessee, and Virginia – two fewer than Eisenhower did in 1956. Nationwide, Kennedy needed strong black support to offset the 52 percent majority Nixon rolled up among white voters. Had not the senator succeeded in regaining 7 percent of the black vote that went to Eisenhower four years before, Richard Nixon would have entered the White House in 1960.

This key segment of the electorate returned to the Democratic Party for a variety of reasons. With the popular Eisenhower out of the race, the proportion of black Democratic support again reached its previously high 1952 level. Because Kennedy's civil rights record going into the contest appeared no stronger than Nixon's, the Democratic nominee's intervention in the King controversy attracted blacks who were inclined to vote Republican or, at the very least, retained the loyalty of black Protestants who opposed Kennedy on religious grounds. But the King incident does not explain the entire matter. In King's home city of Atlanta, Nixon out-polled Kennedy in black districts, though his 54 percent marked a slip of 12 points from Eisenhower's share in 1956. Just as important as civil rights, economic considerations steered blacks into the Democratic column. Kennedy benefited from the recession in the last year of the Eisenhower term. The recession hurt economically vulnerable blacks and strengthened their attachment to the Democratic Party, which promised financial relief from hard times.

The Kennedy Administration and Civil Rights

As in 1948, black ballots contributed significantly in electing a Democratic President, but the prospective rewards remained unclear. Kennedy had delivered ambiguous messages during his campaign. His gesture toward King, his appointment of black advisers, and his pledge to exert strong executive action to remove discrimination in such areas as housing suggested that a great leap forward was about to take place on the civil rights front in Washington. Yet Kennedy had also led the white South to believe that, as Carl Brauer has noted, "he would not favor a reinstitution of Reconstruction." These soothing words had aided Kennedy in securing

50.5 percent of the popular vote in the South, a rise of nearly three points from Stevenson's total in 1956. In all likelihood Kennedy would have done even better in this bastion of Protestant fundamentalism had his religion, much more than civil rights, not been an issue. Furthermore, even if President Kennedy desired to push for new legislation to combat racial bigotry, he faced a Congress in which southern Democrats wielded disproportionate influence through their control of potent committees, their deployment of the Senate filibuster, and their alliance with conservative Republicans to thwart reform measures.

Caught between growing black electoral strength and entrenched southern white political power, President Kennedy ventured circumspectly into the field of civil rights. Like his predecessor, the President opted to concentrate on extending the suffrage to blacks and drawing them into the political mainstream. Where African Americans "are given their rights to participate in the political process," Kennedy asserted, "they do it as free individuals … giving their considered judgment on what is best for their country and what is best for themselves and what is best for the cause of freedom." In the tradition of Eisenhower he placed his faith in the courts to ensure equal voting rights for southern blacks. However, Kennedy instructed the Department of Justice, headed by his brother Robert, to enforce the Civil Rights Acts of 1957 and 1960 more vigorously than had the previous Eisenhower administration. Combining executive and judicial action, the Kennedys hoped to satisfy civil rights proponents without unduly antagonizing southern lawmakers in Congress.

This approach was threatened by rising civil rights militancy in 1961. In May, "freedom rides," aiming to desegregate interstate bus terminal facilities, encountered vicious attacks by southern white extremists. Integrated buses carrying passengers recruited by CORE and SNCC were assaulted and burned outside of Birmingham, Alabama. In Montgomery, a white mob beat the passengers as they departed from their bus. Later a bloodthirsty crowd surrounded a church and menaced the congregants gathered inside to hear Martin Luther King, Jr., voice his support for the protesters. Despite the fact that the Supreme Court had outlawed segregated terminals serving interstate travelers, the Kennedy administration tried to defuse this crisis by urging a cooling-off period during which the civil rights forces would suspend their offensive against Jim Crow. The White House desperately wanted to avoid sending in federal troops to the South for fear of reviving memories of post – Civil War Reconstruction, but the demonstrators refused to comply. In the end, Kennedy dispatched civilian federal marshals to restore peace in Alabama, and the attorney general worked out an agreement with the governor of Mississippi to provide protection for incoming riders before subjecting them to arrest. Finally, the Justice Department obtained a decree from the Interstate Commerce Commission, banning segregated facilities in interstate transportation.

The Kennedy administration attempted to reduce the possibility of provoking further racial confrontations that would again drag the federal government into a clash with state officials. Seeking to channel black protest in a "safer" direction, the Kennedys encouraged voter registration activities. Suffrage drives were a regular feature of American life, and civil rights organizations, such as the NAACP and SCLC, had incorporated them as an essential part of their programs. In contrast to the highly publicized and confrontational sit-ins and freedom rides that often generated violence, voter registration drives promised peaceful, nonconfrontational efforts to place the names of blacks on the suffrage lists. Besides keeping the President from having to dispatch federal troops to Dixie in Reconstruction-era fashion, a voter registration strategy might enhance the fortunes of the reformist wing of the Democratic Party. Additional black voters presumably would support at the national level the party that enfranchised them, and their ballots would also serve to select more moderate officeholders in the South.

The Voter Education Project (VEP) grew out of this convergence of politics and principle. In the wake of the freedom rides, the Kennedy administration believed that "it would be valuable if some of the present energy were channeled into this vital [registration] work." The Justice Department had already begun to file suffrage litigation, and invited civil rights groups to work in this area and collect evidence of ongoing discrimination. Kennedy aides with contacts in liberal philanthropic foundations arranged to obtain financing for nonpartisan voter registration activities. Under the auspices of the Southern Regional Council, a private interracial agency based in Atlanta, nearly $1 million was raised to conduct voter education projects. The council hired Wiley Branton, a black civil rights lawyer from Arkansas, to direct the enterprise, and elicited participation from the major civil rights organizations – the NAACP, SCLC, SNCC, CORE, and the Urban League, an organization specializing in housing and employment programs.

Bringing these groups together was a significant political achievement. Though in agreement with Dr. King's assertion that "if we in the South can win the right to vote it … will give us the concrete tool with which we ourselves can correct injustice," they regarded each other warily. The NAACP viewed itself as the premier organization in the fight for black enfranchisement.

Tenaciously guarding its terrain, the national association looked suspiciously at rival organizations that had recently arrived on the scene. The NAACP particularly worried about competition from SCLC, whose president, Dr. King, exhibited considerable success as a fundraiser and organizer of affiliates throughout the South. Because money was usually a scarce resource for civil rights groups, each agency needed to stand in the center of public attention and earn credit for accomplishments that would attract new supporters and financial contributions. SNCC and CORE posed an additional problem for the NAACP, which feared that their direct-action orientation would foster troublesome, diversionary operations pointed away from the goal of suffrage. Placing its commitment to the ballot first, the NAACP cast aside its misgivings and joined the coalition.

From a different perspective, SNCC also worried about signing up with the VEP. Born out of the sit-in movement and weaned on the freedom rides, the group's members suspected that white liberals and established civil rights leaders wanted to raise the child in their own image. For its part, SNCC was ready to stand among adults and pursue its goals militantly. Though some considered the VEP as a clever means of sidetracking protest, the young activists decided to join the project. The fresh infusion of outside funds for voter registration would save the group the money necessary to continue mass-action demonstrations. Moreover, persuaded by Robert Parris Moses, a soft-spoken, intense, and compelling field secretary from New York City, SNCC viewed voter registration as a potentially radical means of transforming the political and social lives of southern blacks and whites. "In many ways," one SNCC staffer explained, "it seems to me that the voter registration project is even more significant than other forms of protest. The problem is being attacked at its core. A new sense of human dignity and self respect is being discovered."

Whatever reservations SNCC, the NAACP, and the rest of their civil rights comrades harbored, they agreed that the federal government would try to shelter them from racist harm. Without spelling out their intentions, Justice Department officials, who helped arrange for the creation of the VEP, pledged the cooperation of the Kennedy administration in implementing the project. The civil rights representatives attending planning sessions in 1961 left thinking that they could turn to Washington for staunch protection against violent attacks and other forms of harassment from white supremacists. Wiley Branton inferred that "the Justice Department would take all steps necessary to protect federal or constitutional rights" which embraced "the elementary matter of protection."

The Justice Department held a different view. Attorney General Kennedy and his staff wanted to keep the federal government out of the law-enforcement business for political and constitutional reasons. They hesitated to ship troops or marshals into Dixie for fear of alienating powerful southern lawmakers whose cooperation the administration needed to enact its legislative program. Furthermore, they argued that the Constitution left law enforcement in local hands, and they did not want to discourage local responsibility by taking over police powers. Besides, federal lawyers insisted that the national government did not maintain its own police force and that the Federal Bureau of Investigation did not function in that capacity. They envisioned a cooperative partnership between national and state authorities, based on goodwill and mutual trust, and exercised through voluntary compliance rather than coercion. If disputes arose that threatened the constitutional rights and safety of the voter registration workers, the Justice Department preferred to assist them through the courts, not with armed force.

Robert Kennedy had deliberately chosen his top assistant in charge of civil rights enforcement to reflect this viewpoint. He did not want a crusader in the post, and so picked a negotiator. The attorney general passed over Harris Wofford, who had strong civil rights credentials, in favor of Burke Marshall, who had virtually none. Kennedy did not desire someone for the job who had a passionate commitment to racial equality. He explained that he wanted instead a "tough lawyer who could look at things ... objectively." Intending to administer existing suffrage laws more forcefully than before, Kennedy desired the head of the Civil Rights Division to appear neutral and not too closely identified with the civil rights movement. Accordingly, he hoped that the image of evenhandedness would make it easier to deal with southern segregationists, such as James Eastland of Mississippi, who chaired the Senate Judiciary Committee. Marshall fit the bill and said he intended "to make the federal system in the voting field work by itself through local action, without federal court compulsion."

The two-front attack initiated by the Voter Education Project and the Justice Department helped boost political participation in the South. From 1962 to 1964, the VEP accounted for some 287,000 new black registrants, about half of the increase. The Department of Justice supplemented these efforts by filing approximately 50 voting rights suits. Overall, during this period the proportion of southern black registrants jumped from 29.4 percent to 43.1 percent, the steepest rise since 1952 (see Table 3.1). The bulk of the new voters generally came from urban areas in which hostility to black suffrage was less than in the rural black belt and the unusually

Table 3.1   Estimated percentage of voting-age blacks registered in the South,
1940–1964

	1940	*1947*	*1952*	*1960*	*1962*	*1964*
Alabama	0.4	1.2	5.0	13.7	13.4	23.0
Arkansas	1.5	17.3	27.0	37.3	34.0	49.3
Florida	5.7	15.4	33.0	38.9	36.8	63.8
Georgia	3.0	18.8	23.0	29.3	26.7	44.0
Louisiana	0.5	2.6	25.0	30.9	27.8	32.0
Mississippi	0.4	0.9	4.0	5.2	5.3	6.7
North Carolina	7.1	15.2	18.0	38.1	35.8	46.8
South Carolina	0.8	13.0	20.0	15.6	22.9	38.7
Tennessee	6.5	25.8	27.0	58.9	49.8	69.4
Texas	5.6	18.5	31.0	34.9	37.3	57.7
Virginia	4.1	13.2	16.0	22.8	24.0	45.7
All states	**3.0**	**12.0**	**20.0**	**29.1**	**29.4**	**43.1**

Source: David Garrow, *Protest at Selma* (Yale University Press, New Haven, Conn., 1978),
7, 11, 19.

repressive cities like Birmingham, where white extremists resorted to bombs to restrict ballots.

These accomplishments exacted a high price. The failure of the federal government to furnish protection for civil rights workers hampered their effectiveness and engendered their bitterness. Field staff from SNCC and CORE dug themselves into the most hard-core, resistant locales in Mississippi, Alabama, Louisiana, and Georgia and met verbal threats, violence, and intimidation by the police. The supposedly safe act of canvassing potential registrants door to door and accompanying them to the courthouse often converted suffrage drives into direct-action confrontations. The local law-enforcement officers the Justice Department depended on to keep the peace themselves violated the constitutional rights of registration workers. At the mercy of sheriffs who interpreted the law from the grip of a billy club or the handle of a gun, the suffragists pleaded with the Kennedy administration for assistance.

In response, they received sympathy rather than protection. If the FBI appeared on the scene it was not to make arrests but to jot down their observations. In pursuit of interstate car thieves, kidnappers, and bank robbers, the bureau worked closely with local law-enforcement officials, including those in the South, and did not want to jeopardize this cooperation by interfering with traditional racial practices. "You couldn't find those bastards," Timothy Jenkins, a student activist, complained about federal agents in general: "All the force, all the demonstrations of force and intimidation ... were on the side of the local authorities who wore badges and suits, and they had the ostensible perquisites of the state. Our part of the state was invisible – the federal state."

The Justice Department's reliance on the courts did not help the situation. The Kennedy administration had appointed to federal benches in the South a handful of judges who steadfastly resisted its efforts to enforce suffrage laws and shield individuals who peacefully engaged in voter registration activities. Judges like William Harold Cox of Mississippi publicly belittled the claims both of Justice Department lawyers and black litigants who appeared before him. These judges won appointment because the President, as a matter of courtesy, had to clear their names with the Democratic senators from their home states. The potential choices were narrowed even further, for the candidates had to pass through the nomination roadblock set up by Chairman Eastland's Judiciary Committee. Not all of Kennedy's selections behaved poorly, but too frequently the obstructionist jurists presided in precisely those areas where registration workers faced the greatest hazards.

SNCC's Encounter with Mississippi

The experiences of SNCC in Mississippi demonstrated the challenges to black political development. In the Deep South, the civil rights activists struggled to organize blacks in local communities to liberate themselves from oppressive white domination. They saw voter registration not as an end in itself but as the means for black people to obtain power to secure control of their lives. According to Bob Moses, the architect of much of SNCC's suffrage strategy, the real issue was "not only do you gain the right to vote but you begin to change all the other educational values." The ballot could open the way for blacks to determine their own leaders and change the conditions that exploited them. Indeed, to the young radicals politics was the key to rearranging economic and social relations. Lawrence Guyot, an SNCC fieldworker in Mississippi, explained his group's message: "There is a relationship between your not being able to feed your children and your not registering to vote."

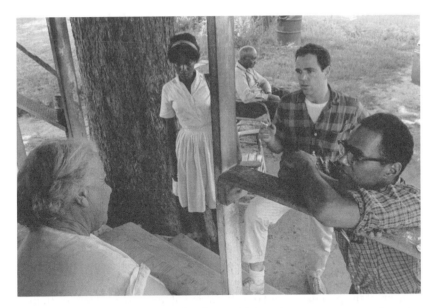

Figure 7 Bob Moses along with other SNCC workers on a voter registration campaign in Mississippi. (Danny Lyon/Magnum Photos)

The key to political organizing in the black belt was first to overcome fear. In the Mississippi delta area, blacks had to muster sufficient courage to make an attempt to register. During the late 1950s and early 1960s, several blacks had been killed in retaliation for their political activities, and their deaths served as a vivid reminder for others who might follow them. Short of murder, white supremacists kept blacks in line through economic intimidation. Plantation owners fired "troublemakers," and stores cut off their credit. In August 1962, Mrs. Fannie Lou Hamer filled out a voter registration form and was fired from her job on a Ruleville plantation immediately after she refused to withdraw her application. The SNCC workers who entered these dangerous areas were also subjected to an array of threats, arrests, and brutality. They grappled with their personal fears even as they joined with those they were trying to mobilize to do collectively what was so difficult to do alone. "To go with friends and neighbors," SNCC field secretary Charles Cobb remarked, "made the attempt less frightening and reduced the chances of physical assault at the courthouse, since cowards don't like to openly attack numbers." Still, the struggle against fear, no matter how successful in persuading blacks to defy racial discrimination, did not confer the right to vote.

While laboring to extend political power at the grassroots level, SNCC fully realized that without federal intervention it could not break the hold of white control over local electoral institutions. In addition to its campaigns of community organizing, SNCC fought the interconnected battle of mobilizing Washington on its side. The group's staff operated in the rural sections where voter registration was certain to arouse racial confrontation. SNCC planned the national dimension of its strategy to focus attention on what was happening in this "other America." Amzie Moore, the longtime fighter for civil rights who had first brought Bob Moses to the Magnolia State, sought to "expose the conditions in Mississippi with reference to people voting ... to uncover what is covered." The civil rights activists counted on newspaper and television reporters to record their plight and influence public opinion in their favor, thereby pressuring the Justice Department to furnish the necessary protection.

Greenwood, Mississippi, sorely tested SNCC's strategy. In LeFlore County, of which this Delta town was the county seat, blacks comprised 64 percent of the population but only 9 percent of the registered voters. In June 1962, SNCC assigned Sam Block to launch a voter education drive in the area. A native Mississippian, the 23-year-old Block had been deeply influenced by the murder of Emmett Till seven years before, which made him realize that one day he had to "do something." After graduating from high school, he left for college in Missouri, joined the air force, and returned home during the time of the freedom rides. He became involved with SNCC through his neighbor, Amzie Moore. Block entered Greenwood alone, without a car, money, or a place to stay. He made contacts wherever people congregated – in pool halls, laundromats, and grocery stores. Through his painstaking canvassing for voter registration he "learned that there were a lot of frightened people in Greenwood. They knew local blacks were being killed in LeFlore County ... and nothing was being done about it."

The SNCC organizer began to whittle down some of this fear. He received help from blacks who had been involved with voter education attempts in the past. Holding meetings in fraternal halls and churches, he taught those in attendance freedom songs that "served as a drawing card ... that seemed to make people want to come back." A local resident expressed the sentiments of many who participated in these sessions: "We have been living in fear, afraid to do something. It is time to do something. The time is now." Having taken the initial step of rallying ordinary yet heroic black folks, Block found he could barely move ahead. The applicants he accompanied to the courthouse failed to pass the literacy tests unfairly administered by the registrars, and the SNCC fieldworker was ordered by the sheriff "to pack your goddamn bags" and get out of town. He stayed, despite constant harassment, arrests, and violent attacks.

When SNCC sent in reinforcements, white resistance grew even stiffer. In October 1962, county officials cut off the distribution of surplus food to some 22,000 residents, contending that the program was too expensive to operate. Block and his companions correctly viewed this action as a reprisal for their voter registration efforts and worried that without the commodities program impoverished black sharecroppers could not survive. In response, SNCC conducted a national food and clothing drive to help the beleaguered farmers get through the winter. In addition to keeping blacks from starving and suffering cold, the drive stimulated their interest in registering to vote. Lawrence Guyot, who was working with Block, recalled how the county government unwittingly assisted SNCC in graphically demonstrating to disfranchised blacks the connection between politics and economics. "It's easy to sell political involvement," he asserted, "when you have that kind of activity by an identifiable political apparatus."

White supremacists provided more brutal lessons about the dangers of voter registration and, hence, confirmed the importance of the ballot. In February and March 1963, whites initiated a reign of terror against SNCC. Arsonists attempted to burn down its headquarters, and unidentified assailants fired shotgun blasts into a car carrying three voter registration workers, seriously wounding one of them. Vigilantes torched several black businesses, burning them to the ground, and aimed gunfire into the homes of two black youths active in the suffrage drive. These attacks spurred the civil rights troops to launch a series of marches in protest at the violence. Direct action and voter registration, which for many SNCC activists originally seemed unrelated, fused in Greenwood. For two weeks, national television cameras spotlighted peaceful demonstrators under siege by the police and their snarling dogs.

As blacks filled the Greenwood jail, they once again exhorted the federal government to intercede on their behalf. Some approached Washington with ambivalent feelings. James Forman, executive secretary of SNCC and one of those arrested, considered "the presence of the federal government as an instrument to be used over the state governments of the South," and expected the Justice Department to protect voter registration workers. At the same time, he doubted federal commitment and believed that suffrage drives would "expose the dirt of the United States and thus alienate black people from the whole system." In part, SNCC had staged the demonstrations, in anticipation of arrests, to force the federal authorities to intervene or else "prove the government was not on [its] side, and thus intensify the development of a mass consciousness among blacks." The VEP, which funded voter registration activities in Greenwood, seconded SNCC's request for federal protection. The agency considered such intervention essential if its projects were to be sustained in hostile southern battlefields.

The Justice Department applied just enough pressure to defuse the crisis, but not with sufficient vigor to satisfy black activists. It stubbornly refused to provide personal protection, and relied instead on the preferred techniques of litigation and negotiation. The Justice Department petitioned the federal district court for an order releasing the imprisoned protestors and enjoining local officials not to interfere with the suffrage campaign. Behind the scenes, John Doar, an attorney in the Civil Rights Division, persuaded the Greenwood authorities to free the jailed demonstrators, and in turn, the department dropped the suit that would have permanently restrained town officials. Having restored some peace to Greenwood, the Justice Department backed off for fear of inflaming white passions anew.

Though the voter registration campaign proceeded, the civil rights forces made little progress in actually enrolling black voters. By mid-1963, some 1,300 blacks in Greenwood had taken the literacy test to register, but officials refused to notify them of the results. Faced with such meager gains and the unwillingness of the federal government to protect the constitutional rights of the fieldworkers, later that year the VEP reluctantly suspended funding for its projects in Mississippi and concentrated its efforts where the returns were higher. Despite these disappointments, such suffrage campaigns as that in Greenwood had a significant political impact. Many of the blacks who encountered the civil rights activists had taken a crucial step toward liberation. They had moved, as a Georgia SNCC organizer reported, "into freedom of the mind, and it is now theirs for life, even if they should never succeed in their efforts to persuade a semi-literate, hostile registrar to put their names on the roll." She succinctly summed up what the movement meant for the political future of the blacks it touched: "They have learned to live with fear, and to advance."

To underscore this point, the civil rights forces in Mississippi devised a novel strategy to turn disfranchised blacks into active political participants. Since 1962, the Council of Federated Organizations (COFO) had coordinated voter registration activities in the state. The NAACP, SNCC, CORE, and SCLC put aside some of their philosophical differences and organizational rivalries to focus their energies on combating the fierce opposition to black suffrage. Out of this cooperative venture the idea for a "freedom vote" emerged. COFO designed a mock-election to accompany the regularly scheduled gubernatorial contest in 1963. The parallel balloting would be open to all black adults, especially the 95 percent who had been excluded from the normal electoral process.

COFO aimed the freedom vote in two directions. By casting ballots in this symbolic election, black Mississippians would send a message to the federal government that they wanted to vote and needed outside help to shatter the racial blockades that hampered them. "The freedom ballot will show," declared Bob Moses, one of the prime movers behind it, "that if Negroes had the right to vote without fear of physical or economic reprisal, they would do so." Yet civil rights activists wanted to achieve much more than Washington's assistance. As director of COFO, Moses envisioned the campaign as part of SNCC's enduring attempt to organize black communities around their perceived needs, in pursuit of their own goals, in behalf of their own emancipation, apart from white control. In holding this independent election, blacks would strike a blow for their political legitimacy. Rejected by white registration officials according to their definitions of political eligibility, black Mississippians intended to demonstrate that they were qualified to vote and seek power on their own terms.

Eighty thousand blacks, nearly four times the number of those registered, vividly staked their claim for recognition as first-class citizens. They marked their ballots in makeshift polling places in locations throughout their communities. In a unified manner they voted for the freedom ticket of Aaron Henry, the black president of COFO who ran for governor, and his running mate, Ed King, the white chaplain at Tougaloo College. Though considered illegitimate by official white standards, these voters and their candidates collectively constructed the machinery to continue agitating for equal political rights and representation. "The Freedom Vote gave Negroes an opportunity to build an organization in every nook and cranny of the State," Henry remarked. "We have an organization now in Mississippi that once we get the vote, we'll be able to direct it."

Martin Luther King, Jr., the SCLC, and the Crisis at Birmingham

While SNCC strove to organize people around the right to vote in rural areas, the SCLC shaped its protest around broader issues of segregation and discrimination in a city notorious for its repression of blacks: Birmingham,

Alabama. Over the years, this steel city had been the scene of numerous bombings and acts of violence against civil rights activists and, most recently, the freedom riders. The commissioner of public safety, Eugene "Bull" Connor, ruled the police with an iron fist and believed that civil rights protesters were Communist dupes who deserved the harsh punishment they received.

The local movement for first-class citizenship was led by the Reverend Fred Shuttlesworth, a founding member of the SCLC. Pastor of the Bethel Baptist Church, Shuttlesworth also headed the Alabama Christian Movement for Human Rights, a group that originated in the mid-1950s after Alabama officials banned the NAACP from the state. Under Shuttlesworth's lead, the organization had attempted to desegregate schools, buses, and government offices in Birmingham. In retaliation against these efforts, the Reverend Shuttlesworth's home and church were bombed, and the minister and his family were attacked and beaten by a mob. Undaunted by threats, Shuttlesworth continued to challenge the city's system of racial apartheid. "I always believed that the minister is God's first line soldier," he remarked bravely. "I should say I'm a battlefield type general like Patton, I guess."

Against this pattern of intimidation, Dr. King, the Reverend Shuttlesworth, and their associates used mass-action strategies to bolster growing, but still underdeveloped, black political influence. In 1962, approximately 12,500 blacks had signed up to vote, about 10 percent of those eligible. This small bloc of voters joined with white reformers in an attempt to unseat the reactionary Connor. Businesspeople and other civic leaders believed the racial violence encouraged by Connor and his henchmen had a harmful effect on the city's economic fortunes and hoped to put a stop to it. They arranged for a referendum to change the form of city government from a three-person commission to a mayor and seven-member council, thereby reducing Connor's power. The measure passed with solid black support, and in the spring of 1963 the coalition of white moderates and blacks defeated Connor's mayoral bid. Instead of accepting his loss at the polls, Connor began litigation challenging the validity of the new government and its newly elected officials. Meanwhile, he retained control over the police.

On April 3, the day after the disputed election, the SCLC orchestrated sit-in demonstrations to desegregate downtown eating facilities and to press for the hiring of black store clerks. These protests had a twofold purpose: to win concessions for Birmingham blacks as part of the ongoing community struggle led by Shuttlesworth and to force the federal government to combat Jim Crow throughout the region. King deliberately picked Birmingham because of the potential for its police, under Connor's command, to respond brutally to protests. To arouse the conscience of the nation, the SCLC deployed nonviolent marches to provoke the expected response from Connor's men. King did not seek to create bloodshed so much as he attempted to dramatize publicly, for newspapers and television to record, the vicious white resistance to racial equality. "You see a policeman beating somebody and with water hoses," Reverend Shuttlesworth declared, "that's news, that's spectacularism."

The protests did elicit white violence. High-pressure water hoses and trained attack dogs were turned on peaceful demonstrators, many of whom were children the SCLC had recruited into the movement. Bombs exploded at the hotel where King was lodged and at his brother's home. These blasts sparked outraged blacks to take to the streets in retaliation, hurling rocks and bottles at the police. Before the city fell into this grip of violence, local civic leaders and federal officials had quietly negotiated with King to forge order out of chaos. The President sent Assistant Attorney General Marshall to mediate between a committee of white businesspeople and black protesters. They hammered out a compromise that called for the desegregation of eating facilities and the gradual hiring of black sales personnel, but left intact the segregation of most public accommodations and the criminal charges brought against black demonstrators, including King. Subsequently, the newly installed mayor, whose election had been upheld by the courts, established a biracial community affairs committee, and the city council repealed its municipal segregation ordinances.

Although much remained to be done, Birmingham witnessed significant change. The demonstrations strengthened the local movement by fostering racial solidarity, and provided tangible evidence that collective action enhanced the influence of blacks in shaping public affairs. To extend the gains derived from direct action protests, civil rights groups mounted voter registration drives to build up budding black electoral clout. By 1964, the proportion of registered blacks had doubled to 20 percent. However far their struggles carried them, they still needed federal support to overcome Jim Crow and disfranchisement. Like their counterparts in Greenwood, blacks in Birmingham continued to face calculated vigilante violence. The culmination of such brutality in Birmingham occurred on September 15, 1963, with the bombing of the Sixteenth Street Baptist Church and the tragic deaths of four young girls worshiping inside.

Meanwhile, the Kennedy administration had continued to venture cautiously into the civil rights field. The President delayed issuing the executive decree on residential desegregation he had promised during the presidential campaign until November 1962. Even then, he limited the order to homes subsidized by federal loans, which left most of the housing market uncovered. Shortly before, the administration had demonstrated its unwillingness to exercise federal might unless given no other choice. Facing a direct threat to a federal court order admitting James Meredith to the University of Mississippi in September 1962, the President finally mobilized sufficient military force to combat racist interference with desegregation. Like Eisenhower in his handling of the Little Rock crisis, Kennedy hesitated to send federal troops to the South, preferring instead to persuade the state to enforce the desegregation ruling voluntarily. On October 1, only after Governor Ross Barnett refused to negotiate in good faith and failed to guarantee Meredith's safety did the President move in the army. This intervention came belatedly after a riot had broken out, resulting in two deaths and over 300 injuries.

The following year, Kennedy showed that he could learn from his mistakes. On June 11, 1963, the administration won a well-publicized battle with Governor George Wallace to desegregate the University of Alabama. With the Mississippi disaster in mind, the President acted more firmly in dealing with Governor Wallace. Carrying out a carefully orchestrated plan, the Kennedy administration dispatched Deputy Attorney General Nicholas Katzenbach and federal marshals to escort two black students, Vivian Malone and James Hood, whose admission had been ordered by the federal judiciary. After Wallace blocked their entry by standing in the schoolhouse door, the President federalized the state National Guard. The six-hour standoff ended when the Alabama governor stepped aside and allowed integration at the Tuscaloosa campus to proceed peacefully.

In the end, President Kennedy went further than his Republican predecessor, Dwight Eisenhower, in pursing racial equality. The political pressure of protest had pushed the chief executive to embrace at least the more moderate goals of the civil rights movement. The disruptive Birmingham demonstrations convinced him that the racial situation in the South had reached a dangerous phase. The crises provoked by civil rights protesters sparked widespread racial confrontations throughout Dixie and even threatened to consume the North. Worried by the escalating violence and the increasing possibility of black retaliation, the President introduced the legislative program he had postponed since entering the White House. The events of the previous two years compelled him to recognize the morality of the civil rights struggle. On June 11, he informed a nationwide television audience that the extension of equal rights to all Americans was an issue "as old as the scriptures and … as clear as the American Constitution." Conflicts in Birmingham and elsewhere, he warned his listeners, required legislation "if we are to move this problem from the streets to the courts." The chief executive's proposals attacked segregation in public accommodations and schools, created a Community Relations Service to mediate racial disputes, authorized cutting off federal funds to local agencies practicing discrimination, and expanded judicial power to speed up voting rights cases. The administration's civil rights measures were timed to restore peace to southern battlegrounds by removing the conditions that had spawned protest. Nonetheless, soothing words alone could not stop violence: only a few hours after the President's address, the NAACP's Medgar Evers was assassinated by a white supremacist in Jackson, Mississippi.

Freedom Votes, Freedom Summer

The Kennedy administration saw its preferred solution to civil rights controversies taking shape in scattered communities throughout the South. In a number of cities, such as Atlanta, Georgia, Tampa, Florida, and Norfolk, Virginia, businesspeople had responded to civil rights turbulence by seeking ways voluntarily to desegregate public accommodations and municipal facilities. These civic leaders recognized that explosive race relations made poor business sense. Seeking to attract outside investments and commercial enterprises to their areas, they took measures to reduce the kind of negative publicity that would tarnish their cities' images, as it had those of Little Rock and Birmingham. A politician such as Mayor Ivan Allen of Atlanta went so far as to support the Kennedy civil rights bill, but this kind of expression by local white moderates was rare. More frequently, they tried to maintain local control over the amount and pace of desegregation in order to forestall federal intervention. Consequently, they accepted sufficient changes to keep their cities relatively quiet and out of the headlines, yet without guaranteeing full equality for blacks.

Also without much fanfare, blacks followed the electoral path to first-class citizenship. In 1964, in Tuskegee, Alabama, a small group of white liberals joined with Charles Gomillion's Macon County Democratic Club, an offshoot of the Tuskegee Civic Association, to elect a biracial slate to city and county offices. By then blacks constituted a majority of the registered voters in Macon County and split about evenly with whites in Tuskegee.

With blacks assuming majority status as voters, Gomillion and his associates favored a gradualist approach in sharing power with whites. They wanted to avoid raising the specter of black domination and hoped to show that the two races could cooperate in governing responsibly. Gomillion hoped this policy would serve as a model for encouraging "whites elsewhere to be willing to appoint or elect qualified Negroes, even in places where Negroes were less numerous than in Macon County." The outcome of elections in his own bailiwick did not disappoint the Tuskegee sociologist. An interracial coalition elected Gomillion to a seat on the board of education, along with three other blacks who won countywide positions. In the city, two blacks gained posts on the municipal council. At the same time, whites retained control of both county and city governments and held the key offices of sheriff and mayor.

This landmark election in Macon County revealed the growing complexity of black politics as the majority of African Americans obtained the vote. Gomillion's strategy had run into serious opposition from within the black community. A group of younger blacks who had come of age during the birth of the civil rights movement in the 1950s challenged the 65-year-old Gomillion and his prescription for racial advancement. These insurgents decried the "pace of social change in Tuskegee [as] unconscionably slow" and argued for the election of as many black candidates as possible. This intraracial split reflected different class as well as ideological perspectives. The Gomillion wing articulated distinctly middle-class values and spoke mainly for the professionals and staff of the Tuskegee Institute and the Veterans Administration hospital. The challengers, many of whom taught at Tuskegee, also came from the middle class but directed their attention to the problems of lower-income and impoverished blacks in the city and the rural sections of the county.

As long as most blacks experienced racial disfranchisement in common, class divisions remained in the background. Nevertheless, class divisions did exist and had already begun to surface in Mississippi as well. The 1963 freedom vote campaign had encountered opposition from some of the state's 27,000 blacks who had managed to register to vote. They resented SNCC's efforts to develop political consciousness among the masses of blacks, which, if successful, might eventually undermine their own leadership. These middle-class blacks had succeeded by playing according to white electoral rules; they considered voting a privilege that should be extended to those, like themselves, who passed the literacy test, as long as it was applied equally. When members of the black middle class opposed

Figure 8   On August 28, 1963, following the introduction of the civil rights bill in Congress, approximately 250,000 blacks and whites marched on Washington to stage a massive rally for jobs and freedom. The demonstration was highlighted by two contrasting speeches. An angry SNCC chairperson, John Lewis, complained that the progress of civil rights was moving too slowly, while Martin Luther King, Jr., pictured above, delivered his optimistic "I Have a Dream" speech for an integrated America. (Getty Images)

racial discrimination they usually did so through "respectable" civil rights groups like the NAACP, which stressed litigation, and not through organizations like SNCC, which they considered disruptive and likely to stir up white hostility. Thus, as Neil R. McMillen has pointed out, in rallying the black masses against white supremacy, civil rights organizers were also challenging "traditional [black] elites once thought to be the natural leaders of their people by the people themselves."

Because racial oppression was so harsh in Mississippi, the civil rights movement generally had been able to submerge class divisions beneath black solidarity. The NAACP had joined SNCC in designing the freedom vote campaign, and one of its leaders, Aaron Henry, had led the insurgent gubernatorial ticket. Following the 1963 mock-election, COFO planned a massive voter registration drive for the next summer, climaxing in a

challenge to the state Democratic Party delegation at the presidential nominating convention in Atlantic City. The project was fashioned to focus
national attention on the blatantly racist means by which white
Mississippians excluded blacks from the suffrage. The planners of the 1964
"Freedom Summer" invited northern white students to the state to expose
them to the dangers blacks experienced every day. White Americans hardly
noticed the deaths of black people, Bob Moses candidly admitted, but "they
would respond to a thousand young white college students" suffering brutality at the hands of Mississippi racists. Like the nonviolent provocation
King practiced in Birmingham, the use of white students did not cause the
violence; rather, it served to dramatize the terror that already existed. It
would take blood spilled by whites, COFO cynically though realistically
reasoned, to prompt federal intervention.

Months before Freedom Summer was scheduled to begin, the
assassination of John F. Kennedy had placed in the Oval Office a new
President, though not a new policy. Upon taking over in November 1963,
Lyndon B. Johnson threw his support behind Kennedy's civil rights bill
and, together with a coalition of liberal lawmakers and civil rights, labor,
and religious groups, had waged a long, fierce struggle that succeeded in
obtaining a stronger measure than the one originally proposed.[1] However,
the new law did not help the political insurgents in Mississippi. Though
it accepted a sixth-grade education as evidence of literacy for the purpose
of voter registration, the statute continued to leave enforcement with
the judiciary, a procedure that proved cumbersome and inadequate.
Furthermore, the Act failed to address the improper application of literacy
tests, which in the past had allowed illiterate or semiliterate whites, but not
blacks, to register. Above all, nothing in the legislation directed the
administration to provide protection for civil rights volunteers engaged in
Freedom Summer.

The murder of three young civil rights workers, James Chaney, Michael
Schwerner, and Andrew Goodman – one black and two whites – on June
21, 1964, finally forced some intervention from Washington. President
Johnson ordered the FBI, which previously had been ineffective if not

---

[1]   In addition to the provisions originally offered by the Kennedy administration in 1963, the
1964 Civil Rights Act prohibited employment discrimination based on race and sex and
created an Equal Employment Opportunity Commission to implement it. The law passed
after the Senate shut off a filibuster that lasted for 57 days. President Johnson signed the bill
into law on July 2.

uninterested in pursuing civil rights offenses, to launch an intensive man-hunt to apprehend the killers. The bureau set up an office in Mississippi and, with assistance from paid informers inside the Ku Klux Klan, arrested 19 men, including a sheriff and deputy sheriff, for commission of the crime. Nevertheless, the Justice Department declined to provide day-to-day protection for the suffragists, who remained in the field to suffer the usual assortment of intimidating tactics: beatings, bombings, arson, and at least three additional homicides.

This racist reign of terror against the freedom fighters did not prevent COFO from organizing blacks into a potent political force. Though relatively few managed to register to vote during the summer campaign, a great many more participated in the formation of the Mississippi Freedom Democratic Party (MFDP). Protesting their exclusion from the process by which state Democrats selected their delegates to the national convention, the Freedom Democrats erected an alternative structure to challenge them. While predominantly black, the reform organization was open to members of both races and included Ed King, the white clergyman who had run with Aaron Henry in the 1963 COFO mock-election. In the style of SNCC, which heavily influenced its creation, the MFDP was the prod-uct of grassroots organizing constructed from the bottom up. Unlike the conservative regulars, the group pledged to support Lyndon Johnson as the Democratic Party's presidential nominee as well as his liberal Great Society platform.

President Johnson counted on widespread black support for his candi-dacy. Since his early career as an opponent of Truman's civil rights program and his middle years as a proponent of lukewarm civil rights legislation, the Texan had grown into a staunch advocate of racial equality. As he climbed higher up the ladder of electoral success, away from the constraints of his southern segregationist constituency, he developed an increasing sense of moral obligation to extend first-class citizenship to blacks. His eth-ical and political convictions meshed with his regional loyalty. A complex man, he believed a resolution of racial problems would liberate his native South, white as well as black, from the burdens of outmoded discriminatory institutions that retarded its economic progress. In the absence of the race issue and the reactionary politics it spawned, Johnson envisioned southern Democratic politicians falling in step behind his reform leadership.

In customary fashion, the President attempted to build a broad con-sensus for his nomination in 1964. The northern, liberal wing of his party backed him solidly, but the South posed some difficulties. Upset with the passage of the 1964 Civil Rights Act and with the expensive social welfare programs that Johnson was preparing for his Great Society, many white southerners were unenthusiastic about their native son. Instead, they seemed to prefer the Republican nominee, Senator Barry Goldwater of Arizona, who had voted against the civil rights law and whose conservative economic views were more compatible with theirs. To stem these potential losses and achieve the biggest possible electoral victory, Johnson came to the convention seeking unity.

The challenge of the MFDP endangered Johnson's plan for a well-ordered convention. Joseph Rauh, a prominent white liberal attorney with connections to organized labor, presented the case for recognition of the Freedom Democrats as the legitimate representatives from Mississippi. He contended that they had been illegally barred from participation in the selection of delegates by the regular party organization and questioned their lily-white rivals' loyalty to the reform principles of the national party. The Freedom delegation backed up its legal right to the convention seats with powerful moral arguments. The most striking presentation came from Fannie Lou Hamer of Sunflower County, the home district of Senator Eastland. She recounted with great emotion the brutality and pain she had suffered from Mississippi law-enforcement officials while working for civil rights. In stirring testimony before the Credentials Committee and recorded by television cameras for a national audience, Mrs. Hamer painted a graphic picture of the outrages happening so frequently in Mississippi and asked her listeners: "Is this America? The land of the free and the home of the brave?"

In this conflict, President Johnson mixed his moral concern for the plight of Mississippi blacks with his political passion for consensus. He hastily arranged a press conference to preempt live coverage of Mrs. Hamer's powerful testimony and put forces in motion to work out a compromise on the Freedom challenge that would appeal to blacks, their liberal allies, and moderate white southerners. He let the reformers know that he would choose Hubert Humphrey, the liberal senator from Minnesota, as his running mate if the latter could settle the dispute without a divisive credentials fight. With the help of Rauh, Walter Reuther, the head of the United Automobile Workers, and Walter Mondale, Humphrey's protégé who sat on the Credentials Committee, the Minnesota senator hatched a plan acceptable to the majority of convention delegates. It extended two at-large seats to the MFDP and named Aaron Henry and Ed King to occupy them. The rest of the Freedom Democrats could attend the convention as nonvoting

Figure 9 In 1965 the Mississippi Freedom Democratic Party contested the election of that state's congressional representatives. The three Freedom Democratic candidates who journeyed to Washington in hopes of replacing the regulars were, from left to right, Victoria Gray, Fannie Lou Hamer, and Annie Devine. The House denied their claim. (Photo © Bettmann/Corbis)

guests. Those state regulars who swore allegiance to the national party would officially represent Mississippi and cast its 44 votes. Furthermore, looking ahead, the Democrats agreed to draw up guidelines to eliminate racial discrimination in delegate selection to the next national nominating convention.

The compromise preserved party harmony at the convention, but it satisfied neither Magnolia faction. Most of the white regulars refused to sign the loyalty pledge and returned home to vote for Goldwater. The Freedom Democrats also rejected the agreement. Believing that they had morality as well as legality on their side, they would not accept a token assignment of two seats while the regulars controlled the votes of the entire delegation. They had not risked their lives merely for a symbolic victory, and further resented the fact that Democratic leaders, not the MFDP representatives, had specifically chosen the two delegates for them. For many of the civil rights organizers, particularly those in SNCC, this whole episode had a souring effect on their relationship with white liberals. They felt sold out by the administration and its allies, who presumed to know what was best for them and to dictate a solution accordingly. They also lost trust in their lawyer, Joseph Rauh, and black leaders, such as Martin Luther King and Bayard Rustin, who favored the arrangement for practical reasons – as a first step toward eventual reform and the best bargain they could get. Despite their loss of faith, most of the Freedom delegation returned home and campaigned for Johnson and future recognition by the Democratic Party.

The convention challenge also produced serious internal strains within the civil rights movement in Mississippi. As John Dittmer has concluded, the Atlantic City affair marked "the beginning of the end of the COFO partnership and the emergence of class conflict as a major destructive force." The debate over whether to accept the administration's offer split the MFDP delegation. Urban middle-class blacks, about one-fifth of the group, tended to favor the compromise in opposition to the largely rural, poor delegates who rejected it. The latter contingent won the opening skirmish, but when the Freedom Democrats returned home the feud continued. Within the state, blacks who were associated with SNCC's increasingly radical vision of grassroots organizing struggled with more traditional elements allied with the NAACP for control over the future course of black politics.

The Triumph of LBJ

President Johnson may have abandoned the most militant blacks at the convention, but he had no intention of ignoring the black electorate. With Barry Goldwater enticing white voters away from the Democratic Party in the South, the President recognized the growing importance of the black vote in carrying Dixie. After Lawrence O'Brien, a top political adviser, returned from traveling through the region during the campaign, he reported to Johnson that "victory in at least four of the states and possibly in six hinges upon the percentage of Negro voters who go to the polls." Because the chief executive would probably garner at least 90 percent of the black vote, the Democrats had to concentrate on getting out the vote. State party leaders like those in Mississippi had discouraged black participation, so it remained for the national organization to mount a suffrage campaign. Under the direction of Louis Martin, the Democratic National Committee sponsored such drives, which, according to Martin, "are better than they ever have been and better than we thought they ever would be." This effort did not prevent Goldwater from capturing five southern states, including Mississippi, but it did help Johnson win the rest of the former Confederacy. Everywhere else, except in Goldwater's Arizona, the President triumphed and racked up huge margins among black voters. They went to the polls in approval, as the *Afro-American* newspaper commented, for one whose record "proves his compassionate concern for people, irrespective of race, creed or color."

Johnson's triumph over Goldwater cemented black voters more solidly than ever before behind the Democratic Party. The trend that started with Franklin Roosevelt, was pushed along by Truman, momentarily interrupted by Eisenhower, and renewed by Kennedy reached landslide proportions under Johnson. As the black electorate grew in influence, so too did its success in shoving civil rights to the front of the national political agenda. In the South, where the majority of blacks still could not vote, protest and community organizing served as the most potent weapons for influencing politics. In different ways, Martin Luther King and the more radical activists in SNCC and CORE recognized that mobilizing blacks from below pressured the national government to act from above. This pincer movement had trapped and wounded Jim Crow, which, though kicking and screaming, nonetheless refused to die.

4

Reenfranchisement and Racial Consciousness

The Selma Movement and the Voting Rights Act of 1965

The distance between Oslo, Norway, and Selma, Alabama, spanned more than an ocean and thousands of miles. For African Americans it represented the difference between dignity and degradation. The winner of the 1964 Nobel Peace Prize, Dr. Martin Luther King, Jr., returned to the United States after obtaining his prestigious award in Oslo and journeyed to Selma in hope of eliminating the gap between the honorific treatment he had received abroad and the lack of respect blacks were accorded at home. Specifically, he sought to do something about the continuing denial of their right to vote. Throughout the former Confederate states, approximately 57 percent of eligible blacks remained off the suffrage rolls; in Alabama, the figure was a more shocking 77 percent; and in Dallas County, where Selma was the county seat, only 335 blacks out of a total population of 15,000 were registered. With this in mind, on January 2, 1965, Dr. King told an audience gathered at Selma's Brown Chapel AME Church what was at stake in the demonstrations the SCLC was about to launch. "When we get the right to vote," he predicted, "we will send to the statehouse not men who will stand in the doorways of universities to keep Negroes out, but men who will uphold the cause of justice."

King's plans capped the 20-year struggle to reenfranchise black southerners. Since the outlawing of the white primary in 1944, civil rights groups and

Running for Freedom: Civil Rights and Black Politics in America since 1941,
Fourth Edition. Steven F. Lawson.
© 2015 John Wiley & Sons, Inc. Published 2015 by John Wiley & Sons, Inc.

the national government had attempted to remove discriminatory barriers impeding black suffrage. Though a combination of litigation, legislation, and voter registration campaigns had yielded much progress, the majority of southern blacks still were disfranchised and were likely to stay so unless state and local officials lost their stranglehold on the enrollment process. Like most of the gains made during the civil rights era, the expansion of black ballots depended upon the power of the federal government in reinforcing the efforts of blacks at the local level, who were already fighting for first-class citizenship.

President Johnson intended to throw his considerable political weight behind renewed efforts to secure the right to vote. The chief executive shared civil rights advocates' faith in the ballot as the ultimate weapon in promoting racial advancement. Once blacks voted in large numbers, he believed, "many other breakthroughs would follow as a consequence of the black man's own legitimate power as an American citizen, not as a gift from the white man." This thinking reflected the willingness of liberals like Johnson to use the federal government to attack racist obstacles in the South, but it also mirrored the more conservative view of the right to vote as a self-help vehicle for uplifting an oppressed group.

In addition to these philosophical considerations, Johnson, the consummate politician, recognized the pragmatic benefits that reenfranchising blacks would bestow. In achieving his landslide victory in 1964, the President had lost the votes of five states in his native South – Alabama, Georgia, Louisiana, Mississippi, and South Carolina. In each of these states, the black enrollment figure was under 39 percent. If the Johnson administration found a way to dismantle discriminatory suffrage procedures, it could boost black registration to offset the Republican inroads Barry Goldwater had made into Democratic ranks in the South. After the election, an official of the Democratic Party reported "that the first step toward getting out a big Democratic vote is to increase [black] registration."

Having already succeeded in obtaining passage of the 1964 Civil Rights Act, Johnson could not afford to rest on his laurels. This landmark legislation continued to leave voting rights enforcement in the hands of the judiciary. Previous experience had proven the courts inadequate in repelling white southern obstructionists. Besides, in the past registrars had not been deterred from signing up white illiterates while excluding those who were black, and the force of any criterion that preserved some standard of literacy would fall disproportionately on the thousands of undereducated blacks who remained disfranchised.

To correct flaws in the existing legislation, both federal agencies and civil rights groups recommended a new approach. On several occasions, most recently in 1963, the United States Commission on Civil Rights suggested that Congress grant the President authority to appoint federal enrollment officers to register qualified blacks. SNCC went even further. Based on its efforts in the impoverished, black-belt South, the organization advocated the complete abolition of literacy tests as a requirement for voting. Either the country must eliminate these qualifications or, as Bob Moses argued, provide blacks with "the right to learn how to read and write *now*." Indeed, in several cases, an unusually progressive federal judge in Alabama, Frank M. Johnson, had ordered the enrollment of black illiterates as voters. Because illiterate whites had managed to register in the past, he decreed that blacks under similar circumstances did not have to prove their ability to read and write in order to qualify to vote.

After his election, in November 1964, President Johnson began seriously to consider his options. Although some White House advisers suggested that the administration forgo proposing any new voting rights legislation for a year, until the South had time to adjust to the recently enacted Civil Rights law, the chief executive forged ahead. After ordering the Justice Department to prepare a new suffrage measure, on January 4, 1965, Johnson delivered the annual State of the Union address and affirmed his desire to "eliminate every remaining obstacle to the right and opportunity to vote."

In the meantime, Dr. King marshaled civil rights forces in Selma to guarantee swift and effective federal action. The unofficial capital of the Alabama black belt, Selma had served as an arsenal and naval foundry for the Confederacy. In 1865, Union forces torched the town, and memories of the Civil War and Reconstruction still burned in the minds of local whites. This section of the state had backed the Dixiecrat challenge in 1948, and the attitude of many white officials toward blacks was summed up by James A. Hare, a Dallas County judge. "Your Negro," he asserted, "is a mixture of African types like the Congolite who has a long heel and the blue-gummed Ebo whose I.Q. is about 50 or 55." James G. Clark, the Dallas County sheriff, practiced the "Bull" Connor brand of law enforcement, showed little patience for civil rights protesters, and seemed genuinely to enjoy roughing them up. Sporting a green helmet adorned with an eagle and a Confederate flag and dressing in the style of the World War II general George S. Patton, Clark led his deputies in poking demonstrators with electric cattle prods, beating them with clubs, and dispersing them with tear gas.

This stronghold of segregation and police-state tactics offered an inviting setting for King and the SCLC to wage a major assault against political disfranchisement. From his previous encounter with Connor in Birmingham, the Nobel laureate had learned that the application of nonviolent pressure would provoke intemperate, racist lawmen to commit acts of brutality. The SCLC's strategy depended on blacks behaving with restraint in the face of such vicious attacks and on television cameras and journalists recording the confrontation so as to prick the conscience of an outraged nation. Injuries and fatalities would very likely accompany this struggle, but King was seeking drama, not bloodshed. By carefully stage-managing events at Selma, by combining disruption with prudence, he hoped to appeal to the larger audience of the public and the more specific one of the President and lawmakers in Washington, DC.

King's troops marched along the trail blazed by SNCC and local black activists in Selma. In 1963, two SNCC fieldworkers had established a beach-head in the town and conducted a voter registration drive that led to the formation of the Dallas County Voters League (DCVL). This indigenous association was headed by Reverend Frederick Reese. A high school teacher and Baptist clergyman, Reese felt strongly that black educators should take an active role in the freedom struggle. Dependent on white school boards and county administrators for their livelihood, many teachers had refrained from becoming actively involved in the movement. Reese believed that his colleagues had both a personal and professional obligation to seek to become registered voters and challenge those who tried to thwart them; otherwise, they could not properly fulfill their responsibility of instructing their pupils in exercising the duties of citizenship.

Amelia P. Boynton joined Reese as a prime mover behind the creation of the Voters League. The widow of the county's black agricultural extension agent, Mrs. Boynton was an independent businesswoman who operated an employment and insurance agency in Selma. Along with her husband, she had actively taken part in civil rights efforts and was especially concerned with efforts to increase black voter registration. Herself an enrolled voter, Boynton was well aware of the discriminatory treatment most blacks suffered. She knew of one official who could barely pronounce the words "constitutionality" and "interrogatory" on a literacy test administered to a black teacher. After the applicant interrupted the clerk to read the words correctly, "the registrar turned red with anger" and flunked her. Boynton had originally invited SNCC into the country to aid the DCVL in mobilizing blacks against such injustices.

Spearheaded by Reverend Reese and Mrs. Boynton, the league sponsored voter registration workshops to encourage blacks to enroll. In the autumn of 1963, together with SNCC, it held a "Freedom Day" rally at the county courthouse that spurred more than 300 blacks to make an attempt to sign up to vote. Instead, the applicants met resistance from the board of registrars and from Sheriff Clark and his deputies, who tried to prevent the would-be enrollees from receiving food and water as they stood for hours waiting on line to enroll. Throughout the following year, SNCC continued to organize voter registration drives in Dallas County but met with scant success.

At the same time, the federal government tackled the registration problem in its usual fashion. Justice Department lawyers had filed suits to restrain Clark from interfering with voter registration activities, and in November 1963, they won a ruling barring county registrars from using the literacy test to discriminate against black applicants. However, this decree failed to deter officials from engaging in biased practices against prospective black voters, and additional legal action to stop them proved unsuccessful. To make matters worse, a local judge issued an injunction blocking the Voters League from conducting mass meetings. By 1965, after several years of frustrating litigation, fewer than 400 Dallas County blacks had managed to register to vote. Acknowledging this failure, Attorney General Nicholas Katzenbach complained of "the inadequacy of the judicial process to deal effectively and expeditiously with a problem so deep-seated and so complex."

The inability of the federal courts to remedy unfair registration practices was matched by the unwillingness of the executive branch to protect suffrage workers from harassment. Adhering to the policy of his predecessors, Johnson refused to deploy federal marshals to Dallas County to safeguard voter registration workers from the menace of Sheriff Clark and his deputies. The chief executive preferred to leave law enforcement under the control of local authorities, barring a total breakdown of public order. In a similar manner, the Justice Department refused to instruct FBI agents to offer relief when they saw the constitutional rights of suffragists under attack. For example, on Freedom Day, October 7, 1963, the FBI merely observed and took notes as peaceful protesters were pushed around and arrested by Sheriff Clark and his men on the steps of the US courthouse. Observing this scene firsthand exasperated Howard Zinn. "For all the good the federal officials did," the historian and adviser to SNCC bitterly commented, "[Alabama Governor] George Wallace might have been President of the United States."

Despite the racist intimidation and the failure of the national government to check it, blacks in Selma refused to retreat. SNCC had helped galvanize the community behind the struggle for political empowerment and set in motion forces for liberation that could not be easily turned back. SNCC's executive secretary, James Forman, celebrated Freedom Day as "the day when a century of Southern fear and terror … had not been able to stop the forward thrust of a people determined … to be free." Nevertheless, SNCC's efforts had sputtered, and local black leaders called in civil rights reinforcements. Their immediate goal was to secure help in registering residents of their own and surrounding counties; nonetheless, in late 1964, when the Dallas County Voters League invited King and the SCLC to Selma, it opened the way for the enfranchisement of the majority of blacks throughout the South.

The second day of the new year brought King to Selma to shape the kind of crisis that would force the federal government to crack white southern interference with black voting. During January and February 1965, the SCLC mobilized blacks in marches to the courthouse, where they would petition to register. At first, a moderate white faction in Selma, represented by the city's director of public safety, Wilson Baker, kept Sheriff Clark and his troops in line. This group, which had taken over political control of the city, believed that brutal suppression of black protest would generate unfavorable publicity and endanger new opportunities for business and civic development. "[T]he social, economic, and industrial complexion of this community," the editor of Selma's newspaper commented, "has suddenly and simultaneously arrived at a point from which there can be no turning aside." Restraint more than racial reform was uppermost on their minds, as Baker declared in referring to the demonstrators: "If we can only get the bastards out of town without getting them arrested, we'll have 'em whipped." Patience, however, was a virtue Clark did not possess, and he soon ordered the arrest of scores of peaceful black protesters.

His tough posture did not deter Selma's blacks; it only united them further. When usually cautious middle-class African-American teachers joined Reverend Reese on a march to the courthouse, they raised black solidarity to a new height. Though the educators did not wind up in jail, on February 1, Martin Luther King, Jr., did. Imprisoned for four days, King directed his aides from his cell to pressure President Johnson "to intervene in some way." Upon his release, he met personally with the chief executive and received assurances that a voting rights bill was in preparation.

Meanwhile, the SCLC attempted to hasten delivery of this promised congressional legislation. In mid-February a night march in neighboring Perry County resulted in the first fatality of the Selma suffrage campaign. In conjunction with the Perry County Civic League, the SCLC had convened a mass meeting and attempted to conduct a peaceful rally, only to come under siege from city, county, and state police. While trying to shield his mother from a beating by a state trooper, 26-year-old Jimmie Lee Jackson was shot in the stomach and later died. Several reporters, including Richard Valeriani of the National Broadcasting Company, were also injured in the melee, thereby ensuring that this police riot received unfavorable publicity from the national media. A series of protests continued throughout the month, and King pledged: "We are going to bring a voting bill into being in the streets of Selma."

In the aftermath of Jackson's shooting, the SCLC began to conceive of dramatically expanding the demonstrations into a march from Selma to Montgomery, 50 miles away. Following the murder, blacks in Perry County discussed the possibility of carrying Jackson's body to Montgomery and depositing it on the steps of the state capitol. "We had to do something," Albert Turner, one of the local leaders recalled, "to point out to the nation the evils of the system." After Jackson's burial, the SCLC picked up on the idea and planned a mass march from Selma to Montgomery to begin on Sunday, March 7. With King having returned to Atlanta that day, one of his aides, Hosea Williams, and the chairman of SNCC, John Lewis, led 600 protesters over the Edmund Pettus Bridge toward the capital city. Before they could get across, however, state troopers and Clark's posse charged into the procession, lobbed tear gas canisters, and clubbed and chased the marchers back to town. Mrs. Boynton, who had previously been roughed up by the sheriff, was knocked unconscious in the assault. "The horses … were more humane than the troopers; they stepped over fallen victims," she wryly remarked.

This display of raw aggression finally provided the SCLC with the provocative incident it needed to mobilize public opinion and secure federal intervention. Television cameras vividly recorded the events of "Bloody Sunday," and the American Broadcasting Company interrupted its network premier showing of the film *Judgment at Nuremberg*, the story of the Nazi war crimes trials, to present footage of the fascist-style behavior here at home.

Throughout this period, King and other civil rights leaders held several meetings with the President and urged him to introduce legislation

Figure 10 Alabama state troopers, wearing gas masks, attack John Lewis on "Bloody Sunday" in Selma. (Photo © Bettmann/Corbis)

immediately to outlaw literacy requirements for voter registration and to authorize the assignment of federal registrars. Johnson intended to support a suffrage measure, but he had several options from which to choose, including taking the slow route of a constitutional amendment. The escalating racial conflict in Selma prompted the chief executive to scuttle any proposal that did not move swiftly to dismantle discriminatory registration barriers. A growing coalition of lawmakers in both political parties called for quick congressional action, and outside of Dixie, civil rights sympathizers held a wave of protests in support of the Selma marchers. In the nation's capital hundreds of marchers demanded that Washington come to the aid of the suffragists, and a contingent from SNCC dramatically mounted a sit-in at the Justice Department to push it in the same direction. Meanwhile, the demonstrations in Alabama and the national outcry they engendered pushed President Johnson to accelerate his legislative timetable, dictated the selection of the most potent legislative option, and created the favorable political climate to guarantee its passage.

Even before the President had an opportunity to move forward, King and his followers precipitated a new crisis. They rescheduled the pilgrimage to Montgomery for March 9, despite the issuance of a federal court decree postponing it. King had not violated a federal judicial order before, but in this instance he was ready to proceed to show that racist violence could not be used to derail the civil rights movement. President Johnson sent to Selma his personal emissary, LeRoy Collins, former governor of Florida and director of the federal Community Relations Service, who carried on negotiations separately with the marchers and the state police and successfully defused the crisis. Accordingly, the protesters walked to the end of the bridge, knelt in prayer, and turned back, while the troopers calmly monitored the situation. This peaceful resolution did not prevent a group of whites from killing one of the returning marchers, the Reverend James Reeb, a white minister from Boston. Brutally beaten while he walked the streets of Selma, Reeb soon died from his wounds.

After federal Judge Frank M. Johnson lifted his ban, the parade finally began on March 21, two weeks after Bloody Sunday. By that time, Governor George C. Wallace refused to furnish protection for the marchers, forcing Johnson to federalize the Alabama National Guard for that purpose. Their presence generally deterred violence but could not prevent one further slaying of a white civil rights volunteer, Mrs. Viola Liuzzo of Detroit, as she rode in her car with a black companion en route to Montgomery to pick up returning marchers. The deaths of Liuzzo and Reeb especially shocked northern whites, including the President.

In the meantime, this renewed round of demonstrations produced the long-awaited presidential proposal on voting rights. On March 15, in a magnificent address to a joint session of Congress televised to an audience of 70 million Americans, Johnson praised the Selma demonstrators as freedom fighters and admonished Congress to allow "no delay, no hesitation, no compromise with" passage of remedial legislation to aid their cause. In one eloquent and memorable moment, he adopted the language of the civil rights movement and promised, "We shall overcome." Two days later, the administration measure reached the halls of Congress.

The Selma struggle had developed along two different fronts. Local movement leaders in Dallas County desired above all to unclog the registration process in their community. As its top priority, the DCVL hoped to place blacks on the voter lists and welcomed any action that brought significant modifications in biased registration procedures. When a federal judge instructed the enrollment board to cease administering literacy tests and to start processing black applicants at a speedier rate, the Voters League considered it a substantial step toward reaching its major goal. In contrast, the SCLC looked beyond the immediate arena and focused on obtaining national legislation to enfranchise blacks throughout the region. King and his aides argued "that if Selma Negroes gained [the right to vote] under special court order or through community agreement ... this would not satisfy SCLC." Nevertheless, the grassroots goal and the broader civil rights aim remained intertwined in support of extending the ballot; only the tactics differed. In the end, the voting rights bill, forged as a result of the Selma campaign, gave each side what it desired.

Johnson's suffrage plan took the forceful approach recommended by civil rights proponents. Instead of a constitutional amendment, the chief executive asked Congress simply to pass legislation that suspended literacy tests, authorized the attorney general to dispatch federal registrars and observers to recalcitrant counties, and empowered the Justice Department to clear in advance changes in state electoral rules that might unfairly burden black voters. Johnson's lawyers had designed these provisions to enforce suffrage expansion through the administrative machinery of the executive branch rather than by the judiciary, where equal voting rights had been stalled for so long. Consequently, the measure contained an automatic triggering mechanism devised to snare only those states and localities that employed a literacy test and in which less than a majority of those eligible had registered to vote or had voted in the presidential election of 1964. As a result of this formula, Alabama, Georgia, Louisiana, Mississippi, South Carolina, Virginia, and sections of North Carolina would come under federal supervision.

Introduced in March, the voting rights bill encountered relatively little difficulty in Congress, and by early August it had become law. The final version followed closely the outline of Johnson's recommendation and also adopted a provision allowing the affected jurisdictions to escape coverage once they proved to the federal district court in Washington, DC, that they had not employed a discriminatory test or device for the previous five years. In addition, the lawmakers issued a finding that the poll tax infringed upon the right to vote, and they directed the attorney general to initiate litigation, which resulted the following year in the removal of the levy in the four southern states that still required it in nonfederal elections. (The Twenty-Fourth Amendment, ratified in 1964, had eliminated the franchise fee in all national elections.)

This landmark legislation emerged in such powerful shape for a variety of reasons. The President displayed a strong commitment to the bill and exercised firm leadership in guiding it through the legislature. His aides worked diligently to round up key votes and keep supporters in line at critical moments. Johnson helped win over to his position the Senate Republican leader, Everett Dirksen of Illinois, which guaranteed bipartisan backing for the administration's version of the measure. The President's task was made easier because of the favorable climate of opinion created by Reverend King's handling of the Selma episode. Southern whites found it increasingly difficult to defend the brutal opposition to black suffrage in Alabama, and their congressional representatives failed to mount their customary fierce challenge to the legislation. A Gallup poll taken during the march to Montgomery reported that 76 percent of the nation favored a voting rights bill; in the South a surprising 49 percent of the sample indicated approval compared with 37 percent in opposition. Democratic Representative Hale Boggs of Louisiana summed up the sentiment of 40 of his colleagues from the South who voted for the legislation: "I ... support this bill because I believe the fundamental right to vote must be a part of this great experiment in human progress under freedom which is America."

The Voting Rights Act resulted in the reenfranchisement of the majority of southern blacks. Within four years of its passage, approximately three-fifths of southern black adults had registered to vote. The most striking gains occurred in the deep South, where resistance to the suffrage had been most harsh. In Mississippi, black registration leaped from 6.7 percent in 1964 to 59.4 in 1968. Similarly, black enrollment in Alabama jumped from 23 percent to 53 percent. In Dallas County, the scene of the Selma demonstrations, the number of registered blacks soared from fewer than 1,000 to over 8,500 within months of the suffrage law taking effect.

The combination of federal power and grassroots activism helped generate the stunning rise in black political participation. The suspension of literacy requirements removed the major obstacle to black registration, and most of the new voters were signed up by local officials who complied with the law. In hard-core areas where blacks still encountered difficulty in securing the ballot, federal examiners intervened to place the applicants' names directly on the rolls. The greatest opportunities for success occurred when federal registrars operated in localities that also experienced voter registration drives. The presence of civil rights organizations laid the basis for progress by building solidarity among blacks and providing them with the strength to confront those risks involved in challenging white segregationists.

The freedom movement bound people together in collaborative projects and broke down some of the helplessness they felt when facing the burdens of discrimination alone. As Mary King, a SNCC staff member, has written about political organizing in Mississippi: "If blacks failed individually they succeeded collectively, because of the learning and experience gained."

However potent the law, the federal government expected the civil rights groups themselves to register the bulk of disfranchised blacks. "Legislation is not self-implementing," the NAACP's Roy Wilkins acknowledged. "There is work to be done." The new law challenged civil rights proponents to undertake a "tedious, unglamorous task" that required "more recruits, more money and more dedication." After 1965, all of those resources were in short supply as the days of large demonstrations and widespread national support for the civil rights movement drew to a close.

To register additional voters, the Southern Regional Council once again formed a Voter Education Project. From 1966 to 1968, this second VEP funded and coordinated over 200 suffrage drives throughout the South. Not only did it help underwrite the costs of well-established groups like the NAACP in conducting enrollment campaigns, the Atlanta-based group also injected money into the efforts of local civic associations, many of which had been spawned or nurtured by the civil rights movement. These projects attempted to empower blacks, individually and collectively, who had not previously felt a sense of political worth. To combat generations of political helplessness, they embarked on programs of basic education to teach lessons fundamental to expressing first-class citizenship. Vernon Jordan, the director of VEP, explained the problem: "Too many of these people have been alienated from the political process for too long a time … and so we have to … teach them what a local government is, how it operates, and try to relate their votes to the things they want."

Rise of Black Power

Heightened racial consciousness, instilled through the freedom struggle and boosted by the Voting Rights Act, swelled even further with the emergence of "black power." A concept that embodied racial pride and solidarity, it partially grew out of the positive experiences of the freedom struggle. The collective engagement of blacks against Jim Crow and disfranchisement through boycotts, sit-ins, freedom rides, voter registration drives, and other political activities fostered self-respect and a feeling of political efficacy. Men and women, boys and girls, who had long been relegated to the sidelines of southern politics, became active agents in reclaiming first-class citizenship and in transforming the structures of oppression. The Montgomery bus boycott, for example, did more than withhold "patronage from the bus; it ... [restored] dignity to the patrons," as Joseph Lowery, an SCLC official, noted. He explained, "prior to the bus boycotts, the determination of our freedom rested with the courts. With the bus boycott, *we* determined it."

The notion of black power also arose from some of the negative consequences of the civil rights struggle. Resistance to racism spawned it, and disillusionment with white liberals nurtured it. The failure of the federal government to protect civil rights workers and the willingness of liberal whites to compromise the Mississippi Freedom Democratic Party's convention challenge in 1964 outraged many black activists. Furthermore, within the South, the constant exposure to violence and harassment faced by black and white civil rights organizers produced enormous tensions between them. Under these circumstances, even the most well-meaning white volunteers were perceived by their black comrades as guilty of paternalism. Middle-class, college-educated whites who journeyed to the South for a march or a voter registration campaign often had superior skills and resources compared to the blacks they worked beside. Their efforts, no matter how unself-conscious or helpful, were sometimes perceived as perpetuating white dominance. "Look at these fly-by-night freedom fighters bossing everybody around," a black SNCC member bitterly commented during the 1964 Mississippi Freedom Summer about white students who could soon return to their comfortable northern campuses.

The black power slogan first gained notoriety in June 1966, on a march initiated by James Meredith to mobilize black Mississippians to register to vote in the wake of the passage of the Voting Rights Act. Soon after the pilgrimage through the Magnolia State had begun, Meredith, whose admission to the state university had sparked a riot in 1962, was shot and wounded. Rising to take up his cause, leaders of SCLC, SNCC, and CORE set out to complete the trek. Along the way, Stokely Carmichael, the chairman of SNCC, pointed out the new direction toward which many blacks were turning. At a stop in Greenwood, Mississippi, he declared that blacks should concentrate on gaining political control over their own communities. Deemphasizing integration and moral appeals to the consciences of whites, Carmichael proclaimed: "The only way we gonna stop them white men from whippin' us is to take over. We been saying freedom for six years and we ain't got nothin'. What we gonna start saying is Black Power."

Figure 11   Martin Luther King, Jr. (front in center) with Floyd McKissick of CORE (to his immediate right) and Stokely Carmichael of SNCC (to his immediate left) on the last leg of the Meredith march into Jackson. (Photo © Lynn Pelham/Getty Images)

Stokely Carmichael was a movement veteran who had grown up in New York City. A senior at the prestigious Bronx High School of Science when lunch counter sit-ins swept the South in 1960, Carmichael joined in demonstrations against Jim Crow. The following year he rode the buses as a freedom rider, was arrested in Mississippi, and served a jail sentence in the state prison at Parchman. In the early sixties, Carmichael attended Howard University and together with several other students formed the Nonviolent Action Group (NAG), an affiliate of SNCC. As a student he was influenced by his reading of Marx and by contact with Malcolm X, the influential Black Muslim minister, whom he invited to speak at Howard. His campus views matured and grew more militant by virtue of his experiences on SNCC battlefields in the Mississippi delta and the Alabama black belt. In May 1966, the articulate and charming 24-year-old Carmichael became chairman of SNCC, replacing John Lewis and signaling a change in direction of the organization toward black nationalism.

The chant of black power voiced both cultural and political aspirations. More of a rallying cry than a systematic program, black power expressed the dual message of racial unity and group self-determination. Heavily influenced by his activities as a SNCC field-worker in Mississippi and Alabama, Carmichael saw the key to liberation in the political organizing of black communities. His personal experiences in the South found reinforcement in his identification with the African struggle against European colonialism. Moreover, Carmichael's reading of America's multi-ethnic history taught him the necessity for minority groups to develop "their own institutions with which to represent their communal needs within the larger society."

In collaboration with Charles V. Hamilton, a political scientist who had taught at Tuskegee Institute, Carmichael attempted to clarify his views by publishing *Black Power: The Politics of Liberation in America*. Combining the moral outrage and toughened perspective of an embittered SNCC veteran with the scholarly analysis of an academic social scientist, this 1967 book rejected integration and criticized the values of white middle-class society as "antihumanist" and "racist." Denying that black power was merely "racism in reverse," the authors argued that blacks had no intention of turning whites into second-class citizens on the basis of their skin color. Instead, Carmichael and Hamilton espoused self-determination and self-identity as the goals of black power: "full participation in the decision-making processes affecting the lives of black people, and recognition of the virtues in themselves as black people." Acknowledging the predominance of race throughout American history, they contended that blacks could not end discrimination on a color-blind, individual basis but could only do so by organizing their own communities around common group concerns. For the present, they ruled out coalitions with whites, including some former allies; however, once blacks had developed independent bases of political and economic power, Carmichael and Hamilton held open the possibility of creating biracial alliances based on mutual interest. Yet if the authors intended their message to be interpreted as pro-black rather than antiwhite, they refused to soothe white sensibilities by guaranteeing that the outcome of black power would be nonracist. "The final truth," they asserted without apology, "is that white society is not entitled to reassurances, even if it were possible to offer them."

The rhetoric of black power produced divisions within the civil rights movement, but its substance exerted widespread appeal among blacks. Julian Bond, the communications director of SNCC, considered black power the logical outgrowth of the freedom struggle. He traced its lineage "from the courtroom to the streets in favor of integrated facilities, from the ... backwoods roads in quest of the right to vote, from the ballot box to the meat of politics, the organization of voters into self-interest units." Dr. King, who participated with Carmichael on the Meredith march, disapproved of the antiwhite connotations of the phrase and the inflammatory remarks that frequently accompanied it. However, he applauded attempts "to build racial pride and refute the notion that black is evil and ugly." As King had expressed many times, most recently in Selma, the ballot offered a critical tool for exhibiting pride and achieving equality. Blacks of more radical persuasions shared this view. Malcolm X, the charismatic black nationalist leader whose ideology differed in most respects from King's, agreed with him that if blacks were fully permitted to exercise their constitutional right to vote they "would sweep all of the racists and segregationists out of office ... [and] would change the entire political structure of the country."

The controversial black power concept had a mixed impact on black political development. On the one hand, it helped to splinter the civil rights coalition and hastened the decline of two of its most innovative components, SNCC and CORE. Having started out firmly committed to interracial cooperation, they became increasingly disillusioned with white liberals and the prospect of blacks gaining their freedom under white leadership. To the extent that whites had a continuing place in the movement, it was to work within their own communities to combat racist attitudes. As these two groups applied black power principles to their organizations and white participation dwindled, they lost considerable institutional and financial backing. Increasingly isolated from mainstream civil rights groups as well as from whites, by the end of the decade SNCC had virtually disappeared and CORE was in serious disarray. Their deterioration deprived blacks, especially in the South, of the kind of imaginative leadership that had rallied many local communities to organize for freedom. Much work remained to be done in registering voters and summoning them to political action, and the departure of these important organizations from the scene made those tasks more difficult.

On the other hand, burgeoning racial pride among African Americans was instrumental in black political mobilization. Following successful completion of the legislative struggle to obtain the suffrage, political activists had to convert the disfranchised into actual voters. Collective action had demonstrated the power of an oppressed group to reshape its political world, and the racial esteem that developed convinced blacks that politics was as much their business as whites'. Traditionally, individuals with little income and education had a low rate of political participation. Concentrated disproportionately at the bottom end of the socioeconomic scale, blacks nonetheless became politically involved at a level above that predicted from their backgrounds. "Organization, with an emphasis on group consciousness and a sense of group efficacy," according to one political scientist, accounted for the difference. In Mississippi, where the black registration figure soared in the years following passage of the Voting Rights Act, a black observer touring the Magnolia State remarked upon the transformation in this way: "It is so good to realize that we are casting aside the feelings of inferiority and shame and realizing what a strong people we are."

The expanded electoral mobilization of blacks further stimulated their interest in competing for public office. This was especially true in areas with a large number of blacks among the eligible voters, where the chances of electing a black candidate seemed high. Just as acquisition of the ballot furnished a necessary step toward advancing first-class citizenship, so did the election of blacks serve as a badge of equality. The running of black candidates both reflected racial pride and presented a stimulus to further black political mobilization. The election of a black to a post in a rural county in Mississippi, the winner asserted, "will give the Negro race the feeling ... like they can progress, and this in itself [will make] more people run for public office."

As southern blacks began competing for a growing number of political positions, they were most successful at the local level. Because blacks remained a clear minority of the state and national electorates, their greatest chances for success came in those towns and counties in which they constituted a majority of the voting-age population. A decade after enactment of the Voting Rights law nearly 50 percent of black elected officials held municipal government posts. The largest number of black officials sat on city councils, and about three-fifths of those were in small towns with a population of under 5,000. This same pattern held true for southern black mayors, approximately 66 percent of whom presided over municipalities with under 5,000 residents.

A raised racial consciousness accounted for much of the support for turning whites out of office and replacing them with blacks; however, part of the explanation stemmed from practical political considerations. In most places in the South, especially where blacks were in the majority, few whites were initially willing to support black candidates or enter into alliances with them. Without white collaboration, blacks had little choice but to go it alone. In Greene County, Alabama, in the rural black belt, a leader of the group of blacks who took control of the government explained the futility of constructing an interracial coalition: "We wanted the government to be polka dot, but the whites wouldn't cooperate, so we had to make it all chocolate."

In a similar manner, blacks constituted a majority of the population in Lowndes County, Alabama, and sought to branch out on their own. After the 1965 Selma-to-Montgomery march, Stokely Carmichael had remained in Lowndes County to help in the political mobilization of the black community. Under the tutelage of SNCC, local blacks formed the independent Lowndes County Freedom Organization (LCFO) to compete against the white-dominated Democratic Party. "To me," John Hulett, LCFO's chairman remarked, "the Democratic primaries ... are something like a gambler who carries a marked card around in his pocket and every now and then has to let somebody win to keep the game going." Choosing the black panther as its insignia, an emblem of fierce racial pride, at the end of the decade LCFO succeeded in electing Hulett to the most critical county office of sheriff.

These triumphs were repeated elsewhere. In Hancock County, Georgia, blacks comprised about 75 percent of the residents and had only recently made inroads in challenging total white domination of their government. In 1964, local black leaders formed the Hancock County Democratic Club to promote voter registration and political education. A combination of civil rights organizing and the passage of the 1965 Voting Rights Act succeeded in enfranchising a majority of Hancock's black electorate. In 1966, this paid off in the election of three blacks to county posts, and two years later blacks captured two of the three seats on the powerful county commission.

Much of the success of black political efforts here could be attributed to John McCown. A civil rights veteran, he had worked with the SCLC and the Georgia Council on Human Relations. In Hancock he built upon the previous voter registration drives of the County Democratic Club and expanded its endeavors to secure federal poverty program benefits for blacks. Riding the crest of expanded black enrollment, in 1968 he became one of the two blacks to win election to the county commission and, for the first time, a black became a probate judge, the most important official at the courthouse. McCown had managed to construct a potent political organization that reduced black fears of participation and provided economic incentives to vote. His message appealed to black pride. "Instead of trying to change the heart of the lady at the welfare department," he declared, "it's better to get in a position to be her boss."

Severe tensions accompanied the transfer of power from whites to blacks, however. The Ku Klux Klan paraded through the streets on election eve, and assorted threats were hurled at black candidates. Once in office, McCown upset whites even further with his vigorous attempts to desegregate public schools and generate black economic development. In addition, McCown's abrasive manner offended whites, and in 1971 relations between the races plummeted to a new low in what was called "the Hancock County arms race." Sparta, the county seat with an all-white government, began to stockpile machine guns, allegedly to protect its residents. In response, the black-controlled county commission ordered its own cache of machine guns and sponsored the formation of a "hunting club." The confrontation ended only with the intervention of Governor Jimmy Carter, who negotiated an uneasy truce between the protagonists.

Nevertheless, verbal sniping continued for the next several years during which McCown was indicted for misusing federal funds. The turbulence finally ended after the outspoken McCown was killed in a plane crash in early 1976. A controversial figure was gone, but black political power remained. Even with McCown's tragic death, blacks still controlled 16 of 18 positions in the government of Hancock County.

In other places blacks who gained political power found some whites willing to cooperate. In 1966, in Macon County, Alabama, the site of historic battles over black reenfranchisement, Lucius Amerson defeated the white incumbent for sheriff. Though Amerson won with solid grassroots black support, he declined to espouse the rhetoric of black power. Upon taking office, he received support from influential whites, including the probate judge and members of the Tuskegee City Council and County Commission. The chairman of the latter body, Allen Parker, helped promote interracial goodwill among officials and labored to enlarge county employment opportunities for blacks. "The public attitude ... has changed tremendously," Sheriff Amerson declared, "and has helped destroy ... the feeling that existed among Negroes as well as whites that a Negro couldn't get cooperation from the white community."

The Macon County model pointed to the direction in which black politics would head. Most black officials recognized the necessity of forming coalitions with whites to broaden their power base. Only at the local level, where blacks were in the majority, could they afford to ignore whites;

and even there, the blacks had to take whites into account to obtain needed economic resources. The towns and hamlets where most black officials operated were impoverished and depended on funds from state and national governments for internal improvements. Outnumbered in these arenas, as a fact of political life they needed to enter into alliances with white lawmakers. Thus, black politicians who first obtained office on the basis of appeals to racial pride nonetheless were compelled to make common cause with whites to achieve their racial aims.

Black Mississippians were also torn between separatist and coalitionist tendencies. For them the civil rights struggle had meant a way not only to secure the right to vote but also to obtain a fair share of political power. Toward these ends, they had created the Mississippi Freedom Democratic Party to stimulate voter registration and gain control of the instrumentality that dominated political affairs in the state. Though interracial in conception – Ed King, the white minister at Tougaloo College was one of its founders – in practice the MFDP reflected black consciousness and supported the election of black candidates whenever possible. "We want to be on the ground level, where the decisions are made about us," explained Bob Moses. "We don't want to [be] mobilized every four years to vote. We want to be in the actual running of things."

This strategy of encouraging independent black political action clashed with the coalitionist approach of the NAACP. Since the campaign to oust Theodore Bilbo from the Senate after World War II, the NAACP had actively struggled to tear down the Magnolia Curtain of racism draped across the state. During the 1950s and until his assassination in 1963, Medgar Evers, along with leaders like Amzie Moore, Aaron Henry, and Hartman Turnbow, had kept alive the voter registration efforts that SNCC and its allies would build upon. The NAACP had collaborated with SNCC in launching the MFDP and its 1964 convention challenge; however, after that event the two groups drifted apart. Alarmed by the growing black power perspective of its rival, the older association chose to join with white moderates and labor leaders to seek national Democratic Party recognition for their state's interracial coalition. In 1968, their protest proved successful, and a biracial Loyalist Democratic group supplanted the MFDP, which soon disbanded, as the chief vehicle for party reform among blacks and whites in the state.

The Democrats expanded black representation in party affairs not only in Mississippi but throughout the South. Wary of the formation of militant, predominantly black Democratic factions in Mississippi and Alabama, they sanctioned the claims of more moderate, interracial delegations, which pressed for seating at the 1968 convention. In addition, the party adopted far-reaching affirmative action guidelines that required "representation of minority groups on the national convention delegation in reasonable relationship to the group's presence in the population of the state." The results were striking. In 1972, at the Democratic presidential nominating meeting, 56 percent of the delegates from Mississippi were black, and in the delegations representing states covered by the Voting Rights Act, the proportion of blacks equaled or exceeded the percentage of blacks in the population.

Although they disdained political separatism, coalitionists tacitly supported their own version of black power as a form of voting power. Charles Evers, who succeeded his brother Medgar as the NAACP's field agent in Mississippi and who mounted several campaigns for political office in the state, urged blacks to "control the ballot of the county ... control the entire county where we are predominant. We don't holler Black Power – but watch it." The NAACP and its black opposition did not disagree so much over ends – political parity for blacks – but over the means to attain it. Each side could have agreed with the view expressed by a black Mississippian who remarked: 'Power is invested in the ballot, and that's why the white man worked like hell to keep you away from it.'

Both the coalition and separatist courses significantly increased black officeholding in the years following adoption of the Voting Rights Act. In 1964, fewer than 25 black elected officials governed in the South, but by the end of the decade the figure had soared to nearly 500. In 1970, the number of elected blacks climbed still higher – to over 700.

Besides yielding these impressive gains, black ballots also helped elect more moderate white officials. In Dallas County, Alabama, shortly after the Voting Rights Act went into effect, newly enfranchised blacks remedied a longstanding political grievance and helped vote Sheriff Jim Clark out of office. In his place they installed Wilson Baker, the Selma law enforcement chief who had vainly tried to forestall violence against civil rights protesters in his city. In 1966, though blacks were not yet strong enough at the polls to beat the segregationist gubernatorial candidate Lurleen Wallace, running as a surrogate for her husband, George, four years later blacks elsewhere joined with white majorities to elect moderate governors in Arkansas, Florida, Georgia, and South Carolina. Racist demagoguery in southern election campaigns was fast becoming a relic.

Despite these successes, southern blacks still encountered a variety of roadblocks to political equality. The formal impediments to voter registration had mainly disappeared, but white officials continued to devise techniques to hamper blacks who had managed to enroll for the suffrage. In 1971, white politicians in Mississippi ordered the reregistration of voters in approximately 30 counties, in many of which a large number of blacks had only recently enrolled. In other sections of the Deep South, local registrars conducted business at inconvenient hours that failed to accommodate the schedules of working-class blacks, and they functioned exclusively at county courthouses too far away for many rural blacks easily to reach.

Malcolm X

Nobody boosted the rise of black power more than Malcolm X. A gifted orator and minister for the Nation of Islam, he preached a message of racial pride that transcended electoral politics, partisan affiliation, and religious sectarianism. Neither a participant in the civil rights movement nor actively engaged in political reform, Malcolm X nevertheless had a profound effect in shaping the direction of the black freedom struggle. While black southerners fought to regain the right to vote and use it to emancipate themselves further, Malcolm spoke for many northern blacks who increasingly believed that legal rights alone would not set them free and who saw the dream of racial equality turning into a nightmare.

Born on May 19, 1925, in Omaha, Nebraska, Malcolm Little grew up in an uncertain environment of racial intolerance and economic hardships. His parents were supporters of the black nationalist Marcus Garvey and his Universal Negro Improvement Association, which promoted black economic and cultural enterprises and a "Back to Africa Movement." (Garvey, a Jamaican who had immigrated to the United States in 1916, had been sent to federal prison for mail fraud and deported in 1927.) White supremacist hate groups chased the Littles out of Omaha to Lansing, Michigan, where vigilantes burned down the family's home. Earl Little died when Malcolm was six, and his mother, Louise, tried unsuccessfully to raise her eight children during the Great Depression of the 1930s. After suffering a nervous breakdown, Louise Little entered a mental institution, and at the age of 12, Malcolm was placed in foster care.

Over the next decade, Malcolm led a troubled life. While still in Lansing, he dropped out of school after the eighth grade. A bright student, Malcolm told his English teacher of his ambition to become a lawyer, only to be advised by him that he should take up carpentry as a more "realistic goal for a nigger." He left Michigan for Boston, where he became a petty criminal dealing in drugs and prostitution. A burglary conviction sent him to prison in 1947, and he remained incarcerated for five years before obtaining parole.

Prison provided the education Malcolm had never finished and transformed him dramatically. In jail he converted to the Nation of Islam, a religious sect which helped him make sense of important issues in his past: his parents' black nationalism, the racial discrimination he had encountered, and the emotional self-loathing that had fueled his criminal activities. Founded in the 1930s in Detroit, the Nation practiced an unorthodox version of Islam by grafting black nationalism onto it. Its spiritual leader, Elijah Muhammad, taught that whites were a mutant race of blue-eyed devils created by a mad black scientist to persecute black people. As the Messenger of God, Elijah Muhammad would free his followers one day when Allah's apocalyptic wrath finally destroyed whites. In the meantime, the Black Muslims, as they were dubbed, offered hope to African Americans that through self-discipline and self-help they could throw off the psychological and economic shackles that kept them in bondage. Rejecting the electoral process, their political program consisted largely of the call for the creation of a separate black state in America.

Leaving jail in 1952, Malcolm became a devoted follower of Elijah Muhammad and the Nation of Islam's most dynamic minister. He dropped his surname and replaced it with "X" in recognition that white slavemasters had obliterated the true name of his African forebears. Though the Nation of Islam had only about 10,000 members in 1960, its message reached beyond a strictly religious audience. In charge of the Harlem Mosque, Malcolm ventured out to neighborhood street corners and dazzled listeners with his fiery sermons in which he denounced whites and called upon African Americans to unite, recover and take pride in their past, and develop their own social, cultural, and economic institutions. He blamed whites for the misery inflicted upon his people, but he refused to accept the role of victim. Instead, he exhorted blacks to cast from their minds the feelings of inferiority instilled by whites, recognize their moral and spiritual worth, and defend themselves from white violence.

Figure 12   Malcolm X addresses a rally in Harlem in June 1963. (AP Photo/Press Association)

To make whites seem less intimidating, Malcolm humiliated them. Small wonder then that whites dismissed him as a hatemonger. The media vilified him, and Malcolm, relishing his role as a gadfly, gave them plenty of ammunition to use against him. For example, in denouncing integration he declared that the only way he wanted to go to the toilet with the white man was if he could "[f]lush him down the drain with the rest of his kind."

He did not reserve his taunts for whites alone. Malcolm also scorned traditional black civil rights leaders as "Uncle Toms" selling out their fellow blacks for the promise of integration. Referring to Martin Luther King, Jr., as a "fool" and a "chump," he condemned nonviolence as cowardly and hypocritical. He asserted that blacks could never gain freedom by refusing to defend themselves from physical attack. Malcolm did not advocate violence as an offensive weapon but only in retaliation against actual assaults – though this distinction was mainly lost in coverage by the hostile media.

The secular dimensions of Malcolm's black nationalist message remained a significant but secondary concern to him until he split from Elijah Muhammad and the Nation of Islam in 1964. (The break did not concern religious doctrine but resulted instead from Muhammad's efforts to rein in his charismatic disciple and Malcolm's questioning whether Muhammad lived up to his own moral teachings.) Presented with new opportunities for growth, Malcolm made a pilgrimage to Mecca, where he saw that devout Muslims came in different skin colors, including white. He visited Africa and the Middle East and returned with a global perspective on African-American liberation. While overseas, he remarked to African leaders: "Our problem is your problem. It is not a Negro problem. This is a world problem; a problem of humanity. It is not a problem of civil rights but a problem of human rights." The racial chauvinism of his earlier thinking was not replaced so much as it was tempered by his new experiences. El-Hajj Malik El-Shabazz, as Malcolm now called himself, never absolved whites of their history of subjugating blacks, but he came to view Caucasians as fallible human beings rather than as incorrigible devils. He would hold whites accountable for their racist behavior, which they could change, but not pre-judge them on the basis of the complexion they were born with. Furthermore, Malcolm began to target capitalism and imperialism alongside race as the chief forms of oppression throughout the world, thereby reassessing the black liberation struggle in economic and political as well as racial terms.

Malcolm did not operate as a political figure in the traditional sense. As a Black Muslim minister he had faithfully obeyed Elijah Muhammad's teaching that Judgment Day rather than the ballot box would liberate blacks and punish whites. After breaking with the Black Muslims, Malcolm began to free himself from the sect's religious straitjacket and develop further the secular implications of his black nationalist beliefs. He dropped his support for a separate territorial homeland for American blacks and advocated instead a "society in which people can live like human beings on the basis of equality." Still, he never let black Americans forget their proud African heritage and sought to dispel racist stereotypes that portrayed the "dark continent" as inhabited by jungle savages. He did this not to promote emigration by blacks to the land of their ancestors but to make them aware of their familial links to nations with a distinguished history and culture.

Making new political overtures, in 1964 Malcolm created the Organization of Afro-American Unity and attempted to establish ties with conventional civil rights groups. His years of berating their leaders kept them from embracing him, but he did find common ground with the younger, more militant activists in SNCC and CORE. In the fall of 1964, he appeared at a rally held in Harlem in support of the Mississippi Freedom Democratic Party and introduced one of its leaders, Fannie Lou Hamer, in his Harlem

Mosque. James Forman, SNCC's executive secretary, remarked that the new directions Malcolm explored "open up possibilities for people who certainly thought the Muslims had something to say but who reject the whole concept of a separate state and religion." Invited by SNCC to come to Selma in February 1965, Malcolm believed his presence would help Dr. King in his campaign for the right to vote. "If the white people realize what the alternative is," he told Dr. King's wife, "perhaps they will be more willing to hear Dr. King."

Later that month in New York City, rival Muslims assassinated Malcolm. Though his thinking was evolving, he died still determined to pursue freedom for African Americans by any means necessary. Increasingly, he saw himself as taking part in a worldwide movement for human rights against exploitation based on race, nationality, and class. His legacy cannot be measured in terms of the organizational structures or tangible programs he bequeathed. Malcolm's main arena of operation was not that of legislative halls or courtrooms. Rather, as the black theologian James Cone summed up: Malcolm "revolutionized the black mind." Whether on a street corner or on the stage at a major university, he functioned as a brilliant polemicist and teacher, instructing his listeners about the necessity of eliminating for themselves what laws and Supreme Court decisions could never fully remove: the badges of subservience stamped by 300 years of white supremacy.

Racial Polarization

As blacks reentered the political arenas of the South, mobilized their forces, and competed for office, the nation witnessed a sharp rise in racial polarization. Even at the height of the freedom struggle, many white Americans sympathized with black integrationist goals but disliked the movement's aggressive, confrontational tactics. In 1963, 64 percent of the whites polled in a nationwide survey had expressed the view that blacks were pushing too quickly for equality. The following year blacks rioted in the northern ghettos of Harlem, Rochester, Jersey City, and Philadelphia, and over the remainder of the decade violent uprisings spread to some 300 cities, involving half a million blacks. The riots consumed millions of dollars in property damage and resulted in 50,000 arrests, 8,000 injuries, and 250 deaths, mostly of blacks. In 1967, in Detroit alone, 43 people were killed, 2,000 were wounded, and 5,000 were burned out of their homes.

The riots reflected both the reawakening of black consciousness and the continued awareness of unresolved grievances. Civil rights battles, while fought primarily in the South, inspired blacks everywhere to identify with the cause of liberation. Though rejecting nonviolence as a tactic, the rioters had taken pride in the willingness of their southern black brothers and sisters to stand up collectively to white racism. In the midst of the conflagration in Detroit, a looter explained what drove him into the streets. In words very much reminiscent of black protesters in the South, he explained that he was looking for "respect as a man, as a first-class citizen."

Outside the South, the law did not require segregation or promote disfranchisement; yet African Americans faced systematic racial discrimination that deprived them of full equality. They had the right to vote and the right to enter public accommodations, but those who dwelled in squalid ghettos lacked decent housing, employment, and evenhanded police protection. Some notable economic improvements had occurred during the 1960s. Median black family income climbed to 61 percent of that earned by whites, the percentage of black families living below the poverty level diminished to 30 percent, and the unemployment rate for married black males dropped to 4 percent by mid-decade. However, these gains did not keep pace with rising black expectations stimulated by the civil rights struggle. Through rioting, many blacks sought to deliver a message of protest to white Americans that focused attention on the seriousness of their plight. They turned to extralegal methods because conventional political channels had failed to resolved their complaints.

The riots yielded mixed results. Many cities responded by seeking ways to relieve the miserable social conditions that fueled the disorders. They took out "riot insurance" by setting up programs to provide job training, recreational facilities, slum clearance, and more effective communication between police and the residents they served. At the same time, city and state governments also devised more punitive measures and put a good deal of their resources into riot control by beefing up their defense arsenals with expensive and powerful weapons.

This latter response mirrored the growing antagonism of whites toward black protest demands. Appalled by the violence and lawlessness, many whites called for a restoration of public order, severe punishment of rioters, and withdrawal of funding for poverty projects that appeared to reward antisocial behavior. Although civil rights leaders such as Dr. King and Roy Wilkins denounced violence, others like SNCC's Stokely Carmichael fanned the flames of discord. Carmichael and his black power associates were not responsible for the spontaneous eruptions that swept over American cities, but their inflammatory rhetoric scared and angered whites. "When you talk about black power," the SNCC chairman declared following a riot in Cleveland, "you talk of building a movement that will smash everything Western civilization has created." This type of provocative statement in tandem with the ghetto riots helped reinforce the menacing connotation that black power had assumed.

The rise of the Black Panther party (BPP) strengthened this image. Adopting the trademark of the Lowndes County Freedom Organization, Huey P. Newton and Bobby Seale, who had met each other in college, formed the organization in October 1966 in Oakland, California. In contrast to the LCFO, the Panthers were not a political party mainly interested in contesting elections. Along with Eldridge Cleaver, a 31-year-old ex-convict and writer who had spent most of his adult life in prison, they denounced capitalism and regarded the ghettos as an exploited colony within the United States. Blending black nationalism and Marxist-Leninist doctrines, the BPP considered itself as the revolutionary vanguard leading the urban masses in the destruction of "the machinery of the oppressor." In the ghetto this meant the police – "the military arm of our oppressors" – which residents frequently saw not as protectors but as the guardians of their misery and the agents of brutality. In fact, most of the summer riots had been sparked by incidents of excessive police force and charges of brutality. The Panthers responded by taking up arms for self-defense and patrolling their neighborhoods to keep watch over the police. In 1967, a bloody confrontation between Newton and the police left one officer dead and the Panther founder wounded and placed under arrest. The next year, another shootout in Oakland killed a BPP official.

Often lost amidst this violence was the broader political program the Panthers advocated. In its original platform, the BPP demanded jobs for the unemployed, decent housing for the poor, and a greater voice for blacks in determining decisions affecting their communities. Working toward these goals, in Oakland and in cities such as Chicago, where they set up chapters, the Panthers instituted free breakfast and healthcare programs to improve neighborhood conditions. They conducted classes in black history and warned against the dangers of drug use, seeking to build racial pride in young black children and to instill confidence in their ability to reshape their lives.

Initially the Panthers put greater emphasis on community organizing than on electoral politics. Their battle cry of "power to the people" called for local control of economic and political institutions based upon armed struggle; nevertheless, by the late 1960s the Panthers had added the ballot as a weapon in their arsenal. Unlike some other black nationalist groups, the BPP formed alliances with white radicals and competed with them for political office in common cause against class as well as racial exploitation. By then, however, the militant actions of the party brought the weight of local, state, and federal governments upon the group, seriously damaging its efforts. Led by the FBI, whose director viewed the Panthers as "the greatest threat to the internal security of the country," government agents infiltrated the group, provoked internal dissension, and shot and jailed its followers. By the end of the decade, the police had killed over a score of Panthers and arrested some 750.

Meanwhile, such strife and the media attention it attracted had fueled a reactionary white backlash against additional civil rights reforms. No one played on the anxieties of whites better than did George Wallace. Having whipped up the antagonism of southerners against desegregation, the Alabama governor transported his racist messages to the North, where they received a favorable reception from those whites who feared that black progress came at their expense. Wallace exploited class as well as racial tensions. He catered to blue-collar workers and excoriated "left-wing theoreticians, briefcase totin' bureaucrats, ivory tower guideline writers, bearded anarchists, smart aleck editorial writers and pointy headed professors." The racial disturbances of the sixties propelled Wallace's presidential ambitions. In 1964, he tested out his antiestablishment, racist appeals by campaigning for the Democratic presidential nomination. His candidacy eventually fizzled, but not before he showed surprising strength among disgruntled white voters in Indiana, Maryland, and Wisconsin.

The increasing bitterness of racial tensions was reflected at every governmental level. In 1966, the Georgia legislature refused to seat Julian Bond as a duly elected representative from Atlanta. Bond had offended lawmakers by supporting SNCC's opposition to the Vietnam war and calling for alternatives to the military draft. A year later, Congress rejected the credentials of Adam Clayton Powell, who had easily won reelection from Harlem. Powell had embraced black power doctrines during the 1960s, but it was financial and ethical improprieties that got him into trouble. In each case, blacks saw white legislators as practicing a double standard of justice and acting unnecessarily harshly. The US Supreme Court ultimately ruled in favor of Bond and Powell and restored their positions to them.

The politics of black power also aggravated racial discord in Ocean Hill-Brownsville, a section of Brooklyn, New York, populated by low-income, poorly educated African Americans and Puerto Ricans. In 1967, under a plan sponsored by the New York City Board of Education in cooperation with the Ford Foundation, the United Federation of Teachers (UFT), and local community groups, Ocean Hill-Brownsville became part of an experimental project in school decentralization. Community activists had complained that the school system was failing to educate their children. Pointing accusing fingers at both insensitive bureaucrats and teachers, the overwhelming majority of whom were white, they called for sweeping educational reorganization to help address the needs of ghetto students. The proposal that was adopted fell short of their objectives, but it did establish school decentralization and called for the election of parents and other community residents to serve alongside teachers on a district governing board.

The experiment resulted in some positive achievements. Communitywide elections gave parents a powerful voice in their children's education that was used to introduce new programs emphasizing racial pride and instilling self-worth – two ingredients often absent from the classrooms and corridors of ghetto schools. As more minority teachers, parents, and paraprofessionals became involved in school affairs, students responded enthusiastically. One pupil recalled her excitement over seeing more black faces: "I mean you felt more accepted. You weren't an outsider in your own school. They were part of your environment. I mean they were Black. You can identify with them and they can identify with you."

However, the children soon got caught up in a power struggle between their parents, the teachers' union, and the central school board. The Ocean Hill-Brownsville governing council, dominated by community residents, and the chief administrator of the district, Rhody McCoy, wanted greater community control over finances and personnel than the union and central board would allow. Albert Shanker, the president of the UFT, favored community participation, but demanded that teachers' job rights be protected. In the spring of 1968, the local governing agency unilaterally ordered the transfer of 13 teachers and seven administrators out of the district, precipitating a confrontation with the union and central board over the issue of due process. When the matter was not resolved over the summer, the UFT took almost 54,000 teachers out on strike in September.

The controversy raged from Labor Day to the middle of November, driving a deep wedge between former allies in the civil rights coalition. Those like Shanker and his union followers who had supported the principle of school integration contended that the Ocean Hill-Brownsville experiment had deteriorated into black separatism. McCoy and his allies,

many of whom were influenced by a growing emphasis on black consciousness, charged that the union constituted a racist obstacle to educational
reform and black self-determination. Although the two sides did not divide
strictly along racial lines – the community board hired a majority of white
teachers as replacements for the strikers, and influential black activists such
as Bayard Rustin supported the union – the conflict exacerbated racial
tensions. The dispute turned even uglier and more divisive when charges
of anti-Semitism surfaced. Most union members were Jewish, and they
were angered by intemperate remarks made by some militants. After an
inflammatory memo referring to Jews as "money changers," "bloodsucking
exploiters," and "Middle East murderers" was distributed in two schools,
the UFT made the already tense situation even worse by reprinting and
circulating the missive to thousands of Jews throughout the city. For its
part, the local governing board denied charges of anti-Semitism, pointing
out that about half the teachers it hired were Jewish. Still, its measured
response to the most vicious displays of anti-Semitism failed to settle the
nerves of apprehensive Jews.

When the nearly two-month-old strike finally ended, the local school
district was placed under state supervision and the union won reinstate-
ment of the dismissed teachers and a new contract guaranteeing employee
safeguards. At the same time, the state legislature enacted a measure that
decentralized all New York City school districts, but it balanced local
participation with limited autonomy for community governing boards. The
educational establishment had prevailed, and had proved itself powerful
enough to resist radical change. Overall, the political fallout from the
dispute poisoned relations between blacks and Jews and between black
power advocates and liberal labor leaders, and left the civil rights alliance
and the electoral coalition behind it badly frayed.

Black militancy and white backlash also delayed passage of new civil
rights legislation. In 1966, the Johnson administration proposed a package
that attacked discrimination in housing and offered federal protection for
civil rights workers. The former provision applied equally throughout the
entire nation, thereby hitting whites in the North close to home. As the
target of civil rights assaults expanded beyond the South, whites offered
greater resistance. In 1966, a presidential aide complained "that it would
have been hard to pass the emancipation proclamation in the atmosphere
prevailing this summer." The hostile political atmosphere continued
through the fall congressional elections, as Republicans increased their representation in the House by 47 seats.

Yet white backlash was not strong enough to kill the civil rights measure. Though President Johnson was deeply disturbed by the outbreak of riots and perceived them as the product of conspiratorial black nationalist forces, he did not retreat from supporting his latest civil rights proposals. He attempted to strike a balance between appearing not to reward the lawless actions of the rioters and backing measures that addressed what he considered to be the legitimate demands of traditional civil rights groups like the NAACP. In this way he could underscore, as one of his aides put it, that "law abiding citizens, black and white, should have and will have the safety and protection of their government." At the same time, he could strengthen the position of his moderate civil rights allies at the expense of their more militant critics. Joining with the NAACP and the Leadership Conference on Civil Rights, a coalition of reform lobbyists, the Johnson administration kept up the legislative pressure; in April 1968, Congress finally passed a Civil Rights Act that featured the controversial fair housing provision. Reflecting the uneasy temper of the times, Congress also enacted a punitive antiriot measure aimed at prosecuting roving black agitators.

This hard-earned legislative victory could not restore unity to the civil rights forces. SNCC and CORE continued down their separatist paths and had little interest in a bill that aimed to promote integration. The SCLC continued to retain its interracial ideals, but broke with the President over his policy of escalating the war in Vietnam. In challenging the administration over this issue, Dr. King parted from his allies in the NAACP and Urban League, who remained loyal to Johnson. King's assassination on April 4, 1968, during the final deliberations on the Civil Rights Act, aided its passage as a tribute to the slain martyr, but also badly weakened the organization that relied heavily on his style of charismatic leadership. In addition to these internal strains that fractured the movement, the Johnson administration greatly accelerated its disintegration from without. The FBI had relentlessly investigated and harassed Dr. King and directed a clandestine counterintelligence program that succeeded in undermining black power groups such as the Panthers.

The Nixon Administration and Benign Neglect

While Johnson struggled to reinforce civil rights moderates at the expense of black radicals, the frustrations of military stalemate in Vietnam combined with antiwar protests at home prompted him not to run for another term as chief executive. The candidates who sought to succeed him guaranteed that African Americans would remain faithful to the party of the President who had achieved more for civil rights than any of his predecessors. Johnson passed the Democratic standard on to his vice president, Hubert H. Humphrey, the liberal stalwart who first led the charge, back in 1948, to swing Democrats behind a strong civil rights platform.

Humphrey's chief opponents did not offer black voters much of an alternative. Though once a firm advocate of the civil rights cause, the GOP nominee, Richard M. Nixon, had charted a political route that moved him away from the search for black ballots toward those of conservative white southerners. In this respect he had stiff competition from George Wallace, who ran on the American Independent Party ticket and whose demagogic rhetoric and obstructionist actions had hampered black racial advancement.

Two black candidates competed as independents. Eldridge Cleaver, the Black Panther, was nominated by the Peace and Freedom Party, a political formation of predominantly white leftists originating in California. The comedian Dick Gregory, who had assumed an active role in the civil rights movement, mounted a campaign that the political scientist Manning Marable concluded was "marked more by political satire than actual political content." Neither candidate had any chance of winning, but each served as an outlet for disaffected black nationalists and white radicals.

In his second bid for the White House, Nixon enthusiastically embraced a southern strategy that would ensure the victory that had narrowly eluded him in 1960. He pursued the same segment of white voters in Dixie that had backed Barry Goldwater in 1964. Besides resurrecting economic positions that attacked the big-spending social welfare programs of Johnson's Great Society, he played on the racial antipathies of conservative white southerners. Speaking out against busing to promote school desegregation, he voiced approval for freedom-of-choice plans that operated to retard full-scale desegregation. In obtaining the Republican nomination over another conservative aspirant, Governor Ronald Reagan of California, he associated himself with Senator Strom Thurmond of South Carolina, the 1948 Dixiecrat candidate, who had subsequently converted to the GOP. The alliance between the two was cemented by their agreement that, if elected, Nixon would slow down school desegregation and voting rights enforcement in the South.

In taking this stand Nixon hoped to undercut potential southern white support for Wallace. The Alabama governor delivered a populist message that echoed the economic and social discontent of working-class whites. To distinguish himself from Nixon and to appeal to a lower-income constituency than that attracted to well-to-do Republicanism, Wallace charged that there was not a "dime's worth of difference between the two major parties." He hammered away on the theme of "law and order," code words that expressed hostility toward black militants, antiwar demonstrators, and the liberal establishment that presumably "coddled" them.

Vice President Humphrey represented that establishment, and only he actively campaigned for black votes. In a chaotic nominating convention racked by antiwar protests, the Democrats awarded unprecedented delegate representation to black southerners and ensured that their influence would expand even further in the future. On the campaign trail, Humphrey blasted Nixon and Wallace for exploiting "fear and tensions that grip significant portions of our people." Instead of a society dedicated to "opportunity and justice," he warned that his opponents would usher in "a fractured and separated society – black against white, rich against poor, comfortable against left-out."

As expected, Humphrey's rivals found a fertile field for their views in the South. The Voting Rights Act had greatly expanded the size of the black electorate in the region, but in the years immediately following its passage had also led to an upsurge in the number of whites registering to vote. Whites constituted some 60 to 70 percent of the newly enrolled electorate. In addition, demographic shifts laid the foundation for white defections from candidates of the national Democratic Party, who were considered too liberal. The influx into the sunbelt of white northerners, many of whom had previously voted Republican, boosted the constituency for the growth of the GOP in the traditionally one-party South. Furthermore, as the South became more urbanized, Republicans drew increasing support from middle- and upper-class whites whose economic interests tied them more closely to the GOP's outlook.

Neither in the South nor elsewhere in the nation were black votes abundant enough to offset white abandonment of the Democrats. Though Humphrey received 88 percent of black ballots, southern whites overwhelmingly lined up behind his opponents. The Democratic candidate received only 31 percent of southern votes, most of them from blacks, a figure that was 19 points behind Johnson's in 1964. Nixon and Wallace divided Dixie's white electorate, each capturing five states and leaving Texas to Humphrey. The GOP contender obtained the support of 35 percent of the region's electorate, a share only slightly larger than Wallace's 34 percent. The Alabama governor cut into Democratic support in the North – working-class whites provided half his total votes – and nationally Wallace obtained 13.5 percent of the ballots cast, the strongest performance by a third-party contestant since 1924. Overall, Democratic defections also helped propel Nixon into the White House. The Republican winner garnered 301 electoral votes and a plurality of 43.4 percent of the popular votes.

President Nixon attempted to deliver on his southern campaign strategy. As Ethel Payne, a black journalist, noted shortly after his election, "Mr. Nixon has no debt to pay black voters." He tried to lift the burden of civil rights enforcement off the South by extending it to the North. The President told reporters, "we finally have in this country what the South has wanted and what the South deserves, a one nation policy." However evenhanded this approach sounded, it aimed to weaken civil rights implementation. The Justice Department's Civil Rights Division would be spread too thin with a staff insufficient in size to monitor and litigate against racial discrimination everywhere in the country. Moreover, many critics believed that in expanding civil rights coverage outside the South, Nixon strategists hoped that disgruntled northern politicians would join southerners in opposing strict enforcement of such controversial desegregation remedies as school busing.

Soon after entering the Oval Office, Nixon sought to reverse policy on school integration of 15 years' standing. In 1969, for the first time since the historic *Brown* decision, federal lawyers appeared in court to support a southern state, Mississippi, in attempting to postpone the implementation of a desegregation plan. Subsequently, the chief executive affirmed his backing for "a truly desegregated public school system" through improvements in the quality of education, rather than by "buying buses, tires, and gasoline to transport young children miles away from their neighborhood schools."

At the same time, the Nixon administration looked to overhaul the provisions of the Voting Rights Act in order to relieve pressure on the South. Most of the important features of the statute were due for renewal after five years, and civil rights advocates favored a simple extension of the law. As with school integration, the President wanted to reshape the measure so that it would extend to the North. Consequently, his attorney general, John Mitchell, requested Congress to scrap the automatic triggering and preclearance sections and in their place authorize the Justice Department to initiate litigation against suffrage discrimination anywhere in the country. The attorney general would be empowered to seek suits halting the imposition of new voting restrictions and to send federal examiners to enforce court orders. Also, the law would suspend the use of literacy tests in the

North as well as the South. "Voting rights is not a regional issue," Mitchell asserted. "It is a nationwide concern for every American which must be tested on a nationwide basis."

Civil rights supporters derided the proposal. They viewed the administration bill as a subterfuge to cripple a law that had proved successful. Having experienced the pitfalls of relying on courts to protect black voting rights, they vigorously opposed a return to the judicial approach. After five years, blacks still encountered suffrage problems in the South, and civil rights proponents wanted attention to remain focused on that region. Clarence Mitchell, the chief lobbyist for the NAACP, attacked the Nixon administration's offering as "a sophisticated, a calculated, incredible effort … to make it impossible for us to continue on the constitutional course that we have followed … in protecting the right to vote."

In general, the Nixon administration did not succeed in curbing civil rights advances. Though blacks had lost political clout within the White House, they still retained influence before the Supreme Court and in Congress. In 1969, the high tribunal rebuked the administration for stalling desegregation in Mississippi, and in *Alexander v. Holmes County Board of Education* it ordered an immediate end to dual school systems. Two years later, the justices sanctioned busing as a remedy for fashioning interracial schools in districts that had practiced segregation by law. Disappointed with the ruling in *Swann v. Charlotte-Mecklenburg Board of Education,* Nixon subsequently requested Congress to pass legislation limiting the use of busing, but the proposal failed. By the middle of the decade, southern schools surpassed those in the North as the least segregated in the country. In the South, 47.1 percent of black students attended schools with a white majority compared with 42.5 percent of northern blacks who did so.

With respect to political rights also, Congress and the courts checked the Nixon administration's racial options. In 1970, lawmakers renewed the Voting Rights Act with its original provisions intact. Literacy tests were again suspended for five years, though Nixon got his way in applying this to the entire country. In addition, the legislation extended the franchise to 18-year-olds. The following year when the attorney general tried to interpret the preclearance provision in a manner that narrowed its operation, Congress stepped in to frustrate him. In the meantime, the Supreme Court defined the scope of the Voting Rights Act very broadly. Beginning in 1969, it decreed that the statute was not only directed toward voter registration but was also meant to include "all actions to make a vote effective." In a series of decisions the judiciary empowered federal authorities to strike down electoral rules that had the purpose or effect of diluting the strength of black ballots. The conversion from single-member districts to at-large elections, the expansion of municipal boundaries through annexation of largely white areas, and reapportionment plans that produced racially gerrymandered districts were regulations of this type.

Given the judicial mandate and under the watchful eyes of Congress, the Nixon administration satisfactorily fulfilled its constitutional obligation to protect black enfranchisement. Whereas White House policymakers may have wished to slow down implementation of the Voting Rights Act, career service lawyers in the Justice Department carried out their enforcement duties in a highly professional manner. Many of these attorneys had held their positions since the Johnson era, and they took their cues from the court and the legislature. Consequently, as William E. Leuchtenburg has noted, "much of the positive activity under the Nixon Administration came not because of the enterprise of Nixon and his immediate aides, but rather from the momentum developed by the federal bureaucracy, a momentum no president can easily halt."

Congress also contained a sufficient amount of pro-civil rights strength to block the chief executive's attempt to appoint conservative southerners to the Supreme Court. In 1969, the Senate rejected the nomination of Clement Haynsworth from Strom Thurmond's South Carolina. A federal judge whose opinions in racial cases had aroused the concern of civil rights groups, Haynsworth was defeated after months of bitter and protracted debate. The next year, the President sent up the name of G. Harrold Carswell to fill the vacancy and was similarly rebuffed. The Florida jurist appeared much less qualified than Haynsworth, a judgment inadvertently rendered by one of his defenders. Even if Carswell "were mediocre, there were a lot of mediocre judges and people and lawyers," Republican Senator Roman Hruska of Nebraska declared. "They are entitled to a little representation, aren't they, and a little chance?" Hearing praise like this, a majority of lawmakers turned down the nominee.

In other areas affecting black advancement, the Nixon administration ranged between moderation and affirmative action. In 1970, one of Nixon's top counselors on domestic affairs, Daniel Patrick Moynihan, a former aide in the Johnson administration, advised the President: "The time may have come when the issue of race could benefit from a period of 'benign neglect.' … The forum has been too much taken over by hysteria, paranoids, and boodlers on all sides. We may need a period in which Negro progress continues and racial rhetoric fades." Accepting this reasoning, the chief executive attempted to encourage economic self-help as the key to racial equality. In conservative fashion, Nixon promoted black capitalism as the cornerstone of black power. Cleverly expropriating his critics' rhetoric, he contended that despite their stridency and seemingly anticapitalist tones, the militants' ideas more clearly resembled "the doctrines of free enterprise than ... those of the welfare thirties – terms of 'pride,' 'ownership,' 'private enterprise,' 'capital,' 'self-assurance,' 'self-respect.'"

To expand minority business opportunities, the President increased funding to the Small Business Administration and the Minority Business Enterprise in the Commerce Department. In 1969, minority firms received $8 million in federal contracts; four years later, they were getting $242 million. Similarly, during this period government aid to minority enterprises leaped from $200 million to $472 million. For the mass of blacks who were destined to remain employees and not employers, the President established the "Philadelphia Plan," which required construction workers' unions involved in federal contracts to sign up and retain a fixed proportion of black apprentices. Befitting his economic philosophy, Nixon's major innovative foray into the field of affirmative action shrewdly shifted the obligation of meeting equal opportunity guidelines away from management and onto organized labor.

Black Caucuses and Conventions

By the end of Nixon's first term, blacks were seeking new ways to increase their influence. While the legislative and judicial branches of the federal government overrode the executive, black politicians organized to boost their leverage in Congress and shape the direction of public policy. In 1969, Representative Charles Diggs, Jr., a Detroit Democrat, organized the eight other black members of the House of Representatives into an informal committee to work with congressional leaders on civil rights and social welfare issues. Two years later, the Congressional Black Caucus (CBC) was officially formed, and functioned as a lobbying group along the lines of other special-interest blocs in the legislative branch. Though it made policy recommendations to expand benefits for blacks, the caucus succeeded mainly in joining with white liberal lawmakers in waging defensive actions to preserve strong enforcement of suffrage legislation and rescue civil rights programs from conservative assault. In addition, the formation of the CBC inspired black elected officials at the state and local levels to establish similar groups, such as the National Conference of Black Mayors, to present a black perspective on policy matters crucial to minorities.

Though not an official member of the CBC, which consisted solely of House lawmakers, Senator Edward Brooke of Massachusetts became its ally. At a time when the overwhelming majority of African Americans preferred the Democratic Party, Brooke was a Republican who belonged to the GOP's moderate-to-liberal wing. Elected in 1966, from a state with a less than 3 percent black population, the former state attorney general declared: "I can't serve just the Negro cause. I've got to serve all the people of Massachusetts." Nevertheless, as the nation's highest-ranking black elected official, Brooke attempted to press upon the White House his concern for civil rights and other items on the CBC agenda during the years his party held the presidency. He had actively campaigned for Nixon in 1968, but his enthusiasm waned as the President tried to put his southern strategy into practice. Consequently, Senator Brooke joined those of his colleagues who successfully thwarted much of Nixon's effort in that direction.

In the face of the Nixon administration's calculated retreat in many areas of civil rights, the most ambitious attempt to unite black political leaders came with the 1972 National Black Political Convention in Gary, Indiana. The meeting grew out of a call by the CBC for the development of "a national black agenda and the crystallization of a national black strategy for the 1972 elections and beyond." The caucus wound up not giving the conference its official endorsement, but individual members did attend. With some cracks in the foundation of unity already surfacing, convention planners emphasized the need for racial solidarity to "transform black political potential into power commensurate with the number of blacks in the United States." The more than 3,500 delegates who attended the sessions from March 10 to 12 adopted a comprehensive set of recommendations for black political and economic empowerment and created the National Black Political Assembly as an independent force for exerting pressure on white political institutions.

Stressing "unity without uniformity," the meetings were presided over by Diggs, Gary Mayor Richard Hatcher, and Amiri Baraka, the poet and black nationalist. The convention secured agreement on most of the items constituting a national black agenda. It approved resolutions calling for increased black congressional representation, community control of schools, a national health insurance program, and a guaranteed minimum annual income. Moreover, the delegates felt exhilarated by the very act of gathering together to shape a political course for African Americans to follow. "I guess the strongest image I have about Gary," an organizer for the Mississippi Freedom Democratic Party remembered, "is the fact that black people were able to mobilize, black people from all walks of life, from all different states, to this one focal point."

However, the highly prized unity failed to last. The convention was torn by divisions between racial integrationists and cultural nationalists and between those who proposed forming a third political party and those who defended working within the existing two-party system. Tensions peaked, however, over the issues of school desegregation and support of the Palestine Liberation Organization, a revolutionary group opposed to Zionism and the state of Israel. When the convention voted to endorse black control of neighborhood schools instead of busing and its promotion of integration and to recognize the right of self-determination for Palestinians, integrationists and supporters of Israel vigorously condemned the resolutions. Succeeding meetings of the Black Political Assembly attracted progressively fewer delegates, black nationalists came to dominate them, and black elected officials abandoned them.

The attempt in Gary to forge black political unity collapsed under the weight of clashing political and ideological interests. Without solid support from established electoral leaders, Representative Shirley Chisholm of Brooklyn, New York, made a futile bid to compete in the Democratic presidential primaries in 1972. Her fellow members of the CBC, along with other prominent black Democrats, refused to line up behind her candidacy. Sexism played a large role in their rejection of her. One black male politician told a reporter, "In this first serious effort of blacks for high political office, it would be better if it were a man." This did not come as a surprise to Chisholm. In her 20 years in local, state, and national politics, she wrote, "I had met far more discrimination because I am a woman than because I am black."

Instead black Democratic officials chose to support the various leading white contenders for their party's nomination. Blacks played a large role at the Democratic National Convention, which nominated Senator George S. McGovern of South Dakota. The coauthor of the convention's newly reformed antidiscriminatory delegate selection rules, McGovern had helped increase the number of African Americans participating in party affairs and the nomination process.

In selecting the liberal McGovern, the Democrats infuriated those who had found the candidacy of George C. Wallace attractive. The primary season had witnessed the explosive presence of Governor Wallace, who vowed to shake the "eyeteeth out" of the Democratic Party. Running a staunchly antibusing campaign aimed at exploiting the white backlash, the Alabama governor defeated ten rivals for the Democratic presidential nomination to capture a victory in Florida with 42 percent of the vote. Wallace's win accurately gauged the mood of the white electorate, as Sunshine State voters passed a nonbinding referendum against forced busing. Fresh from this success, Wallace went on to pile up wins in the normally friendly southern states of Tennessee and North Carolina. The governor delighted crowds with his anti-elitist rhetoric: "If the pseudointellectuals think it is good to bus little children backwards and forwards … the average man doesn't, and there are more of them than there are [of] the pseudos." Northern voters also responded enthusiastically to this message, and Wallace triumphed in Michigan and Maryland and scored strong second-place finishes in Wisconsin, Pennsylvania, and Indiana. Tragedy struck while he was speaking in Maryland, as an assassin's bullet left him alive but paralyzed from the waist down. Unable to continue campaigning actively, the governor saw his powerful bid for the presidential nomination effectively come to an end.

Even without a Wallace candidacy, the results of the 1972 election suggested the sharpening polarization of the electorate along racial lines. Taking his cue from the Alabamian, the President repeated his own opposition to busing, called for a moratorium on additional court-ordered busing until July 1973, and vowed to "end segregation in a way that does not result in more busing." Winning 60.8 percent of the popular vote, Nixon attracted the vast portion of the southern white electorate that supported Wallace and collected the electoral votes of the entire South. Indeed, in his landslide victory, Nixon carried every state except Massachusetts and predominantly black Washington, DC. Ironically, African Americans demonstrated a high degree of the now seemingly elusive racial solidarity in giving the losing candidate more than 85 percent of their ballots.

From the vantage point of state and local arenas, black political progress appeared brighter. Although much remained to be done, following Nixon's reelection the number of black elected officials in the nation stood at over 2,600. Very impressively, the number of minority officeholders in the South climbed to nearly 1,200, up from approximately 875 a year earlier. The rate of increase in black electoral victories was slowing down, but some notable triumphs had occurred. In Selma, Alabama, the civil rights veterans Amelia Boynton and Frederick Reese led the five blacks to win half the seats on the city council. Despite the continued existence of racism in more sophisticated forms, a local black leader contended that "by and large things have improved." Elsewhere in the South in 1972, two blacks, Andrew Young of

Atlanta, Georgia, and Barbara Jordan of Houston, Texas, were elected to the US House of Representatives. For the first time in 70 years blacks from the former Confederate states sat in Congress.

By the time the Watergate scandal pushed Richard Nixon into retirement, southern blacks had managed to make steady political gains within their communities. At the end of 1974, over 1,500 blacks held public office in the South. This figure included an additional congressman from Memphis, Tennessee, Harold Ford, and a growing number of black state legislators. Of the 94 who occupied legislative seats, about 48 were elected in 1974 alone, largely as a result of reapportionment ordered by federal courts and the Department of Justice. Birmingham, Alabama, once the most violently racist of all the major cities in the South, counted 15 blacks in its state legislative delegation. In addition, black ballots continued to serve as an important element in the biracial Democratic Party coalition that elected white Dixie moderates to governor's mansions and the US Senate.

Reflecting the growing number of black elected officials, the Joint Center for Political Studies was founded in 1970 and has continued in operation to the present. (It is now called the Joint Center for Political and Economic Studies.) According to Eddie N. Williams, its president since 1972, the Joint Center grew out of the assumption "that the civil rights movement as we knew it in the '60s was dead, that a new thrust was needed in the '70s, and that there was a great deal to be gained by developing that thrust along the lines of political participation by the citizen and the elected official." Working closely with the Congressional Black Caucus and associations of state and local black officeholders, the nonprofit, nonpartisan group conducts research on policy issues of special concern to black Americans and provides technical assistance to minority officials. The information gathered by this "black think tank" is disseminated largely through its monthly newsletter, *Focus*; a variety of research publications; workshops and educational seminars; and *The National Roster of Black Elected Officials*, which appears annually.

A decade after passage of the 1965 Voting Rights Act, black political influence was widespread but fragile. Renewed in 1970, the suffrage law was becoming a permanent fixture on the American scene. Under the vigilance of the federal government and civil rights groups, many of the impediments to black political participation were being eliminated. With registration of the majority of eligible blacks, attention shifted to making the most effective use of their ballots. Having won reenfranchisement, southern blacks strove to mobilize their communities in the competition for full electoral representation.

The New Black Politicians
From Protest to Empowerment

Civil Rights and the Promise of Electoral Politics

In February 1965, when demonstrations still constituted the central tactic of the freedom struggle, Bayard Rustin forecast the direction in which the civil rights movement would head. A seasoned veteran in the battle for racial justice, Rustin had participated in pioneering freedom rides challenging segregated transportation facilities in the 1940s, served as an adviser to Martin Luther King during the Montgomery bus boycott of the mid-1950s, and in August 1963 had helped organize the celebrated March on Washington for Jobs and Freedom. His civil rights activities had been built around protest, but looking ahead to the future he saw a shift taking place. "Direct action techniques," Rustin observed, "are being subordinated to a strategy calling for the building of community institutions or power bases." As the black struggle evolved from achieving equality of opportunity to obtaining equality of results, Rustin contended that political power, more than the moral force of nonviolent protests, would best fulfill the aims of the struggle.

Few civil rights proponents doubted the wisdom of organizing blacks to increase their political leverage. Although after the summer of 1964 militants increasingly questioned the value of forming coalitions with white liberals and labor unionists, as Rustin urged, they did agree with his premise that blacks needed greater power to reshape economic and political institutions that perpetuated their subordination, even after legal rights were attained. During the 1966 Meredith march through Mississippi, Stokely

Running for Freedom: Civil Rights and Black Politics in America since 1941,
Fourth Edition. Steven F. Lawson.
© 2015 John Wiley & Sons, Inc. Published 2015 by John Wiley & Sons, Inc.

Carmichael emphatically told a crowd of blacks along the route: "If you don't have power, you're begging. We're going to take over and get black sheriffs and black tax assessors." SNCC, the group he led, had helped construct the Mississippi Freedom Democratic Party precisely for the purposes of gaining black control over political decisions affecting their own communities and influencing public policy in the South and the nation.

For different but related reasons, this preference for political solutions also appealed to white liberals. Presidential allies of the civil rights movement had expressed concern about the disruptive effects of demonstrations in provoking confrontations between the races. President Kennedy sought to steer black discontent off the streets and into courthouses, legislative halls, and voting booths. Along with his successor, Lyndon Johnson, he emphasized the right to vote as the chief instrument for blacks to resolve their grievances through regular electoral channels. As black protest took a violent course with the outbreak of urban riots in the mid-1960s, the Johnson administration prescribed the franchise and the election of black officials as an antidote to extremism. "There is more power in the ballot than there is in the bullet," the chief executive declared, "and it lasts longer." White House aides expected black officeholders to counteract the influence of "civil rights kooks" within their communities by offering responsible leadership.

Black elected officials also appealed to conservative whites. Although President Nixon had attempted to blunt enforcement of the Voting Rights Act, at the same time he recognized the value of the growing number of black officeholders who benefited from the measure. When a group of black elected officials visited the nation's capital in September 1969, the President ordered his staff to roll out "the red carpet" for the delegation. According to Leon Panetta (the chief civil rights officer in the Department of Health, Education, and Welfare), the Republican chief executive, like his Democratic predecessors, believed that "elected people were something special." Of all black leaders they "were most worth listening to" because they "clearly represented a constituency." Furthermore, some conservatives suggested that black involvement in government, either as voters or as officeholders, might help calm public unrest. John Patterson, who in the late 1950s had beaten George Wallace for governor of Alabama by outcampaigning him as a segregationist, a decade later came to see the merits of black political participation. "When you allow the nigra to participate in government," Patterson declared in 1966, "you can demand that he obey the law and stay off the streets, but deny him participation ... and you can't make any demands on him at all."

In the post–Voting Rights Act era, blacks who competed for and obtained electoral positions understood the responsibility that had been placed upon them. As one officeholder succinctly put it, he and his elected colleagues represented "the last great white hope for peace in this land." As long as blacks sought to achieve their racial goals within the conventional political system, they conferred legitimacy on the ruling order and devalued other more disruptive tactics, from protest marches to riots. And as long as black candidates did not find their way unfairly blocked in seeking elective posts, they renewed faith in the possibility of minority advancement in peaceful and orderly fashion. But, if their bids for representation were thwarted, the black journalist Chuck Stone noted, "the comparative moderation of the political process will be increasingly disavowed by young blacks as a meaningless exercise in the quest for power."

However, African Americans competed for political office for reasons other than defusing potential racial strife. Rather, they hoped to build upon the legal rights secured through the protest struggle and use them to continue the pursuit of first-class citizenship. "There's an inherent value in officeholding," a black political aspirant in South Carolina asserted. "A race of people excluded from public office will always be second class." Successful black candidates were expected by their constituents to close the gap between the promise of equality and the reality of the inferior conditions they still endured. "As the black politician returns to the scene of politics from years of deprivation," Fannie Lou Hamer declared, "he must restore the democratic principles of shared local control and responsiveness to human needs." From this perspective black elected officials were regarded as champions of their people and, at the very least, they had the obligation to perform in a manner that advanced the material interests of the communities they represented.

The civil rights movement had served as a valuable training ground for the emergence of black politicians. John Lewis, a former chairman of SNCC, who later became a congressman from Atlanta, pointed out that, like himself, "a great many of the people that you see being elected are people that come from the civil rights movement." In the wake of passage of the 1965 Voting Rights Act most blacks who rose to office in Alabama and Mississippi had participated in some aspect of the freedom struggle. Whether through joining in a voter registration drive, marching in a demonstration, signing a petition, or housing a civil rights worker, black candidates had taken the first step toward political liberation. For those who engaged in such efforts, entry into the electoral arena constituted a natural extension of their commitment to toppling the barriers to black equality. As they made the journey from protest to electoral politics, black officeseekers usually carried with them the same concern for helping the oppressed escape from poverty and injustice that had brought them into the movement in the first place. "Virtually every black candidate who runs in the South," one observer remarked, campaigns "with the hope of improving the lot of black people in his community."

In addition to the civil rights movement, President Johnson's Great Society programs paved the way for black electoral competition. Although the funds allocated to fight the "war on poverty" were insufficient to win an unconditional victory, they greatly increased the economic resources available for political organizing. Antipoverty agencies fostered the development of local leaders who gained valuable experience in exercising power and in establishing a political base from which to operate. Through the Economic Opportunity Act of 1964 blacks obtained representation on community governing boards, which furnished training in building necessary political skills, such as bargaining and negotiation. The Community Action Programs (CAPs) decreed that the poor have "maximum feasible participation" in designing and implementing policies directly affecting their welfare. Their presence on antipoverty governing boards, which allocated large sums of money, hampered the traditional control by white mayors over lucrative patronage rewards. Fighting back, the mayors managed to obtain a congressional cutback of the programs within a few years. Despite the controversy raised, the CAPs helped empower the previously disfranchised in many towns and cities in the South as well as the North. "The process of election and service on community poverty boards," the political scientist Robert C. Smith has concluded, "provided a useful socialization experience for blacks in urban politics."

One of the poverty program's recruits who successfully graduated to elective office was Johnny Ford of Tuskegee. The son of a VA hospital employee, Ford had grown up in the town during the heyday of the civil rights movement, before heading off to college in Tennessee. He wound up in New York City in the mid-1960s and found a job as a counselor in Brooklyn's impoverished Bedford-Stuyvesant ghetto. In 1968, he hopped aboard the presidential bandwagon of Senator Robert Kennedy as a staff member, and after the senator's assassination he decided to return to his Alabama hometown. "I've long felt that the South is the real frontier of this nation," he remarked about his decision to move back to Dixie. In 1969, the 28-year-old Tuskegee native became director of Macon County's Model

Cities program, which garnered millions of dollars in federal revenue. From this position he campaigned for mayor and, in 1972, defeated the white incumbent, thereby becoming the city's first black to hold this top executive office.

For many others, however, making the adjustment from civil rights to electoral politics was neither automatic nor easy. The two activities involved different tactics and talents. Though demanding a substantial degree of organization, mass demonstrations depended a good deal on emotional appeals and highly charged targets to rally people. They tended to be episodic and often lapsed quickly after resolution of a particular crisis. In contrast, competition for public office, as a political scientist has observed, "is more mundane and requires both long-term political skills and the ability to consistently draw the black electorate." Candidates had to get elected by spending long hours trying to register voters, campaigning door to door, and shepherding large numbers of people to the polls. Robert Clark, the first black elected to the Mississippi legislature since Reconstruction, explained the challenge: "Just because some folks hear you talk at a rally don't mean they're gonna vote for you. You got to go campaign, talk to 'em, make 'em know you want *each* vote."

The transfer of black politics from the streets to city halls, county court-houses, and legislative chambers frequently had a moderating effect on its practitioners. Once elected, black politicians had to master the techniques of making deals and forging compromises, often settling for solutions hammered more out of pragmatism than principle. Despite the humanistic concerns they often brought to their jobs, black elected officials had to accommodate to the constraints imposed upon them by the traditional political system they entered. Illustrating the aphorism that "politics makes strange bedfellows," some black officials collaborated with powerful whites whose past record on civil rights had been deplorable in order to pry loose economic rewards for their communities. In this vein, during the 1970s Mayor Ford of Tuskegee supported George Wallace in exchange for the benefits that the Alabama governor could deliver. Ford explained the practical considerations that guided him: "It's business with me – no emotion. What you must do is penetrate the system and, once within the system, learn how it works. And then work it well."

Most blacks who successfully entered politics did not abandon their civil rights concerns, but their movement into the electoral mainstream weak-ened some of the radical impulses of the civil rights era. The experience of the Mississippi Freedom Democratic Party was a case in point. The organizers of the MFDP conceived of the group as representing economically dispossessed sharecroppers and domestic workers. In 1968, when the biracial Loyalist delegation from Mississippi gained the authorized seats at the national convention, moderate whites and blacks had replaced many of the original Freedom Democrats. Mrs. Fannie Lou Hamer "felt disgusted" with the newcomers because they "didn't know what suffering is and don't know what politics is about." By the end of the 1970s, this Loyalist faction traded its national recognition for incorporation with the mostly white Democratic regulars, who controlled the party apparatus in the state. Little remained of the original spirit or membership of the MFDP by the time of fusion. Although unity accorded blacks formal sanction as political partners within the Democratic Party, the progressive vision of the early civil rights militants had been tempered in the process.

The admission of blacks into electoral politics in places like Mississippi and Alabama did not displace former civil rights activists so much as it elevated into greater prominence one layer of the black leadership strata. During the height of the freedom struggle, battle zones throughout the Deep South had attracted the most radical elements in the movement to brave the dangers of brutal repression. Fieldworkers from SNCC and CORE had recruited leaders predominantly among poor blacks and built a strong lower-class following in the hope of changing both political and economic relations in the region. The success of the movement in restoring voting rights and in encouraging competition for officeholding cleared the way for the emergence of middle-class blacks to assume a larger role in electoral politics. Equipped with greater educational skills and financial resources, they had the necessary advantages to construct political organizations and wage time-consuming campaigns. The political scientist Lester Salamon, who studied Mississippi very closely, noted one important effect of the transformation of the civil rights crusade: "As the danger of Movement involvement has subsided, the leadership ... has shifted from the sharecroppers and small farmers who spearheaded the battle for political rights to the black professionals who generally stayed in the background until the ball got rolling."

This changing source of leadership should not obscure the positive influence that the civil rights movement had on altering the structure of black politics. Before the era of reenfranchisement, black political leaders who represented their communities usually derived authority from prominent whites. "Clientage politics," as Martin Kilson termed it, linked blacks personally to powerful whites who delivered minimal welfare rewards within the rigid system of segregation. Considering the "over-whelming preponderance of political, social and economic power of the white majority," Everett C. Ladd concluded, "it is hardly surprising that the decision of influential whites as to which of the 'eligible' Negroes were to be leaders was accepted by Negroes themselves." The extension of the suffrage, the racial esteem that accompanied it, and the mobilization that followed it broke the stranglehold of whites over selecting black political leaders and setting their agendas. According to Louis Martin, the noted black journalist and adviser to Presidents Kennedy and Johnson, the Voting Rights Act ushered in a new breed of minority politicians who understood "that political power is generated in the black precincts and does not come from the hands of the great white father."

Obstacles to Officeholding

Blacks stood the best chances of winning election to office where they out-numbered whites, primarily at the local level. Because bloc voting generally characterized the conduct of elections between the races, blacks needed to comprise a clear majority of the population in order to triumph. The size of the black population was one of the most important resources black com-munities possessed in electing members of their race to represent them. As Albert Karnig and Susan Welch found, black candidates usually lost as the black population grew larger, winning only when it reached a majority. Before that point, the growing percentage of blacks posed a threat to whites, who closed ranks against minority-group candidates. Once blacks obtained a majority, they had the raw strength to overcome white opposition.

Still, in many black-majority areas of the South, in order to win blacks needed to comprise at least 60 percent of the population, a figure that indicated an effective voting-age majority. In many places, demographic shifts had resulted in a black population with a disproportionate share of children and the elderly, the former not old enough to vote and the latter less inclined to do so. Migration from rural locales to the cities of the South and North had thinned the ranks of the adults most likely to cast a ballot. Moreover, the continued economic dependency of poor blacks on white employers and creditors as well as the persistence of racial discrimination and of fear and apathy meant that a simple population majority did not always guarantee black electoral success. Old habits died hard: some blacks could be expected to vote for whites because of the deference they had paid them in the past, others may have done so as a consequence of jealousies and rivalries within the black community itself, and some retained a reasoned measure of fear that casting a ballot could still lead to reprisals.

In addition, blacks had to contend with electoral rules that diluted the power of their ballots and hampered them from electing members of their own race. The most significant of these were at-large election requirements. Such arrangements, in which candidates were chosen by voters throughout a wide jurisdiction, frequently resulted in the election of whites and the exclusion of blacks. Even if blacks constituted 40 percent of the total population of a municipality, for instance, in an at-large contest they would almost certainly fail to elect members of their race in proportion to their numerical presence in the community. In switching to elections by ward or single-member districts, black residents greatly enhanced their opportunity to elect black candidates in closer approximation to their strength in the overall electorate. Given the typical concentration of black residents in distinct subdivisions of a city, single-member district elections virtually assured that minorities could maximize their votes and select representatives of their own choosing.

Furthermore, with whites firmly in control of every state legislature, they could reapportion districts to weaken the black vote. Racial gerrymandering kept to a minimum the number of blacks who won election to state houses. For example, in 1971 three adjacent parishes (counties) in Louisiana each had a black population majority. However, when incumbent lawmakers redrew district lines for the state House of Representatives, they refused to form a black-majority district. Instead, they combined two of the black parishes with two predominantly white areas to form a white-majority parish and submerged the remaining black parish within a white-majority district. On the municipal level, white officials attempted to preserve their power by annexing adjacent territory in which a sufficient number of whites lived to once again put blacks in the minority. These sundry practices were often disguised as color-blind regulations, and indeed, at-large elections had first come into existence during the wave of Progressive reform at the turn of the century. Whatever their origins, their continued operation in the South, reinforced by the heritage of racial bias, deprived blacks of an equal opportunity to determine the outcome of elections.

This question of determining what constituted a fair share for minority representation proved especially controversial. Many white liberal allies of the civil rights movement were satisfied with a suffrage solution that removed unfair obstacles to minority registration and provided blacks with an equal opportunity to go to the polls and cast their ballots in a situation free from intimidation. They viewed the ballot from an individualistic perspective and rejected any notion that particular groups, however historically disadvantaged they might have been, were entitled to a share of representation proportionate to their percentage in the population. Accordingly, the federal government should do no more than protect individual black voters from invidious forms of discrimination rather than ensure that black ballots resulted in the election of black officeholders. Suffrage reformers had sought to make the black franchise equal in value to that of whites and then let blacks compete for political power in conventional ways. "If blacks … are able to form political alliances, to have their interests considered by elected officials through threat of political action, and are generally able to secure through their ballots the benefits of citizenship," one white observer remarked, "they are effectively participating in the political process."

Black leaders and their civil rights supporters generally saw the matter differently. They contended that the Voting Rights Act and the expanded registration accompanying it did not confer actual political equality or power. To them the ballot derived importance not principally as a color-blind instrument but as a race-conscious tool to advance the collective goals of African-American communities. Ultimately, blacks aimed to make government more responsive to their needs, and in theory it was possible to obtain greater influence over political affairs by backing white candidates who competed for their votes. However, in reality most blacks preferred representation by other blacks, who they believed reflected their aspirations. Feelings of pride and self-respect were also at stake. The civil rights struggle had succeeded in reawakening group consciousness among blacks, fostering the desire to see members of their own race attain positions of electoral leadership. Short of claiming a right to proportional representation, civil rights stalwarts considered the ratio of black officeholders to the percentage of minorities in the population as a convenient yardstick to measure political equality.

Although the 1965 Voting Rights Act dealt with the right to register to vote and not with the ability to win elections, it did recognize the plight of African Americans in group-centered terms. The law addressed current black disfranchisement by locating its organic roots in the past, and attempted to remedy patterns of racial discrimination against a persecuted group rather than correct specific acts of bias suffered by individuals. The lawmakers devised a statistical formula that automatically identified the presence of racial bigotry and empowered the federal government to challenge the consequences of previously injurious practices. Employing a type of affirmative action, the statute compensated southern blacks for the discriminatory treatment they had received by suspending literacy exams and allowing blacks to register on the same basis as had whites in the past.

The federal courts helped resolve the issue by limiting the operation of at-large elections in the South. Holding back from declaring at-large contests constitutionally invalid, the judiciary nonetheless struck down electoral systems that hampered participation by minorities and constricted their possibilities for holding office. To gauge whether a particular at-large electoral plan was impermissible, judges considered a "totality of circumstances." They looked for a history of racial bias that had excluded blacks from gaining equal access to the electoral process and evaluated whether current electoral institutions perpetuated discriminatory practices of the past. To this end, the courts were less concerned about the original purposes behind the adoption of the election rules and were more interested in ascertaining the effect on black representation. This standard of judgment applied throughout the 1970s and boosted black officeholding in those jurisdictions mandated by the bench to discard their at-large procedures.

Cases from Texas and Louisiana, in 1973, established the precedents. In the Lone Star State blacks challenged the 1970 reapportionment of the state House of Representatives for creating multimember districts in Dallas and Bexar (San Antonio) counties that diluted minority voting power. Only two blacks had ever been elected to the state legislature from Dallas and only five Mexican Americans had represented Bexar County. In *White v. Regester*, the Supreme Court ordered the creation of single-member districts after examining a combination of factors that effectively reduced black electoral opportunities. Accordingly, it discovered a history of racial discrimination and black underrepresentation: the failure of the white-dominated Democratic Party organization to nominate black candidates; the waging of racist campaigns; and the operation of electoral rules that handicapped African Americans and Mexican Americans from winning at-large elections.

Following up this decision, a lower federal court overturned the at-large system of electing members to the school board and police jury in East Carroll Parish, Louisiana. Although constituting a majority of the population of this parish, blacks comprised only 46 percent of enrolled voters, having been barred from registering from 1922 to 1962. Though blacks had managed to win three of 12 contested seats since the initiation of at-large elections in 1968, the court found that the electoral system prevented

African-American voters from achieving more effective representation. The judges acknowledged that barriers to black participation had been removed, but they concluded that "the debilitating effects of these impediments do persist." In rendering its opinion in *Zimmer v. McKeithen*, the judiciary looked at the "totality of circumstances" in uncovering racial bias that denied blacks equal access to the political process. A governmental jurisdiction violated the rights of black voters if it consistently failed to slate blacks to run for office, if its elected officials declined to respond to the interests of their black constituents, and if it adopted procedures that heightened the effects of past racial bias by submerging black voters within large electoral districts and requiring that winning candidates receive a majority rather than a plurality of the votes cast. (Given the prevalence of racial bloc voting, the majority-vote rule hurt blacks particularly where they did not constitute a majority of registered voters.)

These rulings were reinforced by the Justice Department. Under the preclearance section of the Voting Rights Act, the attorney general possessed the authority to reject suffrage changes that had the purpose or effect of discriminating against blacks. This provision pertained only to electoral rules adopted or altered since November 1964. Challenges against procedures fashioned before that date required litigation and were adjudicated as discussed above. Nevertheless, the Civil Rights Division of the Justice Department took its legal cues from the judiciary and refused to sanction switches from single-member districts to at-large elections that weakened the potency of black votes. Along with the courts, Justice Department watchdogs scrutinized reapportionment, redistricting, and annexation plans that potentially minimized opportunities for black representation.

High Hopes, Limited Rewards

As the judicial and executive branches cleared sundry obstacles to minority political participation, southern blacks continued their slow but steady progress in winning public office. In 1976, blacks held 1,847 elected positions in the South, and four years later the figure rose to 2,457. Despite these successes, blacks remained underrepresented in the proportion of offices they won. In 1980, of the more than 32,350 elected officials in the jurisdictions originally covered by the Voting Rights Act, about 5 percent were black. This share trailed far behind the proportion of the black population in the region, which ranged from 18.9 percent in Virginia to

35.2 percent in Mississippi. Moreover, in approximately one-quarter of the black-majority counties no blacks had been elected, a condition that also existed in nearly half the counties with a black population over 20 percent.

The substantial number of blacks who did triumph managed to reap important rewards for their constituents. Though the situation varied from place to place, from rural villages and towns to major urban areas, in general black elected officials delivered tangible benefits that had been long denied to their communities. Routine services, such as garbage collection, paved streets, police and fire protection, and recreational facilities, were upgraded and extended to black residents. Wherever possible, black public officials sought to increase the number of government jobs available through affirmative action programs that awarded contracts to minority businesses and employment to minority workers. They also avidly pursued and obtained federal government grants to fund capital investment for economic development and to expand the distribution of healthcare and social welfare projects in their locales.

The election of blacks pried open access to governmental structures that had been the exclusive domain of whites. Since the late nineteenth century, the disfranchisement of black southerners had made them the object of political attention; however, in regaining the ballot and recovering positions in government, they returned as active political agents. In so doing, black elected officials joined in the formulation and execution of policies, and brought to the attention of their white colleagues issues of special concern to blacks that previously had been ignored. To the extent that knowledge is power, black representatives gained vital information to help shape decision- making and protect the interests of their constituents. "No matter what happened," a black city council member in Florida declared, his white counterparts "knew I was listening to everything that went on."

In addition to these material improvements, blacks gained critical psychological advantages from their empowerment. The presence of black candidates and officeholders stimulated increased black political mobilization, as African Americans turned out with pride to vote for one of their own. This revived sense of self-esteem was aptly voiced by Fannie Lou Hamer. When blacks still sat on the political sidelines, Mrs. Hamer remarked, "some white folks ... would drive past your house in a pickup truck with guns hanging up on the back and give you hate stares." This changed as blacks approached the center of the electoral arena, she pointed out, and "those same people now call me Mrs. Hamer, because they respect people who respect themselves." Furthermore, these feelings of respect and dignity were carried forth by black politicians, who served as valuable role models, especially for the younger members of their communities.

With political reemancipation came raised expectations of what black representatives could accomplish. Because they had been systematically excluded from political participation, southern blacks prized the ballot in the belief that it would advance the goals of their race as a whole and not merely benefit a few. The president of the Savannah, Georgia, branch of the NAACP explained: "Black officeholders ... must be individuals who serve at the pleasure of the black community." Accordingly, black constituents placed demands on their representatives that exceeded the ordinary requirements of the job. Edith Ingram, elected the probate judge of Hancock County, Georgia, in 1968, described the myriad services she performed for the people who regularly came to her office, many of whom were on public assistance:

> I have to write checks for them, pay bills, buy groceries, take them to the doctors, balance checkbooks, certify them for welfare, make doctors' appointments, read letters, answer letters and fix loan papers for houses. A good 85 percent to 90 percent of the work that we do is non-office related work, but these people have no one else to depend on – they trust us, so we do it.

Indeed, many black officials discovered what Richard Arrington found out when he became mayor of Birmingham: "There are the expectations of the black community that expects you to do more than you can do."

Though black officials exerted increasing influence and shared authority, their power was limited in a variety of ways. With a relatively small number of exceptions, black elected officials in most cities and counties of the South and the nation were in the minority and could not deliver political dividends without the cooperation of white colleagues. In such situations minority officeholders had to walk a delicate tightrope in balancing the concerns of their constituents with the need to bargain with their fellow white officials who represented opposing interests. Based on personal experience, State Senator Leroy Johnson of Atlanta stated the problem: "Your position in the black community has to take on a veneer of militancy, but ... you have to be willing to negotiate, to compromise, in order to be effective."

Even in those areas where blacks came to control the majority of government posts, they often lacked the economic resources to affect significantly the material conditions of the impoverished population.

Although the poverty rate among black families declined over the course of the 1970s, from 41 percent to 30 percent, the percentage of poor blacks was more than four times the white figure of 7 percent. At the end of the decade the income of black families was 57 percent that of whites. This represented a slight improvement over the economic situation that existed when the Supreme Court outlawed school desegregation in *Brown*, but marked a downswing from the 60 percent level that prevailed in the years immediately following Johnson's Great Society. Blacks also experienced a higher incidence of unemployment than did whites, and the joblessness of young black male adults reached Depression-era levels.

Lowndes County, Alabama, highlighted the gap between political and economic power. Directed by LCFO, black political participation did improve living conditions, largely through the acquisition of outside federal and foundation grants and the election of a sheriff who attempted to dispense a more evenhanded brand of justice than in the past. But blacks continued to suffer from a disproportionate burden of economic distress. Their median family income rose slightly in comparison with that of white residents, from a ratio of 33 percent to 41 percent. However, their median family income of $7,443 lagged way behind the national average of $18,350 earned annually by whites. Expressing this predicament, the black Sheriff John Hulett remarked: "Until people become economically strong, political power alone won't do."

Though economic prospects remained as bleak for most blacks elsewhere throughout the country, a small but growing segment of African Americans saw their fortunes rise. Expanding opportunities resulting from desegregation and affirmative action programs swelled the size of the black middle class. By the late 1970s, the share of black workers occupying middle-class positions stood at 33 percent, a jump from 13 percent in 1960. For two-income families in which both husbands and wives worked, blacks had just about achieved parity with whites. From this group, with its access to superior economic resources and educational skills, black political leaders emerged. Following reenfranchisement, the representatives of this class, more so than those of lower-income blacks, succeeded in penetrating the structures of electoral officeholding that traditionally had been reserved for whites.

The ascent to power of that class during the 1970s reflected a complex picture of black political development. Themselves only recently risen from the bottom rungs of the economic ladder, middle- class black politicians tended to identify with the plight of their less fortunate brethren. Moreover, the newly acquired wealth of black middle-class families was not fully secure because their prosperity rested more heavily than that of whites on the combined incomes of working wives as well as working husbands and on earnings derived from public sector jobs and those protected by affirmative action regulations. Consequently, they were vulnerable to downswings in the economy and fluctuations in the political climate, especially in a conservative direction. Under these circumstances and because they were products of the same emancipatory forces that shaped the racial consciousness of poor blacks, these middle-class leaders often shared with the former mutual concerns associated with race.

Yet the interests of these politicians also cut across racial lines and embraced concerns they held in common with their middle- and upper-class white colleagues. Urban black politicians, especially in cities that sought to attract economic investment on a large scale, joined with moderate white businesspeople and their representatives to promote lucrative downtown redevelopment projects that favored buildings over ordinary people. In the process, black businesspeople, professionals, and white-collar workers benefited from attempts to revitalize the economy of their cities, whereas poor residents gained little from the private-sector, low-wage service jobs that accompanied urban renewal, and often suffered dislocation as a result of "urban removal." As a result, the black middle class reaped substantial rewards, while considerable poverty persisted among a sizable portion of the black population, a situation that occasioned observers to speak of the appearance of a permanent black underclass.

The "new South" interracial coalition did produce progress, albeit unevenly. The alliance of middle-class black politicians with white corporate and financial elites made sense during the 1970s when American cities were suffering from internal decay and a shrinking tax base. The flight of middle-class whites to the suburbs left behind the poor, who required a large share of public services but who could not afford to fund them. In striking a partnership with influential white civic leaders, black politicians sought to plug the drain on the depleted treasuries they had inherited upon assuming office. They did manage to attract new industries and jobs, and at the very least their presence at the governmental helm ensured that consideration would be given to black concerns as never before. The election of blacks to high public office, according to the political scientist Peter Eisinger, meant that "black interests, *as they are defined by black administrators*, have proved as central as the interests of white capital in the establishment of economic development goals" (emphasis in original).

Black Women Officeholders

Although the majority of black elected officials were men, the 1970s saw a rapid rise of black women officeholders throughout the nation. In 1975, black women comprised 15 percent of all African-American elected officials, a total of 530 out of 3,503 officeholders. Four years later the number of all black elected officials who were female had jumped by 66 percent, and black females held 882 of 4,607 positions. By comparison, the number of black men elected to public office increased from 2,973 to 3,725, a growth rate of 25 percent. Like their male counterparts, black women were most likely to hold government posts at the municipal and county levels and to represent areas with a predominantly black population.

The growing number of black women politicians reflected the impact of the civil rights movement. Black women had played a crucial, though often unsung, role in the freedom struggle. The top leadership positions were usually held by men, and individuals such as Martin Luther King, Roy Wilkins, and Stokely Carmichael were more easily identified by the public; but women both initiated and provided grassroots support for the civil rights protests that transformed the South and the nation. Without the courage, commitment, and vision of Rosa Parks, Jo Ann Robinson, Ella Baker, and Fannie Lou Hamer, to name a few, together with the legions of ordinary housewives and workers who boycotted, marched, sat-in, and went to jail, a widespread freedom struggle could not have been launched and sustained. As with men, in recruiting large numbers of women to its ranks, the civil rights movement inspired pride and encouraged standards of political participation that carried over to the electoral arena. Not coincidentally, by the end of the 1970s a majority of elected black women (51 percent) resided in the South, including Congresswoman Barbara Jordan of Houston, Texas, the primary battlefield and proving ground of the civil rights struggle and the region in which grassroots female leadership first flourished.

Black female politicians owed some of their success to the expanding opportunities generally available to women. Between 1975 and 1981, the number of all female officeholders soared from 7,089 to 16,585, with most of these positions concentrated in local government. The proportion of women holding seats on county governing boards more than doubled, from 456 to 1,205; and from 1971 to 1981, the number of women state legislators tripled, from 293 to 908. By the end of the 1970s, a thousand women were serving as mayors of towns and cities throughout the United States. This extraordinary growth spurt can be attributed in part to the very low level of female officeholding at the beginning of the 1970s. Nevertheless, these electoral accomplishments also owed much to the development of the feminist movement during the 1960s and 1970s. Itself influenced by the civil rights struggle, the women's movement raised an awareness of gender discrimination, provided an egalitarian ideology to challenge it, and stimulated women to attack the barriers blocking their full and active participation as citizens.

The relationship of black women to feminism was complicated by race. Although sympathetic to feminism's liberationist goals, black women activists tended to identify more closely with black men in the fight against racial oppression than with white women, whose skin color was the same as that of the male agents of blacks' exploitation. Whatever male chauvinism black women experienced within civil rights ranks did not stop them from displaying their considerable talents alongside men and developing their skills even further. The importance of black women within the political culture nurtured by the civil rights movement can be seen in the relative figures for black and white female officeholders. Black women constituted a higher percentage of black elected officials than did white women of white officials. In 1979, 18 percent of all black state legislators but only 10 percent of white lawmakers were female.

At the same time, these figures showed that neither black nor white women had reached parity with men. In recognition of both their growing achievements and the distance yet to be closed, women of the two races joined together within the National Women's Political Caucus. Formed in 1971 by Shirley Chisholm, Fannie Lou Hamer, Bella Abzug, and Gloria Steinem, the group promoted racial and ethnic diversity in its membership, challenged racism as well as sexism, and worked for a broad range of political and social reforms of special interest to women.

The importance of the civil rights struggle in serving to empower black women can be glimpsed in the life of Unita Blackwell. A resident of Mayersville, Mississippi, a tiny delta town of 500 people, Mrs. Blackwell was a housewife in her early thirties when she first encountered SNCC workers in the area. Impressed with the group's dedication and concern for developing local leadership, she gravitated toward SNCC and heeded its message: "If you all go and register to vote this is the way to help yourself." It took Blackwell three tries before the county registrar allowed her to register in 1964, and by then she was actively engaged with SNCC in the Freedom Summer campaign and in the creation of the Mississippi Freedom

Democratic Party. A member of the MFDP contingent that failed to win recognition at the 1964 Democratic National Convention, she returned four years later to gain a seat on the revamped biracial delegation from the Magnolia State. After Mayersville became incorporated in 1976, Mrs. Blackwell was chosen as its first mayor. In 1980, she became cochair of the state Democratic Party, the organization that had excluded her on account of race 16 years earlier. Her success illustrates the connection between the civil rights movement and electoral politics, as well as the strength and perseverance of the black women who contributed to the freedom struggle.

Black Mayors in Atlanta and Tuskegee

While noteworthy breakthroughs were occurring among women and in small towns like Mayersville, perhaps more than any other major city in the South, Atlanta, Georgia, reflected the changing currents of black political development in the years following passage of the Voting Rights Act. Characterized by a tradition of electoral activity that succeeded in dismantling discriminatory suffrage obstacles and in stimulating voter registration, black Atlantans already enjoyed a significant measure of influence in municipal politics during the 1960s. This "black Mecca" of Dixie, with its distinguished churches, independent businesses, and institutions of higher learning, had attracted and nurtured a resilient black middle class that included the family of the Reverend Martin Luther King, Jr. Its economic, political, and religious chieftains had allied themselves with white business and civic leaders, who ruled the city with a combination of racial benevolence and paternalism. The kind of racist rhetoric that infected political discourse elsewhere in the South was kept to a minimum, as white candidates campaigned for black ballots to ensure their victories.

Nevertheless, white politicians did not consider the black electorate as an equal governing partner, and they made vital decisions affecting their city without consulting the black community or adequately taking into account the impact of decisions upon it. In 1968, when city officials failed to solicit black advice in the creation of a metropolitan rapid transit system, disgruntled minority voters helped defeat the proposal in a referendum. The plan subsequently passed, but only after blacks were included in a policy-formulating capacity. Furthermore, under white control, urban renewal had meant revitalization of the central business district at the expense of the needs of low-income black neighborhoods.

The transition from moderate black influence to substantial black power began to occur in 1969. That year, white civic leaders split in their choice for mayor, and black voters swung the election to Sam Massell by giving him over 90 percent of their ballots. (He received only a quarter of the white votes.) At the same time, blacks won the post of vice mayor, four seats on the Board of Aldermen, and an additional two seats on the school board. Mayor Massell's administration subsequently fractured its black base of support. Shortly after taking office, the chief executive faced a disruptive strike by predominantly black sanitation workers. Massell upset black leaders, including his vice mayor, Maynard Jackson, in settling the dispute to the disadvantage of the strikers. However, the mayor attempted to patch up his coalition by rehiring the workers and appointing a black to head the Sanitation Department. During the remainder of his term, black politicians devoted their energies to obtaining an increased share of government services and benefits for their constituents and to ensuring that existing programs were administered fairly.

In 1973, black Atlantans were ready to exert a greater measure of control over their city and to reshape the biracial coalition that had governed in the past. They had demographic forces on their side. During the 1960s the composition of the population had shifted in favor of blacks. Over the course of that decade, the number of black Atlantans had increased nearly 37 percent, while that of whites had fallen by 20 percent. In 1970, blacks comprised a 51 percent majority of the city's residents, and three years later they used this numerical advantage to elect Maynard Jackson, who defeated Massell in a racially charged campaign to become Atlanta's first nonwhite mayor. Having guessed that the bulk of the black votes would go to his opponent, Massell reversed his previous campaign form to appeal for white support. Proclaiming Atlanta "Too Young to Die," he suggested that the city would decay under black rule. The *Atlanta Constitution* frowned upon this approach and commented that the incumbent appeared to be "running for mayor of a South African city which practices apartheid rather than the mayor of a fully integrated American city."

Massell's strategy misfired, and Jackson captured 59 percent of the total ballots cast. The heated battle lured to the polls a larger proportion of blacks (67 percent) than whites (55 percent). Jackson received an overwhelming 95 percent of the black vote and, although the electorate generally divided along racial lines, he received 17 percent of the white vote. Together with the mayor's post, blacks won half the seats on the city council and gained a slim one-vote margin on the school board. These victories followed the previous year's election to Congress of Andrew Young, a former assistant to Dr. King. Young had a reputation as a skillful peacemaker and conciliator, and in a district only two-fifths black, he obtained 53 percent of the vote. Nearly every black and about one-quarter of the whites who went to the polls supported the civil rights activist. The triumphs of Jackson and Young demonstrated the arrival of black elected officials as a dominant force in Atlanta politics, but they also indicated that whites still retained significant influence in shaping the outcome of electoral competition.

Only 35 years old when he became mayor, Jackson belonged to a family of distinguished men and women. His relatives included politicians and preachers, a professor, and a performer. His father was a Baptist minister who once ran for a seat on a local school board in Texas. His great-great-grandfather founded the Wheat Street Baptist Church in Atlanta, and his grandfather organized the Georgia Voters League. Jackson's mother had earned a doctorate in French and taught at Spelman College in Atlanta and North Carolina Central University in Durham. One of his aunts, Mattiwilda Dobbs, was a highly acclaimed opera singer. A graduate of Martin Luther King's alma mater, Morehouse College, Jackson obtained a law degree from North Carolina Central and returned to Atlanta to work as an attorney handling cases for low-income clients. The assassinations of Dr. King and Senator Robert F. Kennedy in 1968 helped persuade him to embark on a political career. "I decided the solution to the country's problems had to be in politics," he remarked, "not in violence." He aimed high in his first campaign in 1968, competing for the US Senate seat from Georgia held by Herman Talmadge. Jackson lost by a wide margin, but his strong showing in Atlanta, where he outpolled the popular incumbent, encouraged him to run for vice-mayor in 1969. Four years later, he succeeded in capturing city hall.

Once in office as mayor, Jackson helped deliver important rewards. He reorganized the police department, appointed a black to head the new agency, and increased the number of African-American law enforcement officers. Subsequently, the city experienced a decline in black complaints of police brutality. The mayor also embarked on a vigorous affirmative action program that resulted in the black share of Atlanta's public workforce climbing from 42 percent in 1972 to 51 percent five years later. During this period, the share of contracts awarded by the city to minorities jumped from 2 to 13 percent. In addition, Mayor Jackson instituted a plan giving black firms 25 percent of the contracts for work to expand Atlanta's international airport. Though Jackson disturbed white business and civic leaders with many of these policies and with an aggressive personal style they found abrasive, he could hardly afford to ignore them. To promote urban redevelopment and economic expansion, the mayor needed the resources and expertise white corporate executives and financiers could provide. "Blacks have the ballot box," an Atlanta newspaper editor admitted, "and whites have the money." When a sanitation strike tied up the city in 1977, Jackson treated it even more harshly than had his white predecessor. In a move that could only have pleased influential whites, the mayor took a hardline stance against the work stoppage for higher wages, rejected union demands, and fired the offending strikers. Before he became mayor, Jackson had supported striking garbage workers; however, as official head of the city he placed sound business management practices and fiscal responsibility ahead of the needs of poor wage-earners. He also heeded white demands to remove his controversial law-enforcement chief, and replaced him with a more acceptable black.

The assumption of political power by Mayor Jackson and other black officials improved the overall position of Atlanta's nonwhite population, though it left many nagging problems unsolved. As one scholar has concluded, these accomplishments "often in the face of considerable opposition … represent … a more equitable share for the black community within existing priorities." Still, black leaders did very little to restructure those priorities, which continued to place the poor at a disadvantage. By 1980, 6 percent of black households earned at least $35,000 a year, and more black Atlantans had annual incomes in excess of $50,000 than did minority residents anywhere else in the South. At the same time, however, this premier city had a high incidence of black poverty – 25 percent of black families earned less than $5,000 a year. Overall, one-third of black families lived below the poverty line, compared with 7 percent of whites. Indeed, the diversity of Atlanta's population, reflected in its class structure, sometimes made it difficult for blacks to unite on behalf of efforts to relieve severe impoverishment. For example, during the 1977 sanitation strike, moderate black leaders rallied around the mayor against the demands of workers. In cities like Atlanta, as black political affairs progressed, they became more complicated and pragmatic – pointing to the distance traveled since the height of the civil rights movement, with its moral clarity and solidarity.

Much of this complexity can likewise be seen in the experience of Tuskegee, Alabama. During the 1970s, Mayor Johnny Ford pursued a vigorous policy of obtaining outside money for economic development. At a

Figure 13 Maynard Jackson, shortly before his victory in being elected as Atlanta's first black mayor. (Photo © Bettmann/ Corbis)

time when the Nixon administration was dismantling the apparatus of Lyndon Johnson's War on Poverty, the Tuskegee mayor managed to secure over $30 million in federal and state grants and an additional $30 million from other funding sources. Much of Ford's success as a fundraiser derived from his pragmatic brand of politics. This former campaign aide of Senator Robert Kennedy endorsed Nixon's reelection in 1972, explaining that he wanted to back a winner and have access to power. "It's paying off," he remarked in 1973. "Other places may be losing Federal funds because of cuts, but not Tuskegee. I've prevented that."

The Ford regime directed its efforts to improving basic public services and generating local financial growth. His administration created a new sewage system and expanded police protection. Municipal officials designed an industrial park to attract firms into the area, to serve as the centerpiece of the town's economic revitalization, and to provide jobs for area residents. Plans were prepared for the construction of an oil refinery, a dog-racing track, and an experimental tomato farm.

Unfortunately, many of these efforts failed to produce the anticipated results. Only the racetrack scheme materialized, while the industrial park failed to lure necessary private capital from investors. Although Ford continued to work with willing white leaders, more than half the white population fled Tuskegee, taking with them valuable economic assets that potentially could have benefited the town's growth. In addition, charges of corruption involving black officials, though unproven in most instances, hampered their ability to carry out several of the projects. As in Atlanta, the economic gains flowed to the black middle class rather than to those at the lower end of the economic scale. In 1980, the median income of black families was $10,423, the highest in the black-belt section of the state. Yet the percentage of blacks living in poverty was three times greater than that of whites, and over the decade the median income level in comparison with that of whites had actually dropped from 63 to 60 percent. Black politicians had not found sufficient resources or fashioned an adequate agenda to meet the needs of Tuskegee's most impoverished residents.

These drawbacks notwithstanding, the fruits of black political office-holding in the 1970s cannot be gauged simply in quantitative terms. In Tuskegee, reenfranchisement had empowered blacks to secure a significant measure of control over their lives. No longer did they have to endure the humiliation inflicted by white officials who sought to keep them from registering and who arbitrarily devised gerrymandering plans to limit the effectiveness of their votes. Black Tuskegeans and their Macon County neighbors experienced the pride that comes when the barriers to treatment as first-class citizens are shattered. A government that for generations had been directed by and for whites came to represent the majority of the people it ruled. Political equality did not necessarily translate into economic equality, nor did individual opportunity guarantee that all members of the exploited group would derive benefits equally. But Tuskegee blacks had unprecedented access to a government that had previously excluded them, they more easily identified with governing officials, and they no longer felt so restrained within the tight physical and psychological confines of white supremacy. This experience of liberation meant a great deal to a retired VA hospital worker who had spent most of his life under vastly different circumstances. "Everything's better," he explained. "In the old days, before black elected officials ran the county, most black people steered clear of white enclaves. They used to arrest you over there if you went through, but not anymore."

Black Rule in Cleveland and Gary

While southern blacks were expanding their political power and leverage, their northern counterparts also extended their influence within the electoral arena. These regional pursuits of political equality were both distinct and interconnected. Black northerners, many of whom had migrated from the South during the periods surrounding World Wars I and II, generally faced a less rigid Jim Crow system than existed in Dixie. The residential and school segregation they encountered usually was reinforced by custom rather than by explicit laws. This was particularly true following World War II, when northern whites responded to antifascist democratic ideology and removed some of the racially biased obstacles blocking minority advancement. Discrimination unquestionably remained embedded in northern institutions and practices, but it operated more subtly than in the South.

At the same time, given the freer space that they found in urban centers above the Mason–Dixon line, black northerners had greater access to political representation than did disfranchised or partially enfranchised southern blacks. In cities like Chicago and New York blacks sat on municipal councils and represented their districts in state legislatures and in Congress. When not electing candidates of their own race, blacks cast their ballots to shape the outcome of local and national elections that pitted whites against each other. This type of electoral clout had helped nudge presidents and lawmakers since Franklin D. Roosevelt's time to add civil rights to the national agenda.

Nevertheless, black northerners lacked fully developed political strength. Their votes counted and frequently served to sway the balance of electoral power, but they did not share with whites an equal voice in their governance. In northern cities, political machines advanced the interests of an assortment of white ethnic groups that had arrived there in large numbers before transplanted blacks did. Though political bosses organized blacks as a constituency within their machines, the bosses kept the blacks on the periphery of real power and did virtually nothing to tackle the problems of racism and economic deprivation that pervaded the ghetto. Black politicians served as intermediaries between party organizations and their communities, and occasionally delivered material benefits – patronage jobs, intervention with law enforcement officials, handouts of food for the holidays – but they reflected the unequal power relationships between the races. Even where blacks constituted an integral component of the political machine, such as in Chicago, their leaders provided representation without disturbing the entrenched political and economic structures that perpetuated black subordination.

This form of quasi representation, bereft of independent power, depended on white patrons as the source of authority and dispensers of rewards. Unlike generations of white ethnic groups that had penetrated and captured control of urban political machines as an integral part of their upward economic and social mobility, African Americans faced unparalleled obstacles in taking the same route to success. Though immigrants also encountered discrimination from whites whose forebears had preceded them to America's shores, the newcomers nevertheless shared, in common with the existing residents, the privilege of skin color that relatively quickly lowered barriers to acceptance and assimilation. Blacks, however, could claim no such bond, and by virtue of their race faced uncommon prejudice that kept them on the outside of dominant political institutions. They alone had to wage a fierce struggle merely to obtain the right to vote and other elementary features of citizenship that white Americans from many ethnic backgrounds took for granted.

The new politics that emerged after 1965 increasingly thrust blacks to center-stage as agents of social change and group advancement. Black northerners took pride in the valiant struggles of the southern civil rights movement, which prompted community leaders to turn their attention to the more subtle problems of political and economic discrimination. Civil rights battles in the North focused on securing adequate jobs, quality housing and education, and impartial police protection rather than on Jim Crow and disfranchisement; but, as in the South, black northerners demanded respect and equal treatment in practice as well as in theory. The emancipationist ideology of the freedom movement joined with the social welfare programs of Johnson's War on Poverty to heighten black consciousness of oppression and the possibilities for overcoming it. The Voting Rights Act inspired northern blacks, and after 1970 eliminated literacy tests in the region. More and more black northerners successfully exercised their electoral muscle, as had other ethnic minorities before them.

Yet egalitarian ideals and government programs were not enough. With shifting demographic patterns on their side, the number of blacks in the populations of urban centers rose, and they became serious contenders for public office. In the 1950s and 1960s whites had moved out of the inner cities and into the surrounding suburbs to seek a more comfortable lifestyle, one "uncontaminated" by the presence of incoming black migrants. These pilgrimages produced a sharp upswing in the black proportion of the urban population. In those areas in which blacks approached or actually became a majority of the population they had the most success in dethroning whites from the leadership of dominant political organizations.

Events in Cleveland, Ohio, and Gary, Indiana, demonstrated the changing configuration and complexity of black political development in the North. Between 1930 and 1965, the city of Cleveland lost about 300,000 of its white residents, while the number of blacks increased by over 200,000. As a result of this reshuffling, blacks constituted 34 percent of the total population and composed a slightly higher 40 percent of the city's registered voters. Many of the newly enrolled blacks had signed up during registration drives sponsored by the Democratic Party in preparation for the 1964 campaign against the conservative Republican, Barry Goldwater. Thus, although blacks remained a minority of Cleveland's electorate, they held a large enough portion of the ballots to position themselves to compete for the most important post of mayor.

Until 1965, black voters had thrown their support behind white Democratic mayoral candidates. In 1961 and 1963, they had helped elect Ralph Locher and gained 10 of 33 seats on the city council. Black politicians usually posed little challenge to white rule and chose to consolidate their power within their own districts. They had not developed the idea of uniting black communities around common issues in order to advance the racial goals of their constituents throughout the city. This situation began to alter after the mayor and his administration angered black leaders in their handling of disputes concerning school desegregation, employment practices, and police– community relations. The efforts of local chapters of national civil rights groups, such as the NAACP and CORE, along with a local coalition known as the United Freedom Movement, managed to increase black participation in protest and electoral activities and to raise expectations about the possibilities of running a black candidate for mayor against Locher. Indeed, as William Nelson and Philip Meranto observed, black leaders began to view "electoral politics ... as an extension of the movement; a shortcut to the civil rights goals of housing, education, welfare."

In 1965, Carl Stokes launched a challenge to the mayor that fell short of success but pointed up the chance for future victory. Stokes had grown up in Cleveland's black ghetto, served in the armed forces, and obtained a law degree. He entered municipal government in the late 1950s with an appointment as a city prosecutor, and he first won a seat to the Ohio House of Representatives in 1962. Three years later, after his reelection, Stokes ran for mayor against three white candidates, including the incumbent. Though black Democratic elected officials stuck with Mayor Locher, Stokes won a whopping 85 percent of the minority electorate's votes. With black officeholders lined up behind the Democratic organization, Stokes depended on grassroots groups and volunteers to conduct his campaign. Though he lost, his presence as a candidate succeeded in boosting black turnout at the polls to a record level. Within two years black participation at the ballot box had leaped from 57 percent to 72 percent.

Given the population figures, Stokes's solid base of support in the black community alone was not enough for victory. He needed white allies. In his losing bid, Stokes had garnered 3 to 5 percent of white votes, but he required considerably more to win. The black aspirant looked to white business leaders for backing, and they saw in him an opportunity to heal the city's worsening racial conflicts. In 1966, a bloody riot in the Hough section of the city left four dead and hundreds wounded. Mayor Locher reacted to the violence with a tough law-and-order policy that emphasized more police firepower than programs to deal with the underlying ills that had sparked the uprising. The mayor set the tone for his tough approach by refusing to meet with the visiting Martin Luther King, Jr., or with local black leaders. When Stokes decided again to challenge Locher in 1967, he not only had blacks behind him but he also attracted white businesspeople who believed that his election might calm the racial tensions that posed a threat to their long-range plans for economic development of the city.

In this second try Stokes emerged victorious, to become the first black mayor of a major American city. He patched together a winning coalition consisting of the overwhelming majority of blacks and enough whites to put him ahead. The black candidate reassured whites that he wanted "to get the Negro question out of the way." Once that happened, he asserted, "then we can talk about issues. I'm telling the people my election would not mean a Negro takeover." At the same time, Stokes ran as a black candidate as well as a candidate who happened to be black. "In 1965 when I ran," he declared, "they whispered that I was a Negro. They don't have to whisper today. I am a Negro. I am proud of it. I intend to remain one."

This strategy paid off in the 1967 campaign. First, he defeated Mayor Locher for the Democratic nomination by winning 96 percent of the black vote and 15 percent of the white. This contest again brought out black voters in record numbers, and their turnout at the polls exceeded that of whites by 15 percent. Next, in the general election Stokes defeated his Republican opponent, Seth Taft, by a slender margin of 50.3 to 49.7 percent. Black turnout was even higher than it had been in the primary, and Stokes captured 95 percent of the black votes cast. He also slightly increased his backing among whites by gaining 20 percent of their ballots. In doing so, he had the support of white business leaders, including the publishers of the city's major newspapers. In contrast, Cleveland's working-class ethnic voters deserted him, thereby abandoning their traditional Democratic allegiance in harsh response to the riots and with the feeling that the fruits of black protest came at their expense.

Stokes's victory gave blacks a unique sense of pride, in much the same way as the civil rights struggle in the South had empowered disfranchised blacks. "Stokes was a symbol … for black progress," a city councilman recalled. "You would see old people walking to the polls and perhaps they never voted a day in their lives." He underscored further the stark break from the past that had occurred for blacks: "They considered politics a white man's business. We could have councilmen and judges, but they never dreamed that day would come when a black man would be mayor of the town."

Unfortunately, the hopes generated by the election of Stokes went largely unfulfilled. The mayor did deliver a variety of benefits to his black constituents. His administration built public housing for poor blacks, set up child-care centers and health facilities in minority neighborhoods, and provided funds to stimulate black business enterprise. However, his two terms in office witnessed continuous conflicts with whites, especially city workers, and ongoing fragmentation among blacks. A series of scandals rocked the administration, which was also plagued by several strikes by municipal employees that paralyzed the city and fostered discontent. Contrary to the expectations of his white backers, Stokes's installation in city hall was not

Figure 14   Carl Stokes with his wife, Shirley, after winning election as mayor of Cleveland. (Photo © Bettmann/Corbis)

sufficient to forestall further racial disturbances, though he did have a calming influence when violence again flared in 1968.

The end of his second term saw the black electorate fractured and whites united. The split among blacks was particularly disappointing, and in 1971, upon Stokes's retirement, this division resulted in the election of a white Republican mayor. The grassroots organizations that had united around Stokes to place him in office collapsed, greatly lowering black morale and political participation. During the 1970s, the number of registered black voters decreased by 20,000 and black voter turnout declined drastically – from 75 percent to 48 percent. Blacks still had access to city government, and Carl Stokes's brother, Louis, represented them in Congress, but the promise of a reshaping of municipal politics along progressive lines withered.[1]

Meanwhile, in Gary, Indiana, black political development followed a similar pattern as in Cleveland but proved to be more durable. In this Midwestern home of US Steel, by the late 1960s blacks comprised about

---

[1]   Not until 1989 did Cleveland elect its second black mayor, Michael Smith.

55 percent of the city's population. As whites flocked to the suburbs during the previous decade, Gary's black population rapidly expanded into a majority. Nevertheless, in 1967, whites accounted for 52.3 percent of the city's registered voters compared with 47.7 percent for blacks. Up to that time, the black electorate had thrown its clout behind the local Democratic machine, keeping its leaders in office. For instance, in 1963, two-thirds of the mayor's votes came from blacks, leaving whites to make up only a third of the winning total. In return for this support, black machine function-aries obtained patronage and other spoils; however, the dire economic conditions of their constituents living in the ghettos showed little improvement.

As in Cleveland, civil rights protests of the early 1960s helped alter the structure of black politics in Gary. Community activists engineered direct-action demonstrations to challenge unfair racial practices that the domi-nant machine organization failed to address. These drives mobilized many blacks who previously had been politically inactive, especially those in lower income brackets, and heightened their desire to use the electoral arena to advance racial objectives. Community leaders looked to loosen the hold of the machine on blacks and substitute in its place a political organization directed by blacks and aimed at raising the quality of housing, education, and law enforcement that plagued many inner-city neighborhoods.

The leadership for this assault on the established order came from Richard G. Hatcher. A lawyer and county prosecutor, Hatcher had been active in local civil rights efforts. He served as adviser to the NAACP youth group, provided counsel for a number of local protest associations, and in 1963 headed the Gary contingent to the March on Washington. That same year, he won a seat on the city council with the backing of the Democratic machine. He soon established his independence from party chieftains and lost the plentiful patronage plums they had for distribution to the party faithful. Hatcher also broke with tradition by using his position to promote the broad civil rights aims of the black community. In one of his major accomplishments, he directed the battle to obtain a pathbreaking fair housing law for the city.

In 1967, while Carl Stokes was mounting an insurgent campaign in Cleveland, Hatcher launched his own bid for mayor of Gary. Divorced from the machine, including those black politicians customarily in its ser-vice, he set up a dynamic, grassroots organization of volunteers. Crisscrossing black neighborhoods, Hatcher's workers played upon the racial pride that had been blossoming and delivered the message that the time had arrived to elect a black mayor. They waged an intense drive to boost black voter registration, and over a seven-month period succeeded in enrolling an additional 2,200 names. Though black registration still lagged slightly behind that of whites, the Hatcher candidacy and the hard work behind it managed to stimulate 3,000 more blacks than whites to turn out at the polls. In his Democratic primary contest against two whites, including the incumbent mayor, Hatcher won by capturing about 70 percent of the black vote, while the white electorate split its ballots between his rivals.

The black nominee also prevailed in the general election, where he faced a single white opponent, the Republican Joseph Radigan. Though the candidate of his party, Hatcher failed to receive the endorsement of the regular Democratic organization, which remained deeply suspicious of his independence. Machine leaders not only withheld their backing, but they orchestrated attempts to purge the voter registration lists of 5,000 black names. This chicanery was blocked by the intervention of the Justice Department and issuance of a federal court injunction restoring the names. On election day, Hatcher eked out a slim victory of 1,389 votes, approximately 51 percent of the total cast. He garnered an astounding 96 percent of the black electorate, and owed his triumph to the very high turnout of blacks at the polls. A greater percentage of blacks than whites participated, 76 percent to 72 percent, and in addition to his solid black base of support he obtained 14 percent of the white ballots. Though opposed by most whites, Hatcher scored particularly well in predominantly liberal Jewish districts.

Both Hatcher's candidacy and the determined organizing efforts on his behalf contributed to the victory of Gary's first black mayor. The campaign mobilized many blacks who had felt themselves outside of the electoral process. "People for the first time really began to see how important a vote was," a Hatcher supporter acknowledged, "and that they could control a way of life." Having obtained office, the mayor initiated programs directed at relieving long-neglected problems in the black community. His administration undertook to construct public housing, encouraged affirmative action hiring plans, and recruited blacks for government employment. These benefits underscored for many blacks the connection between electoral politics and minority-group advancement and promoted in Gary's black residents both pride and confidence in government authority. Moreover, unlike the experience in Cleveland,

Hatcher succeeded in solidifying black organizational support behind him and won reelection throughout the next two decades.

Black mayoral candidates also fashioned winning coalitions elsewhere by combining solid black support with a small but sufficient minority of white backers. Such was the situation in Detroit. Though the Motor City had a history of racial strife dating back to the 1943 race riot, it also had a tradition of biracial labor activism, black militancy, and liberal reform. By 1965, Detroit counted two blacks, Charles C. Diggs, Jr., and John Conyers, in its congressional delegation, and one African American sat on the city council. During much of the 1960s the city had been run by Mayor Jerome Cavanagh, a white liberal whose generally enlightened administration was tarnished by the explosion of racial violence in 1967. The urban rebellion helped contribute to white flight to the suburbs. By the end of the decade, blacks comprised 43 percent of Detroit's population. In 1969, Richard Austin, a black accountant and chair of the Wayne County Board of Supervisors, ran for mayor but narrowly lost to his white opponent by a margin of 1 percent. Nevertheless, three blacks were elected to the nine-member city council. (The following year, Austin won election as Michigan's secretary of state.)

In 1973, Coleman Young attempted to become Detroit's first black mayor. During World War II, he had served as a second lieutenant in the Army Air Corps. While in the military, Young was arrested along with 100 black soldiers for trying to integrate an officers' club in Indiana. On the heels of the publicity generated by the protest, the army desegregated this establishment. After finishing his tour of duty, he returned home to work as a union organizer in the automobile industry. However, his left-wing sympathies during the 1940s and 1950s made him the target of both conservative politicians and the powerful, anti-Communist United Automobile Workers. Nevertheless, he demonstrated remarkable political resiliency. By the 1960s, Young had survived the anti-Communist postwar backlash and moved into the electoral arena as a Democratic state senator and party leader still championing liberal and labor causes.

By the time he ran for mayor, in 1973, Young had an advantage that was not available to Austin four years earlier: the number of black registered voters now exceeded that of whites. In the nonpartisan primary, he competed in a field of 19 candidates. No one received a majority, and Young finished second to John Nichols, the white police commissioner. In the runoff contest against Nichols, who symbolized law and order to whites and police brutality to blacks, Young insisted that he would not engineer a black takeover and pledged to "field a team that has balance – racially, ethnically and politically." From the 1.5 million people who went to the polls, he hammered out a slim winning margin of 14,000 votes by mobilizing the overwhelming majority of the black electorate and obtaining about 8 percent of the white ballots.

Though African-American mayors of major cities usually emerged when blacks approached or reached a majority of the population, the election of Tom Bradley in Los Angeles was a notable exception. In a city with only a 15 percent black electorate, Bradley defeated the longtime incumbent, Sam Yorty, in a contest filled with racial bitterness. A former UCLA track star, policeman, and lawyer, Bradley served as a city councilman during the 1960s, representing a district that was two-thirds nonblack. Having lost the Democratic mayoral primary to Yorty in 1969, four years later Bradley fashioned a "coalition of conscience" to triumph over his rival with 56 percent of the vote. In 1973, he captured city hall by gaining 95 percent of black ballots, a bare majority of the Chicano (Mexican American) electorate, and nearly half the white vote – running particularly well among liberal Jews. A source of pride to the black community in a city that was predominantly white, Bradley succeeded in convincing the electorate that his election was a sign of racial progress and an alternative to black radicalism. "The American dream is often verbalized," he asserted, "but it would really have meaning all over the country if a black who believed in the system, who worked and prepared himself for new opportunities, was able to achieve that kind of victory."

The New Challenge

These victories, along with those in Cleveland and Gary, marked the dawning of a new era in black urban politics. For more than a decade after 1967, black mayors took control of city halls in prominent urban areas both in the North and the South. As municipalities acquired black majorities, constructed political organizations to rally the previously disfranchised portion of the electorate, and marshaled economic resources to wage effective campaigns, black candidates triumphed in Newark, Washington, DC, Oakland, Birmingham, and New Orleans. The appearance of black mayors and other elected officials directly opened up government to African Americans on a more equal basis than ever before. In 1974, 1,593 blacks occupied elected positions outside of the South; six years later the number had jumped to 2,455. Although black political leaders made mistakes, and problems of poverty seemed as intractable to them as to their white predecessors, black officials demonstrated that white monopoly control of public affairs could be broken. Henceforth, blacks in towns and cities throughout the nation staked their claim to an equal partnership with whites in governance.

They faced a difficult task, however. In many of the cities in which they ascended to power, blacks inherited a multitude of severe financial problems that limited their options for action. Much of the situation was beyond their command. During the 1970s, structural flaws in the economy produced both recession and inflation that drained tax revenues away from maintaining basic city services, let alone expanding them. Major urban areas teetered on the brink of bankruptcy and needed to be rescued by infusions of state and federal funds. Low-wage foreign competition in the production and distribution of manufactured goods hurt American industry and resulted in plant closures and unemployment in many of the urban locations dominated by black chief executives. Furthermore, the continued migration of whites to the suburbs and the parallel movement of a rising black middle class out of the inner cities left behind an increasingly poor population of blacks unable to contribute to the upkeep of their communities.

In addition, black mayors were hampered in other ways. Those seeking improvements for their constituents often found their efforts slowed by entrenched municipal government employees whose jobs were protected by civil service codes. As a result, changes in personnel to implement new directions in policy could occur only slowly at best and at worst could be thwarted by unsympathetic bureaucrats. Moreover, many issues could not be handled through local initiatives. Cities depended on state and federal governments for funds, but growing conservatism in the 1970s deprived them of political allies to supply crucial material needs. Into the void stepped large corporate investors and financial developers, who in return for their economic assistance steered many municipal projects toward enterprises that created jobs and housing for middle- and upper-class residents to the detriment of the poor.

Despite this sometimes dismal picture, African Americans still found pursuit of electoral power worthwhile. Throughout the nation, a substantial segment of the black electorate benefited from the tangible improvements that increased political strength brought. After 1965, opportunities for public employment and distribution of municipal services had far less to do with skin color than at any time during American history. Furthermore, black empowerment meant much more than could be calculated in dollars and cents. It provided a source of political agency for blacks, breaking down habits of nonparticipation ingrained through generations of racial discrimination. To the extent that the members of any group of people, white or black, male or female, could exert control over their lives in an increasingly complex and technological society, African Americans had joined the ranks of first-class citizens and helped shape the political landscape of the country.

6

Progress and Poverty
Politics in a Conservative Era

The movement of blacks into positions of influence and power in local and state governments, however impressive the gains, was not enough to produce genuine racial equality. Many of the problems blacks encountered were national in scope and required national attention and resources to remedy. Furthermore, the laws placed on the statute books as a result of the civil rights struggle needed federal enforcement, and in the case of the Voting Rights Act, periodic renewal. The economic misery that plagued so many African Americans demanded solutions beyond the purview of local politicians. The burdens inflicted by chronic unemployment, inflation, and inadequate housing and healthcare traversed municipal, county, and state boundary lines and became the responsibility of officials in Washington. Unless blacks and their white allies could shape public policy in the nation's capital to deal with these concerns, the benefits of political empowerment would remain incomplete.

As the fruits of black political mobilization began to ripen during the 1970s, they matured in a climate less nurturing to their continued growth. Black southerners had regained their right to vote with the flowering of liberal reform in the mid-1960s; yet within a decade the nation had moved in a conservative direction that posed serious threats to hard-earned civil rights and social programs and to the initiation of new ones. In the wake of disillusionment over the Vietnam war and racial strife in American cities, Richard Nixon and other conservatives had risen to prominence by deemphasizing racial justice, promising a return to law and order, and pledging economic retrenchment. In this gloomy environment, African Americans

Running for Freedom: Civil Rights and Black Politics in America since 1941,
Fourth Edition. Steven F. Lawson.
© 2015 John Wiley & Sons, Inc. Published 2015 by John Wiley & Sons, Inc.

looked to engage their foes in the national arena in which the vital policies affecting their welfare were forged. The preservation and expansion of electoral victories in local black communities throughout the nation depended on winning battles in Washington to sustain them.

While much needed to be done before blacks achieved the economic equality to accompany their recently gained civil and political rights, in an age of federal retrenchment they were largely forced to fight defensive operations. Although they did wage new skirmishes for racial advancement, civil rights proponents spent much of their creative energies guarding against rollbacks in existing programs. During the Nixon administration, civil rights advocates had successfully petitioned Congress and the courts to maintain strict enforcement of the Voting Rights Act and school desegregation decisions. A bipartisan coalition of moderate and liberal lawmakers, reinforced by determined civil rights lobbyists, ensured that landmark suffrage legislation remained intact and defeated administration-sponsored attempts to circumvent court-ordered busing. On the economic front, the Republican chief executive managed to terminate some of his predecessor's Great Society programs and trim others by turning funding over to the states. But even in this area, in 1973 Congress acknowledged the plight of the poor by adopting the Comprehensive Employment and Training Act (CETA), which provided public service jobs and manpower training to those out of work.

Black Political Influence and the Ford Administration

When the Watergate scandal forced Nixon to resign in 1974, Vice President Gerald Ford stepped in to serve out Nixon's term. A staunch conservative and a veteran of some 25 years in the House of Representatives, Ford had given qualified support to civil rights legislation. As a lawmaker from Grand Rapids, Michigan, Ford routinely voted for passage of civil rights bills extending the suffrage to blacks and challenging racial discrimination in public accommodations and housing. However, in compiling this record he had, like President Nixon, embraced those proposals only after making concerted efforts to soften their impact. As a congressman in 1970, he had lined up behind the chief executive in favor of replacing key provisions of the Voting Rights Act with a version that would have removed much of the weight of enforcement from the white South. His stance in opposition to school busing reflected Nixon's, as well as that of his white constituents who decried imposing this means of remedying racial imbalance in neighborhood schools.

Nevertheless, upon succeeding the disgraced Nixon on August 9, 1974, Ford assumed a conciliatory posture that was absent from his predecessor's final days in office. To restore confidence in the presidency and to bind the wounds inflicted by the Watergate debacle, he sought to reassure some of those who felt most estranged from the White House. These gestures followed earlier attempts "to clear the air" with black leaders while he was still vice president. As Ford later recalled it, disturbed that "the Nixon Administration had closed the door to minorities, particularly blacks," he hoped they would see him as "point man … for dealing with the government; that there was at least one man in the Administration who would listen to them." Unfortunately, when he tried to follow up these meetings by submitting recommendations for action, Nixon's staff ignored him. Within a week of becoming President, he summoned to the Oval Office members of the Congressional Black Caucus, whose chairman, Charles Rangel of New York, called the conference "absolutely, fantastically good."

A short time later, President Ford had sufficient opportunity to show the sincerity of his intentions. Very much on the minds of black lawmakers and civil rights advocates was the upcoming renewal of the Voting Rights Act, whose key provisions were due to lapse in August 1975. For the third time in ten years, Congress had to debate the merits of federal protection of the suffrage and decide whether forceful supervision should continue into the future and for how long. Though southern blacks had taken notable strides in gaining entry to the electoral arena, their political strength was still fragile and depended on continued oversight from Washington to reach its full potential. Remembering the nation's abandonment of the freed slaves at the end of Reconstruction a century earlier, modern-day civil rights supporters worried about the harm that another premature federal withdrawal would cause to the Second Reconstruction's enfranchised blacks.

President Ford appeared to agree with their concern. He okayed the Justice Department's recommendation to extend the Voting Rights Act for an additional five years, thereby choosing not to repeat Nixon's unsuccessful attempt to fasten controversial amendments to it. Acknowledging that southern blacks had made great progress in the decade since passage of the law, the Ford administration noted that the number of black elected officials remained disproportionately low and that evidence of racial discrimination in registration and voting persisted. In taking this position, the chief executive further endeared himself to civil rights advocates by invoking the memory of Dr. King and linking it to the renewal campaign. On January 14, 1975, Ford commemorated the anniversary of the slain minister's birthday by recalling King's leadership in enacting the original suffrage law, which, he remarked, "has helped to open our political process to full citizen participation" and must be "safeguarded."

Boosted by the President and with solid bipartisan congressional backing, the renewal measure headed for sure passage. Compared with previous battles, the current deliberations took place in an atmosphere of relative harmony. Neither the administration nor the liberals disagreed over preserving what had become the most important provision of the statute – the Section 5 requirement for the covered states to clear changes in their electoral laws with the Justice Department before they took effect. There were differences over the length of time desired for extension – the White House favored five years and civil rights lawmakers advocated ten – and the President was reluctant to add to the bill a liberal-sponsored measure to grant language minorities the same protection guaranteed to oppressed racial groups. Nevertheless, unity rather than discord characterized the congressional proceedings. Joseph Rauh, the civil rights attorney who had pleaded the case of the Mississippi Freedom Democratic Party in 1964, summed up the feeling of reformers: "I guess one of the happiest things for us is the broad consensus that has grown up behind extending the Voting Rights Act."

Though southern lawmakers did not abandon their customary opposition to the suffrage bill, they lacked both the passion and strength to mount an effective challenge to it in 1975. Accepting the political reality that the legislation was going to pass in some form, they tried to revive the Nixon administration strategy of expanding coverage of Section 5 nationwide. Moreover, opponents concentrated their energy on designing provisions to make it easier for the southern states to remove themselves from the Act's penalties. Their arguments failed to persuade their legislative colleagues. A proposal for a ten-year extension sailed through the House, and the Senate displayed an unusual enthusiasm for agreement by voting to impose cloture to terminate debate even before southern legislators had the opportunity to wage a filibuster.

Despite this overwhelming show of support, the final outcome became unexpectedly enmeshed in controversy. While the Senate discussed the measure, President Ford suddenly backed away from his firm endorsement of the bill and suggested enlarging its scope to include the entire nation. In offering this last-minute proposal, Ford seemed to be heeding the calls of southern members of his party to take such action. With Republicanism on the rise in Dixie – Goldwater and Nixon had made significant inroads in the once solid Democratic South's presidential vote – the GOP leader looked to the region to help gain his party's nomination and win election in his own right in 1976. His about-face drew a barrage of criticism from civil rights supporters, Democrats and Republicans alike, who charged that his puzzling position confused the issue and put the entire bill in jeopardy. However, Ford's political calculation turned into an empty gesture as the chief executive once again reversed his field. Fearing that his intervention would stall passage of the bill's special provisions before their expiration, the President withdrew his objection to enactment of the original measure. As the presidential fog lifted from the Capitol, both chambers of Congress approved a modified seven-year extension by wide margins.

This victory demonstrated the increasing leverage of southern blacks upon their national representatives. The South's trio of black legislators, Barbara Jordan of Texas, for the bill (as were the 13 black lawmakers from the North); but it was a matter of considerable surprise that 69 of their 105 white colleagues from the region joined them on the final tally. In the Senate, where Edward Brooke, the Massachusetts Republican, sat as the lone black, 13 of 24 southerners lined up behind the measure.

Reflecting the changing pattern of partisan affiliation in Dixie, the party of Abraham Lincoln and the party of Jefferson Davis were trading places. As conservative whites jumped to the Republicans and northern transplants brought their GOP allegiances to the region, Democrats in the South were coming to rely more heavily on the growing black electorate for support at the polls. Though southern Democratic lawmakers did not embrace liberal economic positions that would have benefited African Americans, they had little difficulty in backing a suffrage law that created the very constituency they needed to help keep them in power. This shifting arithmetic led southern Democrats and Republicans to calculate differently. In the House, two-thirds of the southern Democratic bloc supported extension of the Voting Rights Act in contrast to nearly two in three Dixie Republicans who opposed it. A Louisiana lawmaker expressed the sentiments of his fellow Democrats: "We found that the sky did not fall under the 1965 Voting Rights Act, that things worked pretty well in the South, the deep South of the old Confederacy, which readjusted their patterns of voting, readjusted their attitudes toward all people."

In the end, the Ford administration chose to follow the new consensus on voting rights that had developed, but in the more controversial area of school busing the administration pursued the old course laid out by President Nixon. Supreme Court decisions sanctioning busing generated substantial opposition among whites in the North as well as the South. Building upon this hostility, in 1972 the Nixon administration had introduced congressional legislation instructing the judiciary to try to retain the neighborhood school concept and to use busing only as a last resort. The bill passed the House only to die in the Senate. The chief executive kept the measure alive during the remainder of his abbreviated term, and after Ford replaced him, Congress finally approved the proposal. This action delighted the new chief executive, who declared: "I have consistently opposed forced busing to achieve racial balance as a solution to quality education." Furthermore, these words gave encouragement to antibusing opponents such as those in Boston who militantly protested against court-ordered desegregation. Launching school boycotts, holding marches, and fomenting violence, these foes of busing succeeded in plunging the city into turmoil for several years during the mid-1970s.

These attacks notwithstanding, the practical effect of the legislative measure was minimal, because Congress did not have the authority to curtail courts from enforcing the constitutional rights of minority students through busing. In fact, during the Nixon–Ford years nearly 50 percent of black pupils attended desegregated schools in the South, a figure higher than that in the North. And, despite the resistance in Boston, the judiciary remained firm in enforcing its busing decrees. In addition, civil rights lobbyists and their congressional allies defeated a more serious threat to busing than the bill Ford had signed into law. They succeeded in turning back attempts to end court-ordered busing altogether by way of a constitutional amendment, passage of which would have required a two-thirds vote of Congress before ratification by the states.

Beyond salvaging the influential Voting Rights Act and retaining some degree of enforcement of school desegregation, African Americans saw their efforts toward greater racial advancement stall. Blacks used political power to sustain their legal rights of citizenship, but they had far less success in shaping the agenda that would have addressed their economic needs. With fiscal conservatism emerging as the dominant theme in Washington and throughout the country, social programs to stimulate employment, extend health insurance, and furnish housing, which would have aided the working class and poor of both races, realistically did not stand much of a chance. Moreover, the growing inflationary spiral of the mid-1970s, together with rising unemployment – "stagflation," as economists labeled it – brought to a virtual halt the economic gains blacks had been experiencing since the heyday of the civil rights movement a decade before. In 1975, the median income of black families had inched up to 61 percent of whites', but having reached this peak, it immediately began sliding even further away from full equality. Without renewed federal commitment to tackling their economic problems, blacks managed only to fight a rearguard political battle to maintain the status quo.

The Election of Jimmy Carter

The presidential election of 1976 offered dim prospects for meaningful change. The Republican incumbent's performance in civil rights matters, after getting off to a good start, had come to disappoint blacks. Much of the goodwill Ford had created by supporting extension of the Voting Rights Act eroded in his clumsy handling of the bill at its final stage before passage. In addition to his antibusing stand, Ford's position against federal aid to rescue financially troubled cities from bankruptcy upset black activists. They criticized the President for his callousness in allowing major urban centers of the North, which contained substantial black populations, to cut back on municipal social services rather than helping them preserve these programs through an infusion of funds from Washington. In the wake of the riots in the late 1960s and the flight of whites to the suburbs, the cities had become associated increasingly with the presence of impoverished racial minorities whose problems white Americans preferred to ignore. After Ford rejected New York City's plea for relief in 1975, M. Carl Holman, a longtime civil rights advocate and director of the Urban Coalition, contended that many blacks believed New York "would never have been dealt with like that if it had been seen as a city of Wasps [white Anglo-Saxon Protestants]."

Nor had the Democratic presidential nominee identified himself closely with the cities and their black residents. The former governor of Georgia, Jimmy Carter had presided over a largely rural and small-town state. He brought a brand of New South progressivism to the statehouse in Atlanta that emphasized honesty and efficiency in government, streamlining the budgetary process, and upgrading the public education system, which ranked near the bottom in the country. Accordingly, this political and economic modernization fostered an environment hospitable to business investment and growth. In 1976, Carter secured his party's presidential nomination by effectively campaigning in the primaries as an "outsider" from Washington, an image that in the post-Watergate era garnered wide-spread appeal from an electorate disillusioned with national politicians. Weary of "imperial presidents," either of the activist Republican or the Democratic variety, Americans saw merit in the kind of low-expectation approach to government offered by Carter. A self-described conservative in fiscal affairs, the Georgian fit in well with the mood of economic retrenchment and frugality that voters wanted in the nation's capital.

Although Carter's record as governor did not hold out much promise for the extension of costly programs to reduce black poverty, his racial views provided a bit more encouragement for black advancement. However, the case in his favor was hardly clear-cut. Carter had been born and raised in Plains, Georgia, and returned there to live after completing a career in the Navy. During the 1950s and 1960s, he accepted the rigid segregationist practices and nearly total disfranchisement that characterized his home area in southwest Georgia. Never a negrophobe, he did not actively condone Jim Crow so much as he made very little effort to eradicate it. Yet unlike many of his neighbors, this peanut farmer refused to join the White Citizens Council or other states' rights groups opposed to desegregation, and on one occasion in the mid-1960s, he even waged a losing battle to open up his Baptist church doors to black congregants. Nevertheless, elected governor in 1970, he roundly criticized court-ordered busing and endorsed a constitutional amendment to prevent it. He also developed close ties with George Wallace, who he thought had the best chance of defeating Nixon in 1972, and when George McGovern instead of Wallace won the Democratic nomination that year, Carter unsuccessfully tried to extract a pledge from him to relax enforcement of the Voting Rights Act in the South.

While in office, the Georgia governor balanced these positions with others that won black support. In an era when black voters were becoming critical to the election of white Democratic Party officials, New South politicians like Carter (and even some old-style segregationists like Wallace) discarded the racist rhetoric of the past and abandoned irresponsible opposition to the laws of the land that compelled desegregation. The changes wrought by the civil rights movement had made a distinct impression upon Carter, and he accepted them with both a "sense of relief" and "secret gratitude." In effect, the struggle for black equality had also freed many whites from the shackles of racism that kept the South locked into economic and political backwardness. In 1971, Governor Carter had proclaimed the start of a new day: "I say to you quite frankly that the time for racial discrimination is over. No poor, rural, weak, or black person shall ever have to bear the additional burden of being deprived of the opportunity for an education, a job, or simple justice." He matched the symbolism of his eloquent rhetoric with some substance. During his administration, the governor arranged to desegregate the walls of the state capitol by hanging a portrait of Dr. King alongside paintings of distinguished white Georgians, a ceremony that ended with the singing of the powerful civil rights anthem "We Shall Overcome." Moreover, Carter doubled the number of blacks working in state government, increased black appointments to middle-management positions, and signed into law the state's first open-housing measure.

This overall performance won Carter the staunch backing of Dr. King's family and some of the martyred civil rights leader's top associates. Congressman Andrew Young of Atlanta, a King confidant, became an early booster of the governor for the Democratic presidential nomination in 1976. He was joined by the Reverend Martin Luther King, Sr., who remarked that he had "never met a finer person than Governor Carter." Though other black civil rights leaders-turned-politicians, such as Julian Bond, declined to endorse him, Carter held on firmly to his King–Atlanta connections.

The strength of this attachment was sorely tested during the primaries. In Indianapolis, appearing before a largely white audience, Carter reiterated his opposition to racial discrimination at the same time as he defended those "who are trying to maintain the ethnic purity of their neighborhoods." He further stated his disapproval of the government's deliberately "trying to break down an ethnically oriented community ... by injecting into it a member of another race." These comments smacked of the kind of rhetoric that George Wallace had skillfully employed as a presidential candidate in whipping up a white backlash among ethnic groups fearful that black advances would come at their expense. Carter survived this episode by apologizing for any misunderstanding his statement might have caused, which satisfied most black leaders. Representative Young and "Daddy" King rallied around Carter and forgave him for making "a slip of the tongue that does not represent his thinking."

This reaffirmation of support enabled Carter to attract the bulk of black votes in winning crucial primary contests, which carried him to the Democratic National Convention as the frontrunner. There he heard the stirring keynote speech of Representative Barbara Jordan of Houston, the first black to receive the honor of delivering this prestigious address. In 1967, as a first-term Texas state senator, Jordan had come to the attention of President Lyndon Johnson, who invited her to the White

House to participate in a strategy session concerning fair-housing legislation. She impressed the President, as well as her colleagues in the Texas legislature, by combining a concern for civil rights with hardheaded legislative pragmatism. Elected to Congress in 1972, Jordan quickly rose to prominence as perhaps the most eloquent member of the House Judiciary Committee in its televised investigation of the Watergate-related impeachment charges against President Nixon. Chosen to rally the Democratic faithful at the 1976 nominating convention, she declared that her very presence on the podium showed "that the American dream need not forever be deferred." The assembled delegates who heard these words and who subsequently nominated Carter for President included 323 blacks comprising 10.6 percent of the convention members. (In contrast, blacks comprised only 3 percent of the GOP convention delegates who chose Ford as their candidate.) The Democratic reform initiative launched in 1964 was evidenced most vividly in the Mississippi contingent, which contained the highest ratio of blacks to whites of any delegation at the gathering.

Throughout the nomination process and in the subsequent general election campaign, Carter successfully reached out to blacks. A devout

Figure 15 Representative Barbara Jordan of Texas delivering the keynote address at the 1976 Democratic National Convention. (AP Photo/Press Association)

Baptist, he avidly cultivated black support by speaking in black churches and delivering a message his listeners could relate to. Churches had traditionally functioned as key institutions in the political life of black communities, and Carter knew how to tap into their emotional style and felt comfortable in the role of a preacher presenting a sermon. He stressed the themes of redemption and compassion, brotherhood and love, justice and equality, and linked them personally and directly to Dr. King. "I sometimes think that a Southerner of my generation," the Georgian remarked, "can most fully understand the meaning and impact of Martin Luther King's life. He and I grew up in the same South." As Carter's biographer, Betty Glad, concluded, more than any substantive program the candidate offered, blacks responded to him out of "nostalgia for the rhythms and religion of rural Christianity."

Indeed, black ballots proved pivotal in Carter's triumph over Ford. The Georgian eked out a very tight victory over the incumbent, gaining a bare 50 percent of the popular vote and capturing 297 electoral votes to Ford's 241 – the closest margin since 1916. In patching together a coalition of states from his native South, the Midwest, and the Northwest, Carter secured a whopping 90 percent of the black vote. His strongest support came from the southern black electorate, which gave him 92 percent of its ballots. The huge vote that Carter obtained from blacks helped him secure all but one state (Virginia) in the South, where Ford otherwise received about 55 percent of the total white southern vote. When Mississippi, which only a decade before had barred nearly all blacks from the franchise, swung into the Democratic column, Andrew Young gleefully declared: "I knew that the hands that picked the cotton finally picked the president." Nationally the governor piled up 5.2 million black votes, more than triple his slender popular vote margin of 1.7 million.

Blacks flocked to Carter for a variety of reasons. On a personal level, his southern Baptist religious fervor and regional heritage appealed to blacks not only in the South but also to those whose roots extended back to Dixie. Carter credited the civil rights movement with transforming both himself and the South, a message that earned him widespread support from former leaders of that struggle. The key endorsements of Reverend King and Congressman Young, Julian Bond noted, "made Carter legitimate in the eyes of blacks all over the country." Furthermore, Carter ran extremely well among blacks because of his party label. Polls revealed that the Georgian scored heavily with traditional Democrats, and no group exceeded the loyalty exhibited by black Democrats in recent presidential elections. The party of FDR's New Deal and LBJ's Great Society had even greater attraction in 1976, when the unemployment rate under the Republicans had risen to 8 percent and was substantially higher among adult black males.

The important contribution African Americans made to Carter's triumph stood in sharp contrast to the mood of despair felt by many blacks in that bicentennial-year celebration of the Declaration of Independence. Carl Holman detected "a dangerous cynicism," especially among young blacks, who demanded more than the civil rights victories of the past that had brought liberty without equality. "There's a great feeling of being out of it – outsiders in your own country – which was a feeling they began to lose in the sixties," Holman asserted. "And it's come back double-barrelled now." Even before the 1960s ended, the country's urban ghettos had exploded as rioters violently expressed their bitterness in the streets rather than calmly at the polls. Between 1968 and 1972, the black turnout of eligible voters fell. The decline was especially pronounced in the North, where the ballot did not hold the same attraction for blacks as it did for those southerners who had fought a long, difficult struggle to regain the franchise. The traumas of Vietnam and Watergate had heightened this alienation, but the frustration of many African Americans emerged even stronger from the unwillingness of political leaders to grapple with the continuing crises of joblessness, poor health, and substandard housing that gripped black communities. "There is," the political scientist Samuel D. Cook declared in 1976, "a groping for direction, issues, priorities, funds, organization, inspiration, affirmation, protest, and movement."

Yet such assessments did not tell the whole story, as many blacks showed signs that they were not ready to give up on the political system. Since 1972, the number of blacks registered to vote had grown by three-quarters of a million. Civil rights groups such as the NAACP had joined with labor unions, the Democratic Party, and the Voter Education Project to mount active enrollment campaigns to sign up new voters. In the South, blacks narrowed the registration gap between the races from over 40 percent in the mid-1960s to about 11 percent a decade later. Equally as impressive, registered blacks turned out for the 1976 presidential election in growing numbers. This contest brought to the polls about 64 percent of enrolled black voters nationwide, surpassing the 58 percent participating in 1972. The upswing in the rates of black registration and turnout as well as the impact of the minority vote in determining Carter's victory convinced many African Americans that they were still heading in the right direction. No one was more optimistic than John Lewis, the former chairman of

SNCC and director of VEP. "I wish – Lord, how I wish," he commented after the election, "Martin [Luther King] were alive today. He would be very, very happy. Through it all, the lunch counter sit-ins, the bus strike, the marches and everything, the bottom line was voting."

Affirmative Action and Bakke

Having helped elect a President, blacks expected their faith in the electoral system to be suitably rewarded. Not only did they desire to obtain the traditional spoils of victory – jobs and appointments – but they also sought to influence the setting of a public policy agenda that recognized the special needs of their communities. In President Carter they acquired increased access to top-level government positions, but they fell short in steering his administration along a course that would lead to bold new programs.

The President recruited an impressive array of blacks to Washington. Patricia R. Harris, former ambassador to Luxembourg and chair of the Credentials Committee at the 1972 Democratic National Convention, entered the Cabinet as Secretary of Housing and Urban Development. An undergraduate at Howard University in 1943, Harris had participated in an early sit-in demonstration to desegregate a cafeteria in the District of Columbia. The chief executive staffed the Justice Department with Solicitor General Wade McCree, a Harvard-trained federal judge from Michigan, and Assistant Attorney General for Civil Rights Drew Days III, a Yale Law School graduate who had previously handled cases for the NAACP Legal Defense Fund. He chose Clifford Alexander, Jr., an adviser to President Johnson, as Secretary of the Army. Carter, who on the campaign trail had showered praise upon the civil rights movement, appointed several individuals who had played significant roles in that struggle. He selected Andrew Young, one of Dr. King's closest advisers in the SCLC, for the Cabinet-level post of ambassador to the United Nations. From SNCC the President tapped John Lewis to operate Volunteers in Service to America (VISTA), the domestic equivalent of the Peace Corps. (This agency was a division of ACTION, whose associate director was Mary King, a white SNCC organizer.) Named as Assistant Secretary of Labor, Ernest Green 20 years earlier, in 1957, had been part of the courageous group of black students that defied a menacing mob to desegregate Central High School in Little Rock, Arkansas. By the end of Carter's term in office the list of his black appointees had expanded to include 15 ambassadors, 30 federal judges, over 50 sub-Cabinet officials, 110 members of advisory boards and commissions, and 25 members of the White House staff.

Aside from the recognition they conferred, these appointments did not produce bold initiatives in civil rights policy. The most challenging opportunity arose over affirmative action, and the Carter administration acted cautiously. This issue sharply divided the races. Most whites objected to any preferential treatment – reverse discrimination as they saw it – that placed them at a disadvantage in hiring and in admission into graduate and professional schools. They considered any program that established a fixed number of positions, or quotas, for minorities as a violation of the principle of equal opportunity. In stark contrast, the majority of blacks took the opposite position. African Americans argued that on the basis of past discrimination, the effects of which still persisted, they were entitled to compensatory treatment. In their view, this meant the establishment of flexible goals, not quotas, to recruit qualified minorities until a level was reached that indicated they were competing equally. The controversy posed a thorny political hazard for Carter because it split two key elements of his electoral coalition: blacks and Jews. Victims of discriminatory quotas in the past, Jewish Americans deplored any attempt to resurrect quotas even for the purpose of including, rather than excluding, certain groups of people.

The President attempted to walk a fine line on this matter. Having made earnest efforts to increase minority employment in his administration, the chief executive readily acknowledged that blacks suffered from the impact of racial bias, past and present, and pledged "to root out those last vestiges of discrimination in government and set a pattern for the private sector." He disapproved of quota-like regulations that limited access to employment, however, and believed that minorities would benefit in the long run from racially impartial hiring and admission standards.

In this respect, President Carter reflected the position of most white Americans. A 1972 survey had indicated that 82 percent of whites opposed affirmative action plans that favored blacks over equally qualified whites. Nevertheless, 77 percent of those polled approved of the creation of job-training programs for blacks. Like Carter, the overwhelming majority of respondents differentiated between "legitimate" compensatory programs that allowed minority groups an opportunity to compete on an equal level with whites and "unfair" policies that supposedly granted one group preferential treatment over another. These attitudes were hardened by the economic situation of the 1970s, which heightened competition for increasingly scarce jobs and spaces in graduate and professional schools. The decade's economic cycle of recession coincidental with inflation – that is, stagflation, as noted earlier – together with the outpouring into the marketplace of the postwar baby-boomers made whites much less hospitable to racial advancement than in the 1960s, when jobs and educational opportunities were more plentiful.

African Americans generally considered affirmative action from a much different perspective. Having only recently regained their legal right to equality, blacks resented being told to forget their unfortunate history of racial discrimination and to make it on their own without due compensation from the government and the private sector. They refused to believe that such relief could be termed "reverse discrimination" when whites still retained firm control over economic and political power in society. Besides, to blacks racial bias was not so much an individual matter of discrimination as an institutional one allowing whites on the whole to continue to preserve their longstanding advantages. African Americans argued that they would have a very difficult time in ever catching up to the mass of white Americans who had inherited the legacy of superior educational and employment benefits solely on the basis of their skin color. Thus, they contended that "benign" racial classifications were legitimate and proper.

Their arguments received some sanction in the courts. In 1971, the Supreme Court ruled in *Griggs v. Duke Power Company* that "neutral" employment tests were invalid if they perpetuated the effects of prior discriminatory employment practices. The justices found the results of such bias to exist when blacks failed to hold jobs in rough proportion to their percentage in the general population. Yet the issue was far from settled. In 1974, the high tribunal in *DeFunis v. Odegaard* had the opportunity to decide the fate of an affirmative action plan adopted by the University of Washington Law School that applied different entrance standards for blacks and whites. However, because the white plaintiff who charged discrimination had already been admitted to the law school while the suit was pending, the court declared the litigation moot, left the admissions plan intact, and managed to duck the controversial question for the time being.

The issue again surfaced at the medical school of the University of California, Davis, and forced the Carter administration to take action, The university had set aside a designated number of spaces for minority students in order to guarantee their selection. Alan Bakke, a rejected white applicant, sued to gain admission and overturn this procedure. After Bakke won in a lower court, the university appealed to the Supreme Court, where the Justice Department intended to file a brief in opposition to the school's affirmative action plan. Reflecting White House thinking, government lawyers premised their arguments on the principle that "racial classifications favorable to minority groups are presumptively unconstitutional."

Before the department could complete its brief, civil rights advocates inside and outside the administration managed substantially to revise the government's handiwork. Ironically, the original draft that critics found unacceptable had been written under the supervision of Carter's two top black attorneys, McCree and Days. In opposition stood Joseph Califano, Secretary of Health, Education, and Welfare, who was white, and several black officeholders such as Ambassador Young and Eleanor Holmes Norton, the director of the Equal Employment Opportunity Commission. Taking their concerns to the President, they warned him, in Young's words, that the "Bakke case is perceived as a betrayal of the black community by the judicial system." At the same time, the Congressional Black Caucus applied additional pressure on the chief executive and informed him that the Justice brief "irretrievably undermined public and private affirmative action programs." In the wake of these maneuvers, Carter's lawyers, led by McCree and Days, redrafted the brief along lines suggested by its critics. The final version softened the department's anti-quota position, supported university guidelines that took race into account for admission, and suggested that the case be returned to the California judiciary for rehearing. Although the Supreme Court agreed that racial criteria generally were a legitimate consideration in designing affirmative action programs, in this instance it upheld the claim of unfair discrimination and ordered Bakke's matriculation into the medical school.

This episode demonstrated the strengths and exposed the limitations of black political influence during the Carter years. Because the President had had the sensitivity and had felt a political obligation to appoint blacks to important posts in his administration, they were well placed during the Bakke affair to correct Carter from making what Califano called "the most serious mistake … in domestic policy to date." Yet having helped shape this crucial policy matter, black officials and their white allies could not control the ultimate outcome of the decision. The Supreme Court took care of that, and its increasingly conservative orientation, reflecting appointments to the bench made by Nixon, confined affirmative action within narrow boundaries. Though civil rights sympathizers sat on the high tribunal, most notably Thurgood Marshall, the former chief counsel of the NAACP, they did not constitute a majority. Nevertheless, their presence on the court, like that of blacks in the Carter administration, modestly advanced civil rights goals so long as they did not stray too far from the center of the judicial and political spectrum.

The same situation applied in Congress. Throughout the late 1970s the Black Caucus and its white liberal allies made little progress with the majority of lawmakers who believed their constituents demanded fiscal restraint and would not tolerate massive spending to relieve economic distress. For example, the Black Caucus rallied behind a measure aimed at relieving the problem of unemployment, which was disproportionately high among blacks. Before Congress enacted a "full employment" bill in 1978, sponsored by Senator Hubert Humphrey of Minnesota and Representative Augustus Hawkins, a black Democrat from California, conservative lawmakers had turned it into a hollow proposal.[1] Even worse, a national health plan offered by Senator Edward Kennedy of Massachusetts that would have been of great benefit to blacks went unpassed.

Given their optimistic expectations of President Carter, blacks had reason to feel disappointed with his performance. The President, who had campaigned for the White House as a Washington outsider, failed to establish effective relations in dealing with Congress. In this post-Watergate era, the task of leading lawmakers in a more activist, progressive direction would have severely challenged any chief executive, but Carter proved unwilling and unable to marshal his resources toward that end. He had promised the electorate competence, efficiency, and integrity – to restore character and decency to the Oval Office – not new programs for social reform. Further, the slimness of his victory did not furnish a mandate or provide him with the incentive to pursue bold domestic ventures. Still, he might have channeled some of the enthusiasm and energy he displayed in promoting his policy of human rights abroad into efforts at extending civil and economic rights at home. His liberal critics waited in vain for him to guide the nation morally and politically "to an understanding of the demands and subtleties of civil rights in the late 1970s and 1980s."

For black Americans Carter compounded his leadership difficulties by his handling of a controversy surrounding Ambassador Young. The outspoken delegate to the United Nations had become the most visible black representative in the Carter administration. To blacks the former civil rights leader and Atlanta congressman was a source of great pride, but to whites he demonstrated the inability of the chief executive to exercise his presidential

---

[1] The original bill had called for a reduction of unemployment to 4 percent within five years and authorized the federal government to provide "last resort" jobs to reach this target. Instead, the final version relied primarily on the private sector to create jobs and attempted to set a brake on federal spending by establishing a goal of 3 percent inflation within five years.

authority firmly. The UN diplomat had received a great deal of publicity for his comments denouncing the racism of both America's friends and foes abroad as well as for extolling one of the nation's enemies, Cuba, for combating colonialism in Africa. Indeed, Young had served as a forceful advocate within the administration against apartheid in South Africa and for establishing closer ties with newly independent African states. In August 1979, after it became known that Young had held an unauthorized meeting with agents of the Palestine Liberation Organization (PLO), an action contrary to Carter's Middle East policy, the ambassador was forced to resign. The appointment of another black, Donald F. McHenry, to succeed Young only partially repaired the damage to Carter's image in the black community.

In addition, the Young incident once again inflamed tensions between two of the most loyal elements of the Democratic coalition: blacks and Jews. Despite their long history of cooperation within the civil rights movement, since the late 1960s issues concerning affirmative action and the Middle East had strained relations between the groups. Jewish organizations had thrown their considerable weight behind Bakke's challenge to racial quotas, and black activists had called for recognition of a Palestinian homeland, a position they held as an act of solidarity with nonwhite, exploited people and one which they regarded as evenhanded. Blacks considered support for Bakke's case as inimical to their economic advancement, and Jews viewed deliberations with the PLO as a threat to the security of Israel. Proponents from each side worked to defuse the hostility, but events such as those prompting Young's departure heightened the conflict. Shortly after the UN ambassador left his job, tempers again flared. When Jesse L. Jackson, the director of People United to Save Humanity (PUSH)[2] and a former colleague of Young's in the SCLC, met with and embraced Yasser Arafat, the leader of the PLO, he occasioned a barrage of criticism from Jewish organizations.

The Election of Ronald Reagan

Troubled by these political splits, African Americans had even more to worry about in the hard times that had befallen many residents of their communities. Between 1975 and 1980, the median income of blacks compared with whites dropped three points to 58 percent. The proportion of

---

[2]   The name was later changed to People United to Serve Humanity.

blacks without jobs hovered around 14 percent, double the rate for whites. That figure was bad enough, but the 40 percent rate of unemployment for black teenagers, more than twice that of white youths, was even worse. The incidence of poverty among blacks was also greater than for whites, and the situation was deteriorating. In 1980, 33 percent of blacks compared with 10 percent of whites were impoverished. Much of their plight stemmed from the rise of single-parent families headed by women. At the end of the decade, 40 percent of black families lived in such households, and half of them experienced poverty. These deplorable conditions were aggravated by the spiraling inflation of the late 1970s, and the suffering continued as African-American activists could get neither the President nor Congress to exert sufficient leadership to mount a forceful attack on black problems.

Nonetheless, blacks did not abandon their quest for political power. While stalemated in the national arena, they continued their efforts at the local level. The greatest progress came in the South, where the civil rights movement served as a catalyst for political change. By 1980, over 50 percent of all black officeholders, nearly 2,500, resided in Dixie. In 1979, Richard Arrington won election as mayor of Birmingham, the scene of some of the most vicious racial strife during the freedom struggle. In the North and West, black mayors occupied city halls in major urban areas such as Detroit, Gary, Newark, and Los Angeles; and in the nation's capital, Marion Barry, an early leader of SNCC, ran the municipal government. On the downside, the annual rate of increase in the number of black elected officials was on the decline, falling from 13.5 percent in 1977 to 6.6 percent three years later. Moreover, blacks held only about 1 percent of the available elected positions in the nation overall, though they made up over 11 percent of the population. In the Voting Rights Act states of the South, where the minority population reached as high as 35 percent in Mississippi, blacks composed only 5 percent of elected officials.

The prospects for improvement did not appear too bright as the presidential election of 1980 took place. The Democrats renominated Carter after he beat back a challenge from Senator Kennedy, but his chances had been severely damaged by the inability of his government to bring a halt to galloping inflation and to obtain the release of 53 American hostages held in Iran since November 1979. However limited the incumbent's accomplishments in civil rights, a Carter victory offered greater hope for black advancement than did a win by his Republican opponent. Ronald Reagan, the former governor of California and opponent of the 1964 Civil Rights Act, held the states' rights philosophy of the right wing of his party and promised to reduce the federal commitment to civil rights enforcement and the Great Society economic programs that had benefited blacks substantially. He launched his campaign in the South with an appearance in Philadelphia, Mississippi, the location of the murders of three civil rights workers during the 1964 Freedom Summer, where he pledged to "restore to state and local governments the powers that properly belonged to them." These views reflected Reagan's close ties with southern Republicans who had replaced the Democrats in the region as the fiercest opponents of civil rights measures.

Unlike in 1976, the black vote did not save Carter from defeat. Though Reagan won only 51 percent of the popular vote, he overwhelmed his Democratic rival in the electoral column with 489 votes. The incumbent received 41 percent of the popular vote total, with most of the remaining 8 percent going to Congressman John Anderson of Illinois, a liberal Republican running as an independent. Blacks cast the bulk of their ballots for Carter (estimates ranged from 85 to 90 percent), but their votes could not overcome the GOP contender's margins of victory in key industrial states of the Northeast and Midwest and in every southern state except Carter's home territory of Georgia. In spite of their lopsided support for the Democrat, black enthusiasm for Carter had waned. Whereas the turnout of the total voting-age black population was almost 4 percent higher than in 1976, the turnout of eligible registered voters was lower by nearly 3 percent. Because the number of black registrants had increased over the past four years, the percentages meant that many of those who had signed up to vote chose not to cast their ballots (see Table 6.1).

Table 6.1   Estimated national black voter registration and turnout in the 1976 and 1980 presidential elections

	1976	1980
Voting-age population	15,398,000	16,967,000
Number registered	9,024,800	11,400,000
Number of voters	5,784,872	7,000,000
Turnout of registered voters (%)	64.1	61.4
Turnout of voting-age population (%)	37.6	41.3

Source: Joint Center for Political Studies, *The Black Vote: Election '76* (Washington, DC, 1977), 11; Eddie N. Williams, "Black Political Progress in the 1970s: The Electoral Arena," in Michael B. Preston, Lenneal J. Henderson, Jr., and Paul Puryear, eds., *The New Black Politics* (Longman, New York, 1982), 103.

The elections not only thrust a conservative Republican into the White House, but they also spelled defeat for several prominent liberal Democrats in the Senate. Control of the upper chamber shifted to the GOP, which secured a net gain of 12 seats for a total of 53. Among the losers were Gaylord Nelson of Wisconsin, Birch Bayh of Indiana, Frank Church of Idaho, and George McGovern of South Dakota, all of whom had been counted on as civil rights supporters in the past. The new Senate included an additional four Republicans from the South, which mirrored the improved GOP fortunes in the region in presidential and statewide elections. Perhaps as distressing to black reformers as the upsurge of conservatism in the Senate, the Republican majority resulted in the selection of Strom Thurmond of South Carolina as chair of the powerful Judiciary Committee. Though Thurmond had made some accommodations to the black electorate that had swelled in his state since his Dixiecrat bid for the presidency in 1948, he still favored a sharp curtailment in federal spending and a relaxation of civil rights laws in the South.

On a slightly more encouraging note, the elections saw a net increase of one member in the Congressional Black Caucus, bringing its total to 18. Losing one nonvoting delegate seat from the Virgin Islands, the caucus picked up two new representatives from Los Angeles and Chicago. Another two seats passed from one black to another, while the rest were retained by incumbents. (Two years earlier Senator Edward Brooke of Massachusetts had lost his reelection bid for a third term.) Overall, the Democrats kept their majority in the House, 243–192, though the Republicans gained 13 new legislators. At state and local levels, black officeholders grew by 2.6 percent to 5,020, still a modest figure but markedly higher than the 1,185 officials who had held office in 1969.

The Reagan Assault and Hard Times

Reagan's first term witnessed an expected assault on the racial front. The President set the tone of his administration in his appointment policy. Although he selected a black, Samuel Pierce, to sit in his Cabinet as Secretary of Housing and Urban Development, the chief executive disappointed black Republicans by falling short of reaching the number of top-level minority appointments made under Carter. Not merely the quantity but the ideological bent of the appointments troubled civil rights proponents. In making selections the President picked individuals who shared his concern that civil rights programs be limited in scope and not be used to practice "reverse discrimination."

Signaling this shift in direction was his handling of the Commission on Civil Rights. He turned this respected, independent investigative agency, operating since 1957 as a strong advocate for bold racial policies, into an organization that trumpeted the administration's retreat from affirmative remedies to combat the effects of racial bias in employment and education. To preside over this change, Reagan selected Clarence Pendleton as chair of the commission. A black Democrat turned Republican, Pendleton had worked for the Model Cities Program and served as executive director of the Urban League branch in San Diego, California. Despite his background, Pendleton denounced the notion that "all minority progress comes out of a civil rights or social service gun." He opposed busing and affirmative action as "bankrupt" policies, and argued that the "only way for blacks to get a real piece of the action is to get out there and compete in the marketplace and not rely solely on handouts and political favoritism."

As a defender of the free enterprise system and an opponent of restrictive federal regulation, the chief executive sought to weaken government enforcement of affirmative action plans for hiring minorities. Though Reagan intensely disliked compensatory programs, the Supreme Court had upheld, with qualifications, the principle of affirmative action in *Bakke* and in a series of cases following it. As recently as 1980, the high tribunal sustained congressional legislation requiring that at least 10 percent of all federal funds for public works projects go to minority contractors in order to rectify past discrimination. The Reagan administration tried to confine the impact of such rulings. The administration narrowed the coverage of its affirmative action guidelines to exclude federal vendors with fewer than 250 employees whereas previously the regulations had applied to firms with a minimum of 50 workers. According to the secretary of labor, the new standard exempted 75 percent of federal contractors. In a similar vein, William Bradford Reynolds, the assistant attorney general in charge of the Civil Rights Division, signaled an even further pullback from the concept of affirmative action as a legitimate means of promoting the constitutional rights of exploited groups. Reynolds opposed policies that entitled blacks and other minorities to benefits strictly on the basis of their race. Under his direction, the Justice Department office chiefly responsible for civil rights enforcement sought to provide employment relief only to individuals who could prove they had personally suffered from discrimination.

The Reagan administration also damaged civil rights interests by attempting to reverse a longstanding policy concerning racial discrimination in education. Since the 1960s, private academies had sprouted in the South as a refuge for white students fleeing court-ordered desegregation of public schools. In 1970, after the judiciary refused to allow segregated private academies the benefit of a federal tax exemption, the Internal Revenue Service promulgated regulations to carry out that decree. However, in January 1982, the President instructed the IRS to restore tax-exempt status to private schools like Bob Jones University, a religious institution in South Carolina that admitted blacks but banned interracial dating between coeds. The President agreed with the university's claim that removal of the tax exemption interfered with the First Amendment freedom of the school to practice its religious beliefs. Reagan's order, which nonetheless smacked of racism, also stemmed from his conservative opposition to government interference with private enterprise and to the establishment of coercive guidelines for mandating racial quotas in schools. After influential lawmakers and civil rights lobbyists fired a heavy round of criticism against Reagan's proposal, the President backed off. The Supreme Court eventually decided the issue against Reagan's position by approving the original IRS ruling denying tax exemptions to private schools that engaged in racial discrimination even if the policy conflicted with their religious practices.

The major political battle between Reagan and his civil rights opponents occurred over renewal of the Voting Rights Act. For black Americans this landmark law had come to represent one of the last vestiges of federal commitment to racial advancement in an era of diminishing expectations, and they considered the measure essential for continuing to open up government to minority participation. As the Reagan administration slashed the budget with deep cuts in social programs, critics looked to the power of the ballot as a crucial means of challenging these reductions. "The only real safety net that minorities and the poor can rely on is their capacity to influence the political system," remarked Eddie N. Williams, the president of the Joint Center for Political Studies. Toward that end, the suffrage statute had effectively eliminated the major barriers to voter registration, but its enforcement machinery was still necessary to combat a new generation of obstacles – at-large elections, racial gerrymandering, discriminatory annexations – that diluted the strength of minority ballots cast at the polls.

With the Act due for renewal in 1982, with Reagan in the White House, and with Republicans in control of the Senate, the bill's supporters took the precaution of starting their efforts a full year in advance. In addition to undertaking the customary fight to retain the special provisions requiring prior federal clearance of electoral changes and keeping designated jurisdictions from escaping coverage prematurely, the suffragists pursued a new challenge. In 1980, in a slim 5-to-4 decision, the Supreme Court ruled that in suits involving at-large election procedures, civil rights litigants had to prove that a municipality deliberately intended to weaken the vote of minorities. This opinion, in *City of Mobile v. Bolden*, posed a particular problem for blacks because most of the disputed at-large rules had been passed at the turn of the century, and their framers had usually couched their intentions in racially neutral language and in the spirit of reform. In contrast to this burdensome standard of proof, black plaintiffs and their attorneys wanted courts to judge the legality of at-large elections by their effect in permitting or denying blacks the opportunity to choose members of their own race to represent them. Thus, suffrage proponents wanted Congress to amend the Voting Rights Act to direct the judiciary to make discriminatory result as well as intent the standard for proving electoral bias.

The Reagan administration took a position on renewal that conformed with its opposition to race-conscious affirmative action remedies. In October 1981, after the House passed a ten-year-extension proposal containing a provision for an "effects" test in vote dilution suits, the President sought to persuade the Republican-dominated Senate to modify it. The administration and its supporters charged that the bill's result-minded approach would promote proportional representation, which the President warned "would come down to whether all of society had to have an actual quota system" of minority elected officials. Echoing this view, the foes of "preferential treatment" portrayed themselves as standing for the true meaning of civil rights: the "color-blind ideal of equal opportunity for all."

Defenders of the measure denied any design to impose racial quotas on the electoral system. In contrast to the administration's, their view of equal opportunity allowed, indeed required, the government to take racial considerations into account in order to overcome the current effects of past discrimination. They believed that the Constitution safeguarded individual as well as group rights within the political process. The suffrage coalition, composed of the Congressional Black Caucus and civil rights, liberal, and labor groups, insisted that the bill did not sanction proportional representation or quotas, but only enabled the courts to consider whether certain rules had an unfair impact in lowering the chances for minorities to elect candidates of their own race. A civil rights attorney from Atlanta thought it inappropriate to raise the issue of proportional representation, "just as it is also pretty irrelevant to talk about any realistic opportunity within the existing electoral system because black voters had always been shut out, pure and simple."

From this clash of arguments, the Senate hammered out a compromise. Within the Republican majority, a contingent of racial moderates was not willing to abandon blacks, especially in their quest for something so basic to democracy as the right to vote. Led by Robert Dole of Kansas, the upper chamber agreed to an effect-oriented approach that permitted the courts to examine the "totality of circumstances" resulting in the denial of equal electoral opportunity for minorities. In practice, this reestablished the judicial standard in operation before the *Mobile* decision. At the same time, the lawmakers specifically rejected proportional representation as a valid remedy and affirmed their commitment to the Voting Rights Act by renewing it for another 25 years, the longest extension to date.

The final outcome illustrated that despite recent setbacks, blacks still commanded political influence in preserving hard-earned fundamental rights of citizenship. This was particularly evident in the South. With most southern senators refusing to join the filibuster waged by Jesse Helms, a North Carolina Republican, the obstructionist ploy failed miserably. Only four senators from Dixie, three Republicans and one independent, steadfastly declined to approve the measure, and even Strom Thurmond saw fit to cast his first vote ever in favor of a civil rights law. The expanded black electorate in the South, which served as a crucial balance of power in sending legislators to Washington, once again swayed the majority of the region's congressional lawmakers to stand behind the suffrage law. Given this overwhelming mandate, President Reagan signed the bill, praising it as proof of "our unbending commitment to voting rights."

Nevertheless, like Nixon before him, Reagan supported the principle of enfranchisement while attempting to weaken its implementation. Though the Justice Department continued to enforce the statute in conformity with the general policy outlines established by previous administrations, Assistant Attorney General Reynolds interpreted his responsibilities narrowly in clearing electoral procedures submitted by the South. He attempted to raise the standard for demonstrating racial discrimination and to shift the burden of proving it from state and local officials onto the victims. However, as was the case during the Nixon years, civil rights activists successfully persuaded both Congress and the Supreme Court to hold the Justice Department to strict enforcement of the law.

The Reagan administration's policies had a more devastating effect on the economic well-being of blacks than on their political clout. During his first two years in office, Reagan adopted anti-inflationary, budget-slashing programs that succeeded in bringing prices under control at the expense of rising unemployment. African Americans suffered disproportionately. In 1982, over 17 percent of the black workforce could not find jobs, compared with 8.6 percent for whites. The ratio of black families living in poverty jumped from 32.4 percent to 35.7 percent, about three times the figure for impoverished whites. Black poverty continued to be associated with female-headed households: 56 percent of black women (compared with 36 percent of white women) who headed families fell below the subsistence level. The last two years of Reagan's first term brought a measure of economic recovery, but blacks still suffered harshly. Unemployment fell to about 14 percent, and the proportion of the poverty-stricken declined to just under 34 percent. These "improvements," however, did not enable black families to close the gap between their income and that of white families. By the mid-1980s, black families earned a median income of 57.6 percent of whites', a ratio about the same as at the beginning of the decade.

Although part of the deterioration in black material conditions could be attributed to structural defects affecting the American economy in general, the Reagan administration exacerbated the problems. Drastic cuts in or outright elimination of job programs like CETA; reductions in food stamp distribution, health services, and welfare eligibility; and the removal of guaranteed student loans punched holes in the "safety net" of federal assistance to low-income workers and the poor. For instance, rollbacks in educational support were reflected in the decline in black matriculation in four-year colleges from 10.4 percent in 1978 to 9.2 percent in 1984. Not surprisingly then, a 1982 public opinion survey revealed that 85 percent of blacks believed the Reagan administration was going too far in slicing government spending for social welfare programs. In contrast, only 37 percent of whites shared this view.

The President's fiscal policies also accentuated class divisions within the black community. During the 1970s, expanding opportunities arising from desegregation and affirmative action programs had swelled the size of the black middle class, at the same time as the number of poor black families increased. While the share of black families earning more than $50,000 annually nearly doubled – from 4.5 percent in 1970 to 8.8 percent – by the mid-1980s, the number of black households with incomes under $10,000 comprised 30.3 percent of the total, a leap of 11 percent. To achieve middle-class status, black families depended on two wage earners and employment in public-sector jobs to a greater degree than did white middle-class households. The recession and budget cuts of Reagan's first two years in office hurt both the poor who relied on declining welfare assistance and middle-class families dependent upon government employment. But the economic recovery after 1982 mostly aided middle-class blacks who had the skills and educational background to take advantage of the new job openings.

In stark contrast to the majority of African Americans and their elected representatives, some middle-class black professionals and businesspeople endorsed Reagan's conservative brand of government retrenchment and free-market economics. Such notable intellectuals as Thomas Sowell, an economics professor at Stanford University, lent their voices to the attack on affirmative action and welfare programs. Like Reagan, they blamed the enduring poverty in black communities on New Deal–Great Society liberalism. According to their viewpoint, these programs reduced individual incentive to find jobs and fostered out-of-wedlock births and single-parent households. These black "neoconservatives" charged established black political and civil rights leaders with perpetuating this cycle of government dependency and called upon African Americans to help themselves by adopting traditional values of individual initiative, competition, and hard work. Agreeing that black communities should do more to solve their own problems, their opponents responded to this criticism by accusing Reagan's conservative supporters of blaming the victims for the social ills resulting from generations of systematic racism and economic exploitation in the United States.

Harold Washington, Chicago, and the Politics of Renewal

In the political arena, blacks had been struggling to gain greater electoral power in their communities since the early days of the civil rights movement. In the decade and a half following passage of the 1965 Voting Rights Act, black politicians had been striving to put into practice many of the goals of the freedom struggle. Much remained to be done. The damaging impact of the Reagan retrenchment helped reenergize blacks at the local level to seek to gain a fair share of the scarce economic resources available. At the same time, the black electorate looked forward to the possibility of challenging Reagan's reelection and moving the White House in a progressive direction more compatible with their interests and needs.

The city of Chicago provided an excellent opportunity for blacks to lead the way in revitalizing African-American politics. Since the New Deal, blacks had served as clients of the Democratic machine that ran the "Windy City," an arrangement that afforded them some influence in municipal affairs without any real power. Their elected leaders, such as Congressman William Dawson, had faithfully delivered the black vote for the organization's candidates and in return received the spoils of patronage and access to city hall. Their constituents obtained the benefits typically conferred by political machines, but these token rewards for their loyalty failed to make up for city officials' neglect of widespread problems of poor housing, inferior education, and lack of police protection. In fact, black collaboration with the dominant white machine had not prevented Chicago's neighborhoods and schools from becoming among the most segregated in the nation.

For two decades following his election as mayor, in 1955, Richard J. Daley, the "Boss," displayed the power of the machine to manage black politics and stifle challenges to its rule. Daley, who had first won victory largely on the strength of black votes, operated a kind of "plantation politics" that treated blacks as subjects rather than equal ruling partners and placed white interests ahead of black concerns. One of his black critics who successfully broke from the machine described the mayor as a "plantation master ... who keeps his darkies loyal to him by doling out small political favors ... [and] is playing the same old 'divide and conquer' game his forefathers experienced when they made some slaves 'house servants' and kept others out in the field." In the mid-1960s, when civil rights leaders launched a determined attack on racial discrimination in housing and education, Daley drew upon his black machine loyalists to help outmaneuver the insurgents. Even Martin Luther King, Jr., who, in 1966, had been invited by local civil rights leaders to direct the campaign against racism, proved little match for the "Boss" and his entrenched black political allies.

However, during the 1970s black Chicagoans showed increasing signs of independence from machine domination. In 1972, a disgruntled black electorate aided in the defeat of the incumbent state's attorney, Edward V. Hanrahan, a law-and-order candidate. A few years earlier he had authorized a raid against the militant Black Panthers that left two of their leaders dead, including Fred Hampton, and four wounded under questionable circumstances. Black voters also successfully challenged the Daley organization in several congressional and aldermanic contests. The greatest chance for blacks to declare their political independence came only after the death of Mayor Daley, in 1976. In a special election to choose Daley's successor, black voters lined up behind the machine-picked candidate, but three years later over 60 percent cast their ballots for Jane Byrne, who ran without the Democratic organization's backing against the incumbent.

These encouraging signs notwithstanding, blacks still remained subject to the effects of machine rule. The organization had depended on low levels of black participation so that its ward heelers and precinct captains could most effectively control those who bothered to show up at the polls. Furthermore, by placing the party's interests above the needs of the minority community, machine politicians discouraged many blacks from seeing how their electoral participation might make a difference in improving their lives. In 1977, only 27.5 percent of eligible blacks turned out to vote for mayor despite the candidacy of an antimachine black, State Senator Harold Washington. Two years later, the black turnout scarcely climbed to 34 percent. Racial polarization compounded the problem for blacks. In elections that pitted the races against each other, black contestants stood very little chance of attracting white votes to achieve a winning margin.

For blacks the Byrne administration proved to be a severe disappointment. Once installed in power, the mayor made her peace with the Democratic regulars and dashed any hope of reform. Instead, she tried to diminish the voting strength of blacks on the city council, and replaced black appointees on municipal boards with whites. Although blacks had contributed to her mayoral victory, she calculated that her chances for reelection were greater if she mobilized white ethnic voters, who had long supported the Democratic organization. These moves galvanized black activists to oppose the mayor. In June 1982, they mounted a well-publicized and highly coordinated boycott of Byrne's ChicagoFest, a summer festival and exposition designed to promote local business. This successful display of unity encouraged blacks to transform their protest activities into an electoral movement challenging the mayor at the polls. One of the boycott's organizers, the Reverend Jesse Jackson, of Operation PUSH, expressed the anger of blacks who felt neglected by city hall politicians: "We are not bound by Chicago plantation politics. We must aggressively use our dollars and our votes."

Merging protest and electoral politics, Chicago blacks struggled for empowerment with a fervor reminiscent of the civil rights era. As they had in the South during the 1960s, voter registration drives rallied blacks around a common battle for freedom. The task was much bigger than getting people to exercise their civic responsibility of voting; it aimed, as one black leader asserted, "to accomplish a dramatic shift in the political scales in favor of those who have been ignored, used, and abused for too long." Showing the way, an alliance of groups representing Chicago's poorest, most politically disfranchised neighborhoods emerged to conduct voter enrollment campaigns. People Organized for Welfare and Employment Rights (POWER), an organization originally established to protest cutbacks in state welfare funding, spearheaded the registration drives by operating in public assistance offices and unemployment centers. More than 200 community groups helped get their message across to congregations in black churches and to audiences listening to "soul" stations on the radio. Largely as a result of this impressive grassroots coalition, by the fall of 1982 around 150,000 blacks had added their names to the suffrage lists. Moreover, this community-wide campaign succeeded in bringing up the enrollment of eligible blacks to just over 86 percent, a figure that exceeded the 78 percent registration rate for whites.

This surge in enrollment placed blacks in a strong position to unseat Mayor Byrne in her bid for reelection in 1983. By this time, the black population had grown to 40 percent in the city; Hispanics constituted another 12 percent of its residents. As in other places with a large African-American population, black Chicagoans entertained serious hopes for electing a member of their race as mayor. Owing once again to a formidable display of community organizing and group solidarity, blacks chose a consensus candidate to compete for city hall. Under the direction of Chicago Black United Communities, over 30,000 blacks had participated in surveys to determine whom they desired to run. From what amounted to a carefully planned but informal plebiscite, Harold Washington emerged as the top choice from over 90 prominent names.

Washington commanded respect for his extensive political experience. A graduate of Northwestern University Law School, he had served as a member of the Illinois legislature and as a representative in Congress. Once an ally of the Daley machine, he had broken away to establish strong credentials as an independent reformer who spoke out for liberal, consumer, and civil rights causes. Elected to Congress in 1980, he fought for extension of the Voting Rights Act and battled against the Reagan administration's spending cuts for jobs and welfare assistance. In 1977, Washington had run in the Democratic primary for mayor, but with the black electorate poorly mobilized, he received only 11 percent of the total vote. Heartened by the outpouring of new registrants in 1982 and convinced that this time he had a chance to win, the congressman agreed to run. In doing so, he reminded blacks that after years of giving white candidates their votes without receiving an adequate share of power in return, the point had arrived when "it's our turn." Though constructing his campaign on a solid black foundation, Washington fully realized that he needed progressive white and Hispanic votes to win in a city where blacks composed a minority of the population.

Against all odds and predictions, Washington won a narrow victory in the Democratic primary against two prominent white contenders. In addition to Byrne, the congressman faced Richard M. Daley, the son of the former mayor, who considered himself his father's rightful successor. In this three-way contest, Washington captured 37 percent of the ballots to 33 percent for the incumbent and 30 percent for the heir of the "Boss." The white vote divided nearly evenly between Byrne and Daley, while the congressman garnered nearly 85 percent of the black votes. The victor benefited from the outpouring to the polls of newly registered blacks. In 1983, the turnout of blacks in the primary soared to 64 percent of the voting-age population, up from 34 percent in the previous Democratic mayoral race. Approximately 56 percent of Washington's black voters reported that they had registered during the massive enrollment drives of the year before. Though the white turnout rate had also grown since 1979, it had fallen five percentage points behind that of blacks. The winner also secured about 12 percent of the Hispanic and 4 percent of white ballots cast, but their combined votes amounted to slightly less than his margin of victory. Thus, Washington won on the strength of unprecedented support from blacks and the close split in the white vote for his opponents.

Customarily, the winner of the Democratic primary in Chicago was a sure bet to triumph over the Republican in the general election, but when that winner was black all wagers were off. As the earlier contest had shown, the electorate in Chicago voted mainly along racial lines. In a city where whites comprised over 53 percent of the registered voters, unless Washington made greater inroads among whites and Latinos than he had in the primary, he stood a good chance of losing. This was especially true in a showdown with a single white opponent around whom the majority white electorate could unite.

The Republican candidate, State Representative Bernard Epton, made Washington's character and race the dominant campaign issues. Hammering away at Washington's ethics, the GOP nominee attacked his rival's record, which included a conviction for income tax evasion and a suspension of his law license. By the usual standards of Chicago's political morality these indiscretions, for which Washington acknowledged his mistakes, were relatively minor. However, most whites were willing to abandon their party's nominee more so on the basis of his skin color than his ethical transgressions. One of the many Democratic officials who defected from Washington justified his decision in this way: "The people in my area just don't want a black mayor – it's as simple as that." Epton's campaign supporters fed on this racial animosity by adopting the slogan "Epton for Mayor. Before It's Too Late," and by passing out handbills warning in vulgar language that a takeover of city hall would spell doom for Chicago. These negative comments prompted Washington to respond in kind, and he attacked Epton's integrity, his cozy legislative relationship with private insurance companies, and his emotional stability. At the same time, the congressman took the higher road in urging reform-minded white voters to join his campaign assault against the Democratic machine.

On election day, Washington won with a fraction over 50 percent of the votes cast in the closest mayoral clash since 1919. As expected, the voting was polarized by race. The Democratic nominee owed his victory to the nearly unanimous backing (99.5 percent) he received from blacks, which accounted for approximately 77 percent of his total vote. Not only did Washington's candidacy attract solid black approval, but it also succeeded in mobilizing an extraordinarily high black turnout of 73 percent of the voting-age population, surpassing the white figure of 67 percent. In contrast, Epton obtained 95 percent of his ballots from whites, and the Republican candidate won over eight out of ten white Democrats. The victor scored poorly among the city's Irish, Italian, and Polish voters, the mainstays of the Daley machine, who deserted the black Democratic candidate in droves to back Epton. Their racial fears and animosities were strong enough to override their traditional ethnic allegiances to whoever triumphed in the Democratic primary. "They responded to Washington's race rather than to his partisan affiliation," Dianne Pinderhughes concluded. "They became whites, as opposed to Americans of European descent." A disappointed Washington reached the same conclusion. "Ain't it a bitch," he groaned in response to his meager white support, "to be a black man in the land of the free and the home of the brave."

Yet there were key exceptions to the racial division at the polls that helped cement Washington's slender 46,000-vote victory. The triumphant mayor-elect captured almost three-quarters of the Hispanic vote. The more than 45,000 votes marked a stunning jump six times greater than the number he had garnered in the primary. In addition, Washington won a small but sufficient portion of whites to his side. About 12 percent of those who participated provided more than double the number of white ballots

Figure 16 The inauguration of Harold Washington. Cook County Circuit Court Judge Charles Freeman swears in Chicago's first African-American mayor, Harold Washington, during a ceremony attended by 3,000 guests at Navy Pier. Washington, who was 61 years old, succeeded Chicago's first female mayor, Jane Byrne. (Photo © Bettmann/Corbis)

cast for him in the Democratic primary. A large share of these votes came from liberal Jews who put race and religion aside (Epton was Jewish) and welcomed Washington's reform message.

Washington captured the mayor's office, but he did not immediately gain control over the city government. Democrats on the municipal council outnumbered Washington supporters and brawled them to a stalemate. These heated battles reminded one journalist of "Mississippi in 1964, where the Freedom Democratic Party challenged the segregationist regulars." After court-ordered redistricting left the pro- and anti-Washington factions at equal strength, the mayor was able to cast tie-breaking votes in his favor. Like other black mayors in major cities throughout the country, Washington recognized that he needed the cooperation of influential white civic leaders in order to govern, and he brought them into his ruling partnership with blacks, Latinos, and reformers to replace the old party stalwarts.

The mayor promoted the financial development of Chicago, which most profited the city's elites, while at the same time he did not neglect minority economic concerns. He initiated a vigorous affirmative action program in municipal hiring and in awarding government contracts, which aided black businesspeople and professionals. Also, he continued to work to relieve the plight of working-class and poor blacks, who had constituted the backbone of his candidacy and election. Though many problems lingered, the reform mayor took significant steps to increase the availability of low-income housing and provide such public services as healthcare and police protection more equitably than in the past.[3]

Much of the pattern in Washington's election was repeated in the victory of W. Wilson Goode as the first black mayor of Philadelphia, in May 1983. Goode had compiled a strong record as chair of the Pennsylvania Public Utility Commission and as managing director of Philadelphia. In a city in which blacks comprised 40 percent of the population, he competed in the Democratic primary against the former mayor, Frank Rizzo, the darling of the city's white ethnic groups, who had inflamed racial passions during his two previous terms in office. Surprisingly, this contest did not witness the bitter racial rhetoric of the Chicago campaign. In beating Rizzo with 53 percent of the votes, Goode did slightly better than Washington had against Epton. He galvanized black voters into turning out in high numbers. He received 98 percent of their ballots, and secured a small but slightly higher proportion of white crossover support than his Chicago counterpart. Having won the mayoral nomination in this largely Democratic city, the black candidate went on to victory with 55 percent of the vote in the general election against two white candidates. Yet Goode encountered strong racial sentiment against him. The election returns indicated that white ethnic voters in the City of Brotherly Love were just as strongly opposed to Goode as were their ethnic cousins in Chicago to Mayor Washington.

The racial consciousness and solidarity tapped by Washington and Goode in their respective campaigns also were evident in the heightened efforts of blacks throughout the nation to become politically engaged. The victories in Chicago and Philadelphia convinced many blacks that their votes could make a difference. In addition to such positive reinforcement,

---

[3]   In 1987, Mayor Washington won reelection to a second term, but shortly thereafter, he suffered a fatal heart attack. His death occasioned a power struggle in the city council to choose a successor. The black alderman Eugene Sawyer was selected, largely with white support, while the majority of black legislators favored another candidate, Timothy Evans. In 1989, the effects of this battle still divided the Sawyer and Evans forces within the black community, which led to the election of Richard M. Daley as mayor.

African Americans had an increased incentive to vent their negative feelings toward the Reagan administration at the ballot box. The success of the civil rights coalition in strengthening the Voting Rights Act against White House opposition focused renewed attention on the franchise as a key instrument in forwarding black interests.

Spurred on by anti-Reagan sentiments and rearmed with a powerful suffrage weapon, the NAACP, VEP, SCLC, and other organizations stepped up attempts to enroll additional black voters. The largest increases came in the South, where such intensive drives had taken place for over two decades. From 1980 to 1984, black voter registration in the region climbed by 14 percent, with the greatest gains occurring in the Voting Rights Act states of Alabama (37 percent), North Carolina (28 percent), and Mississippi (20 percent). Furthermore, throughout the country black political participation rose in response to active campaigning by black candidates for office and to heated state and local contests in which white politicians cultivated black votes. In the off-year congressional elections of 1982, minority turnout jumped by nearly 6 percent, a notable increase over the figure in 1978. Reflecting this revived spurt of interest, the number of black elected officials nationwide grew by 8.6 percent between 1982 and 1983, the steepest rise in seven years.

One of those winners, Harvey Gantt, became mayor of Charlotte, North Carolina, in 1983. He forged a coalition of blacks and whites to emerge victorious in this white-majority city. His career underscored the close connection between the civil rights struggle and electoral politics. As a youth in neighboring South Carolina, Gantt had participated in the early sit-in protests and become the first black student to desegregate Clemson University, where he received a degree in architecture. His generation, he remarked, is "the group now that are becoming the mayors." Though he had come to substitute negotiations for demonstrations as his preferred tactic, Gantt did not forget the lessons of his previous struggles. "I'm … a believer," the mayor affirmed, "in taking the benefits brought about by … all the other direct-action kinds of things and molding them into long-term, institutional changes that would occur, systematic changes that have occurred in our society."

This political reawakening stemmed from the desire of blacks to continue the process of empowerment that had begun with the emergence of the civil rights movement. As economic conditions deteriorated in the late 1970s and early 1980s, black communities mobilized to obtain a greater share of electoral power in order to meet the unfulfilled material needs of their residents. Though successful in many towns and cities across the nation, for the most part they had been unable to check the wave of political conservatism in national affairs ushered in by the Reagan administration. Blacks and their liberal white allies did hold onto many of their civil rights gains through victories in Congress and the judiciary. But as long as Reagan remained in office, the powerful institution of the presidency would continue to order priorities in a manner that limited advances toward racial equality. At a time when African Americans were flexing their political muscles locally, the goal of capturing the White House and reshaping its agenda became as natural as it was essential.

7

In Search of Legitimacy

In the four decades since World War II, African Americans gradually, though facing grudging opposition, had won a considerable measure of acceptance for their reenfranchisement as full citizens of the United States. Where blacks gained public office, including those at the head of major cities throughout the country, whites generally endorsed the validity of their rule. Undoubtedly, the struggle for political empowerment produced legislative conflicts in Washington and fierce opposition both in the South and the North, as witnessed in Chicago, but, overall, white Americans acknowledged the principle of majority rule and the sanctity of free elections. Whites have largely recognized, that is, the legitimacy of black political representation as an extension of democratic values and the norms of fair play. Moreover, these basic tenets of the political culture received reinforcement from the nation's Cold War ideology, which contrasted American freedom with Soviet totalitarianism. Condemning the Soviet Union for stifling free elections abroad, the United States could not easily tolerate racist restrictions on ballot boxes on its own shores. Besides, federal enforcement of the Voting Rights Act kept in check the resistance of those whites who stubbornly refused to concede the legitimacy of black political power.

Both the considerable progress blacks had made in the electoral arena and their frustration with not having achieved a great deal more prompted black political leaders to focus their attention on the battle for the White House. Within the American political system perhaps nothing reflects the legitimacy of minority-group participation more than competition for the presidency. "The Presidential election is the centerpiece of the U.S. political

Running for Freedom: Civil Rights and Black Politics in America since 1941,
Fourth Edition. Steven F. Lawson.
© 2015 John Wiley & Sons, Inc. Published 2015 by John Wiley & Sons, Inc.

process," the political scientist Mack H. Jones observed, "and therefore every discrete political faction should be expected to use the quadrennial election in some way to advance its interests." To the extent that American political leaders set out broad agendas and debate specific policy objectives, they do so during presidential elections. The chief executive, the nation's highest elected official, plays the key role in focusing attention on a problem, in identifying a course of action to address it, and in rallying legislative and public support behind efforts to solve it. Not since Lyndon Johnson had an occupant of the Oval Office assigned a high priority to the needs of blacks and other exploited groups. Unless the presidency once again became a platform for the cause of racial equality, African Americans would continue to find it hard to catch up politically and economically with other citizens.

Previously, the black electorate had wielded considerable influence in presidential elections and contributed significantly to the winning margins of Democratic nominees, most recently in the election of Jimmy Carter in 1976. Still, no black candidate had mounted a strong challenge for the top office in the land. Representative Shirley Chisholm of New York had actively campaigned in the Democratic presidential primaries in 1972, but her effort attracted scant support. Not only a black, she was also a woman in a nation that simply was unprepared to cast aside considerations of race and gender in selecting its chief executive. Having won reenfranchisement scarcely a few years before, blacks did not constitute a large enough bloc of voters to turn Chisholm's hopes into a serious bid. However, since the early 1970s black political muscle had developed sufficiently to elect mayors of major metropolitan areas as well as a growing contingent of county, state, and national lawmakers.

By the middle of Reagan's first term, the possibility of a black presidential challenge had begun to take shape. Upset by the President's economic policies, which disproportionately raised the level of black unemployment and poverty, influential blacks joined together to map out a strategy to combat those worsening conditions. After several months of discussions, on June 20, 1983, a group of elected officials, known as the Black Leadership Family, sponsored the idea of an African-American presidential bid. The mayoral victory of Harold Washington earlier in the year heavily shaped their thinking. His candidacy had served to mobilize the black electorate in record numbers and at the same time attracted enough Latinos and whites to form a winning coalition. "We've got to be involved in mainstream political activity," Washington declared. "That's what's happening here in Chicago. And that's the lesson that's going out across the country."

In striving for the presidency, blacks naturally looked to compete within the Democratic Party. Though black voters had occasionally supported moderate-to-liberal Republican candidates in local and state-wide elections, since the formation of FDR's New Deal coalition they had stood firmly behind Democratic presidential nominees. In 1980, blacks had accounted for about one-quarter of the ballots cast for Jimmy Carter, and they remained the most loyal element within the Democratic fold. The party of Roosevelt, Truman, Kennedy, and Johnson opened its doors to increased minority representation after 1964; however, many black Democrats believed increasingly that their party had come to take their votes for granted. Given their overwhelming support for Democratic standard-bearers, they expected to obtain more decision-making positions within the party and to fashion programs that more forcefully addressed black concerns. They also worried that Democratic officials, in the hope of recapturing the votes of white conservatives who had become Reagan Republicans, were seeking to modify their position at the expense of the black faithful. Thus, by contending for the Democratic presidential nomination, blacks hoped to boost their leverage within the party and help pick the candidate most sensitive to their interests.

Jesse Jackson for President

With these considerations in mind, the Reverend Jesse L. Jackson chose to launch his candidacy for the presidency. He received inspiration from the example of fellow Chicagoan Harold Washington. The mayor's come-from-behind victory, Jackson concluded, "demonstrated that while some will join us if we assert ourselves, without such aggressiveness no one else will lead our fight for equitable representation." He questioned whether Democratic leaders sufficiently appreciated the contribution blacks made to their party's fortunes. In the case of Washington, top national Democrats, such as Walter Mondale and Edward Kennedy, did not enter his corner until after he had beaten his white rivals in the primary and faced only a Republican hurdle to the city's highest office. Jackson believed that his candidacy would test whether white leaders were ready to accept blacks on an equal basis or whether blacks would continue to play a "Harlem Globetrotter" role, giving the Democratic Party "its soul, its excitement, its rhythm, its margin of victory, and yet not be allowed to set any policy."

Jackson's foray into electoral politics grew out of his involvement in the civil rights struggle of the 1960s. As a student at North Carolina Agricultural and Technical State University in Greensboro in the early 1960s, Jackson had led demonstrations in the city that spawned the sit-in movement. Subsequently, he became a staff member of the SCLC, and established his base of operations in Chicago after Dr. King directed a desegregation campaign there. He headed SCLC's Operation Breadbasket, a project that applied economic pressure on white-owned businesses to open up job opportunities for blacks, and on April 4, 1968, he was part of King's entourage when the civil rights leader was assassinated in Memphis. In the early 1970s, he broke with King's designated successor, the Reverend Ralph D. Abernathy, and created Operation PUSH as his own organization to carry on the work he had begun with the SCLC.

Though Jackson had not held public office in Chicago, he actively participated in its political life and supported the reform forces opposing the Daley machine. At the 1972 Democratic Convention, he was a coleader of the interracial group that successfully challenged the credentials and unseated the delegation headed by the Chicago boss. From his base of operations at PUSH, Jackson initiated economic boycotts, held voter registration drives, furnished campaign workers, and conducted a weekly radio broadcast that publicized concerns voiced by the black community. By linking protest with electoral politics and mobilizing local communities to shape national agendas, he carried on the tradition of the civil rights movement.

A minister himself, Jackson also reflected the close relationship between the black church and African-American politics. During the civil rights movement clergymen had opened their churches to mass meetings and voter registration drives and preached sermons that combined the themes of personal redemption through Christ with social justice through protest. The church was a critical component of the black liberation battle because it was one of the few institutions exclusively under black control and capable of reaching a mass audience. The Reverend Jackson underscored the historic importance of the church in reminding blacks that: "we were not brought from Africa to be white people's slaves. But perhaps [we] were sent here by God to save the nation." His political mission received the endorsement of the National Baptist Convention, the largest black religious body in the country, whose president, T. J. Jemison, had led a pioneering bus boycott in Baton Rouge in 1953.

More than an electoral campaign, Jackson's candidacy resembled a civil rights crusade. It attracted campaign staff such as the Reverend C. T. Vivian, who like Jackson had fought in the front lines of the freedom struggle during the 1960s. Many of those who worked on his behalf did so in recognition "of the unfulfilled objectives of Martin Luther King and the civil rights movement and to warn ... that the movement's earlier gains were in danger." And the candidate clearly tied his current challenge to past civil rights efforts. Shortly before announcing his intention to seek the presidency, at a rally honoring Dr. King and commemorating the twentieth anniversary of the March on Washington, Jackson revived the spirit of that historic occasion by proclaiming: "Our day has come. From slaveship to championship ... [f]rom the outhouse to the courthouse to the White House, we will march on."

Just as blacks once marched to recover the right to vote, they responded to Jackson's campaign by descending on courthouses and registration offices to sign up for the ballot. Jackson stirred memories of civil rights days by embarking on a "Southern Crusade" for voter registration that built upon the intensive local efforts of civic groups and civil rights organizations, such as the NAACP, to enroll additional blacks. He also took every available opportunity to prod the Reagan Justice Department to enforce the Voting Rights Act more vigorously, and he even succeeded in cajoling Assistant Attorney General William Bradford Reynolds to travel to Mississippi and witness suffrage violations for himself. In one notable instance, the persistent Jackson persuaded the usually reticent Reynolds to join him in singing "We Shall Overcome" at a rally. In the 11 southern states some 1.3 million new black voters registered between 1980 and 1984 (see Table 7.1), with a considerable share of them lured out by Jackson's appeal. One survey indicated that 67 percent of recent registrants attributed their interest in enrolling to the Jackson campaign.

His roots deeply sunk into the soil of civil rights, Jackson ventured to cultivate the field of presidential politics. According to a member of his campaign staff, Jackson's "genius lay in linking nonelectoral forms of political mobilization and protest with traditional electoral politics." The minister's charismatic personality, his ability to arouse masses of blacks at rallies and voter registration drives, and his support network in churches throughout black communities furnished him with valuable resources to attract a substantial following. By a wide margin over any other contender, 51 percent of African Americans rated him the most important black leader in the United States. However, the ability to mount effective protests and deliver inspiring oratory would not translate into real victories at the ballot box without a campaign that reached out to a broad segment of the

Table 7.1 Estimated percentage of voting-age blacks registered in the South,1968–1984

	1968	1976	1980	1982	1984
Alabama	56.7	58.4	55.8	69.7	74.0
Arkansas	67.5	94.0	57.2	63.9	67.2
Florida	62.1	61.1	58.3	59.7	63.4
Georgia	56.1	74.8	48.6	50.4	57.9
Louisiana	59.3	63.0	60.7	61.1	65.7
Mississippi	54.4	60.7	62.3	64.2	77.1
North Carolina	55.3	54.8	51.3	50.9	65.4
South Carolina	50.8	56.5	53.7	53.9	58.5
Tennessee	72.8	66.4	64.0	66.1	69.9
Texas	83.1	65.0	56.0	49.5	71.5
Virginia	58.4	54.7	53.2	49.5	62.3
All states	**62.0**	**63.1**	**55.8**	**56.5**	**66.2**

Sources: The 1968 figures are from David Garrow, *Protest at Selma* (Yale University Press, New Haven, Conn., 1978), 189. The remaining figures are from US Department of Commerce, Bureau of the Census, *Statistical Abstract of the United States,* annual (Washington, DC), 1976, 406; 1981, 495; 1982–3, 488; 1986, 257.

Democratic electorate and brought large numbers of voters to the polls. Furthermore, as a civil rights organizer Jackson could devise novel tactics aimed at producing social change from outside the conventional political system, but as an aspirant for his party's nomination he had to operate within the confines of the Democratic organization and play by its rules. Ballots, not ballyhoo, counted in electoral victories.

Jackson acknowledged these political realities and sought to expand his base beyond the black community. He tried to fashion a "rainbow coalition" that attracted the dispossessed of all races – poor whites, Latinos, Native Americans, and Asians, as well as blacks. He hoped to draw upon those elements of the Democratic Party that felt locked out of the process of decision-making. Intending to shift the ideological tilt of the party toward the left, Jackson argued that it could win against the conservative and popular Reagan only by gaining the backing of the millions of Americans who felt disaffected and no longer bothered to cast a ballot. In 1980, Reagan had won in 16 states by a margin of victory of less than 5 percent. A Democratic candidate who enticed higher percentages of ordinarily nonparticipating blacks and whites to the voting booths, he argued, could improve the party's presidential outlook in 1984.

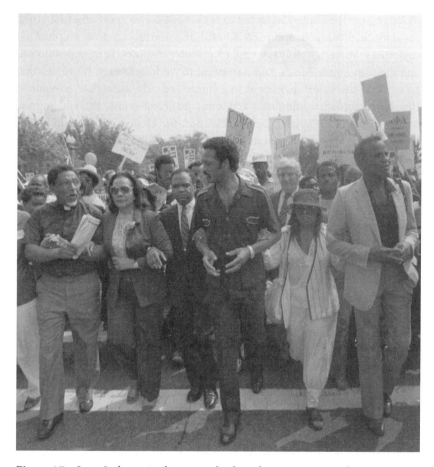

Figure 17 Jesse Jackson, in the center, leading the procession at the 1983 march on Washington. Next to him, from left to right, are Walter Fauntroy, the Washington, DC, delegate to Congress; Coretta Scott King, widow of the slain civil rights leader; Joseph Lowery, president of the SCLC; an unidentified woman; and Harry Belafonte. (AP Photo/Press Association)

Working with an assortment of civil rights activists, community organizers, antinuclear advocates, feminists, and others who championed progressive social causes, Jackson devised a "rainbow" agenda to incorporate into the Democratic platform. In the manner of Dr. King, he attacked a host of ills – racism, militarism, and materialism – that plagued not only blacks but all Americans. Making peace a priority, Jackson criticized Reagan's aggressive Cold War policies and called for stepped-up negotiations with the Soviets, a pledge from the United States not to deploy nuclear weapons in a first-strike capacity, a revamped approach toward the Caribbean that emphasized diplomacy instead of military might to resolve disputes, firm opposition to apartheid in South Africa, and a solution to Middle Eastern hostilities that recognized the Palestinian right to a homeland. The candidate envisioned that peace abroad would foster economic justice at home. By reducing the military budget 20 percent, Jackson claimed, the United States could reallocate its financial resources to create jobs and assist the poor. He would replace Reaganism, with its tax advantages for the wealthy and its deregulation of large corporations, with an economics of compassion that favored working people and the impoverished.

The prominent place that Jackson gave to foreign affairs reflected a long-standing black tradition. Throughout the twentieth century, various black leaders, from W. E. B. Du Bois and Marcus Garvey to Malcolm X and Martin Luther King, Jr., had spoken out about issues connecting African Americans to nonwhite people in the rest of the world. Du Bois promoted Pan-Africanism and a unity of people of color around the globe. Garvey and Malcolm stressed the racial heritage blacks derived from Africa and the Middle East, and King opposed the Vietnam war for the damage it inflicted on nonwhites in Southeast Asia. Black groups, even the moderate NAACP, opposed colonialism in Africa, the Middle East, and Asia and lobbied for the US to oppose imperialism. As recently as the Carter administration, United Nations Ambassador Andrew Young, a former top assistant to Dr. King, had sought to open diplomatic channels to the Palestine Liberation Organization, an enemy of Israel, without success. Moreover, civil rights leaders had used the rhetoric of democracy and freedom associated with two world wars and the Cold War to convince the federal government to extend those beliefs to African Americans at home.

In running for president, Jackson believed the key to changes in domestic and foreign politics came through political empowerment of alienated Americans. Notwithstanding that many of his proposals were considered too radical for mainstream Democrats, the candidate reflected the traditional liberal position that the remedy to social and economic problems rested in the ballot. In this vein, he made vigorous enforcement of the Voting Rights Act central to his campaign. An electorate that was expanded to include more blacks, Latinos, and poor people would presumably enhance the election possibilities of candidates sympathetic to progressive goals. If that happened, Jackson foresaw a chain of events producing sweeping reforms throughout society. For example, responsive elected officials would pass the equal rights amendment, and "since 70 percent of all poor children live in a house headed by a woman where there is no man," Jackson contended, "to enfranchise women is to protect children." Furthermore, he envisioned women workers allying themselves with organized labor to end state right-to-work laws that hampered union organization. Thus, through beefed-up implementation of the Voting Rights Act, a measure originally crafted to help blacks, other exploited groups in society would ultimately gain protection and security.

Jackson's assault on the runoff primary fit in with this line of thinking. Used chiefly in the South, this procedure required that if no candidate received a majority of the vote on the first ballot, a second contest be held between the two top contenders to determine the winner. Generally, this system had come into effect at the beginning of the twentieth century during a period of one-party rule, when victory in the Democratic primary was tantamount to election, although Georgia had adopted it as recently as 1964. It was also part of a package of racially inspired laws that successfully disfranchised black southerners. After blacks regained the right to vote and began competing in Democratic primaries against a field of white candidates, they often found their path blocked by the majority runoff requirement. A black officeseeker might gain a plurality in the first election, especially if whites split their votes among several candidates, only to lose in a head-to-head contest with the remaining white opponent, as the electorate divided along racial lines. Where blacks comprised a minority of the voters their chances of winning a second primary were slim. Keeping in mind that candidates such as Harold Washington might not have won if they had had to survive a runoff primary, Jackson urged the elimination of this practice.

In addition, he wanted to change Democratic Party rules that hampered minority contestants like himself in pursuing the presidential nomination. The Democrats required that primary candidates obtain at least 20 percent of the vote cast in a congressional district to gain a single delegate to the national convention. In only 86 of 425 congressional districts did the black population reach 25 percent of the total, barely enough to aid a black aspirant. Consequently, Jackson sought to convince Democratic leaders to lower the threshold requirement to no more than 15 percent, but they failed to agree. The unwillingness to revise this rule meant that a candidate might not achieve delegate strength approximating his or her primary vote. As it later turned out, Jackson obtained 18 percent of the popular vote, but his share of convention delegates amounted to only 10 percent.

Although the "rainbow" alliance had a distinctly black hue, Jackson's support among blacks was far from unanimous in 1984. A Gallup poll revealed that 59 percent of black Democrats preferred Jackson, but a hefty 34 percent favored Walter Mondale, Carter's vice president, who had strong ties to the liberal-labor wing of the party. Those black politicians most closely linked to national Democratic affairs were less likely to back Jackson, the acknowledged outsider, than an established white candidate like Mondale, who had compiled a good record on civil rights as a senator from Minnesota. They believed that defeating Reagan was the most important goal in 1984, and that the quixotic Jackson certainly had no chance of doing so. Black mayors, such as Coleman Young of Detroit, Richard Arrington of Birmingham, and Andrew Young of Atlanta, along with the heads of national civil rights groups, declined to endorse the Chicago minister. "A black candidacy," the president of the Urban League declared, "would be a counterproductive retreat into emotional symbolism at the expense of realistic coalition efforts better suited to meeting black needs." In contrast, Jackson tended to generate greater enthusiasm from local black officials and community leaders who had few ties to the national Democratic Party apparatus or the power brokers who ran it. Furthermore, he appealed most strongly to younger blacks, whose attachment to the Democrats did not date back as far as that of their elders.

Black opposition to Jackson also stemmed from issues of personality and power. The flamboyant candidate had a reputation for self-promotion, for failing to act as a team player while grabbing headlines to advance his own interests. A prominent black California legislator, Willie Brown, expressed the view of many of those who had doubts about him: "You can't teach Jesse anything. He never has been disciplined." Along with Andrew Young, many members of Dr. King's family and immediate staff refused to endorse their former SCLC associate, who, they believed, had rushed too quickly and indiscreetly to assume the mantle of leadership following the death of the martyred King. Moreover, some black officials who had successfully made the transition from civil rights to electoral politics resented Jackson's attempt to run for the presidency from outside an elected power base. They considered him an interloper, a shrewd protest leader, who threatened their hard-earned leverage within Democratic Party circles and challenged their authority within their own electoral constituencies. Black politics had developed to the point at which its practitioners fought the same kind of "turf battles," as Adolph Reed calls them, as their white counterparts.

The rift among blacks was minor compared with the conflict between Jackson and Jewish voters. Next to African Americans, Jews had been the staunchest supporters of Democratic presidential aspirants. Moreover, Jews had provided more support than the members of other white ethnic groups for black mayoral candidates, such as Carl Stokes, Richard Hatcher, and Harold Washington. Their devotion to liberalism and civil rights notwithstanding, since the late 1960s many Jews had broken with blacks over issues concerning affirmative action and the Palestinian–Israeli struggle (see Chapter 6). Unfortunately, Jackson's 1984 campaign damaged relations between these past allies even further. In an off-the-record remark to a black journalist, Jackson referred to Jews as "Hymies" and to New York City, the home of some 3 million of them, as "Hymietown." When his unguarded comments appeared in a news story in the *Washington Post*, the candidate first denied making them and then apologized, regretting any pain he may have caused and repudiating anti-Semitism.

Even had Jews been inclined to forgive Jackson's slip of the tongue, and most did not appear so willing, the substantive matter of Israel still troubled them. Jackson defended the survival of the Jewish nation, but he also called for the creation of a Palestinian state on territory Israel had captured in a war with its Arab enemies in 1967. This policy, which struck Jackson as evenhanded and essential for peace in the Middle East, was totally unacceptable to most Jewish leaders in its recognition of the radical Palestine Liberation Organization. Extremists in the Jewish community viciously attacked Jackson for what they regarded as his anti-Semitic views, called him a "goddamn dirty Nazi," and picketed his appearances. Aggravating the situation, Minister Louis Farrakhan, the head of the Nation of Islam (the Black Muslims) and an outspoken Jackson defender, labeled Judaism "a gutter religion." Though Jackson denounced this inflammatory remark, he declined to repudiate Farrakhan himself. The candidate explained that he believed in the principle of redemption as embodied by Jesus and that he had tried to reach out and convert people with whom he disagreed, including white segregationists such as George Wallace and Orval Faubus. "Isn't it better," he asked, to bring black militants "inside where we can at least talk to them, perhaps even change them?" Jackson knew that many blacks who were not Muslims, especially those living in impoverished urban ghettos, felt the same anger that separatists like Farrakhan expressed. Consequently, he attempted to walk a very fine political line between blacks and Jews in handling this emotional incident.

In effect, the candidate had to stick with his black base of support, his particular source of strength, whatever the risk of offending Jews and other whites. This fact of political life ensured him representation at the 1984 national convention, but guaranteed his defeat. Indeed, in a field crowded with seven white candidates, Jackson made a respectable showing by running third behind Mondale and Senator Gary Hart of Colorado. He won over 3.5 million primary votes, which included victories in Louisiana and the District of Columbia. He gained a plurality of the popular vote in South Carolina, his birthplace, and in Virginia, and carried 46 congressional districts and seven major cities. In two of them, Atlanta and Philadelphia, Jackson triumphed without the backing of their black mayors, who endorsed Mondale. Ignoring the reservations of some of their political leaders, the overwhelming majority of blacks cast their ballots for Jackson. His figures among blacks ranged from a low of 50 percent in Alabama, where Birmingham Mayor Arrington supported Mondale, to a high of 87 percent in New York.

In contrast, the black candidate picked up only a fraction of the white electorate during the primaries. He averaged a slim 5 percent of the white vote, recording his greatest share, 9 percent, in California. Jackson tended to run slightly higher among whites in states containing the lowest percentages of blacks in the population – a clue that racial perceptions significantly affected voters. Although the evidence is fragmentary, it points to the conclusion that a hard-core one-fifth of whites were unwilling to vote for a black presidential candidate, and a substantial majority of the white electorate were not ready to support one as controversial as Jackson. Even many sympathetic white liberals refused to vote for him because they "felt left out." Believing that Jackson had not forged a true rainbow coalition, they faulted him for concentrating too heavily on solidifying his black support. A white Jackson adviser acknowledged that poor coordination and mistrust "inhibited the campaign's ability to reach out beyond its black core." Nevertheless, Jackson did attract more than three-quarters of a million white votes, which constituted about 22 percent of his total ballots. Given the preponderance of the white majority in the electorate, this showing fell far short of building the winning biracial coalition a minority presidential candidate needed.

Realistically, the black minister never had a chance of obtaining the 1984 Democratic nomination. Though linking together a network of grassroots groups and a dedicated staff to guide their activities, Jackson lacked both an experienced national organization and the funds to operate it. The candidate raised only about $4 million in contributions, with an average donation of $27. This broke down to an expenditure of 99 cents for each vote he won, compared with the $3 per vote the more prosperous Mondale campaign could afford to spend. Starved for adequate resources, Jackson did not have the political capital necessary to defeat entrenched party leaders with their access to superior sources of money and talent. These deficiencies, in turn, reinforced the direction of his strategy. To conserve expenses and deploy personnel efficiently, Jackson had to focus on the black electorate, thereby reducing the possibility that his message would get across to potential white supporters. Without this backing, the rainbow coalition appeared monochromatic.

Yet Jackson accomplished a good deal of what he had set out to achieve. He succeeded in mobilizing unprecedented black political participation. In the South alone, his candidacy sparked 150,000 blacks to add their names to the enrollment lists, and throughout the country black registration reached the level of that of whites. Nationally, about 20 percent of his supporters had decided to vote for the first time in their lives, and in Dixie black voter turnout in the Democratic primaries actually surpassed the rate for whites. He also inspired other blacks to run for office, including a woman in Dallas County, Alabama, who remarked that Jackson "made black people feel they could make a difference." Having a black candidate as a serious contender for the presidency was a source of great racial pride and revived some of the feeling of the civil rights movement that electoral politics could be a tool for social change. "For those who did not have an opportunity to participate in the 'March on Washington', or in Selma," the Reverend Jackson told his campaign followers, "God has provided you another opportunity."

Besides coaxing blacks out to the polls, Jackson's efforts opened the way for future presidential challenges. It brought large numbers of black activists into the electoral process and gave them an inside view of how to conduct a national campaign. They became intimately familiar with Democratic Party rules and learned valuable lessons about fundraising, media relations, and the myriad tasks of preparing a candidate to stump through the country in search of support. Drawing upon the metaphor of baseball, California Assemblyman Willie Brown concluded that Jackson had become the "Jackie Robinson of American politics," and predicted that "a whole lot of little leaguers in many cities and counties" would someday join Jackson in rising up to the political big leagues. The nomination contest had bestowed increased legitimacy on the notion of a black competing for the White House. Lucius Barker, a political scientist and Jackson delegate from Missouri, commented that "Jackson is the first black person to really become a *national political* leader in terms of national *presidential politics*" (emphasis in original). Jackson had communicated to white Americans that blacks were interested in and capable of contesting the presidency and that they could offer leadership for millions of citizens distressed by the lingering problems of economic inequality, racial injustice, and Cold War hostilities exacerbated during the Reagan regime. "[W]e might have learned," the historian John Hope Franklin observed about Jackson's performance, "that it was conceivable that a black man had the qualities to be President." Though the Chicago clergyman had not triumphed in the usual sense, he did earn respect for himself and gained recognition for the political aspirations of African Americans.

Despite these achievements, the Jackson forces had only a slight impact on the 1984 Democratic national platform. Blacks comprised 18 percent of the representatives in attendance and most of them were pledged to the Reverend Jackson. However, with Mondale firmly in charge, they proved no match for the majority of delegates, who rejected the main planks of the "rainbow platform." They did manage to come away with one compromise, convention endorsement of affirmative action goals and timetables, but the convention remained silent on the subject of controversial quotas. Mondale easily won the nomination, with 2,191 votes compared to 1,200 for Senator Hart and 465 for Jackson (higher than his actual number of delegates, which totaled 384). The former vice president counted some prominent blacks on his side. Indeed, he tapped Mayor Andrew Young to speak against Jackson's proposal to curb runoff primaries, an action that engendered a barrage of boos and catcalls from most black delegates. Nor did the black contingent feel much better about the selection of Congresswoman Geraldine Ferraro of New York as Mondale's running mate. Jackson backers applauded the choice of a woman, but they regretted that a black woman had not been seriously considered for the number 2 spot.[1] Still, Jackson did gain a minor concession. The party agreed to establish a fairness commission to investigate complaints about the discriminatory operation of its rules on selecting

[1] Although white female delegates to the Democratic Convention were delighted with the choice of Ferraro, black female representatives were dismayed that no woman from their ranks came under consideration. In August 1984, they expressed their disappointment by forming the National Political Congress of Black Women as a means of exerting independent leverage.

convention delegates, and the group eventually dropped the threshold vote a candidate had to receive from 20 to 15 percent. (At the same time, it minimized the effect of this change by increasing the number of "superdelegates," party leaders chosen outside the primary and caucus system, who could attend the convention.)

Putting aside his disappointment, Jackson lined up behind the national ticket. Considerable sentiment existed among blacks for the Chicago minister to run as an independent, but he declined. Instead, he showed Democratic chieftains that he could play by the rules and abide by the outcome of party decisions. No longer a civil rights leader exclusively, Jackson had to act like a politician who needed to mend his fences in preparation to do battle another day.

He went a long way in that direction by delivering a stirring, emotional address to the convention. Affirming his political commitment to the Democratic Party and to his social mission "to feed the hungry; to clothe the naked; to house the homeless; to teach the illiterate; to provide jobs for the jobless; and to choose the human race over the nuclear race," Jackson called for a coalition of "Red, Yellow, Black, and White" to join together in defeating Reagan in common pursuit of these goals. Toward this end, he attempted to heal the wounds of discord that had festered between blacks and Jews during the campaign. Recalling their mutual sacrifices sealed in blood in the civil rights era and their shared victimization as scapegoats throughout history, the Reverend Jackson denounced racism and anti-Semitism and urged Jewish Americans and African Americans to "turn to each other and not on each other, and choose higher ground." Without erasing all the bruised feelings, this powerful speech did have a soothing effect. Vic McTeer, a black delegate from Mississippi, where Fannie Lou Hamer and the Freedom Democrats had been denied representation 20 years before, felt much of his anger over the Democrats' treatment of Jackson subside after he saw white members of his delegation respond to the address with tears in their eyes and with hands reaching out to clasp those of blacks.

The Reagan Landslide and the Struggle for Black Political Survival

Although Jackson's rhetoric touched deep emotions within Democrats at the convention and the millions watching on television, it could not save the party from defeat. Mondale chose not to assign Jackson a prominent role in his campaign, preferring instead to chase after the votes of traditional white Democrats who had defected to Reagan in 1980. Even the Mondale loyalist Andrew Young griped about the neglect of blacks and called the candidate's advisers "smart-assed white boys and they think they know it all." Jackson dutifully made appearances for the ticket, but even if he had been used more heavily it would have made little difference. Surpassing his performance in 1980, the Republican chief executive won by a landslide. Reagan captured 59 percent of the popular vote and swept 525 of 538 electoral votes, taking every state except Mondale's home territory of Minnesota and the predominantly black District of Columbia. Losing 91 percent of the black ballots cast did not prove much of a handicap for the incumbent, because 66 percent of white voters, up from 55 percent in 1980, enthusiastically backed him. While Jesse Jackson had been mounting voter registration drives among blacks, the Republicans had been busily engaged in escorting new voters into their party. In fact, 60 percent of those citizens voting for the first time selected Reagan over Mondale.

The 1984 election returns indicated the enduring significance of race in determining presidential preferences. The polarization in black and white support for the two contenders continued a 32-year trend. Starting with Eisenhower's victory in 1952, only one Democrat, Lyndon Johnson, had received a majority of white votes. This stood in sharp contrast to the mass of black voters who opposed every Republican challenger during that same period. Conventional wisdom attributed the polarization to Jackson; yet if the black minister's candidacy heightened it did not cause this racial divide. Though Jackson's campaign prompted some whites to jump to the Republicans, the large majority of them simply favored extending the term of a very popular chief executive whose administration had begun to restore economic recovery and national pride. Reagan's financial measures further split blacks from whites in making their presidential choices, as class reinforced racial concerns. Disproportionately harder hit by unemployment and poverty, and still trailing behind whites in average yearly earnings, most blacks found relatively little comfort in the Reaganomic policies aimed at boosting the fortunes of the middle and upper classes. Not surprisingly then, in the South, which had the largest income gap between the races, polls showed 57 percent of whites praising Reagan's economic performance and 87 percent of blacks objecting to it. Consequently, on election day over 70 percent of southern white voters cast their ballots for the Republican.

Despite the huge Reagan victory, blacks did not find the election completely discouraging. In the South, the black turnout rate grew by 5.3 percent

from that of four years before. This increase reflected an even higher rise in
the percentage of blacks registered since 1980. Indeed, in Louisiana and
Georgia the pace of black enrollment exceeded that of whites. Nationally,
the upsurge in participation narrowed the differences between white and
black registration (3.3 percent) and turnout (5.6 percent) to their lowest
points in the post–World War II period. A higher proportion of the total
voting-age black population in the country cast their ballots in this
presidential election than in the previous one. On the down side, however,
the percentage of those who were registered and actually voted had declined
slightly. This situation suggested that the Jackson Democratic primary
campaign had helped swell the pool of available voters, but that the subsequent
contest between Reagan and Mondale dampened their enthusiasm. The
President's conservatism and the challenger's failure to excite African
Americans kept many blacks at home.

Black participation produced mixed results. While Reagan retained the
White House and the Republicans held on to their control of the Senate, the
Democrats picked up one vote in the upper chamber and maintained their
majority in the House. Black votes provided the winning margins for
Democratic senators in Alabama, Illinois, and Michigan as well as for seven
members in the House. Black candidates did not fare so well. Though the
number of blacks serving in state legislatures increased slightly, the
Congressional Black Caucus suffered a net reduction of one seat. In addition
to this loss, six black congressional candidates who were considered as having a chance of winning went down to defeat. As usual, black officeseekers
tended to run most strongly at the local level. In 1984, the greatest annual
increases occurred in the election of black county officials and mayors,
especially in the South, the scene of Jackson's most intensive political efforts
in mobilizing black voters. Yet, as Thomas Cavanagh, a political scientist
and researcher for the Joint Center for Political Studies, suggested, "most of
the black-majority districts may already have black incumbents, making
future gains more difficult to achieve."

The second Reagan administration proved no more promising to African-
American political advancement than did the first. Given the partisanship of
the black vote, the President had little incentive to modify his previous
course. Nevertheless, the Republican administration went further in antagonizing blacks than even its opponents had expected. In the aftermath of
Reagan's reelection, the Justice Department indicted eight long-time civil
rights activists in Alabama on criminal charges that were viewed as an
attempt to roll back black political power. The government contended that

the accused had engaged in vote fraud by improperly soliciting and casting absentee ballots in the heart of the state's black-belt area. Convictions on these felony charges could result in heavy fines and lengthy prison terms.

The cases originated in the region surrounding Selma, where blacks had encountered the greatest resistance to enfranchisement during the civil rights years. Through the efforts of such local leaders as Albert Turner of Perry County, a former SCLC staff member and an organizer of the historic 1965 suffrage march to Montgomery, and Spiver Gordon, a city councilman in nearby Greene County, blacks had won a total of 138 offices and gained control of five county commissions, five school boards, and nine towns. Though the Voting Rights Act had enabled blacks to constitute a majority of the electorate in those rural locations, whites managed to retain substantial influence. They continued to wield economic clout in those counties, which were among the poorest in the state, and they converted their superior financial resources into victories at the polls. Whites held on to the reins of government in five counties and in 33 towns and occupied the top positions of voter registrar, district attorney, and circuit judge. In the fierce political struggle that ensued, absentee ballots often counted as the margin of victory in determining the outcome of elections and thus had been a serious bone of contention for years. Each side charged the other with manipulating these ballots and with engaging in fraud by signing up people without their knowledge and voting in their names and those of individuals who no longer resided in the black belt.

Complicating this interracial conflict, blacks also divided among themselves. Increasingly, black candidates began to vie against each other for office, and in such instances the white minority played a balance-of-power role in deciding the winners. In this section of Alabama, with its history of bigotry and disfranchisement, black leaders eyed suspiciously white attempts to exploit rivalries between black factions. They charged that whites collaborated with disgruntled blacks as a subtle means of reasserting their political hegemony. As a matter of fact, John Kennard, the black tax assessor of Greene County, who had won election with white backing, initiated the complaints of absentee ballot fraud against his black opponents. Kennard, who had been in grade school during the heyday of the freedom struggle in the 1960s and had gone on to graduate from the University of Alabama, headed a group of young insurgents that sought to challenge the rule of blacks identified with the civil rights movement who had governed the county since 1970. Although as a youth he had joined in demonstrations and marches, he felt that the time had come for a change in leadership and strategy. "All this stuff about 'We Shall Overcome' was in the sixties," Kennard asserted, and bluntly rejected the "philosophy among the old-line black leadership that there's something evil and demonic and a master plan in the white community to enslave us."

Conservative whites took advantage of these generational and ideological splits within the black community. Local white Alabamians joined Kennard in persuading the Reagan Justice Department to file charges against Albert Turner and his allies in Perry and Greene counties. The complainants were looking ahead to the upcoming 1986 elections, which featured the bid for another term by Senator Jeremiah Denton, a Republican who had opposed renewal of the Voting Rights Act in 1982. Involved in a close contest with his Democratic opponent, Representative Richard C. Shelby, Denton thought his chances would be stronger if black leaders came under attack and the black electorate felt discouraged from going to the polls. The Republican administration insisted that it was not acting out of political or racial motives, and argued that it was merely seeking to punish one group of blacks for committing fraud against other blacks.

Federal prosecutors denied that they were deliberately intimidating black voters by bringing these suits, but the targets of these trials thought otherwise. They accused Washington of selective enforcement, pointing out that it had not responded in the past to similar complaints filed by blacks against whites. Furthermore, the "black-belt eight" contended that the federal government used heavy-handed tactics in investigating the cases, especially in rounding up for questioning those blacks who had signed the controversial ballots. Many of them were elderly and infirm, and their interrogation by federal agents revived memories of the not-so-distant past when blacks could not register to vote or paid a heavy penalty for doing so.

Ignoring cries of protest from civil rights organizations and the Congressional Black Caucus and their white allies, the Reagan administration persisted in its Alabama prosecutions but obtained only partial success. In the case of three defendants, including Albert Turner, an interracial jury failed to return a guilty verdict. Other trials resulted in hung juries, though several of the accused later pleaded guilty to lesser misdemeanor counts. Only in the case of Spiver Gordon did an all-white jury decide to convict, and even then he was acquitted on most of the charges. Whatever the intention of the Reagan administration, it failed to curtail the determination of Alabama blacks to exercise their franchise: in 1986, the latter won a measure of revenge by pouring out at the polls and contributing to the defeat of Senator Denton.

The Resurgence and Reshaping
of the Civil Rights Coalition

Meanwhile, blacks had salvaged another victory against the Reagan administration shortly before the 1986 congressional elections. Blacks emerged triumphant as they once again bolstered electoral politics with protest to further their goals. Groups of blacks and their white supporters, many of them prominent individuals, took turns picketing the South African embassy in Washington for more than a year, which resulted in arrests on a daily basis. Their persistence and the surrounding publicity generated by the demonstrations had a positive impact on Congress. In mid-September, a bipartisan coalition of lawmakers passed a bill imposing moderate economic sanctions on South Africa. Later that month, President Reagan vetoed this popular legislative measure, which sought to apply punitive action against a nation whose institutions rested on racial oppression and minority rule. In doing so, the chief executive rejected this central item on the black political agenda, an expression of solidarity with a brutally persecuted people of color living on the continent to which African Americans traced their roots. The civil rights movement had cracked the edifice of apartheid and disfranchisement that existed in the American South, and most Americans supported proposals to aid in overcoming these evils in southern Africa. Though the sanctions bill approved by Congress fell short of totally embargoing economic trade with and investment in the racist regime, it went too far for the President, who preferred to dismantle apartheid through a policy of "constructive engagement" that emphasized voluntary persuasion rather than coercion. On October 2, 1986, a month before the legislative elections, the Senate joined the House to register its disagreement with Reagan's approach and repass the bill over his veto. Representative Lynn Martin, an Illinois Republican, echoed the sentiments of more than two-thirds of her colleagues in overriding the President: "The vote matters not because of what it says about South Africa. It matters because of what it says about America."

This victory helped whet the appetite of disgruntled blacks throughout the South and the nation to use the off-year congressional elections to communicate their discontent with the White House. The existence of considerable Republican support for South African sanctions did not sufficiently offset general black hostility to Reagan's GOP administration. The Democrats recaptured control of the Senate by a margin of 55 to 45 seats. According to the Joint Center for Political Studies, Democrats in California and Nevada gained only a minority of white votes but won by obtaining a huge share of black ballots. The same situation prevailed in four contests in the Deep South – Alabama, Georgia, Louisiana, and North Carolina – where black voters tipped the winning balance in favor of Democratic challengers. In two other states, Florida and Maryland, blacks helped expand what otherwise would have been slight victory margins. They did so there by turning out to vote at a rate equaling or surpassing that of whites. Overall, blacks still lagged behind whites in turnout by 7 percentage points, but this marked a significant improvement over the gap of 11 percent in the 1982 off-year congressional elections.

Although the results of these elections demonstrated the rising strength of black political influence in the South since passage of the Voting Rights Act, they also indicated its limits. The triumphant candidates in Dixie gained the overwhelming portion of black ballots, between 80 and 90 percent, and a substantial minority of the white electorate, around 40 percent. Victory depended upon holding on to the bulk of the black electorate while at the same time luring enough white Reagan Democrats into a biracial coalition. Calculating this political arithmetic, successful southern Democrats ran as moderates, very carefully adjusting their messages to attract both liberal blacks and conservative whites. After winning his senatorial election, John Breaux of Louisiana pledged "to remember that he could never have won without the black vote." Nevertheless, the question remained of how responsive Democrats like Breaux would be to black concerns when they also had to consider the political risks of alienating their volatile white supporters. Many southern whites answered with caution. A Raleigh, North Carolina, newspaperman warned: "If black political leaders read too much into the returns of 1986 and do not fashion their agenda with an eye toward winning the next election, they could contribute to a rupturing of the Democratic coalition of which they are a vital part."

The election outcome also suggested that, while blacks were continuing to advance politically, they could not afford to ignore the power of the white electorate. Though blacks secured four additional seats in the House of Representatives, pushing their total to a record high of 23 members, two of these gains were significantly shaped by the decisions of white voters. In Mississippi, Mike Espy became the first black candidate since Reconstruction to represent his state in Congress. The delta district Espy served contained a slight black voting-age majority, but on two previous occasions another black contestant, state legislator Robert Clark, had failed to win sufficient support from white voters and lost. In 1986, Espy defeated the incumbent

Republican by generating a large black turnout in his behalf, nearly doubling his share of white votes to 12 percent, and keeping a significant bloc of whites from voting against him. Many whites who disliked his opponent but could not bear to cast a ballot for a black candidate simply stayed away from the polls, thereby indirectly contributing to Espy's slender 2.3 percent margin of victory.

In the case of the election of Congressman John Lewis from Atlanta white voters played an even more direct role. This contest pitted Lewis, the former chairman of SNCC, against his old civil rights comrade Julian Bond, in the Democratic primary. In this black-majority district, 87 percent of whites threw their support to Lewis, who triumphed while receiving only 40 percent of black ballots. This election reversed the traditional positions of each race at the polls. Previously, when blacks comprised a minority of the electorate, they had lined up behind the white candidate considered the most racially moderate in the field and swung the election in his or her favor. Now the white minority helped elect Lewis, whom they perceived as more temperate than Bond. Elsewhere, in the black-majority city of New Orleans the winning black mayor, Sidney Barthelemy, also failed to win a majority of black votes, but clinched victory by capturing ample support from whites. These triumphant officials faced the delicate task of representing black concerns without offending the segment of the white electorate that had tipped the balance of power in their favor. At the same time, they had to repair splits within the black community that had opened from these intraracial clashes for power, which constituted a natural step in the evolution of black politics.

Although increased competition for public office sometimes proved divisive, blacks generally remained united in their unfinished goal of achieving racial equality. Despite the growing economic stratification within the black polity, middle-class black politicians still tended to identify with the plight of their less fortunate constituents from whom they were only recently removed. "Even those blacks who have 'made it' economically," Thomas Cavanagh reported, "are more likely to support the views of poor blacks than those of well-to-do whites." Having benefited from civil rights and affirmative action remedies, they most assuredly did not want to see those gains weakened or terminated. Public opinion surveys indicated that, in contrast with whites, most blacks favored compensatory federal programs to reverse the economic and social effects of past racial discrimination. Thus, so long as the United States had not become a color-blind society, race persisted as a crucial category for determining political choices.

Black solidarity, reinforced by expanding political clout, brought some notable legislative victories in the final two years of the Reagan era. With Democrats once again in control of both houses of Congress and with several newly elected senators owing their victories to blacks, the prospects for challenging the administration's conservative policies improved. This was especially true when issues involved basic civil rights matters and avoided controversial affirmative action or big-spending measures. The defeat of Robert Bork's nomination to the Supreme Court vividly testifies to this point. A legal scholar and federal judge who had served as solicitor general during Nixon's final Watergate days, Bork had distressed blacks and their white allies by his long history of outspoken opposition to numerous pieces of civil rights legislation and accompanying liberal judicial opinions. Denying any racist motives, Bork had reached these judgments on constitutional grounds and propounded a conservative legal philosophy in harmony with the President's. Whatever the source of Bork's views, civil rights advocates contended that the nominee's ideas fell outside of the judicial mainstream, and they considered him a formidable threat to the advances so recently made. They further believed that his appointment to the high bench would forge a clear majority against extending any future benefits.

The administration and its opponents engaged in a vigorous lobbying campaign to rally public and congressional support for their respective sides. With Democrats having replaced Republicans in control of the crucial Senate Judiciary Committee, Bork's foes succeeded in using the hearings to generate resistance to the nomination. An interracial coalition of civil rights organizations, liberal and labor groups, and pro-abortion feminist organizations, all of which found Bork's positions detrimental to their respective causes, convinced the committee to issue a negative report on the candidate. The full Senate concurred with this recommendation, and critical votes to deny the appointment came dramatically from southern Democrats. In a new version of the "solid South," 15 of 16 Democratic senators from the region voted against the judicial nominee. Though not entirely unsympathetic to Bork's legal reasoning, these moderate and conservative lawmakers were also mindful that this legal scholar aroused deep indignation from their black constituents. The 1986 elections had only recently underscored the political importance of the black electorate and the danger of ignoring its interests. "When the blacks stay with the Democrats," a senior Democratic officeholder in Mississippi remarked, "we can just about win, but when they leave, we can't." To many southern senators, the political risks of supporting the controversial Bork were too great, and they hesitated to stir up past racial animosities. As Senator Richard C. Shelby of Alabama, a moderate conservative who owed his election to black voters, declared: "In the South, we've made a lot of progress. We do not want to go back and revisit old issues."[2]

The revitalized civil rights forces in Washington won another important victory over the President's opposition that also reflected a concern with halting any retreat from hard-earned civil rights gains. Specifically, the One-Hundredth Congress reversed the President in his refusal to restore protections that had been recently whittled down by the Supreme Court in the case of *Grove City College v. Bell.* In 1984, the high tribunal had ruled that under the 1964 Civil Rights Act the federal government could not completely cut off funds to a college for practicing discrimination in some but not all of its activities. In other words, federal sanctions had to be applied on a selective basis specifically against an offending program without penalizing the entire educational institution. This decision represented a setback from the previously expansive interpretation of the law, and the Reagan administration heartily endorsed it. The case involved discrimination against women by Grove City College in Pennsylvania, but its legal reasoning also applied to racial minorities. Subsequently, civil rights and women's groups persuaded lawmakers to pass legislation restoring government authority to remove federal funds from institutions that permitted any discrimination under their auspices. After Reagan vetoed the bill, on March 22, 1988, moderate Republicans, as they had on the South Africa issue, joined the Democratic majority in furnishing the two-thirds vote necessary to override the President. In doing so, Congress expressed its broad agreement for preserving the full scope of the valued Civil Rights Act, which legislators had battled so hard to place on the books in the first place.

While blacks displayed their influence in Washington, they continued to flex their political muscle at the state and local levels. In addition to playing significant roles in deciding the outcome of close elections between white candidates, they boosted the number of blacks holding office. In 1987, there were over 6,600 black elected officials throughout the nation, a rise of 4.1 percent from the year before. For the first time black politicians broke through the barriers that had kept governments lily-white in 71 locales. Among those significant victories was the election of a black candidate as a

---

[2] This civil rights victory was diminished by the eventual confirmation of Judge Anthony M. Kennedy, a conservative considered to have a more flexible judicial temperament than Bork but who nonetheless has consistently voted with the conservative bloc.

supervisor (commissioner) in Fannie Lou Hamer's Sunflower County, Mississippi; the election of the father of one of the young girls killed in the 1963 bombing of a church in Birmingham to a seat on the Jefferson County Commission; and further north, in Baltimore, Maryland, the election of a black as mayor. In addition, black incumbents triumphed as mayors in Atlanta, Birmingham, Chicago, Detroit, Los Angeles, and Philadelphia; and in cities such as Gary and Newark, black challengers defeated the reigning black chief executives.

Nationally, however, African Americans still held only 1.5 percent of elected posts. Though minority officeholding continued to grow steadily, it did so very slowly. As blacks began to fill the available positions in places where they constituted a majority of the population, the opportunities to add to the total number of black officials diminished. There was room for some improvement as the judiciary ordered local governments to convert from at-large to single-member district elections, thereby creating new black-majority jurisdictions. Nevertheless, in many villages and towns in the rural South, blacks had yet to crack white political domination, which was reinforced through tradition and economic dependency. Furthermore, because they were a minority of the population in most cities, in every state, and throughout the nation, blacks needed to attract greater white support to expand their representation. As the 1980s drew toward a close, African-American candidates generally had failed to establish these winning biracial coalitions. Blacks did not occupy any state governor's mansion or hold any US Senate seat, and only some 13 held statewide offices.

Jesse Jackson and the Rainbow Revival

With this mixed record in the background, Jesse Jackson once again sought to expand the horizon of black political opportunity by competing for the 1988 Democratic presidential nomination. This time he was less interested in the symbolism of merely running than he was in actually obtaining the top prize. In this pursuit, he stood upon an even firmer base of black support than in his previous campaign. A poll taken a year before the Democratic Convention showed that 67 percent of blacks preferred Jackson as their first choice for the nomination, whereas no more than 3 percent of those surveyed favored any one of his potential rivals. Unlike in 1984, there was no white candidate in the field who had the liberal credentials of a Mondale or his proven dedication to civil rights. Nor did any aspirant have the former vice president's close ties to the national party establishment that had pulled many black politicians away from Jackson in his first campaign. Under these circumstances and given the substantial backing Jackson commanded among rank-and-file black Democrats, the Chicago minister experienced much less opposition to his candidacy from black leaders this time around. Most notably, former opponents such as Mayor Richard Arrington of Birmingham, Willie Brown, speaker of the California Assembly, and Congressman John Lewis hopped aboard his bandwagon. Some, such as Mayor Coleman Young of Detroit, remained unconvinced, but others, such as Andrew Young, though still not endorsing Jackson, at least stayed neutral.

Yet if Jackson had a realistic chance to improve his performance in contending for the nomination, he had to do more than solidify his black foundation of support. "It's very easy to finish third," Alan Dershowitz, a Harvard Law School professor, said of Jackson's 1984 standing, "if you're black in America, and you're a black candidate seeking a black constituency." To place second and especially first, Jackson had to reach beyond the approximately 20 percent of the Democratic electorate that was securely his. Accordingly, he attempted to broaden his appeal among whites and nonblack minorities, such as Hispanics and Native Americans, and draw a fuller range of colors into his rainbow coalition than he had in 1984. He moved in this direction by bringing in some experienced white political consultants to serve alongside his trusted black confidants. Bert Lance of Georgia, who had helped engineer Jimmy Carter's successful 1976 campaign; John White, former chair of the Democratic National Committee; Ann Lewis, past head of the liberal Americans for Democratic Action; and Jim Hightower, the agricultural commissioner of Texas, were among those Jackson relied on for counsel. Underscoring his commitment to an expanded biracial coalition, he selected Assemblyman Brown to chair his national organization, and picked Gerald Austin, a white political operative who served as campaign manager for Governor Richard Celeste of Ohio, to oversee the organization's day-to-day affairs. The increased visibility of Austin and other nonblacks, Jackson calculated, "tells other people that *they* are welcome" and would raise "the comfort level" for whites.

Jackson aimed his message at diverse segments of the American electorate. He continued to trumpet many of the themes that identified him most closely with black and progressive white concerns: affirmative action, sanctions against South Africa, federally guaranteed full employment, opposition to Reagan's Central American policies, and support for evenhanded treatment of Israeli and Palestinian positions in the Middle East. However, he abandoned or downplayed other issues that had been associated with his previous campaign. No longer did he focus his attack on runoff primaries and party rules establishing a minimum threshold for winning convention delegates, procedures that had a disproportionately negative impact on black and other minority candidates. In general, he attempted to extend the appeal of his progressive agenda to moderate and conservative Democrats who, during the past two decades, had defected from the party or had been turned off from the political system altogether. Jackson explained: "Last time my rhetoric was sufficient to do what I had to do – open up the process, demand room for progressive-thinking people, register new voters. You know there's a right wing and a left wing, and it takes both to fly a plane. My concern is about 85 million voters in neither wing: they're in the belly of the plane."

Jackson raised economic and social issues designed to rally the disaffected behind him. He hammered away at Republican policies that cost factory workers their jobs and lost family farmers their mortgages. Speaking in the language, minus the racism, of white populists of the past, Jackson attacked the "economic violence" that wealthy corporations and their representatives in Washington had perpetrated on the economically disadvantaged. Addressing himself to black and white victims of financial privilege and corporate greed, he asked for the "small fish" to join against the "barracudas." He wrapped this message in a patriotic banner by calling for a "reinvestment in America" that would halt plant closings, stop foreclosures, and create domestic jobs. Furthermore, he highlighted his longstanding concern with the danger of drugs ("Down with dope. Up with hope."), a matter middle-class Americans felt extremely worried about.

These themes struck some responsive chords among white voters. As he hopscotched around the country campaigning in the Democratic primaries and caucuses, he wooed many whites who would not have considered voting for him in 1984. In early April, a *USA Today* poll revealed that 32 percent of whites were more willing to back Jackson on this occasion than four years earlier. Jim Hightower of Texas noted the newfound appeal of Jackson as he espoused his brand of populism: "He is transcending the fact that he is a black candidate. He is gaining white support … from the kind of people who like Willie Nelson – the sort of redneck, lower-middle-class constituency that is out there, and, since Bobby Kennedy and George Wallace, hasn't been voting that much." In one survey, taken in August 1987, 16 percent of rural whites selected Jackson as either their first or second choice for the top spot on the Democratic ticket. Furthermore, Jackson's approach encouraged his rivals for the nomination to shape their campaigns around similar issues dealing with drugs, education, healthcare, and protection for blue-collar workers threatened with layoffs and farmers endangered by foreclosures. Commentators observed that Jackson's popularity had risen as he moved into the party mainstream, but the Chicago minister could equally claim that he had pulled the Democratic center in his progressive direction.

Still, Jackson was stuck with several political liabilities that posed severe problems for him. His position on the Israeli–Palestinian conflict continued to cause him difficulties with Jewish-American voters. He tried to allay the fears of this important segment of the Democratic electorate by pledging to maintain strong US support for the defense of Israel, whose security, he insisted, would not be jeopardized by carefully negotiating recognition of a Palestinian homeland. Jackson also avoided a repetition of the unfortunate "Hymie" incident, and he distanced his campaign from the controversial Muslim minister, Louis Farrakhan. This second time around, Jackson's attempts at reconciliation did bring some Jews into his camp. Indeed, his

Figure 18   Jesse Jackson, flanked by some of his rivals for the 1988 Democratic Party presidential nomination. From left to right stand Senator Al Gore of Tennessee, Congressman Richard Gephardt of Missouri, Jackson, Governor Bruce Babbitt of Arizona, Senator Paul Simon of Illinois, and Governor Michael Dukakis of Massachusetts. (Photo © Wally McNamee/Corbis)

own campaign manager, Gerald Austin, was a Jew who had once been disturbed by the Hymie remark, but now had come to believe that Jackson meant no offense in using the term. However, most of Austin's coreligionists did not forgive Jackson so easily, and instead many apparently agreed with Mayor Edward Koch of New York City that Jews would be "crazy" to vote for Jackson.

Besides his specific problem with Jews, the Chicago civil rights leader generally had trouble convincing whites to endorse him. Whereas many of them thought that Jackson did not have sufficient political experience or that elements of his rainbow platform were too liberal, others indicated that they would not vote for him under any circumstance. Jackson was viewed unfavorably by 38 percent of Democrats, and even if he captured his party's nomination, polls showed him gaining only 27 percent of the total white vote. Personal perceptions and ideology undoubtedly influenced these views, but so too did the fact that Jackson was a black candidate and, therefore, to some extent unacceptable to many whites. The primary contest in West Virginia rudely demonstrated this point when a local resident bluntly informed reporters: "[I] ain't voting for no nigger." Most whites did not display such candor, and though it is difficult to disentangle racial concerns from other factors that generated opposition to Jackson, one may reasonably conclude that race came into play. As a black Jackson supporter lamented after New York's divisive primary: "In the South, if they didn't like you, they told you. In the North, they are just as racist, and just as prejudiced, but they're just a little smoother." Like his populist predecessors before the turn of the century, the black candidate had difficulty in forging an interracial alliance behind common class grievances.

In spite of these drawbacks, Jackson achieved some notable successes in the primaries and caucuses. He ran more strongly than in 1984 among both black and white electorates and out of a field of six white candidates, including several state governors, US senators, and a congressman, he finished second to Governor Michael Dukakis of Massachusetts. Gathering nearly 7 million votes, Jackson won over 1,200 delegates, three times the 1984 number. He scored impressive triumphs in the South by winning primaries in Alabama, Georgia, Louisiana, Mississippi, and Virginia, together with the caucus in South Carolina, his native state. In this region, blacks composed from 33 to 46 percent of the Democratic electorate, and they cast over 90 percent of their votes for Jackson. At the same time, the black candidate beat his rivals by lifting his share of the white vote to 10 percent, up from 4 percent in 1984. Overall, in the former Confederate states Jackson received 28 percent of the popular vote to edge out his closest competitors, Dukakis (27 percent) and Senator Al Gore of Tennessee (25 percent). This showing was remarkable, particularly in a section of the country that until very recently had deprived its black citizens of the right to vote.

In the rest of the country (that is, outside of the South), where blacks generally constituted a smaller proportion of the population and the Democratic electorate, Jackson did surprisingly well. He astonished most political pundits and purveyors of conventional wisdom by winning the Michigan caucus. Forty percent of his total vote came from whites. In addition to capturing black-majority Detroit, despite the opposition of Mayor Young, he won in several predominantly white cities. In a state with a slumping automobile industry and strong blue-collar union membership, his condemnation of plant closures and corporate irresponsibility gained a large following. In this instance, his populist rhetoric was well received. In addition, his personal magnetism, combined with a defense of old-fashioned values stressing the importance of family, upward mobility, and the danger of drugs, prompted many whites to shift, as Jackson put it, "from racial battleground to economic common ground and moral higher ground."

Elsewhere Jackson showed growing support among whites, as his share of the vote greatly exceeded the percentage of blacks in the voting-age population. He came in first in Alaska and Delaware, and finished second by gaining between 20 and 29 percent of the total vote in Connecticut, Indiana, Maine, Maryland, Minnesota, Missouri, Montana, Nebraska, New Mexico, Ohio, Pennsylvania, Vermont, and Wisconsin. He did even better in securing between 30 and 39 percent of the vote in Arizona, California, Colorado, Hawaii, Illinois, Kansas, New Jersey, New York, Oregon, and Washington (see Table 7.2). Although he finished second in the three-way, statewide contest in New York, Jackson triumphed in New York City with 46 percent of the votes and a coalition of blacks, Hispanics, and progressive whites behind him.

Nevertheless, Jackson fell considerably short of his goal. After peaking in Michigan, he lost in nearly all of the remaining primary and caucus elections. Following the bruising New York contest, Governor Dukakis emerged as the clear front-runner, and the field narrowed down to the Massachusetts governor and the Chicago clergyman. Jackson trailed behind his remaining rival in the ensuing head-to-head battles, especially as the white majority rallied around Dukakis. For all of his efforts over the previous four years in diminishing white opposition and even converting non-blacks to his candidacy, Jackson could not persuade a sufficient number of whites to back him.

Table 7.2 Percentage of votes won by Jesse Jackson in democratic primaries, 1984 and 1988[a]

	Blacks in voting-age population, 1980 (%)	Votes (%)	
		1984	*1988*
Alabama (p)	22.9	19.6	43.6[b]
Alaska (c)	3.4	10.6	34.6[b]
Arizona (c)	2.5	15.7	37.8
California (p)	7.1	19.6	35.2
Colorado (c)	3.2	4.2	33.6
Connecticut (p)	6.0	12.0	28.3
Delaware (c)	14.2	9.6	45.8
District of Columbia (p)	65.8	67.3[b]	80.0[b]
Georgia (p)	24.3	21.0	39.8[b]
Hawaii (c)	1.9	4.2	35.0
Indiana (p)	6.8	13.7	22.5
Illinois (p)	12.9	21.0	32.3
Kansas (c)	4.8	3.3	30.8
Louisiana (p)	26.6	42.9[b]	35.5[b]
Maine (c)	0.3	0.4	26.8
Maryland (p)	20.8	25.5	28.7
Michigan (c)	11.7	16.7	53.5[9]
Minnesota (c)	1.1	2.0	19.8
Mississippi (p)	31.0	26.9	44.4[b]
Missouri (c)	9.3	18.5	20.2(p)
Montana (c)	0.2	5.2	22.1(p)
Nebraska (p)	2.6	9.1	25.7
New Jersey (p)	11.0	23.6	32.9
New Mexico (p)	1.7	11.9	28.1
New York (p)	12.4	25.6	37.1
North Carolina (p)	20.3	25.4	33.0
Ohio (p)	9.2	16.4	27.5
Oregon (p)	1.2	9.5	38.1
Pennsylvania (p)	8.1	16.0	27.3
South Carolina (c)	27.3	25.0	54.8[b]
Tennessee (p)	14.2	25.3	20.7
Texas	11.1	16.4(c)	25.0(p)[c]
Vermont (p)	0.2	7.8	25.7[c]

(Continued)

Table 7.2 *(cont'd)*

	Blacks in voting-age population, 1980 (%)	Votes (%) 1984	Votes (%) 1988
Virginia	17.5	26.7(c)	45.1 (p)[b]
Washington (c)	2.4	3.0	34.6
Wisconsin (p)	3.2	9.9	28.2

(p) represents a primary and (c) a caucus election
[a]Primaries in which Jackson obtained at least 25 percent of the vote in either one or both years. Absent from the table is Puerto Rico, where Jackson won the primary with 29 percent of the vote in 1988.
[b]Jackson victories.
[c]Texas and Vermont also had caucuses, and Jackson won both with 40 percent and 46 percent of the vote, respectively.
Source: The Democratic primary election results are taken from *Congressional Quarterly Weekly*, June 16, 1984: 1443, and July 9, 1988: 1894. The caucus totals, also, are from *Congressional Quarterly Weekly*, June 2, 1984: 1317, and June 4, 1988: 1524. The figures on voting-age population are drawn from US Department of Commerce, Bureau of the Census, *Statistical Abstract of the United States, 1984* (Government Printing Office, Washington, DC, 1984), 263.

Whatever their racial views, many white Democrats appeared to harbor sincere doubts as to Jackson's electability. They believed Jackson's views were too far to the left of the political mainstream, and would not bring back to the fold conservative Democrats who had voted for Reagan. Anthony Lewis of the *New York Times* spoke for many of those who found Jackson appealing but a sure loser: 'When I hear liberals talking about their exhilaration at the Jackson candidacy, their delight at its populist character, I worry. That sounds like the gushy liberalism that has got the Democratic Party out of touch with reality before: the reality of the need to win the center."

This hard-nosed perception of Jackson carried over to the decision not to select him as the vice-presidential candidate. Instead, Dukakis chose Senator Lloyd Bentsen of Texas as his running mate. In making this choice the Massachusetts governor sought to revive the "Boston–Austin axis" that had produced victory for John Kennedy and Lyndon Johnson in 1960. Bentsen was a moderate-to-conservative Democrat whose views on many domestic and foreign policy issues diverged from those of the more liberal Dukakis. In balancing the ticket geographically and ideologically, Dukakis hoped to forge a winning majority by prying loose Reagan Democrats and returning them to his column. Blacks decried this strategy because they believed that it took their votes for granted and slighted the Reverend Jackson. They contended that the minister had earned a place on the ticket through his strong showing in the primaries. Jackson was similarly offended, but by the time the Democrats gathered at their convention in July he had come around to endorsing Dukakis and Bentsen.

Although African Americans did not get their first choice for either spot on the ticket, they did significantly increase their representation at the 1988 Democratic Convention. Of those in attendance, 962, or 23 percent, were black. This constituted a one-third increase over the number of black delegates who had sat at the previous convention and comprised the highest number ever to participate in the party's quadrennial meeting. Together with Jackson's white delegates they succeeded in obtaining a few platform concessions on educational and healthcare issues as well as a pledge not to fund the military operations of antigovernment rebels in Central America. They also lent their support to Jackson in gaining a personal commitment from Dukakis to recruit additional blacks to his campaign staff and to policy-making positions within the party. Democratic chieftains also agreed to make some rule changes that Jackson had sought, including a reduction in the number of superdelegates chosen outside of the primary and caucus system.

The highlight for the Jackson delegates came with their candidate's prime-time television address to the convention and the nation. As he had in 1984, Jackson thrilled the audience with his vision of an America that "keeps hope alive" for all of its citizens, no matter how weak or humble, whatever their race, creed, or sex. "We meet tonight at a crossroads, a point of decision," he remarked and went on to ask, "Shall we expand, be inclusive, find unity and power, or suffer division and impotence?" Jackson eloquently answered his own question by pointing out that Dukakis's Greek "foreparents came to America on immigrant ships. My foreparents came to America on slave ships. But whatever the original ships, we are both on the same side now."

Having failed in his bid for the nomination, Jackson nonetheless helped redefine victory. As the influential columnist David Broder noted: "For Jesse L. Jackson … 'winning' has meanings that cannot be captured in primary-election returns or exit-poll numbers." In a poignant illustration of the progress blacks had made, Jackson brought Rosa Parks with him onto the stage of the convention and introduced her to the thousands in the hall and the millions watching on television. Thirty-three years before, she had been arrested for challenging bus segregation in Montgomery, and now she stood beside a leading contender for the presidential nomination. Jackson also reminded the assemblage that only 24 years had passed since another group of Democrats had "locked out" Fannie Lou Hamer, Aaron Henry, and the Mississippi Freedom Democrats from taking their seats at the convention. Now Henry was listening to these words as a member of the Mississippi delegation, an interracial contingent headed by a black man, Ed Cole. Even the site of the meeting inspired thoughts of the momentous changes that had occurred. Jackson pointed out that this gathering was taking place in the capital of Georgia, where Andrew Young now presided as mayor, and where two decades earlier the state legislature had barred SNCC worker Julian Bond from assuming his seat in the legislature because of his objections to the Vietnam war. In this fashion, Jackson vividly connected his own journey as a legitimate contender for the presidency to the triumphs and sacrifices of the civil rights movement in scores of black communities across the nation.

In countless ways, Jackson had become a role model for young blacks who in the future might also aspire to the nation's highest office. Certainly many African Americans had dreamed that one day there would be a black president, but Jackson's candidacy gave new meaning to this hope. Shirley Chisholm's 1972 bid for the Democratic nomination had not attracted much support, even from blacks, whereas Jackson's campaign had drawn a huge black following and considerable interest among whites. Although those who were older might not see a black president in the White House in their lifetime, they took great pride in what Jackson had already achieved. "A five-year-old can look at the T.V. screen and see a black man running for President and have it be credible," a Jackson enthusiast explained. "Jesse has inspired a belief that nothing is unconquerable."

This contest also demonstrated that Jackson was more than a candidate for blacks. His challenge helped transform the attitudes of many whites, and sometimes in a startling manner. In Texas, for example, a white man seeking to have his photograph snapped alongside Jackson mentioned to the candidate that he had marched in Selma. After Jackson retorted that it was nice to be with him again, the fellow replied; "No, you don't understand. I marched with the Klan. I just don't want to be on the wrong side of history again." Although most whites did not experience a conversion this dramatic, those marking their ballots for Jackson in some small way reflected the changes that his candidacy represented. Not a winner in the conventional sense, Jesse Jackson had taken a great stride in gaining political acceptance for himself and for black Americans.

The Election of George H. W. Bush

The 1988 presidential election did little to address, let alone pose solutions for the chronic political and economic problems of African Americans. The Democratic standard-bearer, Michael Dukakis, appealed to voters to judge his competence as an administrator and not his political ideology. Accordingly, for most of the campaign he softpedaled his views as a liberal – the dreaded L word his Republican rival, Vice President George H. W. Bush, hurled against him as an epithet. Though Dukakis did appoint some blacks to his staff, including Ronald Brown, a Jackson campaign aide, and though he recruited Jackson to speak for him, especially in the last weeks of the contest, he did not elevate the special concerns of the black community to the forefront of his political agenda. He set the tone early when he delivered a speech in Philadelphia, Mississippi, mentioning civil rights in passing but omitting any reference to the three Freedom Summer workers who were killed there a quarter-century earlier. Taking note of this omission, the *New York Times* aptly commented: "Ignoring the South's often painful, sometimes proud progress in race relations is a peculiar way to profess leadership."

The GOP ticket of Bush and Senator Dan Quayle of Indiana offered no real alternative, as it pledged to extend Reagan administration policies that 79 percent of blacks found objectionable. In fact, blacks had comprised a scant 2.7 percent of the Republican National Convention delegates who chose their standard-bearers and the Reaganomic platform upon which they ran. If Dukakis could be faulted for sins of omission, Bush was guilty of premeditated racial assault. In shades of vintage George Wallace and Richard Nixon, Bush revived the theme of law and order by casting blacks in the image of criminals. Through highly provocative television ads, he attacked Governor Dukakis for granting a prison furlough to Willie Horton, a black inmate in Massachusetts who escaped from the program and raped a white woman. The Republican candidate never referred to the color of Horton's skin, but he did not have to; the medium vividly conveyed this message for him. As Michael Kinsley, the editor of the *New Republic*, pointed out, whether Bush and his advisers were racially motivated was irrelevant. "Hortonism taps into a thick vein of racial paranoia that is a quarter-inch below the surface of the white American consciousness."

Given the choice of having Dukakis neglect them or Bush insult them, African Americans chose to vote for the Democrat. Nearly 90 percent of the black electorate cast their ballots for the Massachusetts governor, about the same proportion supporting Democratic presidential nominees over the past two decades. Nevertheless, blacks appeared to approach the ballot box with slightly less enthusiasm than in recent years, as their turnout at the polls dropped by about 5 percent of those eligible to participate. (Overall, the white turnout also declined.) In major cities such as Chicago, Detroit, Cleveland, New York, and Philadelphia, the black vote fell by an even larger 10 percent. While blacks continued to line up behind the Democratic hopeful, whites preferred the GOP contender. Bush received around 60 percent of white votes. Though he did not score as well as Reagan, the Republican President-elect won 54 percent of the popular votes and 426 electoral ballots.

Though blacks and Democrats failed to vault their candidate into the White House in 1988, they did better in extending their political power elsewhere. The Congressional Black Caucus added its first representative from New Jersey, and the Democrats gained five seats in the House and one in the Senate. At the state level, the Democrats increased their number by 29 legislators, halting the trend toward the Republican Party that had been taking place throughout the 1980s. One of the black incumbents gaining reelection to the House, Mike Espy of Mississippi, did so in impressive fashion. Espy, who had triumphed with a bare 52 percent of the vote in 1986, walloped his Republican opponent by winning 65 percent of his district's electorate. He improved his performance by sweeping the black vote and obtaining an amazing 40 percent of the ballots from his white constituents. The House also saw Espy's colleague, William H. Gray of Pennsylvania, reach an important milestone in his selection as chairman of the Democratic Caucus. In securing this position, Gray became the first black representative to fill a prestigious leadership job in Congress. (The following year he became House majority whip, ranking third in the Democratic chain of command in the lower chamber.) Moreover, after the election the Democratic National Committee selected Ronald Brown, who had steered Jackson's convention forces and later counseled Dukakis during the campaign, for the post of party head.

In addition, the election returns confirmed the continuing gains made by women of color. Although the annual growth rate was slowing down, between 1979 and 1988 the number of black female elected officials nearly doubled, to a figure of 1,625. In the process, the gap between black male and female officeholders had narrowed. In 1979, there were about four times as many black men as women holding elected posts; a decade later the ratio stood at approximately three to one. Only one black woman, however, Cardiss Collins of Illinois, sat in the House of Representatives (a drop from a high of four in 1975). The majority of women still served in municipal governments and local school boards. Paralleling this upsurge in office-holding was the higher voter turnout rate of black women than men. Black women had not yet caught up with men in obtaining public office (see Table 8.1 in the next chapter), but they had surpassed black men by about seven percentage points in going to the polls.

The 1988 elections underscored the difficulties and possibilities facing African Americans. Staying exceedingly loyal to the Democrats and obtaining new bases of influence, they nonetheless felt that the party welcomed their presidential support but followed a strategy to attract conservative white voters. Surveys indicated that the strength of their partisan attachment to the Democrats was weakening, particularly among younger blacks coming of political age after the peak of the civil rights movement. At the same time, the Republicans showed some signs of trying to entice disaffected black Democrats to their ranks. Below the presidential level a number of Republicans had already fashioned winning coalitions with the black electorate. For example, New Jersey's governor, Thomas Kean, had won office, with 60 percent of the black vote; and George Voinovich attracted 85 percent of black ballots in his victory as mayor of Cleveland. Even President Bush recognized the need to refashion the unflattering image left by his predecessor. Putting aside the offensive rhetoric from his campaign, he called for a "kinder and gentler America" and, in a highly publicized gesture, met with Jesse Jackson to discuss how to bring that about. Yet, until the Republicans offered more than soothing words and proposed meaningful alternatives to the policies of the Reagan administration, they had little chance of significantly improving their standing among nonwhite voters.

8

Hope and Despair
The 1990s

Although African Americans faced a third consecutive Republican presidential regime, they had emerged from the Reagan years with the Voting Rights Act strengthened and extended, affirmative action basically intact, and economic sanctions imposed on the apartheid government of South Africa. True, African Americans obtained these results in spite of Reagan, but as long as the Democrats controlled Congress and the Supreme Court followed precedents upholding civil rights, then African Americans could sustain their political advancement. In fact, throughout the 1980s, the number of black elected officials inched steadily upward, and Jesse Jackson's campaigns for the presidency revitalized grassroots enthusiasm for exercising the ballot. Economically, the black middle class had also made significant gains, and as its ranks expanded some of those enjoying financial success joined their white counterparts in supporting the Republicans as the party of economic opportunity. Thus, as African-American communities became more diverse, the political choices available to them multiplied.

The Election of David Dinkins as Mayor
of New York City

A year after Jesse Jackson's 1988 presidential run came to an end, Democratic voters in New York City elected an African American, David Dinkins, as their candidate for mayor. Because this triumph happened in the nation's largest city, the center of the media universe, it assumed greater significance than if it had come to pass virtually anywhere else. Yet surely as noteworthy

Running for Freedom: Civil Rights and Black Politics in America since 1941,
Fourth Edition. Steven F. Lawson.
© 2015 John Wiley & Sons, Inc. Published 2015 by John Wiley & Sons, Inc.

as the event itself was the fact that it had taken New York more than 20 years to follow the examples set by Cleveland and Gary. In addition, since 1973 Los Angeles, the leading city on the West Coast, could brag about having an African-American mayor. In 1989, the city known as the Big Apple, which prefers to establish the fashionable trends, finally had caught up with its urban counterparts throughout the rest of the country.

Jackson's 1988 campaign had pointed the way toward victory. The civil rights minister, though losing the state to Governor Dukakis, carried New York City with 46 percent of the vote. In doing so, he exposed the vulnerability of Ed Koch, the incumbent mayor completing his third term. Elected in 1976, Koch confronted a desperate financial crisis and helped engineer the city's recovery. However, his administration was marred by a series of scandals involving close political associates, and his flamboyant personality offended many constituents. Among the most upset were blacks and other minorities, who believed that the mayor's programs to restore the city's fiscal health ignored, or even aggravated, the condition of the most impoverished residents of their communities. To make matters worse, in 1988, Koch exacerbated tensions between blacks and the city's large Jewish population by attacking the Reverend Jackson as anti-Semitic, reminding voters that the presidential candidate had termed New York City "Hymietown" during the 1984 campaign. Despite the mayor's bitter opposition, Jackson managed to line up solid black support with sufficient backing from Hispanics and liberal whites to emerge ahead of his two opponents in the city. (Koch allied himself with Senator Al Gore, who came in third.)

Encouraged by Jackson's strong showing, Dinkins, the president of the borough of Manhattan since 1985, challenged Koch's bid for an unprecedented fourth term. Born in Trenton, New Jersey, in 1927, Dinkins served in the Marines and, in 1950, graduated from Howard University with a degree in mathematics. A year later he moved to Harlem and decided to become an attorney. Following his graduation from Brooklyn Law School, in 1956, he pursued a career in politics and served as Democratic Party district leader, state assemblyman, and city clerk, a position he held for ten years before winning election as chief executive of Manhattan. A pensive, soft-spoken individual, Dinkins had a talent for listening carefully before acting and for playing the role of conciliator. He would need to draw upon those skills to forge a winning coalition in a city where blacks constituted less than a quarter of the electorate. His critics called Dinkins indecisive, but almost all agreed that in the rough-and-tumble world of New York City politics, he remained a gentleman – "a political Bill Cosby," as one newspaper dubbed him.

Although neither Koch nor Dinkins sought to attack the other along racial lines, the Democratic mayoral contest took place against a backdrop of growing racial animosities. Trouble had been brewing for some time. The stress of daily life in a city as large as New York strained the limits of racial toleration. The twin problems of crime and drug abuse, nurtured by poverty, took on racial overtones and fostered mutual suspicion. In 1984, when Bernhard Goetz shot four black youths who he believed were trying to rob him on a subway train, many whites regarded him as a hero, a kind of real-life Lone Ranger. The situation grew worse as a number of disturbing incidents followed. On December 20, 1986, a gang of whites attacked three blacks after they entered a pizza parlor in the predominantly white section of Howard Beach, Queens. In trying to make his escape, one of the blacks was struck by a car and killed. A little more than two years later, in April 1989, a white female jogger running in Central Park was raped, beaten, and left for dead by a roving band of black and Hispanic teenagers. Racial friction again reached a peak during the primary campaign for mayor. On August 23, 1989, four black youths ventured into the mainly white neighborhood of Bensonhurst, Brooklyn, to inquire about purchasing a used car. They were assaulted by a mob of whites, one of whom fired a gunshot that killed 16-year-old Yusuf Hawkins. Racial demonstrations followed this tragic incident.

Dinkins won the Democratic primary, but the outcome of the election reflected sharp racial cleavages. In a field of one black and three white candidates, Dinkins gained about 50 percent of the vote and Koch came in second with 42 percent. The nature of their support was markedly different. Blacks constituted 56 percent of Dinkins's total vote, while whites composed 34 percent, and Hispanics 8 percent. In contrast, 89 percent of Koch's vote came from whites, 7 percent from Hispanics, and only 2 percent from blacks. As expected Dinkins ran strongest in New York's minority communities. He captured more than 90 percent of black ballots and a slight majority of Hispanic votes. On the other side, 70 percent of whites stuck with Koch. One of his supporters from Bensonhurst, a community Koch carried by a margin of nearly seven to one, explained her vote for the incumbent: "I'm afraid to have a black mayor."

However, what impressed most observers was not the racial polarization of the electorate but the relative success Dinkins had in attracting white crossover voters. This minority of whites, about 30 percent, constituted a critical element of Dinkins's winning margin of victory. The Manhattan borough president scored twice as well among whites as Jesse Jackson had in 1988. His 25 percent share of Jewish votes was also an improvement over that of Jackson, and was noteworthy because it came against Koch, himself a Jew. Most whites believed that Dinkins would help heal the city's racial wounds, and according to one exit poll 60 percent of whites expected Dinkins to treat both races fairly. In sampling a cross-section of the entire electorate, another survey reported that 91 percent said Dinkins displayed sensitivity to people's needs compared with only 7 percent who thought Koch did so. The impact of the Bensonhurst murder was difficult to measure precisely. Though most voters cited other issues as more important in making up their minds, the Bensonhurst killing probably encouraged a greater number of blacks to go to the polls and reinforced the feeling among whites that Dinkins could help defuse similar racial conflicts in the future. As one of his black supporters remarked: "Dinkins projects the kind of personality that's not threatening to whites and is acceptable to blacks."

Nevertheless, Dinkins had a tough battle in the general election. Successful in uniting Democratic Party leaders, most notably Mayor Koch, behind him, Dinkins still had to keep the white Democratic rank and file in line. In a city where Republicans were outnumbered five to one, the Democratic nominee normally was a shoo-in. However, Dinkins's Republican opponent, Rudolph Giuliani, a former federal prosecutor, waged a fierce campaign to lure white Democrats away from their traditional fold. Besides attacking Dinkins for financial improprieties, Giuliani appealed to racial fears. Behind the moderate Dinkins, he warned, stood the more controversial figure of Jesse Jackson waiting to call the shots.

Dinkins won by a narrow margin of two percentage points – the closest mayoral election since 1905. Despite substantial defections by white Democrats, he held on to 30 percent of the white electorate, including between 33 and 40 percent of Jews. Dinkins ran extremely well among minority voters, gaining more than 90 percent of black ballots and nearly 70 percent of Hispanic votes. Notwithstanding this breakthrough victory, those figures showed the continuing role of racial considerations in determining electoral choices. Yet looked at from a different perspective, the results also demonstrated Dinkins's success in attracting a genuine multiracial coalition. Of the mayor's total vote, approximately 50 percent came from blacks, 30 percent from whites, and 17 percent from Hispanics – a "gorgeous mosaic," as Dinkins called it.[1]

[1] Election day also saw another landmark victory. L. Douglas Wilder, the Democratic lieutenant governor of Virginia, became the first black to be elected governor in the nation's history. In a contest characterized by negative campaigning, but in which the race issue remained in the background, Wilder defeated his Republican opponent by a mere 7,000 votes out of nearly 2 million cast. Race still mattered, however. Many whites who voted for the rest of the statewide Democratic ticket declined to support Wilder, accounting for the closest gubernatorial contest in Virginia's history.

Figure 19 Campaigning for mayor of New York City, David Dinkins stands under a statue of George Washington on the steps of Federal Hall in lower Manhattan. (AP Photo/David Cantor/Press Association)

Dinkins found his job as mayor a difficult challenge, filled with high expectations that were hard to satisfy, African Americans and Hispanics received more appointments to city government and minority businesses obtained a greater share of municipal contracts. Mayor Dinkins served as a source of pride for many black New Yorkers. "When Martin Luther King was alive we had somebody to look up to," a resident of Brooklyn's Bedford-Stuyvesant area declared. "Now the black community is lost. David Dinkins will help a lot." At the same time, however, the plight of the impoverished and the homeless and the problems of crime and drugs remained beyond the grasp of even the most compassionate occupant of city hall to solve. The mayor faced an entrenched municipal bureaucracy resistant to change, powerful corporate developers, tough-minded union leaders, and a shortage of revenue to address issues that were national in scope. Furthermore, Dinkins found it difficult to strike the delicate balance of responding to the special needs of minority communities without losing the necessary economic and political support of the white majority.[2]

Black Conservatism

While most blacks ran as Democratic candidates, the most fertile ground for recruiting African Americans to the Republican Party was found among black conservatives. The challenge proved formidable. At the end of the 1980s, of the 7,300 black elected officials in the nation a mere 76 counted themselves as Republicans. Only three of 439 black state legislators had won on the GOP label. Nevertheless, some promising signs existed. For example, in 1990, Gary Franks from Waterbury, Connecticut, became the first African-American Republican since the New Deal to sit in the House of Representatives. Although blacks continued to identify themselves as loyal Democrats, the strength of their attachment began to wane, especially among younger blacks. Accordingly, the Republican National Committee launched "Operation Outreach" to recruit black voters away from the Democrats.

President Bush did his part to appeal to African Americans by making several high-level appointments. He selected General Colin Powell as head of the Joint Chiefs of Staff, Louis Sullivan as Secretary of Health and Human Resources, and Clarence Thomas, whom Reagan had appointed director of the Equal Employment Opportunity Commission (EEOC), as a judge on the US Court of Appeals for the District of Columbia. Claudia Butts, the White House liaison to the black community, expressed the growing sense of comfort her fellow African Americans felt within Republican circles. "I want to say it loud and clear," this former associate of the right-wing Heritage Foundation exclaimed, "that it's O.K. to be a conservative," and invited black conservatives "to come out of the closet."

---

[2] In 1993, Dinkins failed to win reelection against Rudolph Giuliani, losing by a narrow margin of 51 percent to 49 percent. While his share of the votes among blacks increased, he saw his percentage of white (including Jewish) and Hispanic votes decline. Voters saw him as a calming influence on racial conflicts but considered him a poor administrator of city services.

Since the election of Ronald Reagan in 1980 the fortunes of black conservatives had risen. Some polls estimated that one-third of African Americans considered themselves conservative. If that were true, most did so mainly on cultural rather than economic grounds. Deeply religious, many black Americans followed their fundamentalist Christian denominations in opposing abortion and supporting prayer in the schools. Concerning the policy of busing, blacks had become increasingly weary of their children shouldering most of the burden of being transported outside of their neighborhoods to achieve racial balance, a burden that had not brought educational equality in the classroom. However, Republicans still had a long way to go in making inroads among blacks. Surveys continued to show that the majority of blacks backed the Great Society's liberal programs designed to relieve the poverty disproportionately affecting African Americans. To the chagrin of black conservatives, most African Americans told pollsters that traditional civil rights leaders, such as Jesse Jackson and Benjamin Hooks of the NAACP, effectively represented their views.

Challenging this conventional leadership was a diverse group of black public officials and intellectuals. Their beliefs generally paralleled those of white conservative Republicans who had gained ascendancy under Reagan. Hostile to big government, increased federal regulation, and deficit spending, they emphatically denounced liberalism as a failed ideology. They also joined their white counterparts in criticizing affirmative action, welfare, and busing programs commonly seen as helping blacks, but which they argued caused African Americans great harm. In attacking these crucial items on the liberal agenda, black conservatives gave aid and comfort to the Reagan and Bush administrations, which denied that their policies were conceived out of callousness and racism.

Conservative blacks emphasized self-help, self-esteem, and personal responsibility and scorned federal programs for discouraging individual initiative and enterprise. Part of a longstanding tradition of thinking within black communities, these ideas had been identified with leaders as different as Booker T. Washington and Malcolm X. In this vein, Clarence Thomas asked, "Where does [Malcolm X] say black people should go begging to the Labor Department for jobs? Where does he say you should sacrifice your institutions to be next to white people?" Black conservatives criticized busing for promoting the belief that black students could learn only in the presence of whites and blamed affirmative action for stigmatizing African Americans as unqualified. They maintained that welfare policies undermined the moral fabric of black families, leading to the increase of out-of-wedlock births, crime, and drug abuse. Conservatives further rejected liberalism for what Malcolm would have called brainwashing: instilling in blacks the notion that they were permanent victims and could do nothing to help themselves.

Unlike Malcolm X, however, black conservatives shared a fundamental optimism about America affording blacks a chance for equal opportunity. Alan Keyes, a Reagan appointee and an aspiring presidential candidate, "came to the conclusion that there was something basically correct about the American system." Acknowledging that the civil rights movement had once been useful in overturning segregation and disfranchisement, they saw, according to writer Shelby Steele, "a marked decline in racism." Whatever had happened in the past no longer held relevance for the present. "I don't see any Bull Connors around," a black GOP congressional aide observed, referring to how the country had changed since the 1960s. By implication, then, government-sponsored racism no longer stood in the way of black ambitions, and any failure to take advantage of the opportunities currently available rested with blacks themselves.

These doctrines of self-help, black pride, and moral and community values struck a responsive chord among those worried about the disintegration of black neighborhoods and family life. Indeed, the NAACP and the Urban League began to pay increased attention to these issues. Nevertheless, what left most African Americans unpersuaded was the idea that white racism and its effects had disappeared as a serious obstacle in their lives. They continued to see federal programs, however flawed in practice, as necessary for black progress. After all, slavery and Jim Crow had worked their evils for three centuries, whereas civil rights programs had been around for only three decades.

Black conservatives highlighted the limitations of conventional civil rights wisdom, but they remained blind to their own contradictions. Many of them had benefited from the affirmative action plans they decried. They criticized affirmative action for helping the middle class to the virtual exclusion of the poor, though they spoke from the same middle-class perspective. They pointed out the drawbacks of integration but lived in white neighborhoods and worked in white institutions. Like Booker T. Washington before them, black conservatives drew exaggerated generalizations from their own personal experiences and ignored the restraints still imposed on those unable to overcome the lingering effects of racial discrimination. In advocating self-help as a vehicle for upward mobility they missed what Washington also had overlooked: structural changes in the American economy had empowered large corporations at the expense of individuals living on the economic margins. The loss of once high-paying industrial jobs to overseas and the expansion of employment in the low-wage service sector considerably narrowed opportunities for black self-advancement.

President Bush shared the view of black conservatives against affirmative action. In 1990, Bush vetoed a bill passed by Congress that he believed would impose racial quotas in hiring practices. In 1991, Congress passed a modified Civil Rights Act, designed to remedy a series of Supreme Court decisions that reduced the right of workers to sue their employers for racial discrimination. Assured that the measure did not involve quotas and looking ahead to running for reelection the following year, Bush signed this revised law. The 1991 Civil Rights Act provided for the right to trial by jury on racial discrimination claims and allowed claimants to ask for damages based on emotional distress, while limiting the amount that a jury could award, provisions that reversed recent rulings of the high tribunal. At the same time, Bush undertook an initiative to give black conservatives a voice on the Supreme Court.

The Clarence Thomas–Anita Hill Controversy

Though black conservatives steadily gained a voice in shaping public policy during the Reagan and Bush administrations, they did so without commanding the attention of the general public. Next to Jesse Jackson, Benjamin Hooks, and the Nation of Islam's Louis Farrakhan, African-American conservatives went largely unnoticed outside of intellectual and government circles. This changed dramatically on July 1, 1991, when President Bush nominated Clarence Thomas to replace Justice Thurgood Marshall, who was retiring, on the US Supreme Court. The storm of controversy that erupted over this appointment highlighted the growing presence of black conservatives and their challenge to standard liberal thinking within the African-American community. It also underscored the continued existence of gender as well as race as a divisive political issue in America.

Thomas appeared to embody the conservative message of black self-help. Born in Savannah, Georgia, on June 23, 1948, and raised by his grandparents in the small town of Pin Point from age seven, he gained a strong work ethic from them and received a heightened sense of discipline in the Catholic schools he attended. He graduated from Holy Cross College in Massachusetts in the 1960s, where he protested against racial discrimination

Figure 20 President George H. W. Bush with his Supreme Court nominee Clarence Thomas. (Photo © J. David Ake/Getty Images)

and was an admirer of Malcolm X. He attended Yale Law School and following graduation served as an aide to Senator John Danforth, the Republican attorney general of Missouri. After a brief stint as a corporate lawyer and another tour of duty with Danforth, who had become a US senator, Thomas went to work for the Reagan administration, first as assistant for civil rights in the Department of Education and then as chairman of the Equal Employment Opportunity Commission. In 1990, President Bush tapped this rising black Republican star to serve on the federal appeals bench in Washington, DC.

Having climbed this ladder of success, Thomas interpreted his good fortune solely as the outcome of his own hard work. He denied that race was important. "I have always found it offensive for the government," Thomas stated, "to treat black people differently because of the color of their skin." A friend elaborated on Thomas's thinking: "He made it strictly on the merits, and he resents the notion that he's ever gotten anywhere because he's black." Not shy about expressing these views, during the 1980s Thomas spoke out against affirmative action, busing, and welfare. Evidence abounded to conclude that, as a judge with lifetime tenure, Clarence Thomas would not follow in the liberal footsteps of Justice Marshall.

That is precisely why President Bush nominated him for the post. He could select a staunch conservative for the high court to satisfy his Republican constituency and at the same time undercut Democratic opposition by choosing an African American. Despite the fact that Thomas was far more conservative than most blacks, the majority of African Americans favored his appointment. This contrasted sharply with the position of black organizations such as the NAACP, the Congressional Black Caucus, and the National Bar Association, which opposed his nomination on ideological grounds.[3] Women's groups also mobilized against Thomas because of his antiabortion views. Given the split between civil rights leaders and the black rank and file and the opposition of predominantly white women's organizations, just as the President hoped, Democratic senators had to act cautiously in considering Thomas.

Notwithstanding Bush's and Thomas's comments to the contrary, race did play a significant role in the appointment. The chief executive denied that he selected Thomas because he was black, insisting that merit was his only consideration. However, this justification did not ring entirely true. Had Marshall, the only African American ever to sit on the court, not retired and another position become available, it is highly doubtful that Bush would have chosen Thomas to fill it. Furthermore, even with more than a decade of public service, Thomas had not particularly distinguished himself as suitable for elevation to the high bench. Bush's previous nominee to the court, David Souter, had received a unanimous rating of "well qualified" from the influential American Bar Association, and while Thomas could muster a "qualified" rating, he did not gain a single vote in the top category.

Race figured into Clarence Thomas's success in another important way. Though Thomas denounced affirmative action, he had benefited directly from it. His admission into the prestigious Yale Law School had come as a result of an affirmative action program by the university that recruited qualified minorities, though not necessarily those individuals who scored highest on entrance exams. Whatever Thomas's individual merits, race provided him with the necessary opportunity to gain admission in the first

---

[3] The nominee's race, however, left black groups slow to respond and badly divided. The National Urban League declared itself neutral and the Southern Christian Leadership Conference endorsed Thomas.

place. Other inconsistencies between Thomas's public career and his personal life surfaced. This self-proclaimed admirer of Malcolm X, who said in 1983 that he also respected Louis Farrakhan, lived in an upscale white suburb with a white wife, attended a predominantly white church, and collaborated closely with right-wing Christians in orchestrating his appointment. A critic of an expansive federal government, Thomas had earned his credentials for the Supreme Court post largely through his performance as an official in the Washington bureaucracy. He attacked welfare for destroying personal incentive and cited as an example his own sister; yet she had gone on public assistance, albeit only temporarily, after quitting her job to care for their ailing aunt.

Nevertheless, the politics of the situation favored his confirmation. At his hearing before the Senate Judiciary Committee, the carefully prepared Thomas avoided taking a stand on controversial issues such as abortion, declining to comment because he might be called to rule on the issue once on the court. Though most civil rights organizations opposed him, counted among his defenders was a new generation of black conservatives, many of them professionals and businesspeople, which had risen in the post–civil rights era. As one lawyer expressed it, the engine of the black struggle was shifting gears, signaling that "there are other viewpoints within the black community as to the appropriate vehicle on how to move from one point to the next." In late September 1991, the Judiciary Committee deadlocked seven to seven on whether to recommend confirmation, but the Democratic-controlled Senate seemed inclined to approve Thomas by a slight margin.

Suddenly, the Anita Hill bombshell produced a blast that nearly destroyed Thomas. Hill, a Yale Law School graduate and law professor at the University of Oklahoma, had served as an aide to Thomas at the Department of Education and the EEOC. She had privately revealed to the Judiciary Committee that while she was working for Thomas he had sexually harassed her. She claimed that Thomas used inappropriate language in her presence, made pornographic references, and pressured her for dates. Hill told the committee that she did not want her accusations to become public. Her complaint sprang mainly out of personal, not ideological, concerns. While in his employ, Hill had shared Thomas's conservative outlook, though to a more moderate degree. Thomas categorically denied his former assistant's charges, and his advocates insisted that Hill was at worst a liar and at best a person who could not clearly distinguish social reality from sexual fantasy.

Given the volatile nature of the charges leveled by a woman with an otherwise solid reputation, the all-white male Judiciary Committee convened a second round of hearings after her accusations were leaked to the press. From October 11 to the early hours of October 14, the investigation focused not on ideology but on character and credibility. Televised by the major networks to a very large audience, the hearings pitted Hill against Thomas – two black lawyers, a woman against a man. In the glare of the cameras, Hill recounted the charges she had first voiced privately, in testimony that was both intimate and painful. Thomas followed her, and in equally uncomfortable and grave fashion rejected her entire version of events. Each side produced a stream of character witnesses to bolster its case.

The turning point of the drama came when Thomas summoned racial imagery and mythology in his defense. The same conservative who had criticized civil rights leaders for "bitching, moaning, and whining" and encouraging blacks to see themselves as victims adopted the very tactic he despised. Invoking images from the nation's racist past with its brutal treatment of African Americans, he declared that Hill's comments hurt him deeply because they played into sexual stereotypes about black males. With his anger barely under control, he characterized the televised hearings as a "high-tech lynching for uppity blacks who in a way deign to think for themselves ... that unless you kowtow to the old order ... [y]ou will be lynched, destroyed, caricatured by a committee of the U.S. Senate rather than hung from a tree." In the end, to save his career, Thomas chose to manipulate history and cast himself as a victim of racist slurs.

He did so very effectively. According to surveys, by a two-to-one margin Americans, black and white alike, believed Clarence Thomas over Anita Hill. African-American support for Thomas might have been even greater had many black women not found Hill's accusations so credible. To be sure, these black women also identified with the legacy of racial oppression Thomas had voiced, but they believed that the double burden of race and gender discrimination black women historically shouldered was being ignored, even trivialized. They pointed out that in the past black women themselves had been the victims of sexual abuse by both white and black men. However, because black women had traditionally been stereotyped as sexually promiscuous, as the historian Elsa Barkley Brown noted, "an African- American woman is not likely to be believed if she speaks of unwarranted sexual advances, or will be believed to have been either the initiator or a willing participant." Black female supporters of Hill placed an advertisement in the *New York Times* entitled "African American Women in Defense of Ourselves," which contained nearly 2,000 signatures. Despite

Figure 21   Anita Hill, who accused Clarence Thomas of sexual harassment before Congress and a nationwide television audience. (Getty Images)

the concerns of a large and articulate circle of African-American women, however, most of their black sisters considered racism a greater obstacle to African-American advancement than sexism, and they closed ranks behind Thomas, thereby embracing the racial symbolism of his appointment to the highest court in the land.

With the majority of Americans supporting Thomas's nomination, the Senate voted to confirm. Because of the unusual nature of the proceedings, the Judiciary Committee did not take another vote or make a formal recommendation concerning Hill's charges. Brought before the full Senate in mid-October, Thomas's appointment squeaked through by 52 to 48, the narrowest margin for any Supreme Court justice in history. The majority contained a number of southern Democrats from constituencies in which black votes influenced the outcome of elections. These same lawmakers had voted against the white conservative Robert Bork when blacks registered their disapproval, but they proved willing to support the black conservative Thomas because of his backing from African Americans. In the end, whatever Thomas's stated preference for a color-blind society, he owed his victory to the enduring presence of race as a central feature of the American political landscape.

The 1992 Elections

Elections the following year promised new possibilities for increasing the number of black officeholders, mainly at the national level. The 1990 census required reapportionment of Congress, and southern states such as Florida, North Carolina, Georgia, and Texas stood to benefit from the population growth they had experienced during the previous decade. The Bush Justice Department, backed by civil rights groups, called on the states covered under the Voting Rights Act to redraw congressional boundary lines to expand the number of districts with a majority black population. Not only would African- American representation rise from these majority-minority districts as they were called, but Republicans would likewise gain. Because white Democrats in the South relied on black support for their election, designing new districts by carving out black voters from their former constituencies would likely leave Democratic incumbents vulnerable to GOP challengers.

In addition, the Clarence Thomas–Anita Hill controversy stimulated increased interest among black women in running for office. The image of an all-white, male Senate Judiciary Committee publicly examining the morals of two African Americans upset many blacks. Moreover, the seeming insensitivity to Hill's charges of sexual harassment particularly angered women, both black and white. Fueled by this conflict and worried about the increasing attacks on abortion rights, women's groups fostered political networking and launched fundraising drives in support of female candidates.

Many of the expected gains materialized. More African Americans than ever before, 55, campaigned for Congress. Of these, 39 Democrats,

12 Republicans, and four independents, all the Democrats and one Republican, Gary Franks of Connecticut, won. As a result of these victories the number of blacks in Congress leaped from 26 to 40, and the proportion of black representatives in Washington came very close to matching the 11 percent black share of the general population. Thirteen of the 15 newly elected officials in the House came from the South, mainly from the recently created majority- minority districts.

Black women candidates scored some impressive triumphs. Between 1990 and 1993, the total number of black female elected officials throughout the nation climbed from 1,950 to 2,332, a substantial rise of about 20 percent (see Table 8.1). Female black officeholders continued to make steady progress in closing the gap with their black male counterparts. In 1988, slightly over three times more black men than women occupied elected positions; in 1993, the figure had dropped to just under two and one-half. The overwhelming majority of these women held state and local posts, but following the 1992 elections ten black women, an increase of six, headed for Congress. All but one took seats in the House. This group included Eva Clayton of North Carolina. Typical of those coming to Washington for the first time, Clayton represented a newly created majority-black district fashioned under federal voting rights guidelines. Accordingly, she spoke for one of the most racially integrated constituencies in the country with a black–white voting-age population breakdown of 53 to 47 percent. Representative Clayton received the further distinction of being selected by the incoming class of congressional members, black and white, male and female, as their leader.

Perhaps the most notable victory came in the election of Carol Moseley Braun to the US Senate, the first black woman ever to reach this office. A Democrat from Chicago, Moseley Braun had entered politics working for Harold Washington. She had served in the Illinois General Assembly for ten years, reaching the post of assistant majority leader. After a successful stint as Cook County Recorder of Deeds, she defeated the incumbent senator, Alan J. Dixon, in the Democratic primary and went on to beat her Republican opponent with 55 percent of the vote. Dixon had voted to confirm the nomination of Clarence Thomas, and Moseley Braun had expressed outrage at the spectacle of the televised hearings and the judgment by the lily-white Senate. On taking office, Senator Moseley Braun received an assignment to the Judiciary Committee, one of two women (Diane Feinstein of California was the other) to watch over future judicial appointments considered by that panel.

Table 8.1 Black elected officials in the United States, 1975–2002

	Number of males	Number of females	Male increase (%)	Female increase (%)
1975	2,973	530	–	–
1976	3,295	684	10.8	29.1
1977	3,529	782	7.1	14.3
1978	3,660	843	3.7	7.8
1979	3,725	882	1.8	4.6
1980	3,936	976	5.7	10.6
1981	4,017	1,021	2.0	4.6
1982	4,079	1,081	1.5	9.7
1983	4,383	1,223	7.5	13.1
1984	4,441	1,259	1.3	2.9
1985	4,697	1,359	5.8	10.8
1986	4,942	1,482	5.2	9.1
1987	5,117	1,564	3.5	5.5
1988	5,204	1,625	1.8	3.9
1989	5,412	1,814	4.0	11.6
1990	5,420	1,950	0.1	7.5
1991	5,427	2,053	0.1	5.3
1992	5,431	2,121	0.0	3.3
1993	5,683	2,332	4.6	9.9
1994	5,694	2,468	0.2	5.8
1995	5,782	2,637	1.5	6.8
1996	5,830	2,749	0.8	4.2
1997	5,847	2,809	0.3	2.2
1998	5,944	2,924	1.6	4.1
1999	5,939	2,997	−0.1	2.5
2000	5,921	3,119	−0.3	4.1
2002	6,069	3,401	2.4	9.0

Sources: David A. Bositis, *Black Elected Officials: A Statistical Summary, 2000* (Joint Center for Political and Economic Studies, Washington, DC, 2002), 21. The Joint Center cefased publishing these statistics after 2000. The 2002 figures are courtesy of David Bositis and Richard Hart, and cover the two-year period from 2000 to 2002.

Bill Clinton and the Congressional Black Caucus

The 1992 elections also brought Bill Clinton to the presidency. In running against President Bush, the governor of Arkansas conducted a campaign that generally soft-pedaled the race issue. With Senator Al Gore of Tennessee as his running mate, Clinton followed a strategy that sought to lure Reagan Democrats and traditional southern white supporters back to the party. Aiming to move the Democrats more toward the political center and away from the party's liberal image, he emphasized economic issues over such divisive civil rights matters as affirmative action. This message played well as the nation struggled to recover from a two-year economic recession. Nevertheless, Clinton did not ignore his African-American electoral base and appointed as key campaign advisers Vernon Jordan, former director of the Voter Education Project and the Urban League, and Ron Brown, who had directed Jesse Jackson's campaign in 1988. After 12 years of conservative Republican presidential rule, Clinton, from Hope, Arkansas, inspired in blacks a measure of optimism.

African Americans played an instrumental role in Clinton's election, marking only the second time in the previous 24 years that a Democrat moved into the White House. More than any racial factor, the troubling state of the economy stimulated black support for Clinton. An NAACP official explained: "The economic downturn has escalated to a large degree problems of the African-American community," and a young Austin, Texas, man echoed this sentiment: "We've lost jobs and benefits. Our black children don't have quality schools. Our neighborhoods are full of drugs and crime." Clinton garnered eight out of ten black votes, the highest percentage of any group that supported the new president.[4] About 1 million more black voters participated in 1992 than four years earlier, an upswing generated by a combination of economic woes and the large number of black candidates competing for office. The increased black turnout exceeded Clinton's margin of victory in seven states: Georgia, Louisiana, Maryland, Michigan, New Jersey, Ohio, and Tennessee.

In recognition of the decisive contribution of African-American voters, President Clinton appointed four blacks to his Cabinet. Mike Espy resigned his Mississippi congressional seat to become Secretary of Agriculture. The chief executive swore in Ron Brown as Secretary of Commerce, Hazel O'Leary as Secretary of Energy, and Jesse Brown as head of the Department of Veterans Affairs. Never before in US history had so many African Americans occupied such high-level positions at one time.

More than any of his predecessors, Clinton had to contend with the power of the enlarged Congressional Black Caucus. The group's influence

---

[4] However, a troubling sign for the Democrats was that Clinton received a slightly lower percentage of black votes than had Carter, Mondale, and Dukakis.

had swelled not only because of increased numbers but also because of the important positions some of its senior members held. Ron Dellums of California chaired the House Armed Services Committee; John Conyers of Michigan presided over the Government Operations Committee; and Louis Stokes of Ohio and Julian Dixon of Illinois headed critical subcommittees of the Appropriations Committee. In addition, former SNCC chairman John Lewis of Georgia acted as chief deputy whip and sat on the powerful House Committee on Ways and Means, and one-time Chicago Black Panther Party member Bobby Rush joined the Committee on Banking,

Figure 22 Kweisi Mfume, who headed the Congressional Black Caucus and left Congress to become president of the NAACP in 1995. (Photo © Cynthia Johnson/ Getty Images)

Finance, and Urban Affairs. Containing veteran lawmakers as well as newcomers, the CBC had grown from its early days as a small, cohesive body into a more diverse group representing urban and rural, northern and southern, and predominantly black and majority white districts. Tending to unite around measures that advanced civil rights, affirmative action, and economic benefits for African Americans, the CBC's members nevertheless followed their own interests on issues affecting their particular constituencies.

The chair of the CBC, Kweisi Mfume of Baltimore, attempted to flex its newfound political muscle. A gang member as a youngster, Mfume had turned his life around, changed his name from Frizzell Gray, attended college, and launched his political career as a crusading city councilman. Elected to Congress in 1986, he mastered the skills of coalition-building and political networking. Mfume generally succeeded in keeping the diverse group of black lawmakers together – in 1993, the CBC obtained agreement on over 90 percent of House roll-call votes. He pushed the CBC's agenda, which included cutting military spending and increasing domestic aid for cities and poor rural areas, expanding healthcare to the uninsured, investing in low-income housing, and appointing more minorities to federal offices. "We're not combative," Mfume remarked about the CBC's approach, "but we're not going to roll over." However, Mfume did not run the CBC as a gang lord but as a practical politician. When his attempt to "enter a covenant" with the controversial Nation of Islam raised a howl of protest from supporters inside and outside the group, he quickly retreated.

Lani Guinier

Relations between Clinton and the CBC got off to a shaky start over the nomination of Lani Guinier, as assistant attorney general for civil rights. On April 29, 1993, the President selected Guinier to head the Justice Department's Civil Rights Division. A Yale Law School classmate of the chief executive's wife, Hillary, Guinier had extensive experience in the area of voting rights. She had served as deputy to the chief of the Civil Rights Division during the Carter administration and subsequently worked for the NAACP Legal Defense Fund in successfully litigating cases against racially discriminatory election practices. A University of Pennsylvania Law School professor at the time of her nomination, she had published several provocative law review articles challenging attorneys, judges, and policymakers to reevaluate how best to extend political power to African Americans. These scholarly treatises, originally aimed at a small academic audience, put her nomination in considerable jeopardy.

Conservative opponents of affirmative action programs and of the new black majority voting districts, blasted Guinier's appointment. Disparaged as a "quota queen," a racist in reverse, and an enemy of majority rule, Guinier found herself portrayed as a radical zealot for racial preferences. Newspaper headlines and columnists simplified, sometimes trivialized, her complex arguments, and politicians hopped on the opposition bandwagon. Republican minority leader Robert Dole, offering no evidence that he had actually read her essays, expressed shock that Clinton would choose someone who was a "consistent supporter not only of quotas but of vote-rigging schemes that make quotas look mild." These attacks found support among those with a less obvious political agenda who still questioned whether any race-conscious solutions should be tolerated in a color-blind society.

Guinier's beliefs were less radical and more complicated than her detractors claimed. The law school professor argued that current enforcement of the Voting Rights Act, however well-meaning, would fall short of expanding political opportunity for racial minorities. If anything, contrary to her opponents' charges against her, she had become critical of race-specific voting procedures, which she had once supported, and favored those such as cumulative voting, which did not isolate blacks into separate electoral enclaves. Under a cumulative voting system, voters held as many ballots as there were contested seats. For example, if ten positions were at stake, each voter received ten ballots and could cast them for one or two candidates or spread them among all ten. Guinier reasoned that various interest groups, including those that were racially based, could bloc vote and place at least one of their favored candidates in office. At the same time, she contended, this system would encourage African Americans to form coalitions and exchange votes with other groups in support of mutually acceptable candidates. Furthermore, it was an exaggeration to brand her cumulative voting proposal as radical, because the Reagan–Bush Justice Department had sanctioned its use as a remedy in about three dozen instances, and many business corporations used it in electing members of their boards of directors.

Guinier also expressed concern about the problem of a permanent majority of white lawmakers keeping the black minority from exercising power in legislative and other governing bodies. "At this moment in history," she had written in the late 1980s, "political fairness for blacks means a fair

Figure 23 Lani Guinier, who was unsuccessfully nominated by President Clinton as head of the Justice Department's Civil Rights Division and was described by her critics as a woman with a "strange name, strange hair, strange writing." (Photo © The Image Works/Topfoto)

opportunity to choose their representatives, a fair shake in administrative enforcement that protects minority voting rights, and a fair share of substantive, legislative policy outcomes." She argued that under current congressional rules and procedures it took more than a majority vote to close Senate filibusters, override presidential vetoes, and ratify constitutional amendments. Within this tradition, Guinier wanted to explore the possibility of requiring "supermajority" votes in legislatures on issues of vital concern to racial minorities. Her opponents maintained that this amounted to the same discredited anti-majoritarian ideas that southern secessionists had used to nullify federal laws before the Civil War, whereas her defenders viewed her suggestions as a legitimate attempt to protect minority rights and interests from majority tyranny.

Because President Clinton denied her an opportunity for an ample hearing, only those who took the time to read Guinier's law review articles would have known that her complicated views defied easy categorization. Before the Senate Judiciary Committee could begin its customary deliberations, Clinton withdrew the nomination in June. Though Guinier wanted the chance to defend herself and show that her ideas were being distorted, the President retreated before the conservative attacks and the defection of key Democratic senators who wanted to avoid another bruising confirmation battle like those for Robert Bork and Clarence Thomas. However, Clinton tried to assuage the bitter disappointment of the Congressional Black Caucus, which steadfastly backed Guinier, by personally telephoning Representative Mfume with his decision even before he told the nominee. Mfume remained unpersuaded, as did the NAACP, which pledged "to hold the President's feet to the fire on every vital issue ... to rally support for progressive appointments and programs and to defeat the bigots who have momentarily won the day."[5]

Mending Fences

Mfume and the CBC did keep the pressure on Clinton in seeking to advance their objectives. Although the Democrats controlled Congress, the legislative climate was generally cool toward progressive measures, as evidenced by the failure of the Clinton administration to obtain healthcare legislation. In most respects, the CBC lacked the votes to achieve its aims, but it did succeed in waging defensive battles to force compromises from the President and his congressional leaders. Thus, Clinton's deficit-cutting budget narrowly passed the House in 1993 only after modifications had been made to satisfy the CBC's complaints that the poor were unfairly affected. The President got his crime bill passed, with its ban on certain classifications of assault weapons, following negotiations to meet concerns raised by the CBC. (However, the CBC failed to win approval for provisions related to restricting the death penalty and funding for crime prevention programs for inner-city youths.) Clinton and the CBC did score a mutual victory in winning passage of the motor-voter bill, which expanded voter registration opportunities by allowing convenient enrollment at motor vehicle offices. Overall, Clinton and the CBC maintained an uneasy alliance, with neither of them willing or politically able to abandon the other.

---

[5] The CBC and civil rights groups opposed Clinton's next candidate for the post, John Payton, a black corporation lawyer, who withdrew. Not until April 1994 did Clinton fill the vacancy. He chose Deval Patrick, a former NAACP Legal Defense Fund attorney, who finally won confirmation.

Perhaps the most important and visible triumph secured by the CBC involved foreign affairs. Following the overthrow in 1991 of President Jean-Bertrand Aristide of Haiti, the CBC had pushed for US intervention to restore the democratically elected leader. Just as they had demonstrated their solidarity with the struggle for freedom against apartheid in South Africa, African Americans and their representatives had a special interest in the fate of the predominantly black Caribbean nation. CBC members became particularly irate over what they viewed as a racially discriminatory refugee policy. In contrast to the mainly white Cuban exiles who had received asylum in the United States from Fidel Castro's government, black Haitians suffering under military rule who attempted to flee their homeland were blocked from entering the country. Moreover, the CBC wanted the President to authorize a military invasion of the island to restore Aristide to office.

Under pressure from the CBC and seeking to show his strength as commander-in-chief, Clinton modified his policy. He appointed William Gray, a former congressman from Pennsylvania who had once headed the CBC, as his special adviser on Haiti. The President also reversed the practice of turning back Haitian refugees and prepared to send American troops into combat. As a last resort, he sent a delegation of former President Jimmy Carter, Senator Sam Nunn of Georgia, and General Colin Powell to persuade Haiti's military leaders to step down voluntarily. Only a few hours before US forces were poised to invade, Haiti's rulers resigned and agreed to allow Aristide to return. To the delight of Mfume and the CBC, American forces subsequently landed in Haiti to watch over the successful transfer of power.

On the issue of environmental justice President Clinton also responded to blacks' concerns. Since the early 1980s, black activists had extended the perception of racism to include corporate and governmental policies that placed a disproportionate share of the burden for disposing of harmful industrial wastes on poor and African- American communities. Environmental justice came to mean freedom from pollution and toxic dumping as well as access to clean air, water, parks, recreation, safe schools, and jobs. The issue first received widespread public attention in 1982. Black residents of Warren County, North Carolina, 60 miles north of Raleigh, organized protests against the creation of a 150-acre chemical waste landfill in the county, resulting in hundreds of arrests. One of the leaders, Dollie Burwell, voiced her concern: "I was ticked off. I couldn't believe they'd dump that dirt on us – the landfill's a mile away from the school my daughter Kim went to and down the road from the Baptist Church." Indeed the church, as during the heyday of the civil rights movement, served as the source of Burwell's faith and the center of her organizing drives. Led by Burwell, activists marched, blocked dump trucks, and filed lawsuits, without immediate success. Nevertheless, these protests spawned a movement against environmental racism, a term coined by the Reverend Ben Chavis. A North Carolina activist who provided assistance in Warren County, in 1987 Chavis directed the United Church of Christ in issuing a report, *Toxic Wastes and Race in the United States*, the first study to link toxic dumping and race.

By the time Clinton entered the White House, the movement against environmental racism had accelerated. In 1991, the First National People of Color Environmental Justice Summit met in Washington. Clinton appointed Chavis to his presidential transition team to deal with the subject of "Natural Resources." In 1993, former civil rights leader and Georgia congressman, John Lewis, introduced the environmental justice bill. A year later, in February 1994, with pressure mounting on Clinton to take action, the President promulgated Executive Order 12898. The chief executive directed each federal agency to incorporate environmental justice as part of its mission. He ordered them to address any "disproportionately high and adverse human health, environmental, economic and social effects of its programs, policies, and activities on minority and low-income populations." In addition, the presidential order emphasized the importance of community involvement in the drafting of federal environmental impact assessments. Clinton had taken an important step in responding to the burgeoning environmental justice movement.

The Supreme Court Curbs Redistricting

In the 1990s, continued expansion of black political strength encountered a serious stumbling block in the US Supreme Court. Since the late 1960s, the high tribunal generally had validated state and federal efforts to increase opportunities for minority officeholding. As recently as 1986 in *Thornburg v. Gingles*, a case from North Carolina that Lani Guinier and the NAACP Legal Defense Fund litigated, the court had eased the way for establishing majority-minority legislative districts. It decided that, where racially polarized voting by the white majority made election of African Americans unlikely and black voters were "politically cohesive," the creation of predominantly black election districts was required to remedy the effects of past discrimination. Within a decade of this ruling, however, the court had retreated and upset the very foundation on which its previous opinions rested.

The case of *Shaw v. Reno* also arose from North Carolina. Following the 1990 census and guided by the Justice Department, the legislature adopted a redistricting plan that created two predominantly black congressional districts of among a total of 12 districts in the state. Each district contained a black voting-age population of about 53 percent, though slightly less than half of black voters eligible to register did so. In drawing boundary lines, the Democratic-controlled legislature took into account not only racial considerations but also the desire to protect Democratic incumbents and the need to incorporate similar communities of interest, for example, mainly urban or rural areas. Like many politically designed districts, the first and twelfth in North Carolina had peculiar shapes. One resembled an ink blot splattered in the eastern section and the other a snake slithering across the state for 160 miles from Durham to Charlotte. As a result of this redistricting, in 1992 two African Americans, Eva Clayton and Mel Watt, became the first blacks elected to Congress from the Tar Heel State since 1901.

In 1993, the Supreme Court ruled that North Carolina's congressional redistricting plan constituted racial gerrymandering in violation of the Fourteenth Amendment's Equal Protection Clause. The five white plaintiffs who challenged the serpentine-shaped district that Mel Watt represented claimed that they had been illegally segregated as voters on the grounds of race. Speaking for the tribunal, Justice Sandra Day O'Connor agreed. In a narrow five-to-four decision, she argued that the contour of the twelfth district was so bizarre on its face that it was unexplainable for reasons other than race. Calling the district a version of "political apartheid," a reference to South Africa's odious system of white supremacy, she condemned "racial classifications of any sort" for dividing Americans into competing factions, thereby thwarting the achievement of a color-blind society. Joining O'Connor in the majority was Clarence Thomas, who as a justice began staking out the even more restrictive position that the Voting Rights Act covered only voter registration and not vote dilution issues. However, the court did not take this extreme position and sent the suit back for retrial by the lower federal bench to determine whether the state could defend its redistricting plan in conformity with O'Connor's opinion.[6]

---

[6] At the same time, the court pulled back on affirmative action plans that set aside contracts for minority businesses. In a case from Colorado, *Adarand Constructors v. Pena* (1995), the high bench established a tougher standard for judging the constitutionality of affirmative action programs: they must be "narrowly tailored" to further "compelling state interests."

After hearing the evidence, in 1994, a three-judge federal appeals court upheld the constitutionality of the disputed district. Conceding that race had figured into the state legislature's calculations, the judiciary, in a two-to-one decision, nonetheless ruled that the district was carefully constructed to repair the damage caused by a long history of racial discrimination. Looking at the relevant facts, the court found that the district did not resemble a system of apartheid, especially with a nearly equal racial breakdown in eligible voters. Despite the unusual outline of the district, the court judged it to contain homogeneous political and economic interests. The panel was willing to uphold this admittedly race-conscious redistricting remedy as a necessary means "to break free of a legacy of racial bloc voting that has played a significant part in the inability of any African-American citizen of North Carolina, despite repeated responsible efforts, to be elected to Congress in a century."

Before the Supreme Court could hear a new appeal in this case, it inflicted another damaging blow to black electoral progress. On June 29, 1995, the court overturned a congressional redistricting plan from Georgia, once again by a slim five-to-four margin. This time Justice Anthony Kennedy, a Reagan appointee, spoke for the majority. The case, *Miller v. Johnson*, involved a challenge to the Peach State's eleventh congressional district, represented by Cynthia A. McKinney, the first black woman elected to Congress from Georgia. The state legislature had created the district to satisfy the Justice Department's requirements for enforcement of the Voting Rights Act. African Americans comprised 64 percent of the population of this jurisdiction, one of three predominantly black congressional districts in the state. Justice Kennedy attempted to clarify the court's ruling in *Shaw v. Reno* by emphasizing that the shape of a district, however odd, was not the constitutional basis for overturning it. Rather, Kennedy insisted that race "for its own sake" could not be tolerated as a criterion in drawing district boundaries. In this instance, although the legislature had taken into account political and economic considerations in devising its plan, the court found that race constituted the "predominant" factor in determining the outcome. Echoing Justice O'Connor's opinion in *Shaw*, Kennedy concluded that equal opportunity could never be achieved "by carving electorates into racial blocs."

This ruling elicited a stinging dissent from Justice Ruth Bader Ginsburg, a Clinton appointee. She underscored her dismay with her majority brethren by reading from her opinion in open court, an uncommon practice. Ginsburg criticized the majority for failing to give sufficient weight to the "non racial" reasons used to justify the controversial plan. Further, she declared that state legislatures traditionally had paid attention to groups bound by ethnic ties as a legitimate feature of legislative representation. "If Chinese-Americans and Russian-Americans may seek and secure group recognition in the delineation of voting districts," Justice Ginsburg chided, "then African- Americans should not be dissimilarly treated." In ruling otherwise, she pointed out, the Court had handicapped the very minority group whose history had produced the Fourteenth Amendment and the Voting Rights Act.

Notwithstanding the Supreme Court's rulings in the North Carolina and Georgia cases, questions remained as to whether states might legitimately continue to draw predominantly black districts. Justice O'Connor, in a concurring opinion in *Miller v. Johnson*, took pains to emphasize her belief that race could play a part in legislative decision-making and only extreme examples of gerrymandering would fail to pass judicial scrutiny. Thus, she held out some hope that "application of the Court's standard does not throw into doubt the vast majority of the Nation's 435 Congressional districts, where presumably the States have drawn the boundaries within their customary districting principles." This left open room, however narrow, for states to prove in the courts that the creation of majority-minority districts satisfied nonracial criteria to a reasonable degree.[7]

Republicans Control Congress

The congressional elections of 1994 dealt another blow to the advancement of black political goals. Wielding a "Contract with America," the GOP captured control of both houses of Congress for the first time since 1953. Unlike the situation 40 years earlier, when Republican congressional supremacy was shortlived, this time the party looked forward to a longer period of domination. For the first time since Reconstruction, a majority of southern congressmen counted themselves as Republicans and the Democrats were in retreat in their traditional region of support. The GOP

[7] In 2001, the court ruled that race was not an improper consideration as long as it was not the "dominant and controlling" one. The case involved the same district that North Carolina had tried to redraw several times, and on this occasion, in a five-to-four opinion, Justice Stephen Breyer, a Clinton appointee, contended that the Democratic political affiliation of African Americans rather than race was the predominant concern in the minds of the Tar Heel legislators who created the challenged district.

tide also swept in a second black Republican, J. C. Watt of Oklahoma, who lined up squarely behind his conservative colleagues. Led by Speaker Newt Gingrich of Georgia, the conservative-oriented House attempted to fulfill the obligations of its campaign contract by rolling back welfare programs, overhauling Medicare and Medicaid, and launching an attack on affirmative action. With Democrats in the minority, the members of the CBC lost their prime chairmanships of congressional committees and, like their fellow party colleagues, took a back seat to the Republicans. Underscoring the change in command, the Republican majority in the Senate killed President Clinton's nomination of Dr. Henry Foster, a respected black physician who supported abortion, for the post of surgeon general.

In this hostile climate, some allies of African Americans questioned whether creating more electoral districts for blacks to win would ultimately accomplish their objectives. They attributed a significant part of the huge gains made by Republicans in the South in the 1994 elections to the effects of racial redistricting. Critics of majority- minority districts argued that drawing new boundary lines to create districts in favor of black candidates came at the expense of moderate and liberal white Democrats, who were more likely than Republicans to support black aims. They asked whether African Americans would be better off if, in managing to elect a few more representatives of color, they found themselves part of an ineffectual minority political party. These were valid concerns; however, they created a misleading impression that Democratic losses resulted largely from the mandates of the Voting Rights Act. The rise of Republicanism in the South was part of a larger trend preceding the passage of the 1965 Act. Race surely played a role, but so did economic, demographic, and cultural changes in the electorate. Furthermore, Republicans triumphed in statewide elections in which legislative districts did not figure into the outcome, and they emerged victorious in the North as well as the South. Even if Democrats had retained the seats they lost in the South, the Republicans still would have captured control of both houses of Congress.

Whatever the outcome of these assaults, which gained momentum with the ascendancy of a Republican majority in Congress, African- American political strategists needed to explore new avenues for advancement. Given the political demography of the United States, in which African Americans were a declining segment of the population, the possibilities for establishing a substantial number of new congressional districts that favored black election were limited. Though there may have been greater flexibility and chances for expansion at the state and local levels, these too were restricted.

Much of what could be done to create majority-minority districts had already taken place. Moreover, outnumbered in every state legislature, governmental bodies to which, under the Republican "Contract with America," economic resources increasingly flowed, African-American lawmakers had to find ways to establish meaningful coalitions and devise electoral techniques that linked their constituencies with those who had mutual interests.

Under these circumstances, the ideas of Lani Guinier, which were dismissed during her abortive confirmation battle, merit a closer look. Her proposal for cumulative voting offered one option around the dilemma of race-conscious districting. Instead of packing African- American voters into racially identifiable districts, cumulative voting could give blacks, and other minority interest groups, the opportunity to cast their ballots strategically behind their favored candidates without being confined to racially prescribed boundary lines. How well this would work in practice remains debatable, but Guinier's suggestions pointed the way toward the need for a fuller and more imaginative discussion of how to make representative democracy operate more fairly and inclusively.

Racial Divides

Economic inequality continued to impose a heavy burden on African Americans in the 1990s. Notwithstanding the gains achieved by the middle class, the majority of blacks made little progress in catching up with whites. Twenty-five years after the Kerner Commission warned that the United States was "moving toward two societies, one black, one white – separate and unequal," the median household income of blacks relative to whites had barely increased. From 55.1 percent of the earnings of whites in 1965, the figure had risen only to 59.8 percent in 1990 (Table 8.2). The proportion of unemployed blacks was more than double that of whites, and the percentage of blacks living below the poverty line was triple that of whites. A visit to any of the inner-city ghettos that experienced rioting in the 1960s revealed that little had changed since then, and perhaps conditions had even worsened. Scholars and journalists wrote increasingly about the phenomenon of the black underclass in those depressed areas, a growing group ignored by the government and unaffected by affirmative action. People with little education, they no longer bothered to seek work, lived in poverty and despair, were hooked on drugs, and were virtually unaffected by the presence of blacks governing their city halls. This gloomy picture did not do

Table 8.2 Median household income (current dollars), 1960–2006

	White	Black	Percentage of black to white
1960	5,835	3,230	55.4
1965	7,251	3,993	55.1
1970	9,097	5,537	60.9
1975	12,340	7,408	60.0
1980	18,684	10,764	57.6
1985	24,908	14,819	59.5
1990	31,231	18,676	59.8
2000	43,916	29,667	67.6
2006	50,673	32,132	63.4

Source: US Department of Commerce, Bureau of the Census, *Statistical Abstract of the United States*, 2007.

justice to the millions of blacks in these communities who were working hard to raise their families, struggling to make ends meet, and striving to keep narcotics out of their neighborhoods. Nevertheless, the situation was desperate enough to alarm blacks and whites interested in achieving equality in fact as well as in law.

Violence fueled by continued racial inequalities exploded in Los Angeles, California. In 1992, an all-white jury acquitted several white police officers of beating Rodney King, a black man they were arresting, despite incriminating videotaped evidence of the incident. The verdict sparked a bloody uprising by black and Hispanic residents in south central Los Angeles, resulting in arson, looting, and sporadic attacks on whites. Gunfire killed 53, including eight people shot by law-enforcement agents and two by National Guardsmen. Six died in arson fires and two from stabbings. African Americans paid the highest price, including 25 dead. Sixteen Latinos, eight Caucasians, two Asians, one Algerian, and one Indian or Middle Easterner also perished during the six days before peace was fully restored. The man at the center of the disturbances, Rodney King, helped in reestablishing calm when he went on television on the third day of rioting to raise the poignant and healing question: "Can we all get along?" The following year, King and his supporters won a measure of justice when the federal government tried two of the accused police officers for civil rights violations in the King beating and won convictions.

Economic inequalities based on race underscored the fact that neither whites nor blacks stood ready to abandon their racial identities. This hit home very dramatically in 1995 with the not-guilty verdict in the O. J. Simpson murder trial. Simpson, an All-American college football player, a star in the National Football League, and a part-time actor, was accused of the bloody killing in 1994 of his estranged wife, a white woman, and her male friend in Los Angeles. Whereas whites screamed that the predominantly African-American jury refused to convict a black man with a known record as a wife-beater for the ultimate act of spouse abuse, African Americans rejoiced that justice had prevailed in freeing an innocent black man who was framed by racist cops. Seventy-eight percent of blacks believed that the jury got the verdict right in freeing Simpson, compared with only 42 percent of whites who agreed with the outcome. The fact that the starkly contrasting responses to the Simpson verdict startled so many national leaders, media commentators, and ordinary citizens suggests that the country was long overdue for a serious dialogue on race.

African Americans explored alternatives to relieve their predicament. The Million Man March on Washington in October 1995 brought the largest number of African Americans to the nation's capital, but those assembled did not demand new legislation. Rather, they emphasized the need for black men to close ranks and take a greater role in supporting their families, combating crime in their neighborhoods, providing positive role models for their children to emulate, and taking control of their local political and economic institutions. As successful as the march was in rallying African-American men, it generated sufficient controversy to fuel the fires of racial distrust both within and outside the black community. Yet the Million Man March exposed some of the internal fissures among African Americans. The prominent part played by Minister Louis Farrakhan in organizing the event turned away potential supporters, including Congressman John Lewis of Georgia. A veteran of the 1963 March on Washington and one of the bravest people the civil rights movement had produced, Lewis stayed home because he was distressed by what he saw as Farrakhan's message to "resegregate America." Furthermore, the deliberate omission of black women from the call to march upset many black feminists, whose grievances against racism and sexism once again were pushed into the background. Black leftists and feminists, such as Angela Y. Davis, also complained that black leaders, both radicals like Farrakhan and his moderate opponents, ignored critical issues, including the AIDS epidemic that ravaged black communities in the 1980s and 1990s. During this period, the Congressional

Black Caucus, along with the Nation of Islam, proved reluctant to focus attention on black AIDS patients. Davis and other critics attributed this avoidance to homophobia among black leaders, especially those emphasizing manhood.

Still, without endorsing Farrakhan, a large number of African Americans supported the principles behind the march. For example, the popular comedian Bill Cosby, sounding like Clarence Thomas, agreed that blacks had to cast aside their feelings of "victimhood." In doing so, Cosby favored the promotion of stable, two-parent, families, stressed the importance of education for children, and advocated a disciplined work ethic.

The Second Clinton Administration

In 1996, President Clinton won reelection over his Republican opponent Robert Dole. His notable high-level appointments of African Americans and his close working relationship with the CBC increased his popularity among black voters. In 1995, in the face of judicial decisions limiting the scope of affirmative action and white attacks against "reverse discrimination," the President reaffirmed his commitment to the principle of affirmative action and pledged that he would "mend it, but [not] end it." However, some of his policies had drawn criticism from established black politicians and civil rights leaders, most significantly the Lani Guinier fiasco and passage in 1996 of the Personal Responsibility and Work Opportunity Act, the so-called reform measure calculated to move welfare recipients off public rolls and into jobs within a prescribed five-year period, while cutting funds for food stamps and emergency medical programs. This law severely weakened the social contract between the federal government and the American people first established during the New Deal by curtailing the federal guarantee of protection and care for the nation's most vulnerable and neediest citizens. Nevertheless, the overwhelming majority of the black electorate supported Clinton. He garnered 84 percent of African-American votes, a 3 percent increase from 1992 and a figure vastly higher than for any other group in his winning coalition.

Clinton's reelection did not change the Republican domination of Congress, thereby dooming the prospects of obtaining legislation directed at improving the economic problems of a substantial segment of the black population. By one measure, African Americans made some progress. Blacks had reduced the racial gap in median household income from 59.8

in 1990 to 67.6 ten years later. Most of this growth came from the expansion of the black middle class. In contrast, at the end of the 1990s, approximately 24 percent of African Americans lived in poverty, roughly double the national rate and three times that of whites. African Americans also lagged behind educationally. In 1999, almost twice as many whites received a bachelor's degree as did blacks, 28 to 15 percent. Among blacks, more women than men earned at least a bachelor's degree – 16 percent as opposed to 14 percent. For whites, this was reversed – more men received at least a bachelor's degree (31 percent) than women (25 percent). The figures for African-American men reflected a tragic reality, particularly for youth and young adults. African Americans had a six times greater chance of going to prison during their lifetime than whites and could expect to serve longer sentences for the same offenses. There were more black men in prison than in institutions of higher education. More than 28 percent of African-American men would likely be incarcerated over their lifetime, while whites had only a 4 percent chance of imprisonment. In 1996, African Americans represented 30 percent of all convicted federal offenders despite the fact that they made up only 13 percent of the population. In the decade between 1985 and 1995 the percentage of African Americans under correctional supervision increased 81 percent, creating a "prison-industrial complex." In 1995, it was reported that, on any particular day, almost one in three (32.2 percent) black men in their twenties fell under the authority of the criminal justice system.

The criminal justice system did not operate neutrally in whom it incarcerated for felonies. In 1995, approximately 60 percent of those in jail had been convicted of drug offenses, and African Americans were six times more likely than whites to be arrested for a drug offense. In fact, four in every five prisoners jailed for drug offenses were African- American or Latino. Yet one study concluded that more than three-quarters of drug users were white, but were not prosecuted. Decisions by law-enforcement authorities ranging from what neighborhood to focus on to what type of drug to pursue carry a racial component. Concentrating law enforcement on inner-city neighborhoods, where drug dealing more often takes place outdoors and is therefore easier to prosecute, rather than on suburban neighborhoods, where dealing occurs behind closed doors and requires greater effort by police to uncover, guarantees that prisons will be filled with a higher proportion of minorities than whites. The imposition of higher penalties for possession of crack cocaine, a relatively cheap drug available to the poor, than of powdered cocaine, the choice of the middle-class and wealthy, further discriminates against African Americans. Federal sentencing guidelines mandated five-year prison sentences for being in possession of 5 grams of crack compared to five years for having 500 grams of cocaine.

In contrast to the dismal situation of the poor, the black middle class experienced great gains. By the mid-1990s, 60 percent of black women held white-collar jobs; in the 1940s, the same percentage had been employed as domestic servants. Nearly one-third of African Americans lived in suburbs and black two-parent families earned 13 percent less than their white counterparts. Still, as this last figure suggests, even the black middle class had not achieved economic equality.

One of the most positive political advances during the final decade of the twentieth century came in the gains black women made in winning elected office. By 2000, the number of black women holding elected positions stood at over 3,119, up from 2,332 in 1993 (see Table 8.1). Although the number of women officeholders lagged behind that of black men (5,921), women were catching up fast. In seven years, the number of black male officials had increased 4.2 percent, whereas the number of black female officeholders had leaped by 33.7 percent. Constituting only 6.8 percent of black elected officials in the United States in 1970, 30 years later women made up 35 percent of the total. Most of the progress came at the county level, where black women were getting elected to city councils and school boards. By comparison, white women held 21 percent of all white elected positions. With both racial and gender barriers falling, black women accounted for most of the increase in the number of black officeholders. "Except for a few institutions in the black community," one black elected official explained, "women are accepted in positions of leadership in ways that the larger society does not." Moreover, as noted above, the incarceration rate for black men was skyrocketing, taking them out of the electoral pool, and the percentage of black women attending college exceeded that of black men, further extending the possibilities for women seeking electoral office.

With the partisan legislative balance against him, Clinton resorted to a tactic that other presidents had used when faced with congressional opposition and a shortage of new ideas. Like Harry Truman in 1946 and Lyndon Johnson in 1967, President Clinton appointed a national commission to study race relations and recommend policies to address the problems of discrimination and inequality. At best, the chief executive hoped to generate national support for remedial legislation that would prompt Congress to act; at worst, he could defuse the racial tensions that had surfaced in the Los Angeles riots, the O. J. Simpson trial, and the Million Man March.

On June 13, 1997, Clinton appointed a distinguished, seven-member, national panel to advise him "on matters involving race and racial reconciliation [and to] promote a constructive national dialogue to confront and work through challenging issues that surround race." Clinton also authorized the council to "[i]dentify, develop, and implement solutions to problems in areas in which race has a substantial impact, such as education, economic opportunity, housing, health care, and the administration of justice." The next day, June 14, in a commencement address at the University of California San Diego, the President declared:

> More than 30 years ago, at the high tide of the civil rights movement, the Kerner Commission said we were becoming two Americas: one white, one black, separate and unequal. Today, we face a different choice: Will we become not two but many Americas, separate, unequal, and isolated? Or will we draw strength from all our people and our ancient faith in the quality of human dignity to become the world's first truly multiracial democracy?

The statement reflected the ideology Clinton brought with him to the White House, the one he construed as restoring Democrats to rule as the majority party. Toward this end, he sought to appeal to what the journalist E. J. Dionne called the "language of common citizenship" and an emphasis on "values of generosity and tolerance."

To increase credibility among civil rights leaders, the President selected the eminent African-American historian John Hope Franklin to head the group. Committed to placing his scholarship in the cause of social justice, Franklin had conducted research for the historic *Brown v. Board of Education* decision (1954) and marched during the voting rights campaign in Selma, Alabama, in 1965. In his early eighties, Franklin accepted Clinton's offer to design a racial blueprint to lead the nation into the twenty-first century. In taking this responsibility, Franklin became the first African American to chair a presidential commission on race relations.

Representation on this presidential advisory board reflected the changing face of race in the United States, no longer confined to black and white. The committee included persons of Asian-American and Hispanic-American descent, with the latter group just about to overtake African Americans as the nation's largest minority. Despite its multicultural make-up, the group did not contain a Native American, an omission that evoked criticism from leaders of that community. Nevertheless, the board strove to include ample testimony from Native Americans in its discussions (and Professor Franklin pointed out and took pride in his Cherokee ancestry).

The advisory board encountered even greater criticism from political conservatives for not including them on the panel. There was no shortage of scholars and activists who would have qualified to serve; however, appointing right-wing adherents would have been unprecedented if not counterproductive. Though previous presidents had selected such committees with moderation in mind, they had chosen appointees generally supportive of civil rights. The right-wing agenda conflicted with the main tenets around which racial equality pivoted at the turn of the century: affirmative action, race-conscious voting rights remedies, and government spending to expand economic opportunity. It is true that in creating the advisory board Clinton had called for a dialogue on race in which all Americans should be engaged. Still, neither he nor the panel wanted to have a fractious debate on the subject, which they thought would do more harm than good. The absence of conservative ideologues on the committee did not prevent it from hearing as many diverse points of view as possible, which it did in numerous hearings throughout the country.

On September 18, 1998, the Franklin Commission issued its report, *One America in the 21st Century: Forging a New Future*. The document underscored the growing complexity of racial issues in a multicultural society and the continuing legacy of racial discrimination. No longer a simple matter of black and white, the conversation about race included Hispanics, Native Americans, Alaska Natives, Asian Pacific Americans, and the rising number of offspring of interracial marriages. The panel emphasized the strength of racial diversity at the same time as it promoted national unity. "Our greatest challenge," the report declared, "is to work as one community to define ourselves with pride as a multiracial democracy." The board reported finding consensus among Americans in support of "justice, equality of opportunity, respect, responsibility, honor, integrity, civility, and inclusion," but it also observed that race still mattered in keeping these principles from becoming reality. The Franklin Commission's assumptions mirrored those of Truman's board, the pioneer of presidential studies on race. The panel argued that a fundamental American creed of fairness and morality existed, and the gap between theory and practice could be closed through education, collection and dissemination of information to dispel racial stereotyping, and appeals to the goodwill of all citizens.

Yet the committee did not rely solely on education and conversation to foster change. It also offered specific recommendations for strengthening civil rights enforcement by the government, maintaining affirmative action programs, improving housing, healthcare, and education for the poor, raising the minimum wage, extending collective bargaining for workers, ending racial profiling in law enforcement, strengthening laws against hate crimes, and monitoring the consequences of welfare reform. The committee recognized that much had been accomplished since the end of Jim Crow, but it continued to look to government – national, state, and local – to devise methods to overcome persistent racial inequities that separated whites and racial minorities in their quest for jobs, housing, education, health insurance, and criminal justice.

However, in an era when many Americans had lost trust in government officials and in the ability of Washington politicians to solve their problems, the advisory board put its ultimate faith in ordinary people and the power of reason and persuasion more than in government. Echoing President Clinton's 1996 State of the Union message that "the era of big government is over," the Franklin Commission concluded that "[o]ne of the best tools for forging common ground and developing new understanding among people of different races is dialogue." To that end, the board produced the *One America Dialogue Guide* to facilitate the exchange of ideas, and it compiled a list of civic, religious, and community organizations that interested citizens could join in pursuit of racial and economic justice. It also called for vigorous educational and media advertising campaigns to promote racial reconciliation, and proposed establishment of a permanent President's Council for One America to continue its work.

The report drew mixed reviews. "This board has raised the consciousness and quickened the conscience of America," President Clinton remarked in receiving the report. However, civil rights advocates greeted the document more skeptically. A leading official of the National Council of La Raza, a Hispanic group, noted: "There are not a lot of bold, new or exciting recommendations in the report. But it is important to understand that this is not the final step in the process." Similarly, the director of the Black Leadership Forum praised the board for achieving "a measure of success" and creating "some kind of momentum." The *New York Times* echoed these comments, calling the board's recommendations "modest" and "break[ing] little new ground." The *Los Angeles Times* agreed that the report suggested "too obvious solutions." These assessments were glowing compared to those by conservatives who had criticized the President's race initiative from the beginning and did not change their minds. They found fault with what they considered a limited dialogue. "For this commission, nothing has changed since the 1960s," conservative commentator Clint Bollick groused. "So long as we fail to address such problems as out-of-wedlock births, abysmal inner-city public education and ... violent crime, we will not achieve real equal opportunity."

The committee's report produced very little success. Clinton received it just as he was becoming increasingly embroiled in the controversy over his cover-up of a sexual affair with a young White House intern, Monica Lewinsky. Revelations of this scandal led the press, federal prosecutors, and Republican opponents in Congress to question whether the President had lied under oath about his relationship with Lewinsky and another alleged paramour, Paula Jones. Clinton remained preoccupied with his legal troubles and defending himself from the impeachment charges voted by the House of Representatives in December 1998, three months after the Franklin Commission delivered its report. After the Senate acquitted him in February 1999, Clinton lacked the political resources to press ahead on his commission's race relations initiative. After all, he had barely escaped with his political life.

Nevertheless, over the two remaining years of his term Clinton continued to speak out on behalf of his commission's findings. In February 1999, the President created a White House office to carry on the work of his Initiative on Race to promote ongoing dialogues and explore opportunities to close the gap between whites and blacks. He had far less success in obtaining his annual congressional budget requests to expand programs for minority education, healthcare, and civil rights enforcement. In his 2000 State of the Union Address Clinton reiterated that "the most important fact of life is our common humanity. Therefore, we must do more to tolerate diversity – we must honor it and celebrate it." However, by then Clinton's effectiveness had greatly diminished, and his race initiative ground to a halt.

Still, the sputtering of Clinton's race initiative did not diminish his popularity among African Americans. Blacks stood by the President steadfastly throughout the Lewinsky scandal and his impeachment. No matter the charges against him and whatever personal and legal transgressions he had committed, blacks identified with Clinton as a victim of injustice, accepted him as a reconstructed white southerner, and embraced him in the spirit of Christian redemption. The African-American writer Toni Morrison proclaimed Clinton the "first black president," acknowledging the rapport he had established with African Americans. In 2001, the Congressional Black Caucus honored Clinton at its annual dinner as "the Nation's first black president."

Whether Bill Clinton deserved the honor, albeit symbolic, remains debatable. His administration gave African Americans more than the token presence they had had in the past. The Cabinet as well as government agencies took on the rainbow complexion that Jesse Jackson had sketched out a decade before. The dozens of blacks elected to Congress produced a critical legislative mass that increased their leverage with the White House. The days of a few black lawmakers dotting the Washington scene had ended. Furthermore, the economic recovery that had accompanied Clinton's program of increasing taxes and reducing the deficit benefited middle-class African Americans, for whom the results of the civil rights movement and affirmative action were finally paying off.

Yet amidst these signs of hope, the reality for many blacks remained despair. The middle-class aspirations of African Americans were vulnerable to cutbacks in government spending to balance the budget, as many of their incomes depended on public sector jobs and government services. Attacks on affirmative action, increasingly successful in the courts, threatened middle-class blacks even further. The black poor, whose numbers remained disproportionately high, had lost their access to welfare programs and generally remained invisible to the larger public enjoying the fruits of the surging Clinton economy. In this case, impoverished blacks did not fare much better in cities with black mayors, as Atlanta and New Orleans were among the leaders as areas of black poverty. Finally, the tepid response by politicians and the public to the Franklin Commission report, a document that reflected a moderate and largely inoffensive approach, suggests a great deal about the racial attitudes and complacency that existed at the end of the century. As African Americans faced the new millennium they had good reason to question whether they had reached the limits of their political power.

9

Still Running for Freedom

More than one hundred years ago at the dawn of the twentieth century, the political future looked very bleak for African Americans. By 1900, four decades since the Civil War and emancipation, blacks had virtually lost their voting rights and their opportunity to hold elected office. A century later and nearly four decades following passage of the 1965 Voting Rights Act, the Second Reconstruction appeared over as well. Skeptics feared that African Americans would suffer a similar fate as they had met at the end of the First Reconstruction. In fact, with the turn of the twenty-first century the right to vote once again came under siege, but the gains accompanying the Voting Rights Act would not be obliterated.

The Presidential Election of 2000

The first presidential election of the twenty-first century underlined both the importance and vulnerability of black ballots. The Republican nominee, Governor George W. Bush of Texas, the son of the forty-first President, billed himself as a "compassionate conservative," but staked out a position in opposition to affirmative action. In 1996, a federal circuit court of appeals had struck down the affirmative action plan of the University of Texas Law School. As a result, under Bush's leadership the state adopted a "race neutral" college admissions policy based on financial need and class rank (top 10 percent) of students in high school. "I support what we call affirmative access in the state of Texas," Bush declared and further explained, "But it's

Running for Freedom: Civil Rights and Black Politics in America since 1941,
Fourth Edition. Steven F. Lawson.
© 2015 John Wiley & Sons, Inc. Published 2015 by John Wiley & Sons, Inc.

not a quota. It's not a preference." Such programs were also instituted in California and Florida (under Bush's brother Jeb, the governor of the Sunshine State), and the number of minority students gaining admission to the top-tier state universities dropped sharply in all three states.

Bush's views gained the backing of Ward Connerly. Born in Leesville, Louisiana and a graduate of Sacramento State College in California, Connerly was appointed to the University of California Board of Regents in 1993. An African American whose ancestors included Irish, French, and Choctaws, Connerly led black conservatives against affirmative action. He viewed race-based programs as a form of discrimination, which hampered the ideal of achieving a color-blind society. Connerly organized the campaign to eliminate affirmative action in California through a ballot initiative that would let voters decide its fate. In November 1996, "the Golden State" adopted Proposition 209, which decreed that the "state shall not discriminate against, or grant preferential treatment to, any individual or group on the basis of race, sex, color, ethnicity, or national origin in the operation of public employment, public education, or public contracting." Boosted by this victory, in 1997, Connerly formed the American Civil Rights Institute, which despite its name waged a campaign to expand the objectives of the California movement nationally. A year later, the state of Washington passed a similar measure.

On the campaign trail in 2000, Bush endorsed "the goals of Proposition 209," declaring that he supported "the spirit of no quotas and no preferences." Yet he would not come out and explicitly back the proposition – perhaps an indication of his desire to sell "compassionate conservatism" to blacks. Rather, he preferred "to say it's not what you are against but what you are for. In [Texas] I'm for increasing the pool of applicants, opening the door so that more people are eligible to go to the university system." Nevertheless, in shaping his argument against "quotas" and "preferences," the Republican candidate used buzz words that both distorted affirmative action guidelines and adopted the language of its fiercest critics.

Bush's Democratic rival, Vice President Al Gore of Tennessee, stood on the opposite side of the issue. As Clinton's second in command, Gore had endorsed the Democratic President's efforts to "mend and not end" affirmative action in the wake of court decisions and state referenda limiting its application. As a presidential candidate, Gore spoke out vigorously in favor of its continuation and opposed Proposition 209. In contrast to Bush, Gore contended that "affirmative action isn't quotas. ... Affirmative action means that you take extra steps to acknowledge the history of discrimination and injustice and prejudice." He admitted that he too opposed quotas, but the vice president pledged to retain affirmative action and "make sure that programs are carefully targeted and fair and that they meet the legal requirements."

The candidates underscored their differences in other ways. Bush made it a point to speak at Bob Jones University, a bastion of religious fundamentalism and right-wing Republicanism. In the 1980s the Supreme Court had ruled that the private Christian university could not receive any federal tax exemptions because it practiced discrimination by banning interracial dating. Rather than change its policy, the college relinquished its claim as a tax-exempt institution. At Bob Jones, Bush affirmed "our ideas, Republican ideas, conservative ideas."

Having flaunted his core values, Bush tried to show some compassion to go along with his conservatism. In July 2000, he addressed the NAACP annual convention, which took some courage because, although a nonpartisan organization, the NAACP had little sympathy with the Republican's positions. Avoiding specific issues, Bush extended an olive branch:

> The NAACP and the GOP haven't always been allies. But recognizing our past and confronting the future with a common vision, I believe that we can find common ground. It won't be easy work, but a philosopher once advised, "If given a choice, look for the hard. I would prefer the hard, for only the hard will achieve the good." That's my commitment.

Most delegates remained unconvinced. Instead they gave Al Gore a rousing reception. The vice president, who was a card-carrying member of the NAACP, pledged to support affirmative action and other measures, such as hate crime legislation and increased federal funding for public schools, supported by civil rights proponents. In addition, Gore's campaign was run by Donna Brazile, an African American who had grown up in Kenner, Louisiana and played a leading role in organizing Jesse Jackson's presidential bid in 1984.

In no surprise, Gore won the overwhelming majority of African-American votes (91 percent). Bush's conservative opinions on affirmative action and the economy did not convert many African Americans, even those for whom Bush's religious-based convictions against abortion and for prayer in schools resonated. The election vividly exposed a "racial gap," as a stunning 48 percent difference showed up nationally between black support for Gore and white approval for Bush. Overall, the Democratic candidate won a majority of the popular vote, but lost in the critical electoral vote column by a slim margin of 271 to 266.

The outcome of the election proved that every vote counted, though thousands did not count at all. In a contest this close, numerous reasons might explain Bush's narrow edge. However, more than anything else, the disqualification of black ballots (along with many cast by whites) in Florida altered the results. Out of some 5.8 million cast in the state, Bush officially won by a meager 537 votes.

Bush vs. Gore, Round Two

With the electoral vote count so close and victory depending on the results from Florida, the campaign did not end on election day. Instead, Democratic and Republican lawyers descended on the Sunshine State demanding a proper recount; if necessary they were prepared to extend the battle to the federal courts. The ensuing struggle revealed new forms of black disfranchisement, though revelations of injustices failed to reverse the results of the election.

The election system in Florida abetted disfranchisement, starting with the operation of voting machines. Counties primarily used two kinds of machines: a punch-card system and an optical-scan system. In precincts employing the former, the percentage of ballots recorded as having "non votes" was 3.92 compared with 1.43 percent for districts using the optical-scan variety. The problem with punch-card voting stemmed from a combination of undervotes, in which machines read the ballot card as having no votes, and overvotes, in which the machine recorded multiple votes for candidates running for the same position. In the case of undervotes, the stylus on the machine had not punctured the ballot fully and left "dimples" (slight indentations) or "hanging chads" (a partially ruptured piece of the card). Such ballots were disqualified, although Florida law required election officials to discern the "intent of the voter" from the marking of the ballot, which could be accomplished from manually observing the dimples and chads. Overvotes were likely to occur in places that offered the "butterfly" ballot. In Palm Beach County, with heavily Democratic precincts, voters encountered a ballot that placed candidates for the presidency (ten names) side by side on pages facing each other, thereby creating confusion as to where to place the mark for the desired choice. Many voters punched out more than one space to make sure they had supported the candidate of their choice. Some even wrote the name of their preferred presidential contender on the ballot, but this made no difference if they had punched their cards more than once. In Palm Beach County 6.45 percent of all ballots were discarded mostly because of multiple votes. In this county, the predominantly black precincts of Riviera Beach reached an even higher rate of overvotes at 13 percent.

Although white voters were affected by these confusing procedures, especially in Palm Beach County with its heavy population of Jewish retirees, the greatest burden throughout the state fell upon African Americans. For example, in Duval County, about 19 percent of the votes in four predominantly black districts in Jacksonville, where Gore ran strongly, were discarded, whereas in the city's white precincts, which supported Bush, only 7.5 percent of the votes were disqualified. Similar situations prevailed in Dade County (Miami) and Broward County (Fort Lauderdale).

African Americans suffered disproportionately largely because the institutions shaped by segregation and second-class citizenship continued to

Figure 24 Rev Jesse Jackson leads a march in downtown West Palm Beach with Irma Fleishaman, from West Boca Raton (left), and Joanna Carbone, from Boynton Beach, who both said their votes did not count due to ballot confusion. (Photo © Jason Millstein/Aurora Photos)

discriminate against them. African Americans were more likely than whites to live in poverty, have poorer education, and go to the polls for the first time. Black Floridians were also more likely to live in impoverished precincts that could not afford the most up-to-date voting equipment and continued to use punch-card ballots. The use of confusing ballots sorely tested the reading and comprehension skills of voters, particularly those who had the least education and experience. The Duval County election supervisor admitted as much when he explained that the racial disparity in spoiled ballots came from "literacy." He went on to say, "I mean you have to have certain skills."

Florida election officials were well aware of the problems of outdated machinery, but as one reporter put it, they "kept their fingers crossed for a low voter turnout and a large margin" of victory, neither of which happened in 2000. In fact, the NAACP and local civic groups had mounted an extensive voter registration drive before the 2000 election, which swelled the ranks of black voters. Making the situation worse, the precincts with the greatest difficulties and the most confusion were unable to provide assistance to befuddled voters. Local election workers could not get through to county supervisors to answer questions because the telephone lines were jammed by so many requests for information and computers used for e-mail communications malfunctioned.

Felon disfranchisement also reduced the size of the African-American electorate. Many black citizens, mostly men, did not have the opportunity to register to vote let alone go to the polls on election day. Along with six other states, Florida permanently prohibited released felons from voting. Blacks comprised 58 percent of the 600,000 ex-convicts in this category, and a whopping 31 percent of the black male population in Florida had been imprisoned on felony charges. In Florida, only the governor can restore felon voting rights by issuing executive clemency in individual cases, a procedure that is time-consuming and politically contentious. This left a substantial portion of the Afro-Floridian population disqualified from exercising the suffrage. Before the 2000 election, Florida's Republican Secretary of State Katherine Harris, the state's top election official, implemented the ban on felon suffrage in a manner that excluded more than former prisoners. She ordered a purge of felons from the voter rolls, which resulted in the elimination of citizens who turned out not to have committed any crime. One of them, Willie D. Whiting, had never been in jail and after he was purged expressed how he felt: "I was slingshotted into slavery." Subsequently, he discovered that his name had been confused with that of another and, unlike countless others, he managed to clear up the misunderstanding in time to vote.

These obstacles of poverty and felon disfranchisement represented an insidious form of systemic racism that depressed black voting in this hotly contested election. Overall, about 54 percent of 180,000 spoiled ballots were cast by African Americans. Nine of the ten counties with the highest percentages of black voters had discard rates above the state average. In contrast, of the ten counties with the highest proportion of white voters, only two had spoilage rates above the Florida average. At the precinct level, figures showed that 83 of 100 precincts with the largest number of disqualified ballots were in predominantly black areas.

It is clear that African Americans did not have their votes counted fully and many were not able to vote at all. An accurate tally of their votes might very well have transferred the victory from Bush to Gore. This is not to conclude that the official outcome of the election resulted from intentional discrimination, racial or otherwise, on the part of Florida election officials. A subsequent investigation by the United States Civil Rights Commission, whose chairperson, Mary Frances Berry, was an outspoken defender of racial equality, did not find any evidence "that the highest officials of the state conspired to disenfranchise voters." Even though they discovered numerous examples of voting irregularities, the commissioners would only say that the "state's highest officials responsible for ensuring efficiency, uniformity, and fairness in the election failed to fulfill their responsibilities and were subsequently unwilling to take responsibility." The commission further charged that the failure of Florida officials from Governor Jeb Bush on down "resulted in an extraordinarily high and inexcusable level of disfranchisement, with a significantly disproportionate impact on African American voters."

Bush vs. Gore: Round Three

The initial tabulation of ballots from Florida put Bush ahead by 537, a paper-thin margin. With reports of suffrage difficulties beginning to mount and quickly turning into a deluge, it became clear that the final tally remained in doubt until election officials could conduct a recount. Rather than clarifying the matter, the recount process engendered further confusion and shifted the presidential contest from the polls to the courts, where politics did not end.

The recount did not prove more enlightening than the original vote. Election officials had to discern the intent of voters from ballots with dimples and hanging chads. This produced images widely reported in the media of officials holding up ballots to the light to make sense of the voters' choice. At the same time, Florida Secretary of State Harris attempted to bring the recount to a swift close, seeking to preserve Bush's slender victory. Consequently, Gore supporters went to court and succeeded in extending the deadline for concluding the retabulation of ballots, a time-consuming task that had to be done by hand. Both sides sent high-powered lawyers to Florida to argue their case and steer the course of events in their favor. James A. Baker, former Secretary of State under Bush's father, headed the Republican team and Warren Christopher, Clinton's Secretary of State, led the Democrats. On November 16, nine days after the election, the Florida Supreme Court ruled that Harris could not prevent county officials from continuing to count ballots manually. However, in another instance, the state's highest court decided that if a county (Miami-Dade) did not want to resume the tallying, it did not have to do so. On November 26, despite results from Broward County that reduced Bush's statewide margin to 465 votes and with Palm Beach County officials requiring additional time to finish its recount, Secretary Harris called a halt to the proceedings and certified Bush's victory by 537 votes.

This did not end the conflict, however, because Gore challenged Harris's action in court. On November 27, the vice president asserted, "Our Constitution matters more than convenience," and he asked for "a complete count of all the votes cast in Florida" and claimed that "many thousands of votes … have not yet been counted at all, not once." In response Bush stated, "One of our strategies is to get this election ratified, and the sooner the better for the good of the country." To make this happen, the Bush team had appealed to the United States Supreme Court to overturn the Florida Supreme Court's order that extended the deadline for certifying the vote and permitting a manual recount of the ballots. The justices remanded the case to the Florida high court, where on December 8, a month after the election, a majority of the judges ordered a manual recount of undervotes in all counties where a hand count had not already occurred or been completed, notably Miami-Dade and Palm Beach Counties, where about 45,000 ballots were at issue. Furthermore, the court certified the addition of 483 votes for Gore, which narrowed Bush's lead to 154 votes. In the meantime, the Florida legislature, with a Republican majority, voted to approve the state's 25 electors for George Bush.

The US Supreme Court finally ended the stalemate. On December 12, in an extraordinary evening session, the high tribunal reversed the Florida Supreme Court ruling and brought a halt to the statewide recount of ballots. The justices divided five to four, pitting the conservative wing (Chief Justice William Rehnquist, Anthony Kennedy, Sandra Day O'Connor, Antonin Scalia, and Clarence Thomas) against the liberals (Stephen Breyer, Ruth Bader Ginsberg, John Paul Stevens, and David Souter). In *Bush v. Gore*, the majority based its decision on an expansive reading of the Equal Protection Clause of the Fourteenth Amendment. The high bench argued that allowing counties to recount ballots without sufficient procedural safeguards and uniform standards would constitute "arbitrary and disparate treatment, [and] value one person's vote over another." Yet Florida Republicans had been responsible for the electoral mess in the first place. Their failure to anticipate problems with electoral machinery and effectively resolve them, as well as their purge of voters, a disproportionate number of them African Americans, hardly constituted fairness and equal treatment. Furthermore, with respect to the operation of state election laws and practices, the conservative justices departed from judicial restraint and the usual deference judges paid to the highest state court to sort out these kinds of issues.

Accordingly, in a stinging dissent four justices condemned the majority for "substituting" their views for that of the Florida Supreme Court. In effect, they pointed out that rather than ensuring equal protection, the majority decision deprived thousands of Floridians of the right to vote and to have that vote counted. The ruling, Justice Stevens argued for the dissenters, "effectively orders the disfranchisement of an unknown number of voters whose ballots reveal their intent – and are therefore legal under state law – but were for some reason rejected by ballot-counting machines." They further showed their disappointment with their majority brethren by bluntly concluding: "Although we may never know with complete certainty the identity of the winner of this year's Presidential election, the identity of the loser is perfectly clear. It is the Nation's confidence in the judge as an impartial guardian of the rule of law." Nevertheless, with five justices on the Supreme Court having the final word, George W. Bush became the forty-third President of the United States.

Opponents of the President-elect made one last-ditch effort to bring election irregularities to light and send a message of protest. On January 6, 2005, Representative Stephanie Tubbs Jones, a black Ohio Democrat, argued before a Joint Session of Congress that Ohio's 20 electoral votes should not be certified because of election chicanery. "This objection," Tubbs Jones explained on the House floor, "does not have at its root the hope or even the hint of overturning the victory of the President but it is a necessary, timely and appropriate opportunity to review and remedy the most precious process in our democracy." She managed to persuade only 30 of her fellow representatives to join her, and her request for decertification overwhelmingly went down to defeat.[1]

The Bush Presidency, Part I

The compassionate conservatism of President Bush produced gains more symbolic than substantive for African Americans. The Republican chief executive did make two of the highest level appointments of African Americans in the nation's history. General Colin Powell, who held posts in the Reagan and George H. W. Bush administrations as National Security Advisor and Chairman of the Joint Chiefs of Staff, became Secretary of State. Born in Harlem to a Jamaican immigrant family and raised in the South Bronx, Powell graduated from the City College of New York in 1958, entered the military, and was a decorated veteran of the Vietnam War. In another unprecedented move, the President selected a black woman as National Security Advisor. Condoleezza Rice, a Soviet specialist and former provost of Stanford University, had grown up in Birmingham, Alabama, and lived there during the time of the infamous 1963 church bombing that killed four girls. Bush also chose Rod Paige, the African-American superintendent of the Houston (Texas) Independent School District, as Secretary of Education.

Bush touted diversity in his Cabinet-level appointments as the central measure of civil rights. Diversity may have given decision-making in his administration a different complexion, but it did not provide an adequate substitute for forceful implementation of civil rights policies and federal efforts to combat intractable forms of racism. Bush did not ignore

[1] Two years later, on October 29, 2002, President Bush signed into law a bipartisan measure called Help Americans Vote Act (HAVA). Among its provisions, the law called for an end to punch-card voting systems; established an Elections Assistance Commission; authorized the casting of provisional ballots by contested voters; and required presentation of personal photo identification cards by those seeking to vote at polling places. HAVA produced mixed results and had little impact on the 2004 presidential election.

African-American leaders, but he chose to deal mainly with those who might respond more positively to his message of uplift through self-reliance and faith-based initiatives. Consequently, Bush became the first sitting President since Herbert Hoover not to address the NAACP annual convention, choosing instead to speak to the National Urban League (NUL), which emphasized economic self-empowerment and focused on conciliation rather than protest. In conferring with the NUL and black church leaders rather than the NAACP, the President practiced diversity without satisfying the substantive civil rights demands of most African Americans.

Within the confines of compassionate conservatism, the Bush administration acted to extend educational equality to African-American children. The President was appalled that in the year 2000 "nearly 70 percent of 4th graders from high poverty backgrounds couldn't read at grade level ... [and] 40 percent of minority students failed to finish high school on time." These statistics, Bush contended, pointed to the existence of racial and ethnic bias against disadvantaged minorities, discrimination not produced by law but by the low expectations of government officials and educators of what blacks and Latinos could accomplish. In a stroke of ingenuity, Bush presented educational reform as "a piece of civil rights legislation." In this way, he attempted to shift the civil rights focus from affirmative action with its controversial racial preferences to quality schooling, an idea at the heart of basic American values of uplift and fair play. In campaigning for the presidency, Bush had told the NAACP that he would implement educational reform because "no child should be left behind in America."

The basic elements of Bush's No Child Left Behind (NCLB) legislative proposal consisted of assessment, accountability, and expanded school options. The President refused to put the blame for failing schools on parents and the impoverished circumstances under which families lived; instead, he attributed the major portion of responsibility to school administrators and teachers who did not expect poor children to succeed. He adeptly termed this problem "the soft bigotry of low expectations." Money alone, he argued, would not solve the problem, as the federal government had invested $158 billion dollars in aid to schools. "Just as faith without works is dead," the preacher-in-chief instructed, "money without reform is fruitless." The educational gap would not close without a regular testing regimen to show teachers "where and how to improve."

NCLB legislation drew bipartisan support and it passed the House and Senate by wide margins. The measure, which Bush signed into law on

January 8, 2002, required mandatory annual testing by the states to assess the performance of schoolchildren. The government would issue report cards for each school in the nation based on reading and math scores broken down by race, ethnicity, and socioeconomic status. By "disaggregating" results in this fashion, Bush fulfilled his pledge to minorities to spotlight gaps in educational achievement and move to erase them. Toward this end, the Act provided that if schools failed to meet assigned goals for three consecutive years, they must offer free tutoring services for children who needed them or else allow parents to transfer their children to a better performing school in the district. The law set 2014 as the year for achieving 100 percent proficiency in reading and math for all schoolchildren in the United States, an ambitious goal but one that Bush considered realistic and not merely symbolic.

Bush initially succeeded in casting NCLB as a civil rights victory. Margaret Spellings, the education secretary of the NAACP, called the Act "not just an education law. It's a civil rights law." Robert Gordon, a Democratic adviser to Senator John Kerry, went so far as to praise the Act "as a form of affirmative action [because] States must show that minority and poor students are achieving proficiency … or else provide remedies targeted to the school." Even the US Commission on Civil Rights, whose liberal members usually clashed with the Bush administration, hailed NCLB as ushering in the "most sweeping public education changes in decades."

However, praise for Bush's accomplishment proved short-lived. From the beginning, many conservatives, skeptical of big government and "social engineering," questioned the expense of undertaking a massive, federal overhaul of education. Expressing this concern, conservative scholars Frederick M. Hess and Chester E. Finn, Jr., criticized NCLB as too ambitious and impractical, "a civil rights manifesto masquerading as an education accountability system." The Bush administration gave liberals even greater reason to complain. Having embraced federal-sponsored reform, the President returned to more traditional conservative principles by cutting taxes and thereby reducing the revenue to fund NCLB adequately. A month after the President signed NCLB legislation, he sliced $90 million from its appropriation. Over the next six years NCLB remained substantially underfunded, thereby raising liberal hackles. In 2006, Congressman George Miller, the liberal Democrat from California who had voted for the measure, issued a report card for NCLB: "I would give it an 'A' in terms of the goals that it has set," he declared, but "I would give it an 'F' for funding … and on implementation I would give it a 'C.'"

Unquestionably, NCLB has fallen short of closing gaps in educational achievement among students based on race, ethnicity, and income. Yet Bush deserves greater recognition than he has received for departing from the strictures of conservative ideology to reform education in a manner not witnessed since the 1960s. In so doing he enlarged the scope of the traditional civil rights agenda to include reading and math literacy.

Although embracing diversity and educational reform, the Bush administration opposed affirmative action. Like most conservatives, Bush believed that the federal government had done all it could to extend equal opportunities to individuals regardless of race. Acknowledging that African Americans still faced prejudices, the President and his supporters nevertheless contended that the kind of legalized racism the government could challenge had come mostly to an end. Declaring integration an accomplished fact, they called for a halt to race-conscious policies. "In a society that is genuinely open to black opportunity," the conservative scholar Abigail M. Thernstrom argued, "colorblind principles have no moral competition."

During Bush's first term affirmative action suffered a severe blow from the Supreme Court. In 2003, the justices decided two cases concerning the University of Michigan's admission policies, which narrowed the application of affirmative action while leaving it intact. In fostering diversity in its student body, the university's undergraduate college awarded minority applicants special points in a numerical system that evaluated potential students. In a six-to-three ruling in *Gratz v. Bollinger*, the court struck down the plan because it did not pay sufficient attention to the individual characteristics of applicants and instead applied a rigid formula based on race to evaluate them. In legal terminology, Chief Justice William Rehnquist, speaking for the majority, found that the disputed "admissions policy is not narrowly tailored to achieve [the university's] asserted compelling interest in diversity."

However, on the same day a majority of five justices upheld the University of Michigan Law School's affirmative action admissions policy. In *Grutter v. Bollinger* the court found that in contrast to the university's undergraduate program, the law school admission plan considered race as only one of many factors in selecting students. In her majority opinion, Justice O'Connor upheld the law school guidelines, which emphasized flexibility and assessment of individual characteristics, because they furthered "a compelling interest in obtaining the educational benefits that flow from a diverse student body." The court no longer accepted affirmative action as a method of redressing past racial injustices, but sanctioned tightly drawn versions of it "in order to cultivate a set of leaders with legitimacy in the eyes of the citizenry" and open "the path to leadership ... to talented and qualified individuals of every race and ethnicity."

In the two Michigan cases the Bush administration had submitted briefs opposing the affirmative action plans. Despite the mixed outcomes, Bush considered the rulings a victory. "Today's decisions seek a careful balance between the goal of campus diversity and the fundamental principle of equal treatment under the law," the President remarked, and added that he looked "forward to the day when America will be a color-blind society." However, the Bush administration acted as if this egalitarian moment had arrived. Subsequently, it filed briefs on behalf of white parents in public school districts in Seattle, Washington and Louisville, Kentucky challenging voluntary efforts to desegregate schools to reflect the racial and ethnic composition of the districts. In 2007, the Supreme Court agreed with the Bush administration that the school districts had improperly employed race to assign children, thereby limiting further attempts by school districts to promote desegregation effectively. In practice, these rulings ensured that the President's No Child Left Behind program would operate within the segregated educational systems that continued to exist 50 years after Brown.

As evidenced by the Supreme Court's rulings in voting rights cases from North Carolina, Texas, and Georgia (discussed in Chapter 8), the majority of the court continued to make expansion of black suffrage difficult. Section 5 of the Voting Rights Act required state and local governments covered by its special provisions to submit any electoral changes to the Department of Justice or the federal district court in Washington, DC for "preclearance" before they went into effect. Also, in the past the high tribunal had ruled that for a voting change to be judged suspect it had to "make matters worse for minority voters" than the existing situation. The court referred to this principle as "retrogression." On January 24, 2000, before Bush was elected, in a five-to-four decision, the Supreme Court decided that with respect to Section 5 cases, a voting change could pass muster, despite evidence of racial discrimination, if it did not *intend* to place minority voters in a worse condition ("retrogressive intent") than currently existed. Thus, *Reno v. Bossier Parish School Board* (*Bossier II*) made it more difficult for the Department of Justice to wield Section 5 as a tool for guaranteeing minority voting rights. In the decade of the 1990s, the Civil Rights Division had reviewed numerous submissions of voting alterations and objected to approximately 250 of them on grounds of racial bias. After

Bossier II, the department filed only 41 objections from 2000 to 2004. And, nearly all of these objections were based on discriminatory retrogressive *effect* rather than intent, which proved much harder to determine.

President Bush assigned civil rights a low priority during his first term. Some of this stemmed from his ideological position against affirmative action. Instead, he devoted considerable energy to opposing abortion and homosexual rights, especially gay marriage, and to organizing a White House "faith-based" initiative. The latter was intended to assist and encourage religious organizations in seeking federal funds to combat problems like drug addiction and homelessness. In emphasizing these issues, the President strengthened his conservative political base.

Ultimately, the events of September 11, 2001 (9/11) played a far greater role in the setting of Bush's legislative program than any of his planned strategies. The attack on the World Trade Center and the Pentagon by a group of Islamic extremists from al-Qaeda, a shadowy organization led by Osama bin Laden, a Saudi Arabian national, launched a war against terrorism by the United States. Bush fought this war within the United States by securing passage of the Patriot Act (2001), a draconian internal security measure that expanded government surveillance of and eavesdropping on immigrants and American citizens suspected of engaging in terrorist activities. The 9/11 assaults fomented hate attacks against American Muslims but created unity among most Americans across racial, class, and gender lines. For example, when the Reverend Jerry Falwell, a Christian fundamentalist and Bush supporter, blamed pagans, abortionists, feminists, gays and lesbians, and the American Civil Liberties Union for heaping God's wrath on the United States on September 11, he produced national outrage and quickly apologized.

When President Bush led the nation into war against Iraq in 2003, most Americans approved. In what turned out to be erroneous assumptions, the Bush administration, including Secretary of State Powell and National Security Advisor Rice, argued that Iraq was on the verge of producing nuclear weapons, that its leader, Saddam Hussein, would use them against Israel, an American ally, and that the ruthless Saddam had formed an alliance with al-Qaeda. None of this proved true, but after toppling Saddam, over the next six years over 4,300 American troops were killed in Iraq. As the war dragged on and casualties mounted, approval for the invasion and Bush's handling of the war dropped precipitously to around 33 percent.

African Americans were among the harshest critics of the war. From January to May 2004, less than a year after the war began, the President's job approval rating among blacks slid from an already paltry 20 percent to 12 percent. Although the majority of the Congressional Black Caucus voted to authorize the war, its members became more quickly disillusioned than most. Taking into account the lure of the armed forces for economically strapped blacks, Congressman Kendrick Meek of Florida observed, African Americans "come into the military looking for jobs and wanting to serve their country. … But … many ask, what is the motivation behind the fight?" African Americans constituted 20 percent of the armed services, a higher percentage than their presence in the general population (approximately 12 percent) and their casualty rate in Iraq hovered around 14 percent. With this in mind, in March 2004 Congressman Charles Rangel of Harlem proposed a measure reinstituting the military draft to spread the burden of fighting more widely throughout the population. Without the support of the Bush administration, the bill failed, and African Americans became even more disgruntled with the war. A poll taken in 2004 revealed that 73 percent of blacks believed the war was not worth the casualties; 63 percent favored immediate withdrawal of US troops; and 77 percent thought that to some degree Bush had intentionally misled the country into battle.

The Election of 2004

President Bush had little more chance of gaining black ballots in his reelection bid than he had had four years earlier. Nor did he seek African-American backing in any significant way. In fact, Bush and his chief political adviser, Karl Rove, adopted the strategy of polarizing the electorate while expanding the base of Republican support among economic conservatives and Christian evangelicals. This meant presenting Bush as a strong national security leader in the post-9/11 world, despite the growing quagmire in Iraq, and as a defender of fundamental moral values with respect to the traditional definition of the nuclear family, the right to life (excluding the death penalty), and faith in Divine intervention on America's behalf. If religiously conservative African Americans, especially among Baptist denominations, found this appealing then they could hop aboard the Bush bandwagon. More likely, however, they would reject the President on economic grounds, as the black unemployment rate grew from 7.5 percent in 2001 to 11 percent the following year. By 2004, the black poverty rate had swelled from 20 to 24.4 percent. Bush further antagonized civil rights leaders by refusing to speak before the NAACP annual convention in July

2004, even though he had appeared there four years earlier. Accordingly, the NAACP chairman, Julian Bond, a former SNCC activist and Georgia legislator, condemned Bush's prosecution of the war in Iraq and affirmed that "blacks are increasingly angry about the economy and the war."

African Americans had a greater choice among potential Democratic presidential candidates. The field included two black contenders: the Reverend Al Sharpton, the controversial minister from New York City, and Carol Moseley Braun, the former senator from Illinois. Born and raised in Brooklyn, New York, Sharpton had gotten his start as a civil rights leader in 1969 when Jesse Jackson appointed him youth director of Operation Breadbasket. Nearly two decades later, he had become an outspoken presence in New York City, alienating whites and irritating city mayors by relentlessly charging police brutality against minorities. In 1986, he loudly defended the allegations of a 15-year-old black woman who claimed that she had been raped in a New York City suburb by six white men, including a few policemen, charges that later proved false. The sharp-tongued gadfly also led demonstrations through white New York City neighborhoods in Queens and Brooklyn after blacks were attacked by whites. Sharpton had not run for public office before, but Moseley Braun had served in the Illinois legislature for ten years before her election to the US Senate in 1998. After declining to run for reelection, she cast her eyes on the bigger prize of the presidency. She received encouragement from Donna Brazile, Gore's 2000 campaign manager, and the mainly white National Organization for Women. "I think she should run and we should have [a] woman running this year," Brazile asserted.

Neither Moseley-Braun nor Sharpton showed the strength of Jesse Jackson in 1988. Sharpton received 27 delegates in his primary campaign, but he fell short of victory in two important contests, South Carolina and Washington, DC, with heavily African-American electorates. The majority of black votes in these primaries went to the frontrunners, John Edwards and John Kerry in South Carolina and Howard Dean in the District of Columbia. Although Sharpton voiced issues directly connected to black economic and political concerns, he was perceived more as a protest candidate than as someone who had a real chance of winning. Congressman James Clyburn of South Carolina, a member of the Black Caucus, shared this view and threw his backing in the state behind Kerry. Nevertheless, Sharpton did wield some influence. He agreed to endorse Kerry and in return the Massachusetts senator pledged to help pay off Sharpton's campaign debt and vigorously support affirmative action and federal programs to challenge police brutality and racial profiling. Unlike Sharpton's campaign, Moseley-Braun's never got off the ground and was handicapped by the failure of her backers to raise the necessary financial support in her behalf.

Senator John Kerry won the Democratic Party nomination and black organizations rallied around him to encourage a high voter turnout among African-American voters. The National Coalition on Black Civic Participation (NCBCP) adopted the theme of "Unity '04." Consisting of 165 groups, both black and white, including the NAACP, National Urban League, the National Rainbow Coalition, the Congressional Black Caucus, the United Auto Workers of America, and People for the American Way, the NCBCP sponsored voter registration and get-out-the-vote drives throughout the nation and especially in places where the black vote could make a critical difference. Also, the National Coalition partnered with the Lawyers' Committee for Civil Rights under Law to recruit over 15,000 attorneys to monitor polling places on election day and prevent a repeat of the problems associated with the 2000 election. There was no doubt that the overwhelming majority of African Americans would cast their ballots for Kerry over Bush. However, compared with national security issues

Figure 25 Democratic presidential contenders John Kerry, Al Sharpton, John Edwards, and Dennis Kucinich debating in New York City on February 29, 2004. (Getty Images)

stemming from the 9/11 attack and the war in Iraq, civil rights achieved only minor importance in the campaign. Indeed, concerns were raised not so much about the treatment of African Americans as that of Muslim Americans, who had become the target of racial profiling and harassment. Still, Kerry backed affirmative action and promised that African Americans would not be disfranchised as they had four years earlier. He vowed to the NAACP convention: "We will enforce the law. We're not only going to make sure every vote counts, we're going to make sure that every single vote is counted." In contrast, the only civil rights issue the Bush campaign focused on was gay rights. The administration and its supporters spoke out forcefully against same-sex marriage, which the Massachusetts Supreme Court had sanctioned in February 2004. As part of its electoral strategy, the Bush team endorsed election day referenda in 11 states against gay marriage, including in the vital battleground state of Ohio, to mobilize its conservative base to turn out at the polls. (The measures passed in all 11 states.)

The outcome of the election proved disappointing to African Americans and other Democratic supporters. Bush won reelection again by a slim margin, though not as close as that in 2000. He garnered 50.7 percent of the popular vote to Kerry's 48.3 and defeated his opponent, 286 to 252, in the electoral vote. Bush had an easier time in Florida than four years before, winning by a comfortable margin of nearly 400,000 votes. Also, Republicans added to their victory by picking up four seats in the Senate and two in the House.

Not all the news, however, discouraged African Americans. Their overall turnout rate for this hotly contested election was 60 percent, the highest since 1968. The black vote increased by 25 percent and reduced the gap with white voter turnout from 2.9 percent in 2000 to 1.4 percent in 2004. Black ballots made the critical difference in Kerry's victories in Michigan, Pennsylvania, and Wisconsin. Nevertheless, Bush did pick up black votes nationally, however slight, gaining two percentage points over the 9 percent he received in 2000. Apparently some black voters, particularly religious fundamentalists, responded positively to Bush's emphasis on faith-based initiatives and opposition to abortion and gay marriage. A black women Democrat in Florida explained why she voted for Bush: "I believe he is a Christian. I admire him because he's not for gay marriage and he's pro-life. He's strong in his morals."

Still, Bush's reelection did not occur without considerable controversy. Ohio with its 20 electoral votes replaced Florida as the main source of contention. Both parties mounted intense voter registration and turnout campaigns, and data from exit polls placed Kerry ahead of Bush.

Nevertheless, the President won by 118,000 votes, and the discrepancy between the exit polls and the actual vote cast suspicion on the legitimacy of the Republican victory.

A close inspection of the results did not change the outcome but it raised serious complaints about the role played by state Republicans in whittling down the size of the black vote. Secretary of State J. Kenneth Blackwell, the African-American version of Florida's Katharine Harris, failed to inform 34,000 ex-felons that they could vote and the Republican official made it difficult for voters to cast provisional ballots. In Franklin County, which contains the city of Columbus and Ohio State University, the Republican-controlled election board withheld voting machines from predominantly black wards and shipped them to the white suburbs. Not surprisingly, turnout was higher in most of the districts that Bush won than in those in which Kerry emerged as winner.

Perhaps the most egregious attempt to disfranchise black voters resulted from the practice of "caging." Toward this end, Ohio Republicans sent registered letters to recently enrolled voters chiefly in minority neighborhoods, and then challenged 35,000 people who refused to accept the mailing or presumably did not live at the address listed. In sending out these letters, Republican challengers had no evidence that the intended recipients had violated Ohio's voting requirements; in effect, they were chosen because they were black (though some white Democrats also appeared on the list). This racially biased scheme was eventually struck down by the judiciary, but it more than likely resulted in intimidating blacks from voting.

The Bush administration cooperated with such disfranchising methods in Ohio and elsewhere. The Justice Department applied considerable pressure on US attorneys to investigate suspicions of false voter registrations. One of those attorneys, David Iglesias in New Mexico, a state Gore had carried in 2000 by fewer than 400 votes, failed to find any objections or prosecute cases of alleged Democratic vote fraud. As a result, Republican state politicos bitterly complained to Karl Rove, and Iglesias and seven other attorneys were subsequently fired, apparently with the approval of the White House.

Despite the Ohio irregularities, Kerry did not make a concerted effort to contest the results. The day after the election on November 3, Kerry formally conceded victory to President Bush. "In America, it is vital that every vote count, and that every vote be counted," Kerry declared:

> But the outcome should be decided by voters, not a protracted legal process. I would not give up this fight if there was a chance that we would prevail. But it

is now clear that even when all the provisional ballots are counted, which they will be, there won't be enough outstanding votes for us to be able to win Ohio.

There was just no way to prove definitively that Kerry's 118,000 vote deficit could be erased by recounting disputed ballots or factoring in possible votes from people who for one reason or another – long lines, polling place challenges, unreliable technology – did not cast a ballot.

Black Political Progress

The 2004 Bush victory dismayed African Americans, but blacks could look elsewhere for notable successes. One of the most heartening was the election in 2001 of Shirley Franklin as the first black female mayor of Atlanta. The city in which a succession of black mayors had governed since the mid-1970s had fallen on hard times, in large put due to mismanagement and corruption. Under her leadership, Atlanta restored its reputation as the bastion of southern black progressivism.

Franklin provided a direct link between the protest tradition of the civil rights era and the succeeding period of hardboiled, competitive, electoral politics. She earned her college degree at Howard University in the 1960s, when Howard supplied a good deal of talent for the civil rights and black power struggles. As an 18-year-old in 1963, she attended the March on Washington with her mother. After obtaining a master's degree in sociology at the University of Pennsylvania, she worked at the US Department of Labor and taught political science at historically black Talladega College in Alabama. In 1978, Franklin joined the administration of Maynard Jackson, Atlanta's first black mayor, and served as commissioner of cultural affairs. This marked her first foray into government and launched a distinguished career. Under Mayor Andrew Young, Jackson's successor, Franklin became the nation's first chief administrative officer, giving her the opportunity to manage a city budget of $1 billion and 8,000 employees. Among her duties she guided construction of the new Hartsfield International Airport and a new city hall and municipal court buildings. In 1991, after Maynard Jackson made a comeback and won a third term as mayor, Franklin became his executive officer for operations. At the same time, she was appointed to the Atlanta Committee for the [1996] Olympic Games. In 1999, Democratic Governor Roy Barnes appointed her to the Georgia Regional Transportation Authority, which she served as vice-chair.

In 2001, Franklin ran for mayor of Atlanta, the first time she competed for elective office. She sought an office that had been recently rocked by scandal. Mayor Bill Campbell, Jackson's successor, used his position to reward his friends and business partners by ignoring official contract bidding procedures and sound financial practices. (In 2006, he was convicted by a federal jury for tax evasion and sentenced to 30 months in prison.) With her outstanding record as an administrator, Franklin ran against Robb Pitts, an experienced politician and president of the Atlanta City Council. With three other candidates in the contest, Franklin still managed to win a majority of the vote (50.23 percent) and avoid a runoff election. Atlanta now had at its helm a five-foot-one-inch divorced mother of three who dyed her hair platinum blond – a sharp contrast in image from previous mayors.

Atlanta had shattered the race barrier for mayor nearly 30 years before, and Franklin's victory signaled a new breakthrough for women. Majority-black cities such as Hampton, Virginia, Camden and Irvington, New Jersey, and East Point, Georgia, had elected African-American women as mayors. But Atlanta was the only one of two (Minneapolis was the other) of the 100 largest cities with this distinction, even though one in five cities in the United States were led by women mayors. Franklin was astutely conscious of her role in history. In her inaugural address in January 2002, she drew inspiration from pioneering black women such as Harriet Tubman, Mary McLeod Bethune, and Madame C. J. Walker, and asserted: "I proudly represent all the women who have worked in the fields, toiled in the kitchen, fought for our rights and challenged our society." In living up to this tradition, she had her work cut out for her.

Taking over city hall in 2002, Franklin's most immediate challenge was to wipe out the budget deficit of $82 million left by Campbell. In a symbolic gesture, she reduced her salary by $40,000 to $101,000 and more substantially cut the mayor's staff by 50 percent, slashed nearly 800 government jobs, and succeeded in canceling the deficit. She also took on the daunting task of repairing the city's aging infrastructure. Dubbing herself the "Sewer Mayor," Franklin persuaded voters to pass a $3.2 billion reconstruction of Atlanta's crumbling water and sewage systems. She also directed police to begin walking beats and patrol neighborhoods, which helped lessen crime. In a move most conventional politicians avoided as the kiss of death, Franklin raised the municipal sales tax 1 percent and increased property taxes by 50 percent. Her "no-nonsense" actions, however financially painful they may have been, did not diminish her popularity. Polls gave her a

75 percent approval rating. "I'm kind of an unconventional politician," Franklin said, stating the obvious. "I've always been interested in the policy and not in the political strategy." Having restored trust in local government, in 2005 Franklin easily won reelection to a second term with more than 90 percent of the vote. That same year, *Time* magazine named her one of the five best big city mayors in the US and she won the John F. Kennedy Profiles in Courage Award, the only sitting mayor ever to receive this honor.

Franklin's success did not stand alone, and despite the results of the 2004 presidential election African Americans picked up some key victories. In addition to the 39 African Americans who sat in the House of Representatives, three new black representatives won, increasing their number to 42. Emanuel Cleaver, Kansas City's first black mayor, was elected to the House from Missouri, along with Wisconsin state senator Gwen Moore of Milwaukee and Al Green, a former NAACP official and judge from Houston, Texas. All sitting black members of Congress retained their seats except for Denise Majette of Georgia, who ran unsuccessfully for the US Senate. Nevertheless, she was succeeded by Cynthia McKinney, a former congresswomen ousted by Majette two years earlier.[2] In another notable comeback, former Virginia governor L. Douglas Wilder won election as mayor of Richmond; showing that he had lost none of his appeal, he captured nearly 80 percent of the vote.

The most significant victory, however, came with the election of Barack Obama to the US Senate from Illinois. Obama belonged to the post–civil rights generation of African-American politicians, and his background did not fit the traditional profile. Born in 1961 in Hawaii to a mixed-race family, Obama had a white mother who grew up in Kansas and an African immigrant father from Kenya. His parents met at the University of Hawaii, where both were students, married, and had one child. After Barack Obama, Sr., returned to Kenya, leaving his American family behind, the two-year-old Barack lived with his mother and her parents in Hawaii. When his mother remarried and moved Barack to Indonesia, he stayed in Jakarta for four years, but returned to Hawaii and resumed living with his grandparents. The Aloha State had a mixed-race population, but relatively few African Americans, which left Obama feeling isolated and torn between the two cultural streams that flowed through his blood. As a teenager, he used alcohol, marijuana, and cocaine, Obama recalled, "to "push questions of who I was out of my mind." Following his high school graduation, he

[2]   In 2006, the outspoken McKinney lost to another black candidate, Hank Johnson.

attended Occidental College in California for two years before transferring to Columbia University, where he received his degree in 1983.

Obama moved to Chicago in 1985 and became a community organizer, his first real opportunity to work closely in and identify with the African-American community. For three years he strove to improve living conditions in the Altgeld Gardens housing projects, an impoverished neighborhood filled with crime and unemployment. Obama came to realize that grass-roots change had its limits without the necessary political support from state and federal governments. Reform involved shaping public policy and changing the law, so Obama attended Harvard Law School, graduating in 1991. He was an outstanding student and the first African American elected president of the prestigious *Harvard Law Review*.

After returning to Chicago, practicing civil rights law, and teaching part-time at the University of Chicago Law School, Obama shifted his attention to running for office. While attending Harvard, he had found the time to direct a voter registration drive that signed up over 100,000 blacks in support of the candidacy and eventual victory of Carol Mosely Braun, the first black woman to win a seat in the US Senate. He later won election to the state senate and served for eight years. He viewed his role as a politician and organizer, "part teacher and part advocate, one who does not sell voters short but who educates them about the real choices before him." A Democrat, he succeeded in working with the majority Republican Party and passing the Earned Income Tax Credit, which provided over $100 million in tax cuts to working families. Obama also supported an expansion of early childhood education programs, videotaping of police interrogations in all capital cases, ethics and welfare reform, and a law to monitor racial profiling. He did not abandon the high ideals with which he entered the legislature, but he supplemented them with a healthy dose of practicality in a body that thrived on power politics. Besides the art of compromise, the ex-community organizer learned "that forming relationships a lot of times was more important than having all the policy talking points in your arsenal. That most of the time the people at the state level ... are moved as much by whether or not they trust you and whether or not they think your values are sound as they are by graphs and charts and numbers on a page." Based on his excellent record, in 2000 he sought higher office but failed to unseat the incumbent congressman Bobby Rush, a former member of the Black Panther Party.

This disappointment did not last long. In 2004, Obama ran for the US Senate. After winning the Democratic primary in a tight contest, he ran into a stroke of good fortune. With no incumbent in the race, Obama was slated to oppose the Republican nominee, Jack Ryan. However, Ryan dropped out in the midst of a messy divorce that revealed lurid sexual behavior. With only three months left in the campaign, Republicans nominated Alan Keyes, a black conservative diplomat, scholar, and occasional candidate for political office, including the presidency. Keyes lived in Maryland where he had unsuccessfully run for the Senate, but managed to establish legal residency in Illinois in time for the campaign. These two African-American candidates posed a stark contrast on the issues. Obama supported abortion rights, federal aid for stem cell research, and public education, whereas Keyes opposed the first two and favored school vouchers that could be applied to private education. Illinois voters resoundingly backed Obama, giving him 70 percent of the vote.

Before Obama gained his landslide victory, he came to national prominence at the 2004 Democratic presidential nominating convention. He delivered a stirring keynote address that brought the delegates to their feet. Entitled "The Audacity of Hope," his address recounted his life story, a child of black and white parents who gave him the African name Barack, meaning "blessed," because they believed "that in a tolerant America your name is no barrier to success." He chose words to heal racial, gender, and cultural divisions polarizing Americans politically into "Blue States" (Democrats) and "Red States" (Republican). Binding together the American people in all their diversity into one shared community was his audacity of hope:

> It's the hope of slaves sitting around a fire singing freedom songs; the hope of immigrants setting out for distant shores; the hope of a young naval lieutenant bravely patrolling the Mekong Delta; the hope of a millworker's son who dares to defy the odds; the hope of a skinny kid with a funny name who believes that America has a place for him too.

This speech reflected Obama's appreciation of what W. E. B. Du Bois called "two-ness" or the double consciousness of hyphenated Americanism, experienced by most inhabitants of the multiethnic United States. Obama readily embraced his African roots as well as his blood connections to white America, optimistically believing that the two could be woven together in celebration of the nation's variety of cultures. Furthermore, in the post-9/11 era, he spoke out against the war in Iraq and for protection of civil liberties. After all, he remarked in another campaign speech, "I don't just have to worry about my own child. … It's not enough that I am part of the

African-American community. I've got to worry about the Arab-American family that [Attorney General] John Ashcroft is rounding up, because I might be next." This powerful address reflected ideas Obama had thought long about and expressed in *Dreams for My Father: A Story of Race and Inheritance*, a memoir published in 1995 and which few read at the time. It is here that he describes how he had to "learn to slip back and forth between my black and white worlds, understanding that each possessed its own languages and structures of meaning." Despite obstacles to overcome, the confident Obama became "convinced that with a bit of translation on my part the two worlds would eventually cohere."

Not only did Obama, a relative unknown until then, inspire Democrats at the convention and those who watched its proceedings on television, he increased his political stock by campaigning for his party's congressional candidates throughout the country. Because the outcome of his own senatorial campaign was never in doubt, he could afford the time and money to travel throughout the country. He raised $1.2 million for Democratic senatorial contests and donated $225,000 from his own campaign war chest. John Kerry and other candidates invited him to campaign for them, and he delighted audiences wherever he appeared, coming across as an authentic American, seemingly transcending race. After Kerry's loss and even before he began his Senate term, Obama emerged as one of the new stars of the Democratic Party and a legitimate presidential contender in 2008.

The Bush Presidency, Part II

On the civil rights front, blacks gained little from the second Bush presidency. The chief executive continued to rein in affirmative action programs, and the Justice Department deemphasized civil rights enforcement. The department extended the administration's concern for conservative religious values by making protection of religious freedom a top priority in a manner once reserved for conventional civil rights cases. Under Attorney General Alberto Gonzales, who replaced John Ashcroft in 2005, the government supported the position of groups that wanted public schools to send home religious literature with their children; argued for the exemption of places of worship from local zoning laws; and pressed for the expansion of the definition of religious freedom under the First Amendment. In readjusting its mission, the Justice Department gave less attention to cases involving hate crimes, racial profiling, and voting rights. "Not until recently," Brian K. Landsberg, a law professor and former attorney in the Justice Department commented, "has anyone considered religious discrimination such a high priority. No one has ever considered it to be of the same magnitude as race or national origin."

The Bush administration sought to diminish enforcement of civil rights in general, and voting rights in particular, in other, less visible ways. More so than previous administrations, Democratic or Republican, the Bush Justice Department used a political litmus test in hiring staff that reflected its ideological positions. By the time Bush became President career civil rights lawyers in the Justice Department, especially in the Voting Section, had succeeded in enforcing the statutes passed at the height of the civil rights movement in imaginative and aggressive ways. As with most bureaucracies, career civil rights attorneys had provided continuity in enforcement no matter which political party occupied the White House. However, serious conflicts between political appointees and career officials arose in the Bush administration, thereby weakening enforcement. Joseph Rich, an attorney in the Civil Rights Division (CRD) of the Justice Department for 37 years, bitterly underscored this point: "I was there in the Reagan years, and this is worse." Between 2003 and 2007 more than 70 percent of CRD lawyers left the department, many of them forced to take early retirement, while others departed because of disagreements with department leadership. At the same time, those who stayed increasingly found their recommendations ignored and power diminished.

Making matters worse, the administration sought to crack down on alleged voter fraud, often targeting black communities with heavily Democratic majorities. The GOP's support for "caging" schemes in Ohio and elsewhere in the 2004 presidential election was part of the campaign to challenge increased black voter registration. Although government prosecutors filed 120 cases and obtained convictions in 86, a federal commission that studied electoral chicanery found that the pervasiveness of fraud was greatly exaggerated. Most of the problems stemmed from ignorance, confusion, and error rather than criminal intent to undermine fair elections. They were "isolated acts of individual wrongdoing" and not part of "organized schemes to subvert elections." For example, in 2004, Kimberly Prude registered to vote in Milwaukee and cast an absentee ballot in the presidential election. Convicted four years earlier for cashing a counterfeit check, she had been placed on six years' probation. She mistakenly believed she could vote because she was out of jail. Told by her probation officer that she could not vote, she asked local authorities to cancel her ballot. Her efforts were to no avail, and she was prosecuted and sent to jail. A federal appeals judge found "this whole prosecution mysterious." Judge Diane P. Wood declared: "I don't know if the Eastern District of Wisconsin goes after every felon who accidentally votes. It is not like she voted five times, she cast one vote."

Following a provision in the Help Americans Vote Act, the voting assistance law passed in 2002, the Justice Department backed use of voter identification cards to combat alleged fraud. To this end, in 2005, the Republican-dominated Georgia legislature adopted a voter identification law. Under the regulation, a prospective voter needed a government-issued, photo identification card, such as a driver's license, to take to the polls. Opponents argued that the requirement placed an unfair burden on impoverished Georgians, many of them black, who did not own a car or who could not afford the $20 for the approved identification card. Despite the advice of attorneys in the Civil Rights Division, the Attorney General okayed the law under Section 5 of the Voting Rights Act. The 11th US Circuit Court of Appeals ruled otherwise. Judge Harold A. Murphy compared the law "to a Jim Crow-era poll tax that required residents, most of them black, to pay back taxes before voting" and struck down the measure. In response, the state legislature made it easier for Georgians to obtain photo identification and at no cost. The Secretary of State also began a concerted program to inform registered voters of the need to obtain the photo card. With these efforts in mind, on September 6, 2007, Judge Murphy ruled that civil rights challengers had not proved that the law placed "an undue or significant burden" on the right to vote.

This decision foreshadowed a Supreme Court ruling the following year that dealt opponents of government-issued photo identification a severe blow. In 2005, the state of Indiana passed a law requiring voters to submit a United States or Indiana photo identification card at the polls. If a person did not have one, they could receive one free or vote provisionally pending obtaining one within ten days. The state claimed that it required such proof to prevent voter fraud, though it did not show that individuals stole other people's identity in voting. The challengers of the law argued that the burden of producing a photo identification fell most heavily on racial minorities, low-income people, and the elderly. In a six to three decision in *Crawford v. Marion County Board of Elections*, the court upheld the law in ruling that it did not impose an undue burden on prospective voters.

New Orleans and Hurricane Katrina

The Bush administration's civil rights enforcement policies greatly disturbed African Americans, but for blacks and their allies, the defining moment of the second Bush term came eight months after the presidential inauguration. During the last week of August 2005, a raging hurricane named Katrina hurled through the Caribbean and into the Gulf of Mexico, taking dead aim at the city of New Orleans. The eye of the storm just missed the Crescent City but left in its wake unprecedented devastation in New Orleans and along the Gulf Coast in neighboring Mississippi and Alabama, from which residents have yet to recover. In the face of such an immense natural catastrophe, it could be expected that substantial misery and dislocation would follow. However, the response to this disaster reveals much about racial politics on the local, state, and national levels and the ways in which human beings exacerbated the suffering inflicted by nature.

New Orleans was one of the great tourist destinations in the United States. Known as the birthplace of jazz and host of the annual Mardi Gras celebration, the city attracted state, regional, and national conventions to its famed Bourbon Street in the French Quarter, where tourists enjoyed fine dining and reveled in the "anything goes" atmosphere. Besides tourism, which brought in $5 billion a year, the port of New Orleans carried on a lively $13 billion annual trade, especially in the cruise ship business. Though the oil industry still existed, it had peaked in 1970 and declined precipitously thereafter. In 2004, the Crescent City contained about 444,515 residents, the thirty-fifth largest city in the United States. African Americans composed approximately 67.5 percent of this population. Despite the hoopla and high living that most tourists experienced in the French Quarter, the city displayed only the veneer of opulence. The median household income in 2004 was $27,355, about $8,000 less than that in Louisiana. At the same time, the proportion of residents living below the poverty line, 27 percent, exceeded that of state and national averages. Reflecting the reality of economic hard times, the population of the city had dropped by 40,000 since 2000.

Since 1978, African-American mayors had governed the Big Easy. The first to win election to city hall was Ernest "Dutch" Morial, a civil rights attorney, a state judge, and the first black elected to the state legislature. He ran against a white candidate and came out ahead at a time when whites still constituted a majority of registered voters. Morial succeeded in capturing an overwhelming majority of the black electorate and about 16 percent of white ballots, mostly middle- and upper-class liberals. Serving two terms (the city had a two-term limit), he concentrated on rejuvenating the downtown business section, renovating the city's waterfront, and balancing the municipal budget. His efforts created new jobs, and he helped minority businesses through affirmative action programs that allowed blacks to compete for and obtain a greater share of city government contracts.

Succeeding Morial in 1986, Sidney Barthelemy also served two terms. A New Orleans native, Barthelemy had studied to become a Catholic priest at St. Joseph's Seminary in Washington, DC. Instead of entering the priesthood he returned to New Orleans and received a master's degree in social work at Tulane. He headed the city's Department of Welfare in the early 1970s, and in 1974 Barthelemy was elected the first African American since Reconstruction to sit in the Louisiana Senate. He then won a seat on the New Orleans City Council, where he frequently quarreled with Morial. Upon Morial's retirement, Barthelemy competed against a black candidate, William Jefferson, in a city that now had a majority-black population. Gaining only a minority of the black vote (43 percent), he captured the large majority of white votes, reversing the pattern that first brought Morial to power. The new mayor faced a host of economic problems, including a slump in the oil industry and an unemployment rate of 11 percent. He worked closely with white business interests and built up the tourist industry by attracting the 1988 Republican National Convention and the 1993 NCAA Final Four basketball championship to the Big Easy. However, his attempts to promote land-based casino gambling proved a bust.

In 1994, Marc Morial, Dutch's son, succeeded Barthelemy. He had worked in Jesse Jackson's campaign for the Democratic presidential nomination in 1988, and three years later was elected to the state senate. Two white candidates ran against him for mayor, Mitch Landrieu, also the son of a former mayor, and Donald Mintz, in a racially charged contest. Morial won a runoff against Mintz with 54 percent of the vote, and in a manner reminiscent of his father, he captured an overwhelming majority of the black vote and a minority of the white vote. The younger Morial continued to promote tourism by fostering construction of 14 new downtown hotels, expanding the convention center named after his father, improving municipal streets, returning a professional basketball team to the city, and bringing the National Football League "Super Bowl" to the Louisiana Superdome. He also appointed an adroit black official, William Pennington, to run the police department, and the level of violent crime fell by 60 percent. In addition, he followed up his father's affirmative action programs by ensuring that 35 percent of city contracts were awarded to minority-owned firms and attempted to attract more black police officers and city workers by enforcing the rule that such employees live within city boundaries. Although his popularity remained very high during his two terms, he failed to persuade voters to change the city charter and allow him to seek a third term. His record was not flawless, however. Longstanding charges of corruption in the police department and other city agencies plagued him, and the boom in tourism failed to spread throughout the general economy or trickle down to the burgeoning population of poor people.

Following Morial in 2002, Ray Nagin burst on the scene. A native of New Orleans like his predecessors, and like Marc Morial a product of the post–civil rights era, Nagin received an undergraduate degree from Tuskegee University in Alabama and a master's in business administration from Tulane. He earned his living as vice president of Cox Communications, a cable company, and had not played an active role in politics. When he did take part, he hedged his bets. He appears to have contributed $1,000 to the first election campaign of President George Bush, as well as to Democrats running in the state. Contending for mayor in 2002 as a Democrat, the first time he had ever competed for elective office, Nagin campaigned as a reformer, promising to wipe out corruption and put city government on a sound financial footing. He ran independently of New Orleans's traditional black political network, and in a crowded field of candidates won the opportunity to compete against William Pennington, Marc Morial's popular chief of police. Subsequently, Nagin rode to victory with 59 percent of the vote, 85 percent of the white vote and 45 percent of the black. Both Nagin and Barthelemy demonstrated that in a new era of majority black politics, winners were still dependent on white votes.

Nagin, who had never been a liberal, did not suddenly turn into one. Recalling his 2002 campaign, he acknowledged: "I got attacked. I was called 'Ray Reagan.' And that white man in black skin stuff." He tended to cozy up to the oil, gas, and shipping interests and real estate developers at the expense of the growing number of poor folks who inhabited the city. He did, however, have a flair for publicity, which he demonstrated in embarking on an anticorruption crusade in the Taxicab Bureau and Utilities Department, firing workers in wholesale fashion, prosecuting officials, including one of his cousins, and approving a raid on the house of Marc Morial's brother. In the end, these actions led to the conviction of what one newspaper called "a motley collection of cabbies, vehicle inspection agents and low-level bureaucrats." Mayor Nagin was more successful in attracting media attention for his anticorruption efforts than in communicating with other blacks with political influence. Whereas Nagin wielded his axe to chop down the framework of corruption in municipal government, he refused to extend an olive branch to the city council, a move that backfired politically. He presented new plans and legislative proposals without first consulting elected council members, who expressed their pique by refusing to pass them. And, while Nagin talked about cleaning up police corruption, the murder rate, which had dropped 50 percent under Morial, soared to ten times the national average.

Even before Hurricane Katrina struck New Orleans, the city lacked the financial revenue and political leadership to deal with the problem of poverty, which affected over a quarter of its residents. The glitter of business-growth and tourist-related projects hardly scratched the surface of providing decent-paying jobs, good schools, improved housing, safe streets, and affordable healthcare for the people who needed them. Like many cities, the Big Easy had two sides – one that housed prosperous whites and the smaller black middle class, and the other in which the black poor lived. New Orleans was a microcosm of urban American, a metropolis split along lines of race and class.

Hurricane Katrina made that perfectly clear. The story of this tragic storm has been widely chronicled and its details need only to be briefly outlined here. At 6.10 a.m. on Monday August 29, 2005, Katrina, a Category 4 hurricane (on a scale of 5) whose winds were clocked at 145 miles per hour, swept over New Orleans and the Gulf Coast. The Crescent City suffered damage from the high winds, torrential rains, and a rampaging storm surge, but it did not experience severe flooding until torrents of water from Lake Pontchartrain burst through several weakened levees. Forty-nine percent of New Orleans lies below sea level, and in some low-lying areas, the water rose to 20 feet, swamping homes and businesses.

Approximately, 90 percent of New Orleanians escaped the city before the storm hit. Those who did not evacuate or who had chosen not to leave fled to the attics and roofs of their homes, and some 45,000 people evacuated to the Superdome and the Ernest Morial Convention Center. However, these shelters offered little comfort or solace to those who occupied them. Food, water, toilets, and medical care were in short supply, and corpses began to pile up outside the buildings. It took nearly a week for authorities to remove all the people from these facilities, board them on buses, and send them to safer shelters outside the city. As the days dragged on without much relief and with frustrations and anger mounting, violence and looting broke out on the drier streets of the city. Desperate people grabbed vital supplies off vacant store shelves and others stole not-so-vital televisions and appliances that obviously would be of no use until electricity was restored. Yet the enduring image from the hurricane remains the suffering of tens of thousands of ordinary people, displaced from their homes, who had lost everything, pleading for someone to rescue and assist them, and baffled as to why it was taking so long to do so. And these were the lucky ones; over 1,400 New Orleanians perished in the storm. Slightly more than half the dead were black, which meant that a significant number of whites also died (many of whom lived in the wealthy lakefront district susceptible to flooding). However, given the racial composition of the city and the predominance of photographs and videos of black faces anxiously seeking help, Katrina became an episode associated mainly with African Americans and the poor.

Figure 26 New Orleans residents appeal to be rescued, September 1, 2005. (AP Photo/David J. Pool/Press Association)

As Americans throughout the nation watched in horror the round-the-clock television coverage of the disaster unfolding, one thing became obvious – there remained a sizable population of poor black people in this country. The tragedy spotlighted race and class as matters of life and death. In this majority-black city, it was natural that African Americans would endure greater hardships, but numbers alone do not tell the whole story. Blacks suffered most because they were disproportionately poor. Many blacks remained in the city with the storm approaching not because they were irresponsible and chose to, but because they did not own automobiles and could not afford to pay the fares to exit on a plane or train. Also, they lived in places such as the Lower Ninth Ward precisely because their vulnerability to flooding made homes there less desirable and cheaper. Housing in the city continued to reflect patterns of racial discrimination associated with the Jim Crow era, which exposed African Americans to the daily vicissitudes of crime, poor education, and health hazards, and confined them to neighborhoods most likely to suffer the consequences of a hurricane. The damage inflicted by Katrina was not so much random as historically engineered. According to Chester Hartman and Gregory D. Squires, "if nobody is allowed to return to damaged areas, New Orleans will lose 80 percent of its black population, compared to just 50 percent of its white population."

In the searing words of one commentator at the time, the bodies of Katrina victims "reveal and shatter the conservative fiction of living in a color-blind society." Once again, the country seemed ready to discuss the enduring impact of race and poverty, as it had done when President Clinton created a race initiative commission a decade before. Once again, however, after much rhetoric and soul-searching, and numerous conferences and publications, the nation moved on to other business. But before it did, the hurricane in all its ramifications became a political football.

From the moment the levees broke, flooding the city and trapping its remaining residents from leaving, politicians and journalists began playing the blame game. And there was plenty to go around. The greatest responsibility for making this disaster worse fell on the shoulders of President Bush. His administration, built upon the conservative notion that the government that governed best governed least, botched the job of preparing for the storm and relieving the distress that accompanied it. Bush budget cuts had hurt the Army Corps of Engineers, the group responsible for constructing and maintaining the levees, and the Federal Emergency Management

Figure 27 The media highlighted race in ways shown by the captions that originally accompanied these photos. The one on the left read "A young man walks through chest deep flood water after looting a grocery store in New Orleans." The one on the right said "Two residents wade through chest deep water after finding bread and soda from a local grocery store after Hurricane Katrina." (AP Photo/ Dave Martin/Press Association)

Agency (FEMA), the organization in charge of disaster relief. Moreover, the federal government had ample warning of the catastrophe waiting to happen.

Experts had long pointed out the consequences of a major storm striking New Orleans, and FEMA had sufficient time to prepare. Part of the problem was structural. Following 9/11, Bush along with Congress folded FEMA into the new Department of Homeland Security, and in this reorganization, the agency received a lower priority than those fighting terrorism. The President made matters worse by appointing political cronies to head FEMA. Under Clinton, the organization had been run effectively by James Lee Witt, an experienced emergency relief official, who streamlined FEMA and elevated it to a higher status within the government. At the time of Katrina, however, the agency was run by Michael Brown, who had little experience in disaster management and whose appointment had lowered morale in the career staff. Brown seemed clearly over his head in dealing with the monumental chaos Katrina produced, but his boss, Michael Chertoff, the head of Homeland Security, did not perform any better. He was slow to heed warnings of impending disaster, even ignoring pleas for help from the hapless Brown. As a result, FEMA did not have adequate supplies or manpower on the scene to handle the crisis adequately. Not until Wednesday, August 31, did Secretary Chertoff formally declare Katrina an "incident of national significance," paving the way for the Department of Homeland Security to coordinate operations on the scene and get things moving. Yet Chertoff continued dragging his feet, never fully coming to grips with the dimensions of this extraordinary tragedy that was drowning one of America's most culturally distinctive cities.

In addition, Bush fumbled the ball on the field of symbolism. The President hesitated to cut his vacation in Texas short and take charge. It took him two days to fly over the affected region in Air Force One and another two days to pay a visit to the hardest hit sites in Alabama, Mississippi, and Louisiana. In a television interview on Thursday, Bush tried to explain the government's slow response: "I don't think anybody anticipated the breach of the levees," a statement based more on confusion or ignorance than veracity. On Friday, September 2, he made the widely reported gaffe on his inspection visit, when he greeted FEMA's director and told him for the press to hear, "Brownie, you're doing a heck of a job." Unfortunately for the President, nobody believed him, and his own statement contradicted the facts. Not surprisingly, on September 9, Chertoff relieved Brown of his duties on the Gulf Coast, and a week later "Brownie" resigned.

Democratic Governor Kathleen Blanco of Louisiana performed little better. On the first evening after the hurricane struck and with reports of flooding mounting, Blanco spoke with President Bush and acknowledged that the state needed help. "We need everything you've got," she implored. However, the governor did not provide any specific requests, so Bush refrained from responding vigorously. Perhaps Blanco should have been more decisive in making her request to the chief executive, but the president should have already gotten this kind of information from FEMA. He did not because communications between Brown and Chertoff were spotty. Clearly, Blanco, a first-term, recently elected governor, lacked experience in such matters. Despite numerous warnings over the years and exercises to gauge New Orleans's capacity to withstand a powerful hurricane, Blanco had not sufficiently prepared the state government to offer emergency assistance. Yet she did not remain immobilized. When FEMA buses had not arrived in the city two days after the storm, she issued an executive order to send vehicles to New Orleans. Blanco also sent in over 13,000 National Guard troops, however belatedly, who managed to oversee the evacuation of displaced citizens from the Superdome and convention center. These soldiers were later supplemented by a contingent of US Army troops finally authorized by the President. Blanco, however, declined to sign an agreement allowing the Bush administration to federalize the Louisiana National Guard troops stationed in the Crescent City. She feared that doing so would give the Republicans political ammunition to shift the blame for the misery from the White House and place it squarely upon her Democratic shoulders.

Finally, New Orleans Mayor Ray Nagin bears considerable responsibility for the tragedy. A political neophyte who distanced himself from the African-American establishment, Nagin lacked the experience and political sagacity to use the power of his office creatively and to the fullest. A Democrat, he had endorsed Blanco's Republican rival in the 2003 gubernatorial election, thereby causing a breach that had not healed. Nagin's first misstep came on the evening before the hurricane blew ashore. Advised by the director of the National Hurricane Center to declare a mandatory evacuation of the city, the mayor hesitated because he did not know whether he had the authority to do so (he did). Instead he called upon New Orleanians to abandon the area voluntarily, and not until the levees broke did Nagin make the evacuation mandatory. With the city's plan for disaster relief in disarray, the mayor did take some action by rounding up municipal buses to transport people to the Superdome, a "facility of last resort," and calling upon churches to send cars to rescue their congregants. Yet the city had not stocked the Superdome or Morial Convention Center with basic supplies, which led to a great deal of discomfort and distress for those gathered inside. Furthermore, with electricity out, telephone lines down, and cellular service disrupted, unlike his storm-ravaged counterparts in Mississippi, Nagin did not quickly dispatch a senior aide to communicate directly with the governor or top FEMA officials. Nagin and Michael Brown met only once during the first four days of the disaster.

Nagin seemed overwhelmed by the burden of leadership. When the storm hit, he fled city hall and retreated to the relative safety of the downtown Hyatt Hotel, a high-rise structure opposite the Superdome. In the immediate aftermath of the storm, he refused to cross the street and speak to people flocking to the sports stadium or lend his efforts to rescue operations, which would have had a mostly symbolic but positive effect. His actions usually came one step too late: not until Tuesday did he order mandatory evacuations, and on Wednesday, August 31, he declared martial law and deployed the police from its rescue mission to curb the violence and looting that had erupted. During the week, the mayor seemed to fluctuate between bouts of depression and aggressiveness. A number of those who observed him closely, including Governor Blanco, thought he was having a "meltdown." Some evidence of this came on Thursday. Appearing on CNN, he desperately pleaded for reinforcements. "I need troops, man," he reverted to the language of the streets. "I need troops, man. I need five hundred buses, man." Later that day on a popular local radio talk show, he called in and lashed out at both state and federal governments for not sending in troops to bail out the city. "I don't want to see anybody do any more press conferences. Put a moratorium on press conferences," he scolded the President and the governor and bluntly admonished, "Now get off your asses and do something and let's fix the biggest goddamn crisis in the history of this country." Having said his piece and hung up the phone, the mayor broke down and wept.

The next day a still angry and charged-up Nagin met with President Bush and Governor Blanco on Air Force One. He rehashed the outrage he had expressed over the radio, and told them, "you two need to get together on the same page, because of the lack of communication, people are dying in my city." These words allowed Nagin to blow off more steam, but they did not change the situation (though the President gave him the opportunity on board the plane to take his first shower since the hurricane). Earlier that day Congress had approved $10.5 billion in aid for New Orleans and Bush had ordered 30,000 soldiers to New Orleans. The following week, on Wednesday, September 7, with the crisis abated but far from resolved, Nagin abruptly left the Big Easy, leased a house in Dallas, and spent six days there. Perhaps trying to recover from the stress inflicted by Katrina, he nevertheless gave the impression that he was abandoning the city. Before leaving, he claimed on a national television program that "it wouldn't be unreasonable to have 10,000 deaths," a prediction greatly exaggerated.

Clearly, this catastrophe was mishandled up and down the political chain of command, but the failures of the Bush administration did the most harm. The White House had the capacity but not the will or the skill to contain the damage inflicted on New Orleans. Some of this involved political considerations. Bush worked better with the governors of Mississippi and Alabama, both Republicans, than he did with the Democratic Blanco. Louisiana was not as reliable a Republican state (it had a Democratic governor and one US senator) as the other two, and if Blanco came out looking poorly, this would benefit GOP electoral prospects. (Indeed, Blanco decided not to seek a second term.) However, some critics attributed Bush's shortcomings to personal racism. This accusation was voiced most prominently at the end of the first week following the storm. On a nationally televised benefit show to raise money for Katrina victims, the hip-hop singer Kanye West told the audience, "You know it's been five days [without aid], because most of the people are black. ... George Bush doesn't care about black people."

This judgment, born out of anger and frustration in the immediate wake of the tragedy, missed the mark. Many whites living in the path of Katrina's worst destruction, in Louisiana and Mississippi, suffered as much as African Americans in New Orleans and were likewise ignored by Bush. In an interview on "Meet the Press" on September 4, Aaron Broussard, the white president of Jefferson Parish, Louisiana, exclaimed: "We have been abandoned by our own country. Hurricane Katrina will go down in history as one of the worst storms ever to hit an American coast, but the aftermath of Hurricane Katrina will go down as one of the worst abandonments of Americans on American soil ever in US history."

Katrina had a catastrophic impact not because of any insidious racial belief of the President and the officials around him. All those in command, including the city's African-American mayor, performed poorly; the storm's mishandling was not personal. The hurricane dramatically revealed that the country may have conquered legal inequality, but the debilitating effects of race and class remained embedded in American institutions, which had been slow if not impossible to change in the post–civil rights era. The legacy of racial discrimination had pulled a disproportionate share of blacks into poverty and left them less able to flee the storm's wrath, thereby exposing them more fully to the incompetence of their elected representatives.

Katrina underscored the weakness of the conservative philosophy of self-help and reliance, as well as conservative hostility to government. The tragedy revealed dramatically how broadly government intervention was needed, especially for those impoverished and with little means to escape or cope with this overwhelming disaster. President Bush failed to see racism as institutional and its solutions as requiring much more than personal sympathy. Senator Barack Obama recognized this when asked whether the administration's response was evidence of racism. "I do not subscribe to the notion that the painfully slow response of [the Bush administration] was racially-based," Obama replied. "The ineptitude was colorblind." Instead, the senator attributed Bush's failures to "indifference" to poor communities in general and New Orleans in this specific instance.

Race also affected perceptions about government reactions to the event. Two weeks after the "Great Deluge" a Cable News Network (CNN) poll revealed a yawning gap in views between blacks and whites about the handling of the storm. Sixty percent of African Americans interviewed said the federal government's rescue operations moved too slowly compared with only 12 percent of whites who thought so. Thirty-seven percent of blacks held Bush primarily responsible for the poor response and 20 percent blamed Nagin. The reverse was true for whites: 29 percent held Nagin to blame and 15 percent said Bush. Despite the triumphs of the civil rights movement, centuries of racism sharply divided the way blacks and whites interpreted reality. Hurricane Katrina reinforced this racial divide.

Community action groups such as the Association for Community Organizations for Reform Now (ACORN) rushed in to fill the void left by national, state, and local governments, especially on behalf of the poor. The national organization and its local affiliates pressured New Orleans officials to rebuild the Lower Ninth Ward for its displaced residents and not abandon it to create wetlands. ACORN persuaded the city to allocate $145 million to assist homeowners in the neighborhoods of the Lower Ninth. The group also took the lead in building new storm-resistant housing in the hardest-hit areas. ACORN conducted protests and held rallies to campaign against the demolition of low-income and middle-class houses. In addition, ACORN staff engaged in voter registration and get-out-the-vote activities, helping to mobilize the black electorate for the 2006 mayoral race. Still, non-governmental organizations such as ACORN and Habitat for Humanity could only do so much with limited private funds, a fraction of the resources that were needed to restore New Orleans as it existed for the majority of its residents before Katrina.

Unfortunately, over the next few years the situation hardly improved for the residents who remained in New Orleans and on the Gulf Coast and for those who have returned in the years following Katrina. After many promises, local, state, and federal governments failed in restoring New Orleans to its previous condition or made much of an impact in doing so. Caught up in the quagmire of the Iraq war, the Bush administration did not display any sense of urgency in revitalizing the Crescent City, which remained a shadow of its former self. Mardi Gras festivities resumed without missing a beat, the French Quarter managed to regain tourists, the wealthy built condominiums on higher ground, but the Lower Ninth Ward and other black neighborhoods remained something of a ghost town. Estimates of the Crescent City's population in mid-2007 ranged from 255,000 to 274,000 or from 50 to 55 percent of the pre-Katrina figure. (In 2012 the population had grown to 369,250, about 81 percent of its pre-Katrina figure.) The Big Easy had lost nearly half its population but not its mayor. In 2006, Nagin faced a field of over 20 candidates, all but two of whom were white, competing for his office. The incumbent was reelected primarily by rallying what was left of black voters living in the city (approximately 58 percent of the population) and displaced voters who either cast absentee ballots or voted in an authorized polling place outside city limits in Louisiana. To obtain the majority of black support, which Nagin had not received in the last election, he insisted that despite the dislocation of many of its African-American residents, New Orleans would always remain a "Chocolate City." Consequently, the mayor succeeded in gaining 80 percent of the black vote and retained enough white voters (20 percent) among those he had catered to in the past, thereby defeating Mitch Landrieu, the state lieutenant governor, in a runoff. In doing so, Nagin squeaked to victory with 52 percent of the vote, the lowest winning margin for mayor in over 50 years. New Orleans had its "Chocolate Mayor," but the welfare of its citizens had hardly improved.[3]

In contrast to its handling of the Hurricane Katrina catastrophe, the Bush administration showed greater compassion for suffering in Africa, an area of special interest to black Americans. The President saw the international component of his compassionate conservatism as government assistance to fight epidemics in Africa. Many of the religious groups that composed Bush's political base were committed to fighting poverty and ending genocide in Africa in places such as the Darfur region of Sudan. According to Representative Donald M. Payne of New Jersey, the black congressman and top-ranking Democrat on the House International Relations Subcommittee on Africa: "The evangelical community raised the awareness of HIV and AIDS to the president. When the Bush administration came in, HIV and AIDS were not an overwhelming priority. Now we have seen a total metamorphosis." Still, action to relieve suffering in Africa proved of little comfort to those in New Orleans and failed to provide any political lift for the President among African Americans.

Reversal of Political Fortunes

President Bush's popularity sharply declined after his reelection. His polling numbers plummeted as American casualties soared to over 3,000 in the Iraq war and the prospects for achieving the administration's goals looked

---

[3] Bound by term limits, Nagin left office in 2010 and was succeeded by Mitch Landrieu, the first white mayor to serve since 1978. Three years later, a federal grand jury charged Nagin with 21 counts of corruption, including wire fraud, conspiracy, bribery, money laundering, and filing false tax returns related to his time as mayor. In 2014, a jury found Nagin guilty of all but one of the 21 charges.

unlikely. In addition, the White House's bungling of the Katrina rescue and rebuilding operations prompted voters further to lose trust in the President. Republicans also got hurt from a scandal involving accusations that a Florida GOP congressman, Mark Foley, had sent sexually explicit e-mail messages to male congressional pages, calling into question the party's commitment to moral values.

With Republican midterm electoral prospects growing dim, President Bush made an overture to black voters, a group that he had virtually ignored in the past. A year before the Voting Rights Act was scheduled for renewal in 2007, the President supported bipartisan legislative efforts to reauthorize its special provisions, including Section 5, for an additional 25 years. In recognition of the contributions African-American women made to the cause of civil and voting rights, the statute was entitled, the "Fannie Lou Hamer, Rosa Parks, and Coretta Scott King Voting Rights Reauthorization and Amendments Act of 2006." Moreover, Congress took the opportunity to remedy the problem that recent Supreme Court cases had caused for Justice Department enforcement of the Voting Rights Act. The revised statute stipulated that a voting change motivated by any discriminatory purpose, whether "retrogressive" (as *Bossier II* had dictated) or not, should be rejected. Lawmakers passed the measure by huge margins.

The Republicans' belated efforts did not pay off; protracted war, Hurricane Katrina, and scandal cost the GOP control of Congress. The 2006 congressional elections gave Democrats a 233 to 202 majority in the House and a 51 to 49 margin in the Senate.[4] Whereas 48 percent of all white voters cast their ballots for Democrats, 87 percent of black voters did so. This victory meant a great deal to the 43 members of the Congressional Black Caucus, all Democrats, now in the majority. Having built up seniority, African-American lawmakers claimed their rewards. James E. Clyburn of South Carolina became House whip, the third highest-ranking leadership position; Charles Rangel of New York City took over as chair of the House Ways and Means Committee; John Conyers of Michigan headed the House Judiciary Committee; Benny Thompson of Mississippi presided over the House Homeland Security Committee; and Juanita Millender-McDonald of California sat atop the House Administration Committee.

Another key gain was the election of Deval Patrick as governor of Massachusetts. Raised in a single-parent family in inner-city Chicago,

[4] Two independents, Joseph Lieberman of Connecticut, Gore's vice-presidential running mate in 2000, and Bernard Sanders of Vermont, a socialist, participated in the Democratic Caucus.

Patrick graduated from Harvard College and Harvard Law School. He worked for the NAACP, and in 1994 President Clinton appointed him assistant attorney general in charge of the Civil Rights Division, where he stayed until 1997. After serving in the corporate boardrooms of Texaco and Coca-Cola, he decided to run for governor in 2006. Winning the Democratic primary with 50 percent of the vote over two white candidates, Patrick handily defeated Karen Healey, outgoing Republican Governor Mitt Romney's second in command, with 56 percent of the vote. The first Democratic governor in 16 years and the commonwealth's first African American to occupy the state house, Patrick had run on a platform of hope and inclusion.

Not all the news turned out well for African Americans. Democratic Congressman Harold Ford, Jr., of Tennessee lost a close, bitter contest for the US Senate in which Republicans used highly charged ads stirring up the potent mixture of sex and race. In other contests, a black Democrat from Mississippi, Keith Erikson, failed to come close to unseating US Senator Trent Lott, and a black Republican from Maryland, Lieutenant-Governor Michael Steele, lost the Senate contest to Democrat Benjamin L. Cardin. In Ohio and Pennsylvania, black Republican candidates competed for governor and lost, failing to attract a significant portion of the black electorate to the GOP. Beyond elections for public office, African Americans suffered some stinging defeats at the polls. Ward Connerly, the determined black foe of affirmative action, bankrolled referendum drives against the use of race-sensitive programs. Voters in Michigan, where the Supreme Court had recently upheld a limited affirmative action plan for the University of Michigan Law School, voted overwhelmingly (58 percent to 42 percent) to ban the use of race in any way to promote minority admissions in education.

However, a significant longer-term trend of black empowerment must be highlighted. As African Americans regained the ballot and electoral office in the South, state officials reopened unsolved civil rights murder cases from the 1960s. Prosecutors now had to answer to a black electorate and juries were no longer all white. The federal government had tried culprits for several killings in the 1960s, but they had been charged with violations of civil rights statutes and not murder. From 1994 to 2007, Mississippi and Alabama, where the most infamous crimes had taken place, finally brought an assortment of murderers to trial. In a manner resembling ongoing efforts to bring ex-Nazis to justice no matter how much time had lapsed since World War II, state prosecutors charged now elderly, but once lethal, men for their past misdeeds. In 1994, Byron de la Beckwith, who had stood trial twice before, was convicted of assassinating Medgar Evers 31 years earlier. In 1998, another Mississippi jury found Sam Bowers guilty of the 1966 murder of Vernon Dahmer, an NAACP official active in suffrage drives. In 2001, Thomas Blanton went to prison for life after an Alabama jury convicted him of murdering four girls in the infamous Birmingham church bombing of 1963. The next year, his Ku Klux Klan accomplice, Bobby Frank Cherry, suffered the same fate. In 2005, a judge sentenced 70-year-old Edgar Ray Killen, one of the last surviving participants in the killings of James Cheney, Mickey Schwerner, and Andrew Goodman during the 1964 Mississippi Freedom Summer, to 60 years in prison on manslaughter charges. And in 2007, former Klansman James Ford Seale was convicted and sentenced to serve out the rest of his life in jail for participating in the murders of two Mississippi black men he believed were engaged in civil rights work in 1964.

Blacks had experienced some victories and suffered some blows during the Bush years. By 2008, the right to vote had been battered but remained strong. Yet the greatest test of black political advancement lay ahead in the quest of Barack Obama for the presidency.

10

Toward a "More Perfect Union"
The Obama Presidency

The future of black electoral politics remains unsettled a decade and a half into the twenty-first century. To an extent unfathomable in 1941, African Americans exert considerable influence in local and national affairs; yet, old patterns of discrimination still linger. The process of empowerment has moved ahead in many areas, but not at the same rate and often in a halting fashion. The notable achievements of the civil rights struggle often obscure the political dilemmas that continue to perplex African Americans and their allies. Questions remain as to whether conventional electoral politics can resolve the fundamental economic problems experienced by blacks and other impoverished Americans. These problems result not from individual acts of bigotry but from the enduring presence of discrimination deeply entrenched in key institutions throughout the centuries. Finally, African Americans face the future knowing that they are no longer the nation's largest racial minority; Hispanic Americans now hold this distinction and their percentage of the national population continues to grow. The election of Barack Obama as president marked a milestone in black political history, while at the same time revealing the persistence of race as a barrier to equality for many African Americans.

The Obama Candidacy

The best chance for an African American to gain the highest office in the land and reshape the future of the United States rested in the candidacy of Senator Barack Obama for president. With only three years in the US Senate, Obama

Running for Freedom: Civil Rights and Black Politics in America since 1941,
Fourth Edition. Steven F. Lawson.
© 2015 John Wiley & Sons, Inc. Published 2015 by John Wiley & Sons, Inc.

experienced a meteoric rise. The Illinois senator had far greater appeal among whites than did Jesse Jackson in his campaigns for the presidency. Too young to have engaged in celebrated civil rights struggles, Obama offered a fresh face on the political scene. Moreover, by succeeding in two racial worlds, he drew potential support from millions of blacks and whites.

In 2007, as Obama weighed his options in running for president, Africans Americans needed an economic as much as a political boost. Blacks had a median income of $30,939, compared with $50,622 for whites. Three-quarters of white households owned their own homes compared with 46 percent for blacks. Approximately 24 percent of African Americans lived in poverty, nearly double the national rate of 12.3 percent, while only 8 percent of non-Hispanic whites lived in poverty. Approximately 20 percent of African Americans lacked health insurance; the rate for all Americans was around 4 percent lower.

Yet Obama did not run for the White House mainly to help racial or ethnic minorities. He proclaimed a much broader vision. When it came to politics Obama thought in universal rather than race-specific terms. In his campaigns for the presidency in the 1980s, Jesse Jackson had tried to assemble a broad "Rainbow Coalition" of different races and ethnic groups to fight for economic goals that united women and men, the poor and the middle class. Despite attempting to extend his political base, Jackson still came across as "a race man," a candidate who represented and spoke chiefly for black voters. Unlike Jackson, Obama came of age after the civil rights movement of the 1950s and 1960s (he was not born until 1961) and although influenced by it he presented himself as a politician who addressed issues beyond race. Indeed, he used his opposition to the Iraq war, which he voiced before becoming a US senator, to distance himself from other Democratic contenders for the presidential nomination.

In many ways, transcending racial concerns came naturally to Obama. The son of an interracial marriage who grew up in multi-ethnic Hawaii, where race was not conceived in strictly black and white terms, Obama could appeal to the American electorate as a proud symbol of diversity who embodied the tradition of many cultures coming together to form one nation. In an interview on National Public Radio in 2007, Obama acknowledged that his background made it easier for him "to speak in universal terms" rather than in "very race-specific terms about the plight of the African-American community." He agreed with his University of Chicago colleague, the sociologist William J. Wilson, who had argued for several decades that with the end of the civil rights movement and the loss of industrial jobs in the US to foreign competition, class had replaced race as the most significant detriment to economic mobility. Consequently, Obama favored government policies that created good-paying jobs and increased educational opportunities for all Americans and supported greater public investment in human capital, health care, and infrastructure to achieve these ends.

Not only did Senator Obama believe that a universal approach was more desirable than a race-oriented one as a matter of policy, but he judged that it constituted "good politics" as well. "It would be difficult for an African American to be elected president in this country," the Obama pollster Cornell Belcher reported, "However it is not difficult for an extraordinary individual *who happens to be African American* to be elected president" (emphasis added). Obama modeled himself after Harold Washington, the black mayor of Chicago in the 1980s (see Chapter 6), where Obama worked as a community organizer. In a majority-white city with fierce racial divisions, Washington had forged a cross-racial coalition to gain victory. One of Washington's principal advisers, David Axelrod, a white journalist turned political consultant, became part of Obama's inner circle. As the political scientists Rogers Smith and Desmond King point out, Obama sought to forge common ground between those whites who preferred a color-blind society but would support some race-conscious policies to promote black progress and African Americans who favored targeted racial measures but "who would be willing to see them put on the back burner if progress is indeed being achieved through other means."

Accordingly, Obama attempted to minimize the impact of racial issues by convincing whites that if elected he would serve as president of all the people. He acknowledged that although "rooted in the African-American community," he did not feel "limited by it." He avoided hot-button issues like affirmative action, which he described in his second book, *The Audacity of Hope* (2006), as "a useful, if limited tool to expand opportunity to under-represented minorities."

As part of this race-defusing strategy, Obama aimed to convince whites that the burden of making up for past wrongs and extending racial progress did not fall solely upon them. He did this through "tough love," instructing African Americans to accept "personal responsibility" for improving their lives without using injustice and poverty as excuses for holding them back. He singled out black men to accept their filial duties as husbands and fathers and stop acting "like boys instead of men." In stressing personal responsibility and self-help, Obama stood within the long African-American religious tradition of promoting racial uplift, racial pride, and caring for the poor and underprivileged. Obama and his wife, Michelle, attended Trinity United Church of Christ in Chicago, where pastor Jeremiah Wright delivered messages of community outreach to help blacks overcome poverty, disease, and substandard living conditions.

Obama did not play the role only of scold; he made it clear that the plight of African Americans resulted from centuries of white racism, and the government had an obligation to overcome the effects of past discrimination. While highlighting black responsibility for curing social ills might ease guilty white consciences, it failed to acknowledge the structural components of racism – disparities in employment opportunities, healthcare, education, and sentencing for crimes; profiling; and residential segregation. In walking a fine line between self-help and government intervention, Obama attempted to reassure whites without alienating blacks.

This did not prove easy. Initially, African Americans remained wary of his candidacy. By the end of 2007, polls showed that only about 50 percent of blacks believed Obama shared their values. This wariness stemmed from a variety of sources. Some African Americans voiced skepticism that Obama, by virtue of his biracial family background and his early upbringing in Hawaii, had truly shared the experience of being black with its legacy of slavery and Jim Crow. The critic Stanley Crouch conceded that Obama "has experienced some light versions of typical racial stereotypes," but he doubted that the senator could "claim those problems as his own – nor has he lived the life of a black American." Former presidential candidate Reverend Al Sharpton agreed: "Just because you are our color doesn't make you our kind." Others questioned whether Obama, an inexperienced politician on the national scene, could be elected president and instead backed the candidacy of Hillary Clinton, the former first lady and senator from New York. She and her husband had built up an extensive network of political relationships among black elected officials during President Clinton's two terms, and it continued afterwards. While Jessie Jackson did not endorse either candidate, Hillary Clinton won important endorsements from congressmen John Lewis of Georgia and Charles Rangel of New York, and former congressman and mayor of Atlanta Andrew Young, along with many other members of the black political establishment. Polls taken in 2007 reported Hillary Clinton running far ahead of Obama among registered black Democrats, 57 percent to 33 percent.

Early doubts about Obama's "blackness" proved misdirected. Although Obama actively appealed for white support and moved easily between black and white constituencies, he never accepted the notion "that we live in a colorblind society." Writing in *The Audacity of Hope*, he asserted, "To say that we are one people is not to suggest that race no longer matters." He went even further in his response to an NAACP questionnaire of presidential candidates, insisting that "to suggest that our racial attitudes play no part in the socio-economic disparities that we often observe turns a blind eye to both our history and our experience." When correspondent Steve Kroft of the television program *60 Minutes* bluntly asked Obama when he decided he was black, a question that was both patronizing and on the minds of many blacks and whites, the senator responded with his usual poise. "Well I'm not sure I decided it," Obama replied and then coolly stated the obvious, "If you look African American in this society, you're treated as an African American." Whether he chose it or not, Obama considered himself a proud black man, married to an intelligent and strong African-American woman whose roots went back to slavery, and together they raised their two African-American daughters.

Adding to his sense of blackness, Obama embraced the legacy of the southern civil rights movement. As a college student in California in the early 1980s, Obama joined in demonstrations against the racist apartheid regime in South Africa. Later at Harvard Law School he carried around volume one of Taylor Branch's magisterial history of the civil rights movement, *Parting the Waters* (1988), and affirmed it was "my story." Presenting himself as the heir to Martin Luther King, Jr., in March 2007 he proclaimed that King and his "Moses Generation" had taken African Americans 90 percent of the way to racial equality. It was left to Obama's "Joshua Generation" to go the rest of the way. He looked to the civil rights movement for inspiration and proclaimed as his role models John Lewis, Bob Moses, Fannie Lou Hamer, and Ella Baker, all associated with the Student Nonviolent Coordinating Committee, the vanguard of the southern civil rights movement. Although Obama acknowledged the influence of the black nationalist Malcolm X, he admired him more for his "repeated acts of self-creation" than for his ideology. A black candidate such as Obama seeking the presidency might recognize Malcolm's importance to African Americans, but to compete successfully he had to identify with King, who had entered the pantheon of all-American heroes, rather than with a so-called "angry black man." Obama explained why this made perfect political sense. "It may give us [African Americans] psychic satisfaction to curse out people outside our community and blame them for our plight," he told a black audience, "but the truth is, if you ... [want] to get things accomplished politically, you've got to work with them [whites]."

Obama's racial ideology mirrored his general approach to economic and social problems – they both reflected pragmatism. In the brief time he had served as senator from Illinois, Obama had compiled a liberal voting record. However, he was more comfortable seeking bipartisan solutions than refusing to compromise ideological principles. As Thomas Sugrue has noted, Obama "had developed a patchwork quilt of social politics." From the left he advocated government-sponsored job creation, healthcare extension, educational opportunity, and clean, renewable energy. He stitched this agenda to the centrist program enacted by President Clinton in ending the New Deal-Great Society system of welfare. Obama aptly summed up his political orientation: "Since the founding, the American political tradition has been reformist, not revolutionary, what that means is that for a political leader to get things done, he or she should ideally be ahead of the curve, but not too far ahead." This blend of ingenuity and caution made Obama difficult to classify. Terms like "pragmatic progressive," "progressive pragmatist," "visionary minimalist," and "conservative revolutionary" have been used to describe him, but most agree with George Packer that "Obama pursues large goals in a way that offends the deepest values of as few people as possible." In fact, before running for president, Obama bragged of his ability to remain "a blank screen on which people of vastly different political stripes project their own views."

Obama vs. Clinton

Those who questioned whether the nation had made sufficient racial progress for a black man to compete successfully for the American presidency received a preliminary but affirmative answer from the results of the Iowa caucus in early January 2008. In the first contest to pit the eight Democratic candidates against each other, Barack Obama came out on top with 37.6 percent of the caucus votes, with Hillary Clinton running third. The outcome was crucial in demonstrating Obama's crossover appeal in a state where blacks constituted less than 5 percent of the population. Obama's resounding victory gave established black politicians who had not supported him some cause to rethink their assumption that he could not win. Shirley Jackson, the mayor of Atlanta, who had earlier declared her neutrality, jumped on Obama's bandwagon after Iowa. However, John Lewis and Charles Rangel remained Clinton supporters and Jesse Jackson remained undecided, though his son, Congressman Jesse Jackson, Jr., campaigned for

Obama. The other 39 members of the Congressional Black Caucus were split down the middle between Obama and Clinton.

As African Americans began to reevaluate Obama's chances in the wake of Iowa, he established once again that he could attract a significant number of white votes. In a field of seven candidates, he came in second to Clinton in New Hampshire, doing so in a state with a tiny African-American electorate. Nevertheless, the contest in the Granite State raised the specter of the race issue that would divide the Democratic frontrunners in the months to come. During the campaign, Clinton, in maintaining that she was better qualified to serve as president than Obama, did so in a round-about way that seemed a slight to African Americans. "Dr. [Martin Luther] King's dream began to be realized," she asserted, "when President [Lyndon] Johnson passed the Civil Rights Act. It took a president to get it done." Clinton was not attempting to diminish the civil rights leader, whom she greatly admired, but trying to underscore the importance of presidential leadership and distinguish herself from her rival. Implying that it would take more than a charismatic black man to get things done, her remarks came, as the *New York Times* editorialized, "perilously close to injecting racial tension" into the campaign.

Racial controversy erupted more unmistakably in South Carolina. In the Palmetto State blacks constituted 50 percent of the Democratic Party electorate, which provided an opportunity to answer the question whether a decisive number of black voters would rally around Obama. The response was a resounding yes, as Obama won more than 80 percent of the black vote and defeated Clinton and seven others in the primary with a muscular 55 percent of the vote. For the first time in the primary season, Obama had a chance to identify with black audiences, not as the Harvard Law School graduate and university professor, but as someone who came out of their community and spoke their language. Referring to his opponents, mainly Mrs. Clinton, before a black audience, he communicated in a style very familiar to them: "They are trying to bamboozle you. It's the old okie-doke. Y'all know about the okie-doke, right …They try to bamboozle you. Hoodwink ya. All right, I'm having too much fun up here." This was Obama at his best in moving between two worlds. However, not everyone appre-ciated this. Bill Clinton, who was campaigning tenaciously for his wife, griped to reporters about the results and tried to minimize them. "Jesse Jackson won South Carolina in '84 and '88," the former president reminded the press corps, suggesting that like Jackson, Obama had only a limited appeal based on racial solidarity. His words suggested that the former president was trying to "blacken" Obama, thereby marginalizing him. Not only did Clinton disturb many African Americans who thought of him as an "honorary brother," but he was wrong in his assessment. Obama ran very well throughout all of South Carolina, winning all but two of 46 counties. He captured about 25 percent of the white vote, but even more significant, he won a majority of white voters under the age of 40.

On February 5, the hotly contested "Super Tuesday" races in 22 states resulted in Obama and Clinton splitting the delegates, which strengthened Obama's credibility, since Clinton had expected to come out on top and lock up the victory. Obama's strength rested with African Americans and younger voters fired up by the Illinois senator's campaign for change, under the slogan "Yes we can." Winning over 80 percent of black voters, Obama clearly had convinced them that he could win. After Obama captured the Georgia primary on Super Tuesday, Congressman John Lewis switched his support from Clinton to Obama, a monumental defection that carried great weight among whatever doubtful black voters remained. Besides heeding the message of his home state constituents, Lewis left no doubt that Obama was a worthy heir of the black freedom struggle. "Barack was born long before he could experience or understand the movement," Lewis explained, "He had to move towards it in his own time, but it is so clear that he digested it, the spirit and the language of the movement."

Not surprisingly, Obama lost to Senator Clinton among white women, many of whom were excited by the prospect of electing a woman to the White House for the first time in history. He also received fewer votes from white men and Latino and Asian-American voters in New York, New Jersey, California, and the Southwest. Nevertheless, he went on to win 11 straight primaries and caucuses following Super Tuesday and by the end of February, he led Clinton in both the popular vote and convention delegate count.

Having locked up the black vote, Obama struggled to pry away white voters or ethnic minorities from Clinton. In a nationally televised debate three weeks after Super Tuesday, the moderator Tim Russert of NBC asked Obama if he accepted the announced support of Louis Farrakhan, the controversial head of the Nation of Islam. Obama responded that he had not sought Farrakhan's endorsement and denounced the Black Muslim minister. Clinton jumped in to insist that Obama should not simply "denounce" but "reject" Farrakhan's endorsement. He replied that he saw no real difference between the words, and agreed to both reject and denounce Farrakhan's backing. The Nation of Muslim minister did not respond to Obama's remarks in kind and urged blacks to ignore these attempts "to hurt

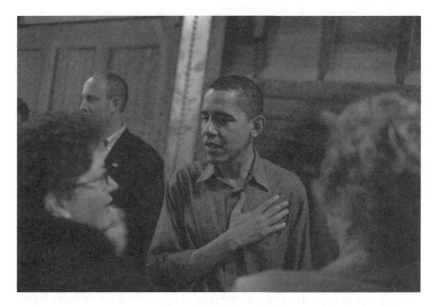

Figure 28   US senator and presidential candidate Barack Obama talks to local voters after a town hall meeting in Chariton, Iowa. (Photo © Callie Shell/ Aurora Photos)

Mr. Obama politically." Still, Farrakhan missed the point. Clinton did not aim her remarks at blacks; rather she directed them to whites.

Around the same time in late February, Clinton supporters posted a photo on the internet designed to heighten suspicions that Obama was a secret Muslim. In 2006, Senator Obama had visited his father's native Kenya and was photographed wearing African garb, which he had put on as a goodwill gesture. Obama campaign managers accused the Clinton camp of fueling misinformation about their candidate's religion and birthplace, thus feeding into the notion that Obama was an outsider, someone to be feared as not really an American.

In March and April, Clinton gained considerable strength by beating Obama in several primaries in key battleground states. In Ohio, she put together a winning coalition of white women and working-class white men to triumph in a state suffering heavily from unemployment. Obama inadvertently bolstered Clinton's appeal among this latter group. At a fundraiser in San Francisco he tried to explain the disaffection among white working-class voters and his difficulties in gaining their support. "So it's not surprising that they get bitter, Obama remarked. "They cling to guns and religion or antipathy to people who aren't like them … as a way to explain their frustration." Clinton seized on these comments, portraying them as elitist, insulting, and "not reflective of the values and beliefs of Americans." Although Obama quickly apologized and insisted that he meant to demean no one, the damage was done. Clinton went on to win the important Pennsylvania primary, a state with high unemployment. In May, after Clinton won Indiana, another bellwether of white working-class support, she gloated that Obama's appeal was weakening among "hard-working Americans." In case anyone did not understand whom she meant by "hard-working," she added "white Americans."

The greatest threat to Obama's standing among the majority-white electorate erupted over the candidate's relationship with his pastor, Jeremiah Wright. As head of the predominantly black Trinity United Church of Christ in Chicago, Wright had mentored Obama and deepened his Christian faith, presided over his marriage to Michelle Robinson, and baptized their daughters, Malia and Sasha. Obama borrowed the title of one of Wright's sermons, "Audacity of Hope," as the title of one of his books. Despite this close personal relationship, the two men differed in style and perspective. In the prophetic ministerial tradition of Dr. King, Wright held up a mirror to America to highlight the gap between its promise of equality and justice and the reality of continuing racial discrimination. His preaching of a black-centered theology focused on liberation of the poor and dispossessed, those at the bottom of society for whom Jesus Christ had suffered. Under Wright's leadership the church extended beyond an institution of worship and operated more as a center of activism in promoting the social gospel. Trinity United ran day-care programs, established prison outreach to black inmates, and encouraged testing for HIV-AIDS, a disease on the rise in black communities.

Wright delivered his sermons in passionate if not impolitic language. In one such homily on April 13, 2003, Reverend Wright, a veteran of the US Marines, condemned America for its treatment of black people and other minorities; for its criminal justice system that discriminated against African Americans with its unequal sentencing standards; and for its building of bigger prisons instead of better schools. But in his peroration, Wright went too far:

> The government wants us to sing "God Bless America." No, no, no, not God Bless America. God damn America – that's in the Bible – for killing innocent people. God damn America, for treating our citizens as less than human. God damn America, as long as she tries to act like she is God, and

she is supreme. The United States government has failed the vast majority of her citizens of African descent.

These words came back to haunt Obama, whose campaign attempted to soft-pedal racial conflict. As David Plouffe, the candidate's campaign manager, observed, Wright's statements "threatened to undermine the profile we had spent fifteen months building": Obama as a "steady" and "pragmatic" leader who bridges "racial divides." In fact, the Obama team had decided as early as February 2007, when the senator officially announced his candidacy for president, to keep his controversial minister in the background because of Wright's fiery sermons. All remained quiet until 13 months later in March 2008, when videos of some of Wright's sermons, including his "God Damn America" tirade, surfaced. Television shows broadcast excerpts from them nationally, and they went viral on the internet. Coming at the midpoint of the Democratic contest and threatening to wipe out his narrow lead over Clinton in subsequent primaries and caucuses, these revelations forced Obama to make the kind of speech on race that his campaign had previously avoided. However, Obama was well prepared. "I already know what I want to say in this speech," he told his closest advisers. "I've been thinking about it for almost thirty years."

On March 18, 2008, in Philadelphia, the birthplace of the Constitution, Obama placed his pastor's remarks in context before a televised national audience. Although he distanced himself from his minister's "pessimism" about race relations, he still tried to explain the sources of Wright's disturbing views. Thus, he reminded his listeners, "So many of the disparities that exist in the African-American community today can be directly traced to inequalities passed on from the past." He then personalized the insidiousness of discrimination by recalling the racial prejudice of his beloved white grandmother who had helped raise him. He recounted how she had "once confessed her fear of black men who passed by her on the street, and who on more than one occasion has uttered racial or ethnic stereotypes that made me cringe." That said, he could no more disown her for these remarks than he could Reverend Wright for his; nor could he "disown the black community."

Having explained the burden of racial discrimination to whites, in typical Obama fashion, he turned to African Americans and pointed out that whites too had grievances. "Like the anger within the black community," he asserted, "these resentments aren't always expressed in polite company." Working-class and middle-class whites, he explained, "don't feel that they have been particularly privileged by their race"; rather, "[t]hey've worked hard all their lives, many times only to see their jobs shipped overseas or their pension dumped after a lifetime of labor." Such economic resentments fueled their concerns over school busing to achieve racial balance and affirmative-action programs that they believed came at their expense. In effect, Obama equated the expression of white anger with black rage. In the manner of King Solomon, Obama, the historian Peniel Joseph wryly commented, "blamed both sides equally for a predicament that blacks have largely no part in creating."

Obama called upon all Americans to find common ground, the ecumenical approach to resolving differences that defined the candidate. Rather than dwelling on past grievances, he urged all Americans to join together and move toward "the more perfect union" that the founding fathers had envisioned. He wanted to transform race from a source of contention to an opportunity "to come together and solve challenges like health care, or education, or the need to find good jobs for every American."

In delicately balancing his remarks to appeal both to whites and blacks, Obama generally achieved his political aim of defusing the Wright issue. The *Dallas Morning Herald* praised the address for its "unflinching, human, and ultimately hopeful" qualities and declared "this remarkable address was one for the history books." Yet the controversy still had some life. "Just imagine," Hillary Clinton remarked, "if my pastor from Arkansas said the kind of things [Obama's] pastor said … This race would be over." Perhaps had the Wright story broken earlier, before mid-March with the majority of primary and caucus contests over, its impact would have been greater. Still, Reverend Wright would not retreat. He refused to follow the path of Louis Farrakhan and help Obama by remaining silent. Instead, more than a month after the Philadelphia address, this proud man licked his wounds publicly in an address to the National Press Club in Washington, DC. Not only did he compare US military efforts in Iraq and Afghanistan to "terrorism," he denounced Obama for criticizing him "based on electability, based on sound bites, based on polls." This time his strident remarks proved too much, and Obama and his family withdrew from Trinity United Church.

In addition to race, gender played a critical role in the campaign. The National Organization for Women and leading feminists, such as Gloria Steinem, enthusiastically backed Hillary Clinton, the first woman to seek the presidency who had a chance of winning. Steinem penned an op-ed piece in the *New York Times* arguing that "the sex barrier was not taken as seriously as the racial one." This launched a contest between Clinton and

Obama supporters over who would achieve the distinction of running first as Democratic candidate for president, an African American or a woman, which then turned into an argument concerning which group had suffered greater oppression historically. The disagreement reminded commentators of the split between the civil rights leader Frederick Douglass and the suffragist Elizabeth Cady Stanton in the post–Civil War era over whether African Americans should get the right to vote under the Fifteenth Amendment without including women. In a modern version of this battle, Geraldine Ferraro blasted Obama. The Clinton fundraiser and the first woman nominated by a major political party for vice president in 1984 claimed that "if Obama was a white man, he would not be in this position. And if he was a woman he would not be in this position. He happens to be very lucky to be who he is. And the country is caught up in the concept." The Illinois senator responded politely but sardonically that being an "African American man named Barack Obama" was hardly a political asset. "Anybody who knows the history of this country I think would not take too seriously the notion that this has been a huge advantage, but I don't think it's a disadvantage either," he declared. Ferraro refused to back down and shot back at Obama. "Every time that campaign is upset about something," she fumed, "they call it racist. I will not be discriminated against because I'm white." It was now Clinton who found an ally too controversial, and Ferraro resigned from her campaign.

As the primary season drew to a close in June, both candidates chalked up additional victories – Clinton in Texas, West Virginia, and Kentucky and Obama in North Carolina, Nevada, and Oregon. After tabulating these results, Obama had a narrow lead among pledged delegates, though Clinton had accumulated more popular votes. Obama attracted African Americans, young whites between the ages of 18 and 29, and big city dwellers. Clinton countered with the support of white women and working-class men, seniors, Latinos, Jews, and suburbanites. Most telling, in a pattern that would repeat itself in the general election, racial outlook provided the most serious fault line between Obama and Clinton backers. In 24 of 36 states with exit poll data, Obama lost the majority of the white vote in landslide proportions. "The impact of racial attitudes on individual voter decisions … was so strong," according to social scientists Michael Tessler and David O. Sears, that it appeared even greater "than the impact of racial attitudes on Jesse Jackson's more racially charged campaign" in 1988.

The hard-fought contest left neither candidate with the required 2,117 votes to win. The decision remained in the hands of "superdelegates." Eight hundred and twenty-four superdelegates, consisting of Democratic members of Congress, governors, state officials, and party functionaries, have a vote at the convention. Superdelegates comprised about 20 percent of convention delegates.[1] In the end, the majority of the superdelegates supported Obama and provided his margin of victory for the nomination. They did not want to appear to have stolen the nomination from the candidate who had won more delegates in the primaries and caucuses.

On August 28, 2008, Obama stood in front of a crowd of 84,000 people gathered at the Democratic National Convention in Denver, Colorado and accepted the nomination of his party. In his address, the first African American nominated for president by a major political party noted the significance of his accomplishment. He pointed out that 45 years ago, on that very date, 250,000 blacks and whites had journeyed to the nation's capital to march for freedom. Without mentioning him by name, he praised Martin Luther King, Jr. – "a young preacher from Georgia" – for refusing to fan the flames of anger and frustration and instead affirm that "in America, our destiny is inextricably linked, that together our dreams can be one." Amidst a growing economic crisis and two wars, Obama reinforced his optimism in "the promise of America, the idea that we are responsible for ourselves, but that we also rise or fall as one nation, the fundamental belief that I am my brother's keeper, I am my sister's keeper."

Obama vs. McCain

In the general election, Obama and his running mate, Senator Joseph Biden of Delaware, squared off against the Republican nominees, Senator John McCain of Arizona and Governor Sarah Palin of Alaska. The economic calamities of the Great Recession of the Bush years, including rising unemployment, mortgage foreclosures, bank collapses, and tumbling prices on stock exchanges, shaped the Democratic ticket's assault on President

---

[1] The system of superdelegates was instituted in 1984 to give party stalwarts a voice in the nomination. The convention had to resolve a thorny issue involving aborted primaries in Michigan and Florida. The Democratic National Committee penalized both states for holding primaries earlier than stipulated. Clinton won in both states, but Obama, following party rules, took himself off the ballot in Michigan and did not campaign in Florida. Accordingly, the delegate vote from these two states would not be tabulated. At the convention, with his nomination assured by the superdelegates, Obama agreed to allow the votes from these two states to count for Clinton.

Bush and the Republican Party, as did Obama's pledge to end the Iraq war. The outcome of the election largely hinged on these issues, but race continued to play a significant role.

At first, this did not seem the case. McCain, a distinguished veteran of the Vietnam war and considered something of a maverick within his party, threw the Reverend Wright issue out of bounds. The Republican presidential candidate took the high road. At a town meeting in Minnesota, when a woman told him that Obama was an "Arab," the Arizona senator was taken aback and informed her she was incorrect. After a man tested McCain's patience by saying he would be afraid to raise a child in America if Obama were elected, McCain responded forcefully that his rival was a "decent person and not a person you have to be scared of as president."

Nevertheless, racist sentiments continued to surface along the campaign trail. To the chagrin of McCain, some members of the crowds he addressed called Obama a "Nigger," cartoons lampooned Obama as an "ape," and bloggers circulated digital messages teasing that if the African American won he would cater festivals at the White House with fried chicken and watermelons. Perhaps these remarks represented the attitudes of a small number of racist outliers, but they reflected a more troubling concern when they came from Republican officials. Representative Lynn Westmoreland of Georgia called Senator Obama "uppity," a word long used to disparage blacks and keep them subordinate. Even more disturbing was the rhetoric of vice-presidential candidate Sarah Palin, the second woman nominated for this high office by a major political party. Palin was known for her brashness and limited fund of information about domestic and world affairs. She used fears of Muslims as terrorists to attack Obama in surrogate racial terms. A candidate who many Republicans incorrectly claimed was a Muslim and not a Christian and whose surname sounded like the first name of America's number one enemy, Osama bin Laden, provided a target for Palin's shrill charges that Obama did not see "America as you see America, and as I see America." Recalling the McCarthyite era of the 1950s and its obsession with those considered "un-American," Palin insisted that Obama was "palling around with terrorists who would target their own country."[2]

---

[2] She was referring to William Ayers, a member of the Weather Underground in the 1960s who engaged in violence against American institutions. Ayers had become a university professor in Chicago and served on a civic committee with Obama. In fairness to Palin, Hillary Clinton had raised the issue of the Obama–Ayers relationship in the primaries.

Palin did not use crude racial language but she did not have to. Her remarks reinforced the image of Obama as "the Other," someone black with a foreign name. As an Associated Press reporter wrote, Palin avoided overt racism, "but there is a subtext for creating a false image of a black president" as "not like us." In the later stages of the election when McCain was trailing, he joined Palin in linking Obama to so-called terrorists. This desperation upset General Colin Powell, George W. Bush's former secretary of state and an old friend and ally of McCain. Once mentioned as a Republican presidential contender, Powell came out in support of Obama.

When this heated campaign ended, the country had elected Barack Obama president. He won a convincing victory over McCain by a margin of 53 percent to 46 percent, the first Democrat since Jimmy Carter to win a majority of the popular vote and the largest margin for a Democrat since Lyndon Johnson won the White House in 1964. Capturing 28 states and the District of Columbia, the Illinois senator trounced his opponent in the electoral college 365 to 173. He came out ahead in the key battleground states of Ohio and Florida and moved Virginia and North Carolina out of the Republican column for the first time since 1964 and 1976 respectively.

Obama triumphed by expanding his winning coalition in the Democratic primaries. With an African American at the top of the ticket, black voters gave him around 95 percent of their ballots. Not only did African Americans throw their overwhelming support behind Obama, they turned out in record numbers at the polls: some 2 million more than in 2004, a jump from 60 percent of registered voters to 66 percent, equaling white turnout for the first time. Black women voters made up the bulk of this increase. The black electorate now comprised 13 percent of the total, up two percentage points from four years earlier. In addition, he won a majority of voters under age 30, exceeding the total for the Democratic candidate, John Kerry, in the previous presidential contest by 12 percent. Along with these groups, Obama picked up support from most Democrats who voted for Hillary Clinton in the primaries. Women, comprising 53 percent of general election voters, backed Obama with 56 percent; the candidate did amazingly well among unmarried women, who gave him 70 percent of their ballots. In contrast, white women in general cast only 41 percent of their ballots for Obama. Thus the main strength of his female support derived from black women and other women of color. In addition, the winner garnered 67 percent of the Latino vote (9 percent of the total electorate), a gain of 9 percent for his party since 2004, and 62 percent of Asian Americans.

Not surprising, the President-elect showed uneven support among whites. He did manage to obtain 43 percent of the white vote, which was 2 percent more than Kerry had. Although a majority of white men voted for McCain, they gave Obama 47 percent of their votes, a higher percentage than did white women. Those calling themselves "independents" backed the Democrat by a margin of 8 points. But Obama won only a meager 34 percent of white Protestants and an even lower 24 percent of white evangelicals. Still, Catholics provided him with 54 percent of their vote and Jews an overwhelming 86 percent.

Yet the tell-tale sign that race still mattered came in the South, the region with the most tortured racial history. Obama won every section of the country except the states of the Old Confederacy, where McCain trounced him. In Alabama and Mississippi, Obama received 10 percent and 11 percent of white votes respectively. One white Alabama women explained her dismay over Obama's victory: "From where I'm from, this is going to give [blacks] the right to be more aggressive." He did slightly better in Louisiana (14 percent), Georgia (23 percent), and South Carolina (26 percent). Even in winning North Carolina, Virginia, and Florida, Obama lost the white vote. Underscoring the continued presence of racial polarization in the electorate, African Americans throughout the South cast their ballots for Obama by percentages ranging from 92 to 99.

Many ingredients figured into the election of President Obama. The worsening economic distress accompanying the Great Recession played a huge role, as did the weariness of Americans with the Iraq war. The McCain-Palin ticket proved a weak one because the former did not excite the conservative base and the latter turned off independent voters with her strident comments and obvious lack of preparedness for the second highest office in the land. Indeed, the number of Republican voters dropped by 1.3 percent between 2004 and 2008 while the Democratic vote increased by 2.6 percent. Equally as important, the changing demography of the country aided Obama. In 1976, whites had constituted 89 percent of the presidential electorate compared to 74 percent in 2008. And, across racial and ethnic lines, first-time, mainly young voters cast their ballots for Obama over McCain by a lopsided margin of 71 to 27 percent. Obama inspired these young voters by generating hope of a brighter future. His campaign also made ample use of new digital technologies to get his message across to young people, who communicated increasingly through cell phones and social media sites on the internet. Organizing at the grass roots and through cyberspace, the Obama team found untapped sources of campaign revenue from small as well as large donors and succeeded in outspending the Republicans.

Most of all, Barack Obama won because he overcame the burden of the nation's racial history. With African Americans solidly behind him, he appealed to a sufficient number of white voters, mainly liberals, moderates, and independents, as a person both black and not-so-black. The child of a white woman with roots in the Kansas heartland and an educated Kenyan who sought educational opportunities in the United States, Obama presented his story of success in a way that whites accepted within the traditional narrative of American exceptionalism. Indeed, Abner Mikva, a former Democratic congressman and judge, could see in Obama the hallmarks of his immigrant parents. In an expression his mother used, he described this African-American Christian as a *yiddishe neshuma*, "a Jewish soul … a sensitive, sympathetic personality … who knows where you are coming from." This explains his appeal in part to newer immigrants, especially Latinos. New Mexico Governor Bill Richardson, of Mexican ancestry, elaborated on Obama's attraction to Hispanics in speaking "to them not as an ethnic group but as American voters pursuing the American dream." Moreover, although Obama accepted the legacy of the civil rights movement as essential to his victory, he did what he could to assure whites that he would represent the entire country as a president who just happened to be black. "His success," the legal scholar Randall Kennedy concluded, "was predicated on neutralizing racial resistance while keeping to a minimum complaints that he was playing the race card."[3]

Whatever this triumph meant to whites, African Americans considered it even more of a joyous and monumental occasion, a secular blessing bestowed on them after centuries of suffering. Gathering by the tens of thousands in Grant Park in Chicago, they stood side-by-side with their white allies to hear the President-elect speak on the night of his victory. Bringing tears to their eyes, Obama exclaimed:

> This is our moment. This is our time – to put our people back to work and open doors of opportunity for our kids; to restore prosperity and promote

[3] The daughter of the President who had first signed the Voting Rights Act into law, Luci Baines Johnson wrote that she had been too young to vote for her father in 1964, but she was delighted to cast her ballot for Barack Obama, who supported the same causes of "social justice and equal opportunity to quality education, decent health care, and a cleaner environment for all Americans" as her "Daddy." Recalling the words of Dr. King, she praised Obama for succeeding "because of the content of his character, not the color of his skin."

the cause of peace; to reclaim the American Dream and reaffirm that fundamental truth – that out of many, we are one; that while we breathe, we hope, and where we are met with cynicism, and doubt, and those who tell us that we can't, we will respond with that timeless creed that sums up the spirit of a people – Yes, we can.

African Americans also celebrated around the country. An Atlanta woman whose grandmother was born a slave proclaimed, "For me to see this happen means there is hope for America." Bernard Lafayette, who had risked his life in civil rights battles as a staff member of SNCC and SCLC, compared Obama to Dr. King for "reaching out to one's enemies and seeking reconciliation." In similar fashion, the award-winning author Alice Walker placed Obama not only next to King but also to Nelson Mandela, the South African freedom fighter, and called his election "a profound moment."

Amidst this exuberance, other voices urged caution. The election of the first black president did not guarantee sweeping changes. Robert Newby, an African-American sociologist, pointed out that "electoral politics and revolutionary, or movement politics, are a different breed of cat." Stating the obvious, Newby noted that had Obama been a revolutionary, he would not have won. Still, he found encouragement that the new president would "struggle for decency." Robert C. Smith, a black political scientist, went even further. He warned that Barack Obama reflected the limitations of electoral politics in the post–civil rights era. He contended that, since the late 1960s, black political leaders had become incorporated into the mainstream, which had rendered them largely ineffective in addressing the problems of urban decay and entrenched black poverty. According to this critique, black candidates like Obama spend too much time pursuing racial and political integration, which has benefited middle-class blacks but left poorer blacks marginalized. Nevertheless, these cautionary words did not deter the excitement occasioned by the election of the nation's first African-American president.

Black Man in the White House

Upon entering the White House on January 20, 2009, Obama once again took up the theme of national unity and American exceptionalism. At his inauguration he paid homage to the black freedom struggle by including civil rights veterans Congressman John Lewis and Reverend Joseph Lowery on the dais in front of the capitol dome where the President was sworn in. In his inaugural address, Obama underscored that "a man whose father less than sixty years ago might not have been served at a local restaurant can now stand before you to take a most sacred oath." With this nod to black pride, he spent most of his time pledging to deal with the economic, political, and social problems that faced all Americans, while promising to pursue peace through strength in fighting terrorism from abroad. "The question we ask today is not whether our government is too big or too small," President Obama declared, "but whether it works, whether it helps families find jobs at a decent wage, care they can afford, a retirement that is dignified. Where the answer is yes, we intend to move forward. Where the answer is no, programs will end." And looking overseas, he warned "those who seek to advance their aims by inducing terror and slaughtering innocents, we say to you now that, 'Our spirit is stronger and cannot be broken. You cannot outlast us, and we will defeat you.'" This was standard fare for any American president, including one who happened to be black.

Obama's initial Cabinet-level appointments reflected his principle of running a government that looked like all Americans. They included six women, most notably Secretary of State Hillary Clinton, four African Americans, two Latinos, two Asian Americans, and two Republicans.[4] In his first two years, 25 percent of his nominations for seats on the lower federal courts went to African Americans, a higher figure than for any previous chief executive. His two appointments to the US Supreme Court went to a white woman, Elena Kagan, and a Latina woman, Sonia Sotomayor.

Many commentators insisted that Obama's presidency marked the beginning of a "post-racial" society. In fact, this assessment came mainly from conservatives who used it as a political argument to end the remnants of affirmative action and other policies they referred to as "racial entitlements." Those who did not vote for him now reshaped the meaning of his election. According to Juan Williams of the Fox News Channel, with Obama's election the "idea of black politics now tilts away from leadership based on voicing grievance, and identity politics based on victimization and anger. In its place is an era in which it is assumed that talented, tough people of any background will find a way to their rightful seat of power in mainstream political life." Even more to the point, Dinesh D'Souza, a

---

[4] This total takes into account appointments that have Cabinet rank but are not considered heads of Cabinet agencies: Ambassador to the United Nations, Administrator of the Environmental Protection Agency, and United States Trade Representative.

staunch opponent of Obama, applauded his victory for affirming "we are now living in a post-racist America."

Yet race hardly disappeared as an issue. During Black History Month in February 2009, Obama's attorney general Eric Holder, an African American, spoke publicly to commemorate the occasion. More bluntly than his boss would have articulated it, Holder argued that as long as Americans refused to admit that racism lay at the heart of the country's "soul," they would remain "a nation of cowards." He may have used strong phrasing, but his recommendation was hardly unreasonable – he called on Americans of all races to engage in dialogue. Nevertheless, Holder's remarks raised the political hackles of conservatives, and the President had to backtrack, if only slightly. "I think it's fair to say that if I had been advising my attorney general, we would have used different language," Obama explained. But he went on to elaborate, "I think the point that he was making is that we're oftentimes uncomfortable with talking about race until there's some sort of racial flare-up or conflict, and that we could probably be more constructive in facing up to the painful legacy of slavery and Jim Crow and discrimination."

A few months later, the President returned to some of the themes raised by Holder. In a speech to the NAACP annual convention in Atlanta, Obama reaffirmed that the US had made great racial progress since the 1950s and he saluted the legions of civil rights activists for making the country "a more perfect union." He did not stop there, however. Denying that his election had signaled a post-racial society, he enumerated the remaining forms of racial discrimination that African Americans faced. The most important of these did not involve blatant acts of personal bias, but stemmed from built-in, structural inequities that disadvantaged minorities with respect to education, healthcare, housing, and criminal justice. Still, he reaffirmed his universalistic legislative strategy to provide relief for all Americans, which in turn would help blacks who were hardest hit by unemployment and lack of access to healthcare. At the same time, Obama warned his largely black audience that government could not solve all their problems; that African-American leaders had to rally men and women in their communities to heal themselves. "We've got to say to our children, yes, if you're African American, the odds of growing up amid crime and gangs are higher. Yes, if you live in a poor neighborhood, you will face challenges that somebody in a wealthy suburb does not have to face," the chief executive asserted, "But ... that's not a reason to give up on your education and drop out of school. No one has written your destiny for you. Your destiny is in your hands – you cannot forget that. That's what we have to teach all of our children. No excuses." His speech received great applause, because rather than talking down to African Americans, as some black critics had accused him of doing, the President understood from history that change would come through self-help as well as government intervention. It remained a matter of getting the balance right.

While trying to focus his attention on reviving the economy and providing universal health insurance, the President had to deal with another racial brouhaha that forced him once again to demonstrate that his loyalties were not confined to African Americans. On July 16, 2009, Henry Louis Gates, a distinguished professor of African-American Studies at Harvard and a well-known public intellectual, returned from an overseas research trip to his home in Cambridge, Massachusetts. As he and his driver tried to unlock his front door, which had jammed, a neighbor who suspected that a burglary was in progress called the police. Gates managed to enter his home shortly before police arrived and questioned him about his presence in the house. Thinking himself the victim of racial profiling, Gates got into an argument with the white police officer and was arrested for disorderly conduct. This minor, local incident evolved into a national story. Although police soon dropped the charges, a reporter asked President Obama at a press conference about the episode. Admitting he did not have all the facts, the President, who knew Gates personally, stated "that the Cambridge police acted stupidly in arresting somebody when there was already proof that they were in their own home." More importantly, he pointed out that this incident was only one in a long history in the country of African Americans and Latinos being stopped by law enforcement disproportionately. "That's just a fact." After these remarks proved controversial – a Pew poll reported 41 percent disapproval and 29 percent approval – the President invited Gates and the arresting officer to the White House for a friendly chat over beers. However, rather than turning this summit into a "teachable moment" on the criminal justice system and race, Obama, who was busy trying to get his health insurance bill passed, let the matter drop.

A more disconcerting sign that race continued to matter came as Obama's political opponents increasingly flaunted their disrespect for him as president. On September 9, 2009, Obama was in the midst of addressing a joint session of Congress on his healthcare proposal when South Carolina Republican Congressman Joseph Wilson twice shouted, "You lie." Wilson, who had led the effort to keep the Confederate flag flying atop the South Carolina capitol, did apologize. However, the broad meaning of this incident remained evident. As Maureen Dowd, the *New York Times* columnist, wrote, people like Wilson "can't believe a black man is president and will never accept it." President Jimmy Carter, a native southerner who understood politicians such as Wilson, agreed that the animosity toward Barack Obama "is based on the fact that he is a black man, that he's African American." Characteristically, Obama chose to accept the congressman's apology and move on. However, this incident signaled even greater racial animus to come.

The greatest hostility came from the Republican Party and its media cheerleaders. Much of it could be attributed to normal political posturing, especially in an era of hyper-partisanship dating back to the administrations of Bill Clinton and George W. Bush. It was not enough for Republicans to disparage Obama's philosophy as "socialist," however mistaken the label. Many of their attacks reflected a deeper racial antagonism toward him. Conservative radio talk-show host Rush Limbaugh mocked Obama as a "halfrican American" who "is more African in his roots than he is American." Dinesh D'Souza, who apparently had abandoned his view of Obama as a post-racial president, claimed in his book *The Roots of Obama's Rage* (2010) that the black chief executive's supposed "hostility" to the US came from the "anticolonial impulses" of his Kenyan father. The journalist Jonathan Alter diagnosed the purveyors of such nonsense, which included many others, as suffering from "Obama Derangement Syndrome."

This political disease infected the members of the so-called "birther movement." Despite overwhelming factual evidence to the contrary, birthers charged that Obama was not born in Hawaii but in Kenya. Because only native-born Americans could become president according to the Constitution, they demanded that Obama release his birth certificate as proof that he held his office legitimately. Yet proof did not make any difference even when presented. Birther antipathy had no grounding in reality, but stemmed instead from Obama being black and having a father who came from a Muslim country (though Barack Obama, Sr., was more of an atheist than a Muslim). Polls taken in 2010 revealed that 40 percent of Republicans could not identify the President's place of birth and more than 50 percent believed that Obama sympathized with those who wanted to impose Islamic law around the world, including in the US. Some well-known people stoked these birther fires. Donald Trump, the real estate developer, television self-promoter, and on again-off again Republican candidate for president, not only questioned Obama's citizenship, but also offered the President $5 million for his favorite charity if he produced his college and passport applications, implying that they would reveal his true place of birth. More a publicity stunt, the President did not dignify it with a response.[5]

The racial divide also showed up in the stark contrast between whites and blacks over Obama's job performance. In a November 2010 Gallup poll, 37 percent of whites approved of Obama's handling of the presidency compared to 90 percent of African Americans who rated him favorably. True, partisanship helped shape these very different assessments, but the gap was far too large to discount the influence of race. Racial antipathy spilled over into policy decisions. Although the President acknowledged that African Americans would benefit greatly from his plan to extend health care to the 40 million Americans who did not have insurance, he insisted on "Meet the Press" in 2009 that the reforms were "not about race." His statement did not matter. Fox News Channel host Glenn Beck denounced Obama's affordable healthcare legislation as a form of "reparations," and Republican Congressman Steve King from Iowa claimed that the President "favors the black person." These charges reflected widespread sentiment among Republicans. The political scientist Michael Tessler found that "racial attitudes had a significantly greater impact on health care opinions when framed as part of President Obama's plan than they had" during the earlier debate over President Clinton's failed healthcare proposals in the 1990s. In other words, whatever position the President took would generate opposition "according to racial predispositions."[6]

In the face of both partisan and racial opposition, President Obama accomplished a great deal in his first two years in office. Democrats had majorities in the Senate and the House, but they did not give Obama free rein to impose his will. In the House some 52 Democrats belonged to a moderate to conservative faction, many elected from swing districts, who shared Republican views on taxes and spending. A similar but smaller group appeared in the Senate, and because of the upper chamber's unique filibuster rule, it would be difficult to obtain the 60 votes necessary to pass

---

[5]   During the 2012 presidential election, the Republican candidate, Mitt Romney, managed a roundabout reference to the birther claim. On a trip to Michigan where he and his wife were born, Romney told crowds that he loved "being at home," and then hurled a scarcely veiled jibe at Obama, "No one's ever asked me for my birth certificate."

[6]   President Obama thought that by framing legislation in universal terms he could keep race out of the discussion. "We have to deal with the specific problems of different groups – blacks, women, gays, lesbians, immigrants," he confided to Al Sharpton, "in a way that doesn't allow people to put these wedges [divisions] in."

legislation.[7] For their part, Republican legislators proved much more ideologically united than the Democrats and sought to keep Obama from scoring any political victories. Yet they could not thwart the President, who had numbers and an electoral mandate on his side.

As a result, in Obama's first two years in office his administration guided important legislation through Congress in a manner not seen since the days of President Lyndon Johnson. The American Recovery and Reinvestment Act (ARRA), popularly known as the "stimulus," injected nearly $800 billion into the economy, creating some 3 million jobs on projects that would improve roads, highways, and transportation; fund states and municipalities to enable them to keep teachers, police, and other essential employees on the payroll; computerize and store health records for greater efficiency; and reconfigure federal buildings to make them more energy efficient. Also, the President poured over $4 billion in stimulus money into a newly created Race to the Top program, which awarded funds to states that met high performance-based educational standards. Another major part of the stimulus, approximately one-third of its total, went for tax cuts for the working and middle classes. Liberals within the President's own party would have liked the Obama administration to wage a fiercer battle to gain much larger funding, but without the support of Republicans (only three GOP senators voted for the stimulus) the President probably got as much as possible. At any rate, the ARRA helped bring the Great Recession to a halt, in contrast to Great Britain where the Conservative government instituted austerity rather than stimulus measures, only to worsen the economic situation.

Obama's legislative scorecard also contained a number of other victories. The President implemented the Troubled Asset Relief Program begun in the Bush administration to bail out banks and other financial institutions from collapse, but he also signed the Dodd-Frank Act, which established the most extensive regulation of Wall Street since the New Deal. The Fair Pay Act reversed a Supreme Court decision that made it more difficult for women to sue their employers for pay discrimination. The Children's Health Insurance Reauthorization Act, twice vetoed by President George W. Bush, extended health insurance coverage for children. A Hate Crimes Prevention Act expanded existing law to include crimes against lesbians,

---

[7]   From July 2008 to January 2010, Democrats did have a majority of 60 in the Senate but then lost it after the death of Edward Kennedy of Massachusetts and his replacement by a Republican in a special state election.

gays, and transsexuals. The Fair Sentencing Act closed the gap between penalties for possession of crack cocaine, associated with black use, and powdered cocaine, identified with whites, reversing the harsher punishment for crack. The Omnibus Public Lands Management Act overturned Bush administration policy and protected millions of acres of western lands from private development. Obama also won legislation to extend unemployment benefits to workers still having trouble finding jobs, and he gained legislative approval to rescue the automobile industry from bankruptcy, thereby keeping tens of thousands of industrial workers on the job. Many homeowners had been hard hit in the housing bubble that produced high-interest mortgages. Under Obama about a million homeowners received assistance; however, this helped only about one-tenth of those in need and fell far short of the financial bailouts to the banks and auto industry. The President did sign a law making student loans more affordable, and expanded Pell Grants for students who otherwise did not have enough money to attend college.

Of all his legislation, Obama's signature accomplishment and the one that has proven most controversial is the Affordable Care Act (ACA), commonly known as Obamacare. Liberals had supported some kind of national health insurance plan since the 1940s, when President Harry S. Truman proposed one to Congress. Condemned by the American Medical Association as "socialized medicine," Truman's recommendation died in the legislature. President Johnson had succeeded in enacting Medicare and Medicaid to provide government medical insurance for the elderly and the poor. President Clinton, with the assistance of his wife, had made the expansion of health insurance a top priority, but suffered a stinging defeat. President Obama ran on a platform that revived the idea of expanding health insurance, but he was forced to compromise to win bipartisan support in Congress. His administration backed a measure similar to the one devised in the 1990s by the Heritage Foundation, a conservative think tank, and signed into law by GOP Governor Mitt Romney in Massachusetts. Obamacare added two important provisions, however: parents could carry their children under their policies until they reached the age of 26; and insurance companies were prevented from denying coverage to people with preexisting conditions.

Despite the conservative nature of the ACA, Republicans attacked it. They blasted it as "socialistic," even though health insurance remained in the hands of private companies. Sarah Palin charged falsely that under the law government "death panels" would be set up to determine whether elderly patients or children with conditions such as Down syndrome "were worthy of medical care." No Republican in Congress voted for the Act, even with conservative fingerprints all over its conception. Because President Obama supported it, the GOP sought to deny him any political victory that would help his reelection. At a secret meeting of Republican lawmakers on the evening of Obama's inauguration, Representative Paul Ryan of Wisconsin had voiced this strategy of opposing the President steadfastly: The "[o]nly way we'll succeed is if we're united." Nevertheless, the President had the votes to enact what *New York Times* columnist David Leonhardt called "the most sweeping piece of federal legislation since Medicare passed in 1965."

While racking up these legislative victories, the President effectively wielded his power as commander-in-chief. He succeeded in winding down American engagement in the Iraq war, while expanding military operations in Afghanistan. Obama also rescinded approval for the use of "waterboarding" in interrogating suspected terrorists, a practice used during the Bush administration which he considered a form of torture and contrary to international law. In 2011, the President launched the secret operation in Pakistan that resulted in the killing of America's number one terrorist enemy, Osama bin Laden. At the same time he retained and expanded the use of unmanned, armed drones to hit enemy targets abroad, which did not always prove precise and led to the tragic deaths of innocent civilians. Moreover, the President failed to close the Guantanamo Bay detention center in Cuba, which he had promised to do during the campaign. The facility housed nearly 800 prisoners captured during the wars in Iraq and Afghanistan who were considered dangerous terrorists and held as enemy combatants. Many were held for years without trial and were subject to brutal treatment. While some Obama supporters criticized the drone program and the continued existence of the Guantanamo Bay prison, they all applauded the commander-in-chief's repeal of the "Don't Ask, Don't Tell" policy initiated under the Clinton administration, which prohibited discrimination against gays as long as they remained closeted. The approach had proved unworkable and Obama discarded it in favor of integrating gays and lesbians openly into the military services.[8]

The President's race-neutral approach toward legislation evoked some criticism from within his own party. Members of the Congressional Black

---

[8]   The President also instructed the Justice Department to stop defending another Clinton-era law, the Defense of Marriage Act, which barred gay spouses of same-sex marriages in states that legally recognized them from receiving federal benefits.

Caucus, a group Obama had once belonged to as a senator, complained that the administration's efforts failed to target for relief groups such as African Americans, which suffered the most from economic hardship. Black lawmakers, as well as their white liberal allies, questioned whether Obama's legislation, however well intentioned, would sufficiently ease the plight of those mired in poverty. They had a point. In December 2009, black unemployment stood at about 16 percent, twice that of white Americans. Over the three-year period from 2007 to 2010, black family wealth fell by 31 percent, nearly three times the decline for whites (11 percent). Because African Americans had obtained the more risky subprime mortgages to buy their homes – the major source of wealth for most Americans – during the housing bubble, they suffered disproportionately from the collapse. In 2011, over 27 percent of African Americans lived in poverty, up from 25 percent in 2009, and nearly triple that of whites (9.9 percent).

Aware of these inequities, Obama nevertheless held firm to his strategy of universalism. "My general approach," he declared in 2009, "is that if the economy is strong that will lift all boats." Denying that he could single out African Americans and other minorities for special treatment, he reasoned, "I can't pass laws saying I'm just helping black folks. I'm president of the entire United States." He was right to the extent that such legislation would have had little or no chance of passing in a Congress filled with Republican roadblocks and centrist Democrats who refused to back the President. Furthermore, with every move he made examined under a racial microscope by his opponents in Congress and the media, Obama had to maneuver cautiously.

His African-American detractors remained unconvinced. Cornell West, a philosopher and cultural critic at Princeton University, scorned Obama as a "puppet of corporate capitalism." Another university professor and public intellectual, Michael Eric Dyson, charged that the "president runs from race like a black man runs from a cop." Bob Herbert, the *New York Times* columnist, agreed when he wrote, "President Obama would rather walk through hell than spend his time dealing with America's racial problems." Even more emphatic, the political scientist Robert C. Smith insisted, "At the end of his presidency, if one asks what difference the first black president made for the material well-being of African Americans, the answer will be none."

Many African Americans shared these concerns about the President's refusal to address issues of poverty and race, but most blacks did not waver in their support. Whatever complaints they may have had with Obama's performance most blacks chose to keep to themselves, thereby hoping to protect him from Republican, right-wing attacks. "Nobody," Congressman Emanuel Cleaver of Missouri explained, "wants to do anything that would empower the people who hate the president."

African Americans remained loyal even after the Obama administration committed a clear racial injustice. Shirley Sherrod worked for the US Department of Agriculture as its first black director of Rural Development in Georgia. Her father had been murdered by white men in the 1960s, a crime that went unprosecuted. She and her husband, Charles, were dedicated veterans of the civil rights movement in southwest Georgia and subsequently turned their attention to building farm cooperatives to improve the economic lives of rural blacks. In March 2010, Shirley Sherrod appeared before a gathering of the NAACP in Georgia and in an emotional speech explained how the movement had transformed her. Before beginning her current government job, back in the 1980s she started out committed only to blacks, so when a white farmer sought her help to stave off foreclosure, she directed him to a white lawyer. The attorney proved unhelpful and when the farmer returned again seeking her help, she realized that her obligation was to the poor, white as well as black, and assisted him in rescuing his farm. The point of her story was that she had come to realize that the struggle was between the haves and the have-nots, regardless of race.

What began as an inspirational talk about biracial cooperation turned into a lesson in manipulating bigotry. The talk had been videotaped, and Andrew Breitbart, a notorious right-wing blogger, edited it to make Sherrod sound as if she promoted racial bias rather than opposed it, converting her speech into an example of reverse racism. In his haste to defuse this racial controversy, the secretary of agriculture fired Sherrod before she could defend herself. After the truth came out exposing Breitbart's deception, Obama finally got involved, phoned Sherrod to apologize, and offered her a new job, which she refused. Instead of standing up to purveyors of racist mischief, the Obama administration initially backed off to avoid triggering a white political backlash.

Obama tried to do better on another matter of importance to African Americans. In his first year in office the President and his family delighted African Americans by visiting Ghana, the leading democratic nation in sub-Saharan Africa. There he took in sites memorializing the African slave trade that sent millions of blacks to the Americas, including the United States. Four years later he made a similar trip with stops in Senegal, Tanzania, and South Africa. Ironically, during his two trips Obama avoided traveling to Kenya, the home of his father, because the country's president had been indicted for war crimes by the International Criminal Court. Nevertheless, for the Obamas and African Americans these travels fueled great pride and reinforced their connection to their African ancestry. The Obama administration also provided billions of dollars in aid to Africa and extended the considerable efforts of President Bush to fight malaria and HIV-AIDs.

These efforts, however laudable, fell short. The Obama administration had very little success in achieving its broader, more tangible goals of promoting democratic governments, protecting women's rights, and reducing hunger in Africa. It was more concerned with defense issues on the continent. To this end, the US provided military and economic assistance to overthrow the Libyan dictator Muammar Gaddafi, established drone bases in Niger, and struck at terrorists in Somalia. Still, Obama remained as tremendously popular in Africa as he did among African Americans in the US.

The Shellacking of 2010

Having retained support among African Americans, the biggest political test for Obama and the Democrats came in the 2010 midterm elections. The results proved disastrous for the President. The party in control of the White House usually suffers some losses in such contests, but the Republicans gave the Democrats what Obama admitted was a "shellacking." The GOP gained a whopping 63 seats in the House for a total of 242, the party's highest number since 1946, and a majority of the lower chamber. The Senate stayed in the hands of Democrats, though they lost six seats. Democrat losses went even deeper. Before the 2010 elections, Democrats held the majority of state governorships and state legislatures. Following these contests, Republicans won 23 of 37 gubernatorial races, adding 11 new governors for a total of 30 out of 50 states, and capturing a majority of state legislative seats. This meant that in the wake of the 2010 Census, Republicans would have the opportunity to reapportion state and congressional districts in a greater number of states than would Democrats, guaranteeing more safe districts for members of their party. As a result, there would be fewer competitive seats up for election in the House of Representatives for years to come, thereby boding poorly for the president's legislative agenda.

In light of the Obama administration's numerous accomplishments over the first two years, what explains this monumental defeat at the polls? Jobs headed the list. Although the President's policies had rescued the financial system from collapse and ended the Great Recession, large numbers of Americans did not feel much improvement. A month before the midterm elections, unemployment stood at 10.2 percent, a rise of 2.5 percent since Obama's inauguration. This figure did not reflect those who had stopped looking for work, which would have placed the percentage even higher. As a consequence, Democrat support from the white working class dropped by 30 percent, a decline of 20 points from 2008. Also, turnout had a great deal to do with shaping the outcome. Not unexpectedly for an off-year election, some 50 million fewer people voted in 2010 than had in the presidential contest, but who stayed home was critical. The coalition that had brought Obama to office failed to show the same enthusiasm for Democrats in this election cycle. Only 12 percent of 2010 voters were under 30-years-old, a drop of 6 percent from two years earlier. The black and minority share of the electorate fell by 3 percent. African Americans remained overwhelmingly faithful to Obama and the Democratic Party, but with their unemployment rates double that of whites, many lost interest in going to the polls. Young and nonwhite voters still voted Democratic, but they did not turn out in sufficient numbers to counter Republican gains among whites and the elderly. The percentage of voters over the age of 65 shot up by five points and the percentage of white voters grew by one-third. Had this been the composition of the voting electorate in 2008, one commentator observed, John McCain would have won the presidency.

Obama deserves part of the blame for failing to rally his Democratic forces. Many Americans did not fully comprehend what he had accomplished. Fewer than 10 percent knew that the administration's stimulus package included a tax cut. Moreover, most of the provisions of the Affordable Care Act that mandated coverage for all Americans would not go into effect until 2014, four years after its passage. Given continued Republican attacks on the law, Obama should have spent more time using his talents as a communicator to explain how the Act would work and clear up misunderstandings. And once the Act passed, the President was too slow in focusing attention on a jobs program to deal with rising unemployment. Many voters believed that the administration had done more to bail out banks and automobile companies than to provide jobs and help keep them in their homes. Also, Obama and the Democrats would have had to prove the negative proposition that the economy would have been even worse without the stimulus and other measures, a difficult idea to demonstrate. The President accepted responsibility for the outcome of the elections, agreeing that he had not concentrated enough on "persuading people … making an argument that people can understand."

If Obama's accomplishments did not generate much enthusiasm among Democrats, they aroused tremendous anger from his political enemies. Before the 2010 elections a Gallup poll reported that 68 percent of Republican voters were highly motivated to turn out at the polls compared to 44 percent of Democrats. Much of the Republican zeal came from the Tea Party. This group had formed with a variety of grievances three months after Obama assumed office. Distrusting elected officials in general, they believed that the Republican Party had reneged on its principles of cutting the size of government, lowering taxes, and eliminating budget deficits and the national debt. They wanted to restore the Republican Party to its core doctrines, but their prime target was Obama, whom they considered the most severe threat to the nation. To them Obamacare was a form of undeserved welfare for the poor and those unwilling to work. Even the limited efforts of the Obama administration to provide assistance to people on the verge of losing their mortgages drew Tea Party ire for helping "losers" and "rewarding bad behavior." Its faithful also denounced the government bailout of banks, Wall Street financial institutions, and automobile companies as a form of corporate welfare coming at the expense of small businesses.

The fact that soaring deficit and debt increases as well as the bank rescue had begun under President Bush without triggering the creation of the Tea Party suggests a more personal motivation for its rise. A largely white group – only 8 percent of its members were nonwhite – many of its supporters cringed that a man named "Barack Hussein Obama," a black man with a Muslim father, occupied the White House. Some of this racial and cultural rage came out in their rallying cry – "Take Our Country Back." To one of its Texas supporters this meant taking it back from President Obama, the "cokehead-in-chief," who she scorned as being in the grip of "demonic possession."

The greatest source of strength for the Tea Party emerged in the South. Sixty-three percent of its membership was located in that region compared to 19 percent in the Midwest, 16 percent in the West, and 2 percent in the Northeast. The states with the highest number of Tea Party representatives came from Texas, Florida, Louisiana, and Georgia. Polls showed that around half of the South supported the Tea Party. In a sense, many of the southern Tea Party faithful represented a neo-Confederate revival that gained momentum in the wake of Obama's election. Governor Robert F. McDonnell of Virginia, who spoke at his state's Tea Party convention in 2010, declared April as Confederate History Month to commemorate "the sacrifices of the Confederate leaders, soldiers, and citizens during the period of the Civil War." Omitted from the decree was any mention of slavery, which Douglas Wilder, Virginia's first African-American governor, found "mind boggling."

In 2010, the Tea Party mobilized within the ranks of the GOP to combat the reputed presidential devil and his disciples. These right-wing Republicans started out as a loose network of hundreds of grassroots organizations with populist, conservative roots. Besides their enthusiasm, they depended on outside funding from influential and wealthy Republicans such as Charles and David Koch, whose charitable foundations supported free-market, antigovernment, and libertarian causes. The Fox News Channel provided unlimited coverage of the Tea Party and helped publicize its campaigns. In 2009, Glenn Beck, one of its most popular program personalities, told viewers that President Obama possessed "a deep-seated hatred for white people or the white culture." A year later, the Tea Party helped engineer the stunning Democratic defeat in the midterm state and congressional elections. According to exit polls, 41 percent of those who voted favored the Tea Party. Forty-four Tea Party Republicans won congressional seats, five in the Senate and 39 in the House, including two African Americans (Allen West of Florida and Tim Scott of South Carolina), though another 85 Tea Party candidates lost.

In the wake of the electoral upheaval, the President seized the opportunity to make more legislative advances while Democrats still had majorities in both houses of Congress. His first priority was to broker a deal to stimulate the economy and job growth while easing the pain of those still without jobs. He succeeded in getting the lame duck Congress to extend unemployment benefits, expand the school lunch program, reduce payroll taxes for Social Security, and renew tax cuts begun in the Bush administration. Turning to foreign affairs, he obtained ratification by the Senate of a treaty with Russia reducing nuclear weapons.

Obama vs. Romney

As expected, President Obama did not achieve significant legislative victories once the Republican-controlled House returned in January 2011. Even in the Senate, where Democrats held a slim majority, Republicans blocked legislation through the filibuster, in effect requiring a supermajority of 60 to do business. Senate Minority Leader Mitch McConnell admitted the kind of cooperation Obama would receive from Republicans: "The single most important thing we want to achieve is for President Obama to be a one-term president." House Republicans took this message to heart and over the next two years voted to repeal Obamacare over 40 times, to no effect. House Republican Speaker John Boehner of Ohio, who had worked with Democrats in the past, largely kowtowed to the Republican Caucus dominated by out-spoken Tea Party members and their sympathizers. Wielding the threat of shutting down the government over raising the debt ceiling, Republicans forced the President to accept mandatory spending cuts amounting to about 3 percent. This so-called sequester deal put a break on economic growth as the country was recovering from the Great Recession, hurting education, infrastructure, scientific and medical research, and conservation initiatives.

During the long lead-up to the next presidential election, Republican candidates jockeyed in their primaries and caucuses to see who could condemn Obama most strongly. Chiefly they appealed to the party's base of rock-ribbed conservatives and Tea Party enthusiasts. Obamacare served as their main target. Even Mitt Romney, who as governor of Massachusetts had approved a similar program, attacked Obama's version as unsuitable for the nation. The sluggish economy, partly the result of the Republicans' forced cutbacks in government spending, provided GOP contenders with political ammunition against the President. Unemployment hovered around 8 percent during the first half of 2012, and family income was 8 percent lower than a decade earlier.

With the economy only slowly recovering, race did not weigh as a political issue as heavily as in 2008. By 2012, President Obama was now a much better known figure with three years of governance behind him. As the President acknowledged, "You can only elect the first black American president once." Still, Republican challengers took verbal jabs in questioning the President's loyalty to an ideal America. Fox News Channel commentators claimed that Obama was too quick to apologize for American actions overseas, and Romney picked up this theme. "We have a president right now," the governor asserted, "who thinks America's just another nation. [But] America is an exceptional nation." It apparently did not matter that Obama had never conducted what Romney termed an "apology tour" – though he did acknowl-edge past American mistakes in foreign affairs – and had articulated the concept of exceptionalism in his speeches many times. Newt Gingrich, former speaker of the House of Representatives and a contender for the

Republican nomination, revived controversial racial images. Calling Obama the "food stamp president," he advocated changing child labor laws so African-American youths could learn the value of work and get paid for custodial and other jobs in their schools. In a similar vein, another candidate, Rick Santorum, former senator from Pennsylvania, declared, "I don't want to make black people's lives better by giving them somebody else's money. I want to give them the opportunity to earn the money." The Republican field did include a black candidate, Herman Cain, the former head of Godfather's Pizza and a favorite of the Tea Party, and he too sprinkled his attacks against the President's leadership with well-worn charges that Obama was a socialist, Marxist, and un-American.

After a protracted and bruising Republican contest, Romney emerged as the presidential nominee and selected Congressman Paul Ryan from Wisconsin, a leader of the conservative wing of the party, as his running mate. The GOP convention that nominated them consisted of only 47 black delegates out of 2,286, a decline from 167 in 2004. (Of the 5,551 delegates to the Democratic convention 1,452 were black.) They built their campaign around the same themes Republicans voiced during the primaries, attacking Obamacare as the chief example of big government regulation and waste, emphasizing continued high unemployment and economic stagnation, and criticizing Obama's leadership at home and around the world.

Portraying himself as an experienced businessman and job creator, Romney suffered a severe setback when a video recording surfaced of a private speech he gave to wealthy donors in Florida. In it, he wrote off Obama supporters as the 47 percent of the population "who are dependent upon government, who believe that they are victims, who believe that government has a responsibility to care for them, who believe that they are entitled to health care, to food, to housing, to you name it. That that's an entitlement … These are people who pay no income tax." This proved a huge mistake (and a factual one as well, for many of the 47 percent were subject to payroll taxes for Social Security and Medicare) as the Republican candidate seemingly wrote off a large percentage of the American electorate. At the same time, it highlighted Democratic attacks on Romney as an out-of-touch multimillionaire, a member of the top 1 percent of Americans whose wealth, in contrast to most Americans, had grown in the past decade, and the recipient of benefits from provisions in the tax code that allowed him to pay a lower percentage in taxes than those in the middle class.

At the same time, Obama exercised his power as chief executive to reinforce his electoral base. Although Latinos had supported him in 2008, his administration had deported some 1.5 million undocumented immigrants, most of them Hispanic. With the election coming, in June 2012 the President granted temporary amnesty from deportation to thousands of young immigrants illegally settled in the US. In contrast, Romney responded that he would end these reprieves and urged the approximately 11.5 million undocumented residents to "self-deport." Also in 2012, the President made historic overtures to gays and lesbians. Initially, a proponent of civil unions instead of marriage for same-sex couples, in May 2012, Obama changed his mind and supported marriage equality for gay and lesbian couples. Lest he offend Americans whose religious beliefs drove their opposition to same-sex marriage, he invoked religion and morality to explain his conversion. "The thing at root that we think about is, not only Christ sacrificing himself on our behalf, but it's also the golden rule – you know, treat others the way you would want to be treated." In contrast, the Republican candidate affirmed that his opposition to gay marriage had not "evolved," and he continued to believe that marriage was a relationship between a man and a woman.

Foreign affairs gained some attention in the final weeks before the election. Obama's record in ending one war in Iraq and bringing another in Afghanistan to a close made him a difficult target for Republicans to attack. The killing of Osama bin Laden by Navy Seals made Republican efforts even more problematic. Their best chance arose in September when Islamic militants attacked the US consulate in Benghazi, Libya, killing the American ambassador and three others. Romney charged that the Obama administration misled the public about the incident and should have provided greater security for the diplomatic mission. This criticism did not stick because Obama demonstrated that he was in command of the situation, and most American voters were focused less on military actions abroad and more on economic issues at home.

Race played only a small part in the campaigning of the two candidates, but it figured greatly into Republican electoral calculations to cut down the number of Obama voters. In 2008, the Supreme Court in a case from Indiana had validated state legislation requiring government-issued photo identification for voting (see Chapter 9). As a result, Republicans in other states drew up and passed similar legislation as if they were combating an epidemic of voter fraud and had to use photo identification to inoculate the electorate. The real impetus behind such measures was to weaken Democratic Party fortunes at the polls. A good deal of research demonstrated that minorities and college-age students – those most likely to vote

Democratic – were least likely to have government-issued identification. The Brennan Center for Justice at New York University Law School reported that approximately 25 percent of African Americans did not possess a photo identification card. Although Nate Silver, a respected political statistician, estimated that identification laws reduced voter turnout by a mere 2 percent, this loss of likely Democratic voters could swing victory toward Republicans in close elections.

Republicans revealed their hand with further attempts to suppress voting in their favor. After the 2010 midterm election, Republican-dominated state legislatures adopted measures to reduce the number of days for early, in-person voting, which black voters had utilized to a considerable extent; to inhibit groups such as the League of Women Voters from conducting voter registration drives, which tended to enroll twice as many minorities as nonminorities; and to eliminate the possibility of registering and voting on election day, a procedure used frequently by college students. By 2012, 16 states, including the battleground states of Ohio, Florida, Virginia, Pennsylvania, Wisconsin, and Colorado, had adopted an assortment of these techniques.

This strategy of voter suppression backfired. The blatant partisan and racial intent behind such legislation aroused African Americans to mobilize registered voters, help those without the proper identification cards to obtain them, and challenge these disfranchisement laws in state courts before they did damage in the election. "Black people vote when they are proud or angry," Reverend Sharpton observed. "They were proud in 2008 and angry in 2012." If African Americans had grown somewhat complacent after Obama's landmark victory, Republican attacks on the President and attempts to limit the black vote for him four years later pushed them to the polls in record numbers. "We are accustomed to people trying to deny us things," an NAACP official remarked, "and … and sometimes you wake the sleeping giant." For the first time in the history of presidential elections, blacks turned out at a higher rate than did whites, 66.2 percent to 64.1 percent. An estimated 1.8 million more African Americans voted in 2012 than in 2008, compared with a decline of some 2 million whites.

Black voters were only one element accounting for President Obama's reelection triumph. The President won the popular vote 51 percent to 47 percent and carried the electoral college by 332 to 206, smaller than four years earlier but nonetheless substantial margins. His coalition of African Americans, Latinos, young people, women, and gays held together and helped give him 5 million more votes than Romney. The gender gap had widened in four years as women were now10 percent more likely than men to vote for Obama, three points higher than in 2008. Blacks supported Obama with 93 percent of their ballots; Latinos gave him 69 percent, and Asian Americans 74 percent. The latter two groups comprised the fastest growing segments of the American population, which boded well for the Democrats. In addition to race, gender, and ethnicity, class shaped the outcome. The President ran well ahead of Romney among voters with a family income of under $50,000, while the Republican scored heavily among those earning over that amount. Racial polarization still existed. Obama won only 40 percent of the white vote, 3 percent less than in 2008. However, this did not matter as much because the white share of the total electorate fell to 72 percent, a steep drop of 2 percent since the last election. Obama captured only 45 percent of independents, a turnabout from four years earlier when he won 52 percent of their vote. Yet like whites, independents experienced a falloff in turnout at the polls.

Whatever the breakdown of the statistics, Obama won an impressive victory. No president in the modern era had gained reelection with an unemployment rate near 8 percent (though it had declined slightly under that figure by election day). In the end, Obama won because Romney could not convince voters that he would provide better leadership for the country either at home or abroad. Exit polls revealed that 52 percent of respondents believed the nation was headed in the wrong direction, which should have aided Romney, but the majority thought that Obama "cares more for people like me" and speaks more clearly for the middle class. A majority of Americans decided that they still had a better chance to improve their lives with the incumbent than with the challenger who disparaged them as "takers" and had difficulty showing that he empathized with their plight. With this triumph, Obama displayed, as Jonathan Alter pointed out, that he could not be viewed as a "historical fluke." More so than in 2008, Obama finally gained recognition as a president who happened to be black and not just a black president – something he had sought all along.

President Obama's Second Term

Despite his decisive victory, the President still faced gloomy prospects for his legislative agenda. As a result of the elections, Republicans retained their majority in the House, whereas Democrats increased their lead in the Senate. Given the continued presence of hyper-partisanship, the prospects for the President making headway on his economic programs appeared very dim. Yet not having to run for reelection did provide Obama greater leeway than he had in his first term to speak out more on race and gender equality as the nation's educator-in-chief.

His second inaugural address gave him the opportunity to do so. In 2008, he had taken the oath of office by placing his hand on Abraham Lincoln's Bible; four years later he added Martin Luther King, Jr.'s Bible to the swearing in. In his address, he combined populist phrases from the Constitution – "We the people" – with egalitarian language from the Declaration of Independence – "all of us are created equal." With the African-American civil rights struggle and the women's liberation movement in mind, the President declared that the nation's journey toward equality would not be complete "until our gay brothers and sisters are treated like anyone else under the law – for if we are truly created equal, then surely the love we commit to one another must be equal as well." The President also reaffirmed the continuing need to protect the right to vote, "until no citizen is forced to wait for hours" to cast a ballot. Obama sketched out broadly his second-term progressive agenda to include legislation dealing with immigration reform, climate change, and poverty.

Still, House Republicans continued to thwart Obama's efforts. Following the mass shooting at an elementary school in Newtown, Connecticut in December 2012, which killed 20 children and six adults, the White House backed a new round of gun-safety measures. Although gaining a majority in the Senate, the bill did not garner the filibuster-proof 60 votes to pass. Despite public support for gun regulation, the powerful National Rifle Association lobby prevailed. Immigration reform attracted greater support in the Democratic-controlled Senate, including from a few outspoken Republicans, but eventually suffered the same fate as gun control. After the upper chamber passed a comprehensive immigration bill that offered undocumented residents a pathway to citizenship while increasing border security, House GOP leaders refused to bring it up for consideration. In addition, rather than concentrate on job creation or relieving poverty, which Obama increasingly promoted, Republicans worried more about rising deficits and the national debt. In a battle over the budget, House Republicans shut down the federal government for over two weeks until a compromise could be brokered. Republicans continued to hammer away at Obamacare as well. When the national website to enroll applicants for health insurance crashed in

October 2013, the President suffered a major political blow and saw his approval ratings plunge. The President's legislative program remained stalemated for the rest of the year, though lawmakers finally agreed to a budget deal designed to avoid another government shutdown.

Nevertheless, President Obama did have several high-profile chances to address the issue of race more forcefully than he had during his first term. One of these opportunities grew out of the killing of an unarmed black youth named Trayvon Martin by a white man in Sanford, Florida in 2012, before his reelection. In February of that year, the 17-year-old Martin, wearing a sweatshirt and hoodie over his head, was walking after dark to his father's residence, which he was visiting. Another homeowner, George Zimmerman, a white neighborhood watch leader of Hispanic descent, thinking that Martin looked suspicious called the police. Identifying Martin as black, he told the Sanford police dispatcher, "These assholes they always get away." Rather than waiting for police cars to arrive as instructed by the dispatcher, Zimmerman, who was armed with a handgun, followed Martin. A scuffle broke out during which Zimmerman claimed that his life was threatened and, in response, shot and killed the young man. Originally the Sanford police concluded that Zimmerman had not committed any crime because under Florida's "stand your ground" law he had the right to defend himself. However, after howls of protest from the NAACP and widespread criticism in the media, the Florida governor appointed a special state prosecutor who charged Zimmerman with second-degree murder.

At the time of the shooting the President commented only briefly on the case. Without expressing any opinion on Zimmerman's culpability, and pleading for a fair and comprehensive investigation, he offered his sympathies to Martin's parents and acknowledged, "You know if I had a son, he'd look like Trayvon."[9] The case raised serious questions of racial profiling and racial inequities in the criminal justice system. A study by one of Florida's leading newspapers, the *Tampa Bay Times*, reported that those claiming the "stand your ground" defense were more likely to "prevail if

---

[9] Yet even these empathetic remarks drew political flak. Running at that time for the Republican nomination for the presidency, Newt Gingrich questioned Obama's racial fairness. "Is the president suggesting that if it had been a white who had been shot," he asked, "that would be okay because it wouldn't look like him?" Contrary to Gingrich's allegations, the President recognized all too well that as a matter of record most black victims of homicide came at the hands of other blacks. This problem greatly concerned him and civic leaders in black communities who worked toward reducing gun violence.

Figure 29 Justice 4 Trayvon signs outside the Seminole County Courthouse during the George Zimmerman trial in Sanford, Florida, in 2013. (AP Photo/Phelan M. Ebenhack/Press Association)

the victim is black." Of the defendants charged in such cases in the Sunshine State, 73 percent of those who killed an African American received no penalty compared with 53 percent of those who killed a white person.[10]

The Obama administration seized the opportunity to address these issues more forcefully in 2013 after a jury acquitted Zimmerman. Following the verdict in mid-July, Attorney General Holder in a speech before the NAACP recounted his father instructing him as a boy on how to conduct himself if the police or other whites stopped him. He thought those conversations had become a thing of the past, but the Martin case proved him wrong. Like his father before him, he now had to sit down for "the conversation" with his own 15-year-old son. A few days later, the President followed up by expressing his distress. He held an impromptu presidential briefing with reporters to deliver a message that spoke more poignantly about race than at any time since the 2008 campaign. Without questioning the outcome of the verdict,

[10] In one such case, a black woman, Marissa Alexander of Jacksonville, was convicted and sentenced to 20 years in prison for firing a warning shot at her estranged husband, who she feared was about to harm her. Following the Zimmerman verdict and increasing attention to her case, she won a new trial.

Obama explained why African Americans looked at this issue differently than did whites. He counted himself among the overwhelming majority of African-American men who shared the experience "of being followed in a department store" or getting on an elevator and seeing "a woman clutching her purse nervously and holding her breath until she had a chance to get off." Added to this pain, blacks were well aware of the long history of "racial disparities in the application of criminal laws – everything from the death penalty to enforcement of our drug laws." The President did not propose any new federal programs to deal with these issues, but he did offer words of advice. Americans, the President remarked, needed to give African-American boys "the sense that their country cares about them and values them and is willing to invest in them." The President's comments to reporters, though justifiably gloomy, ended on a more characteristic note of optimism, "Along this long, difficult journey, "we're becoming a more perfect union – not a perfect union, but a more perfect union."

The gap between a perfect and not-so-perfect union soon grew wider. In *Shelby County, Alabama v. Holder* the Supreme Court heard a challenge to the constitutionality of key provisions of the Voting Rights Act. The formula covering jurisdictions for special federal oversight of voter registration and elections (Section 4) as well as submission of suffrage laws for federal preclearance (Section 5) dated back over three decades. Delivering a serious blow to the Voting Rights Act, the high court in a 5 to 4 vote ruled that its coverage formula, Section 4, was no longer valid, and affected jurisdictions no longer had to submit voting changes to Washington before going into effect. Remaining intact, however, was Section 2 of the Act, which protected the right to vote through litigation anywhere in the country. This offered small consolation because court remedies generally proved expensive and time-consuming.

A mainly white suburb of Birmingham, Shelby County had a considerable history of racial bias in voting. Between 1975 and 2008, the county's election laws had been found racially discriminatory 20 times. The most recent instance had occurred in 2008 and involved the redrawing of a local town's voting boundaries. The black population had risen by 3 percent, but under the redistricting proposal, the sole majority-black district was eliminated and black voters reshuffled to predominantly white districts. This type of racial gerrymandering usually resulted in a Justice Department objection, which occurred in this situation. The town held the election with its new districts anyway, and as a result, the lone black incumbent lost. The election was declared invalid, but two years later, lawyers for the county brought litigation challenging the two key special provisions of the Voting Rights Act.

The heart of the case involved whether racial minorities in 2012 still faced discriminatory obstacles to voting in states covered under the Act. Speaking for the majority of five on a bitterly divided court, Chief Justice John Roberts contended that the country had changed greatly with respect to race relations since 1965. It had elected an African-American president, and in the 2012 presidential election, black voter turnout in five of six states originally covered by Section 4 exceeded that of whites. He further noted that Selma, Alabama and Philadelphia, Mississippi, two cities that had played a significant role in civil rights history, had elected black mayors.[11] Roberts went on to advise that if Congress wanted to extend federal oversight over state and local elections, it should do so based on current data. Responding for the minority of four, Justice Ruth Bader Ginsberg declared that the court "errs egregiously" in overriding Congress's well-established decision-making power concerning voting rights. Acknowledging the political progress African Americans had made, Ginsberg pointed out the significant body of evidence of continued electoral bias in the covered states. Fighting racial disfranchisement, she observed, "resembled battling the Hydra. Whenever one form of voting discrimination was identified and prohibited, others sprang up in its place." The racist monster still existed, she argued, and Congress had ample power to try and slay it.

As Ginsberg charged, the majority reached its verdict in the face of a great deal of evidence to the contrary. In renewing the Voting Rights Act in 2006, Congress conducted 21 hearings over ten months, gathering 12,000 pages of testimony. Most of the voting rights challenges adjudicated in the federal courts as late as 2006 occurred in the jurisdictions covered by the Act's formula. It was true that suffrage infractions based on race took place in other locations (which were adjudicated under Section 2 of the law), but minorities had a greater chance of winning in the covered jurisdictions. And in the year before the Shelby decision, the Justice Department had objected to discriminatory election laws in Texas, Florida, and South Carolina among other covered states. Also of significance, six of nine targeted states (Alabama, Georgia, Mississippi, South Carolina, Texas, and Virginia) had passed photo identification provisions for voting compared

---

[11] Protests in Selma in 1965 led to passage of the Voting Rights Act, and outside of Philadelphia three civil rights workers were murdered during Freedom Summer in 1964.

with only one-third of states in the remainder of the country (most notably, Ohio, Pennsylvania, and Wisconsin).

In pronouncing a premature end to the ongoing struggle against racial disfranchisement, the chief justice's opinion appeared inspired by a long-standing political agenda. In the 1980s, Roberts had worked in Ronald Reagan's Justice Department and argued for weakened enforcement of the Voting Rights Act. In tune with the conservative ideology of the Republican administration, he advised against "intensive interference" into "state and local [election] processes," and warned against implementing the law in any way that established quotas for the election of black candidates. He had not changed his views after reaching the Supreme Court. The legal analyst Jeffrey Toobin wrote that Roberts's mission on the high bench was "to declare victory in the nation's fight against racial discrimination and then to disable the weapons with which the struggle was won." Joining him were his ideological companions on the court. Antonin Scalia viewed the Voting Rights Act as the "perpetuation of racial entitlement," and Clarence Thomas, the sole African-American justice, insisted that the entire Voting Rights Act was unconstitutional.[12]

In predictable fashion, within hours of the announcement of the court ruling, Texas reinstated its photo identification law, which a federal court had previously rejected for imposing "strict, unforgiving burdens" on minority voters. The Lone Star State measure excluded photo identification cards issued by colleges and employers, but allowed con-cealed handgun licenses to serve as proof. North Carolina adopted equally restrictive proof for voting and pared back days for early voting and eliminated same-day registration and voting. In the wake of this fresh round of disfranchisement, the editorial page of the <i>New York Times</i> called for "a new coalition as loud and as angry as the voices of 1965 – to demand that Republican lawmakers join Democrats in restoring fairness to the election system."

[12] In <i>Northwest Austin Municipal Utility District No. 1 v. Holder</i>, decided the first year Obama took office, the court had foreshadowed its opinion in <i>Shelby</i>. Although declining to rule on the constitutionality of the coverage formula and preclearance requirement, the jus-tices unanimously approved a district north of Austin, Texas for bailout from coverage under the Voting Rights Act's special provisions. Nevertheless, speaking for the court, Justice Roberts hinted that unless Congress revised Section 4 to take into account more current election data, the court might void it. "The statute's coverage formula is based on data that is now more than 35 years old," Chief Justice Roberts wrote, "and there is considerable evidence that it fails to account for current political conditions."

Congress's response aroused little hope. Although Republican House member John Sensenbrenner of Wisconsin supported new legislation and Majority Whip Eric Cantor of Virginia urged his colleagues to find a "responsible path forward that ensures that the sacred obligation of voting in this country remains protected," the lower chamber conducted a single day of hearings chaired by Trent Franks of Arizona, one of only 33 members opposed to renewing the Voting Rights Act in 2006. To find a solution, Congress would have to devise a new coverage formula based on current voting data that would apply uniformly throughout the country. Or, it could reinforce a little-used provision of the Act – Section 3 – that extended preclearance coverage to localities judged by the federal courts to have discriminated intentionally against minorities. Because racial intent is difficult to prove, to make this so-called "bail-in" provision more effective, Congress would have to allow courts to accept evidence of a contested voting measure's discriminatory effect, a standard much easier to prove. So far this has not happened.

With the chance of congressional action slim, the Obama administration pursued other options. The President gave a pep talk to a group of black leaders he summoned to the White House. "The Voting Rights Act is not dead," the President said, "it's not even critical, it's just wounded." Al Sharpton who attended this meeting found these words reassuring. Attorney General Holder voiced deep disappointment with the Supreme Court ruling and promised that Justice Department officials would "use every tool at our disposal to stand against such discrimination wherever it is found." Speaking of the stated rationale behind the adoption of photo identification laws, Holder insisted, "This whole notion of voter fraud … is really a solution in search of a problem." Carrying out his pledge, the attorney general filed litigation against voter restriction laws in Texas and North Carolina, seeking both to void them and to return these states to preclearance coverage.

In the short run, *Shelby* mobilized minorities to organize suffrage campaigns to assist voters in obtaining photo identification cards in states that required them and sign up new voters to defeat state lawmakers who supported voter suppression. The most promising opportunity emerged in North Carolina. In the 2010 midterm elections Republicans had swept control of both houses of the legislature and two years later they won the governor's office. As a result, Tar Heel politics shifted far to the right. Having voted for Obama in 2008, the state moved into the Romney column four years later. In 2013, the legislature passed a series of measures, which the governor signed into law, cutting social services for the poor, shrinking funds for public education, reducing taxes on the wealthy, and relaxing regulations for purchasing guns. Having enacted this arch-conservative economic and social agenda, lawmakers turned their attention to improving Republican electoral fortunes in the future. As noted above, the state enacted a package of voter suppression bills aimed at reducing the number of voters most likely to cast ballots for Democrats, particularly minorities and young people. Opponents of these measures called them "Screw the Voter Act of 2013."

These measures triggered a counter-mobilization of African Americans and their white allies. Led by the state NAACP and its president, the Reverend William S. Barber, II, protesters organized "Moral Monday," a weekly march to the capitol building in Raleigh to "dramatize the shameful condition of our state." These peaceful demonstrations attracted thousands of people, many of whom, including students and faculty at area universities, were arrested for trespassing in the legislature. Although state officials did not reverse course, Reverend Barber built Moral Monday into a grassroots movement throughout North Carolina, holding rallies, voter registration drives, and political education campaigns from the Atlantic coast counties to those in the Piedmont and the mountains. In this way, he planned to revive the civil rights movement of the 1960s "from Montgomery up, from Raleigh up, from congressional districts up." As Barber envisioned, such pressure from below was as essential in the new millennium as it had been in the 1960s to achieve racial equality.

Local and national forces soon merged to commemorate the fiftieth anniversary of the 1963 March on Washington. On August 24, Reverend Sharpton, as head of the National Action Network, and Martin Luther King, III, heir to his father as president of the Southern Christian Leadership Conference, held a celebration of the original march in front of the Lincoln Memorial where Dr. King gave his historic "I Have a Dream" speech. For the tens of thousands of people who attended in 2013, the dream remained to be fulfilled. The main targets of this march included voter suppression and stand-your- ground laws, inequities in the criminal justice system, and the high unemployment rates among African Americans and other minorities. "Fifty years after the original march for jobs and justice," Sharpton observed, "we have a new version of the same issue." Congressman John Lewis, who as chairman of SNCC spoke at the 1963 demonstration, vowed to the crowd, "I am not going to stand by and let the Supreme Court take the right to vote from us."

Although the President did not attend this event, Attorney General Holder did. Holder, whose sister-in-law Vivian Malone had been the first to integrate the University of Georgia, told those gathered on the National Mall that King's struggle must continue "until every eligible American has the chance to exercise his or her right to vote unencumbered by discrimination or unneeded procedures, rules, or practices." A few days after this gathering, he turned his attention to the criminal justice system and issued an order to federal prosecutors to avoid long, mandatory prison terms for low-level drug offenses. As a White House counsel explained, "part of that focus just by definition is on race behavior because of the sheer statistical, disproportionate numbers of African American men who are impacted."

President Obama did join another, smaller commemoration of the original march in Washington initiated by Dr. King's daughter, the Reverend Bernice King. Held on August 28, the same day as in 1963 and at the same site, the gathering attracted two former presidents, Jimmy Carter and Bill Clinton, the daughters of two former presidents, Caroline Kennedy and Lynda Johnson Robb, civil rights leaders John Lewis, Andrew Young, and Joseph Lowery, and members of the King family. In his keynote address, the President repeated King's famous words that the "arc of the moral universe may bend toward justice," but, he pointed out, "it doesn't bend on its own." Instead, building on the gains that King and the civil rights movement achieved "requires constant vigilance, not complacency." Still, as he had done in the past, the President warned African Americans that they shared responsibility for improving their lives, that they had "agency in our own liberation." He pledged government assistance, for example, in raising the minimum wage, but he argued that blacks could not use poverty as "an excuse for not raising your own child, and the bigotry of others was no reason to give up on yourself." In balancing talk of liberal government intervention with black self-help, Obama was emphasizing the same notion of agency that in the past had driven the civil rights movement forward.

African Americans had made substantial progress since the 1963 March on Washington, but they continued to lag behind whites in a number of key economic areas. With respect to education, the gap between the races in obtaining a high school education had narrowed from 24 percentage points to seven. Life expectancy rates of blacks and whites had nearly converged, and even more remarkably, black voter turnout in presidential elections exceeded that of whites. Although the gap in poverty levels had declined by five percentage points, the gap in homeownership had widened by the same number. Worse yet, the gap between black and white median household income and median household wealth had expanded significantly to the detriment of African Americans. Little wonder then, that on the eve of the March on Washington commemorations, a Pew Research survey found that only 32 percent of African Americans believed that "a lot" of progress had been made since 1963 in achieving racial progress, compared to 48 percent of whites who shared this belief.

Assessing Obama

After five years occupying the highest office in the land, Barack Obama remained something of an enigma to friends and foes alike. As Bill Keller of the *New York Times* noted, supporters and opponents continued to see what they wanted to see in this son of Kansas and Kenya. He could be "a prophetic Martin Luther King, Jr." or "a pent-up Black Panther waiting to explode." Much of the mystery stemmed from Obama himself. As a person with a composed and cool demeanor, someone who dislikes the glad-handing, ingratiating culture of the nation's capital, he projects a standoffish quality that makes it hard to know him. Although there is an abundance of information on the public record to judge this presidential author of two books and countless speeches, reading through them only reinforces the ambiguities of this biracial man. He is African American, but governs mainly as a president who happens to be black. He has a liberal record mediated by a strong pragmatic impulse. He is an heir of the civil rights movement but a politician born too late to experience it and not bound by it. Obama is many things – an either/or formulation does not do him justice – legal scholar, professor, husband, father, sports fan. Above all, however, he is a politician and not a civil rights activist leading a movement. Valerie Jarrett, the presidential assistant who knows Obama as well as does anybody in his political inner circle, agrees that he "felt the responsibility to pick up the baton not as a civil rights leader, but as president of the United States."

Perhaps Obama best expressed who he is at a memorial service for Nelson Mandela in South Africa in December 2013. The President recalled that he had joined his first protest in college against apartheid. It is instructive to identify the qualities Obama found most inspiring about Mandela. He cited "the importance of reason and arguments; the need to study not only those who you agree with, but those who don't agree." Furthermore,

Madiba, as South Africans called Mandela, "was not afraid to compromise for the sake of a larger goal." Finally, Obama praised the South African leader for having the gift of "recognition that we are all bound together in ways that are invisible to the eye; that there is a oneness to humanity," what South Africans call *Ubunto*. In selecting these virtues for emphasis, Obama reaffirmed what he saw as the best characteristics in himself: measured reason, empathy, compromise, and universalism.

In evaluating Obama in the White House, it is essential to understand that even the greatest presidents only make history to the extent that powerful, established institutions permit them to. Personal agency can achieve wonders but it is always limited to some degree. Obama has had to deal with a divided Congress that has become increasingly partisan and polarized. This largely reflects the political transformation of the South from a conservative Democratic into a conservative Republican region and the disappearance of moderate Republicans as a significant political force anywhere in the nation. Obama's victory in 2008 did not produce a willingness for bipartisan cooperation within the ranks of the GOP. Instead, the emergence of the Tea Party, determined to save America from Obama, pushed it further rightward. Meanwhile, Obama inherited a conservative Supreme Court that was unsympathetic to the continued expansion of the political and social reforms in the 1960s and 1970s, most notably the Voting Rights Act.

It is also important to recognize that in contrast to Abraham Lincoln, Franklin D. Roosevelt, and Lyndon B. Johnson, Obama lacks a necessary ingredient for progressive change – the support of a mass, nationwide social movement. Lincoln had the abolitionists, Roosevelt had the labor unions, and Johnson had the civil rights movement. The electoral movement that resulted in Obama's victory in 2008, spurred by young people and disseminated through grassroots organizing and the internet, has shown few signs of developing into a sociopolitical movement of broader significance. However, there are some hopeful indications that this could change, as witnessed in Moral Mondays in North Carolina, organizing around the Trayvon Martin killing, and the mobilization to commemorate the March on Washington. History shows that progressive change is most likely when grassroots social movements and capable national leaders operate in tandem. However capable Obama may be, he has yet to encounter his social movement – or create one. The ferment on the right that found expression in the Tea Party underscored the wholly different political contexts in the 1860s, the 1930s, and the 1960s from the 2010s.

Clearly the transformation of protest into electoral politics and the election and reelection of an African-American president have not solved the interlocking dilemmas of race, class, and gender. Black critics such as the political scientists Frederick C. Harris and Robert C. Smith view Obama's ascendency to the White House as lessening the motivation to confront "racial inequality head on." His dogged determination to preside as president of all the people and meet economic and social challenges through universal, race-neutral policies, they argue, has left a disproportionate share of the black population behind, as yawning gaps in wealth, jobs, education, and criminal punishment continue to show. The accuracy of this criticism notwithstanding, given the changing demography of the United States and the decline of African Americans as the nation's largest minority group, blacks must make shrewd alliances with those groups that share their vision of change. This is especially true at the state and national levels, where the proportion of the African-American population is far lower than can occur at county and precinct levels. In such contests, and the presidency is certainly one, candidates have to cross racial lines and craft a broad, common, agenda that addresses the needs of their constituents as much as political reality and circumstances allow.

In his second term the President has shown promising signs of greater urgency in pursuing a progressive agenda. He has confronted racial challenges more forcefully than in his first term, as seen in his responses to the Trayvon Martin case and assaults on voting rights. The President has used his "bully pulpit" increasingly to spotlight growing income inequality, notwithstanding falling unemployment and rising economic recovery. At the same time, he has shown renewed interest in immigration reform and climate control legislation. And despite the challenges of implementing comprehensive healthcare reform, he has continued to insist that the core aim of the ACA is crucial to a humane society: affordable healthcare for *all* Americans.

An important achievement to highlight as the nation moves ahead into the twenty-first century is the impact of Barack Obama's election on African Americans, especially young people for whom a black man in the White House is reality not prophecy. Before her husband decided to campaign for president, a somewhat reluctant Michelle Obama asked him what he would accomplish by running. Heading the list, Obama replied, "When I raise my hand and take that oath of office there are millions of kids around the country who don't believe that it would ever be possible for them to be president of the US. And for them, the world would change in one day." The importance of this symbolic achievement should not be underestimated. Whatever the tangible results he has achieved, and they are substantial, perhaps one of his greatest, as the journalist Ta-Nehisi Coates writes, "has been an expansion of the black imagination to encompass this: the idea that a man can be culturally black and many other things also – biracial, Ivy League, intellectual, cosmopolitan, temperamentally conservative, presidential." The political travails of the Obama presidency demonstrate that while America has not yet entered a post-racial age, it has moved far enough so that being black no longer disqualifies a citizen born in the US from becoming president.

Bibliographical Essay

The entries noted in the following pages are meant to be a select list of the works upon which this study is primarily based. A full citation appears only at the first referral to the source. My main purpose is to provide the reader with a guide to the available published literature and the themes that they raise; therefore, manuscript sources are omitted. I have made a few exceptions in noting unpublished doctoral dissertations and conference papers that were of particular help.

Preface

A very useful discussion that distinguishes between the civil rights movement and the black freedom struggle and calls for a focus on local communities is presented in Clayborne Carson, "Civil Rights Reform and the Black Freedom Struggle," pp. 19–32 in *The Civil Rights Movement in America*, ed. Charles W. Eagles (University Press of Mississippi, Jackson, 1986).

Chapter 1

Two anthologies that furnish a background for the general study of African-American history and black politics are Darlene Clark Hine, ed., *The State of Afro-American History: Past, Present and Future* (Louisiana

State University Press, Baton Rouge, 1986) and Michael B. Preston, Lenneal J. Henderson, Jr., and Paul Puryear, eds., *The New Black Politics: The Search for Political Power* (Longman, New York, 1982). Useful surveys on the civil rights movement and on black politics can be found in Matthew Holden, *The Politics of the Black "Nation"* (Chandler, New York, 1973); Manning Marable, *Black American Politics; From the Washington Marches to Jesse Jackson* (Verso, London, 1985); Milton D. Morris, *The Politics of Black America* (Harper & Row, New York, 1975); Hanes Walton, Jr., *Invisible Politics: Black Political Behavior* (State University of New York Press, Albany, 1985); Lucius J. Barker and Jesse J. McCrory, Jr., *Black Americans and the Political System* (Winthrop, Cambridge, MA, 1976); Harvard Sitkoff, *The Struggle for Black Equality, 1954–1980* (Hill & Wang, New York, 1981); Robert Weisbrot, *Freedom Bound: A History of America's Civil Rights Movement* (Norton, New York, 1990); and Rhoda Lois Blumberg, *Civil Rights: The 1960s Freedom Struggle* (Twayne, Boston, 1984).

W. E. B. Du Bois, *The Souls of Black Folk* (New American Library, Chicago, 1973) demonstrates the importance of the ballot as a key weapon for black liberation. On the influence of the New Deal on the development of black political strategies, there are two excellent monographs: Harvard Sitkoff, *A New Deal for Blacks* (Oxford University Press, New York, 1978) and Nancy J. Weiss, *Farewell to the Party of Lincoln: Black Politics in the Age of FDR* (Princeton University Press, Princeton, 1983).

The impact of World War II is covered most extensively in Neil A. Wynn, *The Afro-American and the Second World War* (Holmes & Meier, New York, 1975) and in several surveys of life in general on the home front. Among them are Richard Polenberg, *War and Society: The United States, 1941–1945* (J. B. Lippincott, Philadelphia, 1972) and John Morton Blum, *V Was for Victory: Politics and Culture during World War II* (Harcourt, Brace, Jovanovich, New York, 1976). Richard M. Dalfiume, "The 'Forgotten Years' of the Negro Revolution," *Journal of American History*, 55 (June 1968): 90–106, is a seminal article on the origins of the civil rights struggle; Harvard Sitkoff, "Racial Militancy and Interracial Violence in the Second World War," *Journal of American History*, 58 (December 1971): 661–81, explores the moderating influence white liberals had on the development of black protest; Lee Finkle, "The Conservative Aims of Militant Rhetoric; Black Protest during World War II," *Journal of American History*, 60 (December 1973): 692–713, extends Sitkoff's analysis to the black press; and Peter J. Kellogg, "Civil Rights

Consciousness in the 1940s," *The Historian*, 42 (November 1979): 18–41, notes the transformation of liberal thinking toward support of racial equality. Dominic J. Capeci, Jr., has examined outbreaks of racial violence and the response of the federal government in *Race Relations in Wartime Detroit: The Sojourner Truth Housing Controversy of 1942* (Temple University Press, Philadelphia, 1984) and "The Lynching of Cleo Wright: Federal Protection of Constitutional Rights during World War II," *Journal of American History*, 72 (March 1986): 859–87. Herbert Garfinkel, *When Negroes March* (Atheneum, New York, 1969) investigates A. Philip Randolph, the March on Washington Movement, and the FEPC; and Allen M. Winkler, "The Philadelphia Transit Strike of 1944," *Journal of American History*, 59 (June 1972): 73–89, comments on the FEPC's efforts in resolving racial strife during a labor dispute. Jervis Anderson, *A. Philip Randolph: A Biographical Portrait* (Harcourt Brace Jovanovich, New York, 1972) provides a flattering account of the labor leader and protest innovator. Catherine A. Barnes, *Journey from Jim Crow: The Desegregation of Southern Transit* (Columbia University Press, New York, 1983) covers wartime challenges to segregated transportation and shows the continuity of those efforts with later civil rights struggles.

Quintard Taylor, *In Search of the Racial Frontier: African Americans in the American West 1528–1990* (Norton, New York, 1998) is a very useful book on African Americans in the West, as is Gretchen Lemke-Santangelo, *Abiding Courage: African-American Migrant Women and the East Bay Community* (University of North Carolina Press, Chapel Hill, 1996). Jules Tygiel, *Baseball's Great Experiment: Jackie Robinson and His Legacy* (Vintage, New York, 1983) is a social history of the racial integration of America's premier sport. There are a number of informative books on the Tuskegee Airmen, including Lynn Homan and Thomas Reilly, *Black Knights: The Story of Tuskegee Airmen* (Pelican, Gretna, La, 2001), Alan J. Gropman, *The Air Force Integrates, 1945–1968* (Smithsonian Institution Press, Washington, DC,1998), Lawrence Scott and William M. Womack, Sr., *Double V: The Civil Rights Struggle of the Tuskegee Airmen* (Michigan State University Press, East Lansing, 1992), and Charles Dryden, *A-Train: Memoirs of a Tuskegee Airman* (University of Alabama Press, Tuscaloosa, 1997). August Meier and Elliott Rudwick, *CORE: A Study in the Civil Rights Movement, 1942–1968* (Oxford University Press, New York, 1973) details the emergence of a major civil rights group, which pioneered direct-action forms of protest that would become popular in the 1950s and 1960s. Adam Fairclough's, *Race and Democracy: The Civil Rights Struggle in Louisiana*

1915-1972 (University of Georgia Press, Athens, 1995), divides the struggle for black equality in the Pelican State into two stages and credits World War II with playing the largest role in promoting racial change during the first phase.

For continued discrimination against African Americans left unresolved by World War see David H. Onkst, "'First a Negro ... Incidentally a Veteran': Black World War Two Veterans and the G.I. Bill of Rights in the Deep South, 1944–1948," *Journal of Social History* (Spring 1998), and Jennifer E. Brooks, *Defining the Peace: World War II Veterans, Race, and the Remaking of Southern Political Tradition* (University of North Carolina Press, Chapel Hill, 2004). Thomas J. Sugrue offers the classic account of racial discrimination and economic inequality in the North in the postwar years in *The Origins of the Urban Crisis: Race and Inequality in Postwar Detroit* (Princeton, Princeton University Press, 1998). The long legal struggle of blacks to topple the white primary as a means of gaining access to the most meaningful elections in the South is amply described in Darlene Clark Hine, *Black Victory: The Rise and Fall of the White Primary in Texas* (KTO Press, Millwood, NY, 1979) and Steven F. Lawson, *Black Ballots: Voting Rights in the South, 1944–1969* (Columbia University Press, New York, 1976). The battles against the poll tax are discussed in Hollinger F. Barnard, ed., *Outside the Magic Circle* (University of Alabama Press, University, 1985), which is the autobiography of Virginia Foster Durr, a leading southern white liberal reformer; and in a scholarly study by Frederic D. Ogden, *The Poll Tax in the South* (University of Alabama Press, University, 1958).

The attempts of southern blacks and their allies to use their restored ballots in the postwar period were first chronicled by Henry Lee Moon, *Balance of Power: The Negro Vote* (Doubleday, Garden City, NY, 1948), and more recently by Robert Korstad and Nelson Lichtenstein, "Opportunities Found and Lost: Labor, Radicals, and the Early Civil Rights Movement," *Journal of American History*, 75 (December 1988): 786–811, Robert Rogers Korstad, *Civil Rights Unionism: Tobacco Workers and the Struggle for Democracy in the Mid-Twentieth-Century South* (University of North Carolina Press, Chapel Hill, 2003), and by Patricia Sullivan, *Days of Hope: Race and Democracy in the New Deal Era* (University of North Carolina Press, Chapel Hill, 1996). On the uneasy relationship between blacks and labor, see Michael Honey, *Southern Labor and Black Civil Rights: Organizing Memphis Workers* (University of Illinois Press, Urbana, 1993).

Mississippi and the significance of the Bilbo episode are presented in James W. Silver, *Mississippi: The Closed Society* (Harcourt, Brace, & World, New York, 1966) and in Lawson, *Black Ballots*. Detailed studies of black politics in local communities are contained in C. A. Bacote, "The Negro in Atlanta Politics," *Phylon*, 25 (December 1955): 333–50; Everett Carll Ladd, Jr., *Negro Political Leadership in the South* (Atheneum, New York, 1969) [Winston-Salem]; Korstad and Lichtenstein, "Opportunities Found and Lost" [Winston-Salem]; and William H. Chafe, *Civilities and Civil Rights* (Oxford University Press, New York, 1981) [Greensboro]. Focused at the national level, Harvard Sitkoff, "Harry Truman and the Election of 1948: The Coming of Age of Civil Rights in American Politics," *Journal of Southern History*, 37 (November 1971), analyzes the pivotal balance of power wielded by northern black voters in Truman's presidential victory and its implications for the future. The story of the Southern Conference for Human Welfare is detailed in Thomas A. Krueger, *And Promises to Keep* (Vanderbilt University Press, Nashville, 1967) and Linda Reed, *Simple Decency and Common Sense* (Indiana University Press, Bloomington, 1991). Early white moderates and liberals are covered in John Egerton, *Speak Now against the Day* (University of North Carolina Press, Chapel Hill, 1994).

Literature on the role of women and the civil rights movement is growing. Steven F. Lawson, "Civil Rights and Black Liberation," pp. 397–413 in *A Companion to American Women's History*, ed. Nancy A. Hewitt (Blackwell, Oxford, 2002), provides an overview. Christina Greene's *Our Separate Ways: Women and the Black Freedom Movement in Durham, North Carolina* (University of North Carolina Press, Chapel Hill, 2005) offers a provocative reinterpretation of the civil rights movement as a women's movement. For material on Pauli Murray consult her memoir, *The Autobiography of a Black Activist, Feminist, Lawyer, Priest, and Poet* (University of Tennessee Press, Knoxville, 1989). For Grace Towns Hamilton see Kathryn Nasstrom, "Down to Now: Memory, Narrative, and Women's Leadership," *Gender and History*, 11 (April 1999): 117–24, and Lorraine Nelson Spritzer and Jean B. Bergmark, *Grace Towns Hamilton and the Politics of Southern Change* (University of Georgia Press, Athens, 1997). Darlene Clark Hine has written about Mabel Stauper in *Black Women in White: Racial Conflict and Cooperation in the Nursing Profession, 1890–1950* (Indiana University Press, Bloomington, 1989). See also Peter Ling and Sharon Monteith, eds., *Gender and the Civil Rights Movement* (Rutgers University Press, New Brunswick, NJ, 2004) and Lynne Olson, *Freedom's Daughter: The Unsung Heroines of the*

Civil Rights Movement from 1830 to 1970 (Scribner's, New York, 2001). The notion of women as "bridge leaders" comes from Belinda Robnett, *How Long? How Long? African-American Women in the Struggle for Civil Rights* (Oxford University Press, New York, 1997). For one of the most important women in the civil rights movement see Barbara Ransby, *Ella Baker and the Black Freedom Movement: A Radical Vision* (University of North Carolina Press, Chapel Hill, 2003) and Joanne Grant, *Ella Baker: Freedom Bound* (Wiley, New York, 1999).

Chapter 2

Historians are in general agreement that President Truman furthered the civil rights agenda of African Americans, but they remain divided as to how effective and determined he was in achieving those goals. William Carl Berman, *The Politics of Civil Rights in the Truman Administration* (Ohio State University Press, Columbus, 1970) and Barton J. Bernstein, "The Ambiguous Legacy: Civil Rights," pp. 269–314 in *Politics and Policies of the Truman Administration*, ed. Barton J. Bernstein (Quadrangle, Chicago, 1970), take a critical view of Truman's performance and find fault with his leadership as well as with liberalism in general. A more favorable view of the President and his civil rights accomplishments is presented by Donald McCoy and Richard T. Reutten, *Quest and Response: Minority Rights and the Truman Administration* (University of Kansas Press, Lawrence, 1973) and by Robert J. Donovan, *Conflict and Crisis: The Presidency of Harry Truman, 1945–1948* (Norton, New York, 1977). For additional insights into the Truman presidency by a contemporary civil rights leader, see Walter White, *A Man Called White* (Viking, New York, 1948). Weiss, *Farewell to the Party of Lincoln*, and Sitkoff, "Harry Truman and the Election of 1948" (both cited in Chapter 1) also offer judicious comments on the political dimensions of civil rights.

Postwar political developments in black communities are treated in Hugh D. Price, *The Negro in Southern Politics: A Chapter of Florida History* (New York University Press, New York, 1957); Ladd, *Negro Leadership*; Moon, *Balance of Power*; Korstad, *Civil Rights Unionism*; Korstad and Lichtenstein, "Opportunities Found and Lost"; Chafe, *Civilities and Civil Rights*; Bacote, "The Negro in Atlanta Politics" (all cited for Chapter 1); Alton Hornsby, Jr., "The Negro in Atlanta Politics, 1961–1973," *Atlanta Historical Bulletin*, 21 (Spring 1977): 7–33; David J. Garrow, ed., *The*

Montgomery Bus Boycott and the Women Who Started It: The Memoir of Jo Ann Gibson Robinson (University of Tennessee Press, Knoxville, 1987); and J. Mills Thornton, "Challenge and Response in the Montgomery Bus Boycott of 1955–56," *Alabama Review*, 33 (July 1989): 163–235. For a major reinterpretation of the bus boycott as a women's movement see Danielle L. McGuire, *At the Dark End of the Street: Black Women, Rape, and Resistance – A New History of the Civil Rights Movement from Rosa Parks to the Rise of Black Power* (Knopf, New York, 2010).

The comments of William H. Chafe concerning the negative effects of anti-Communism on racially progressive labor unions appear in *The Unfinished Journey: America since World War II* (Oxford University Press, New York, 1986). Mary L. Dudziak's *Cold War Civil Rights: Race and the Image of American Democracy* (Princeton University Press, Princeton, 2000) reveals a more positive side of the Cold War's impact on civil rights. Adam Fairclough, "The Preachers and the People: The Origins and the Early Years of the Southern Christian Leadership Conference, 1955–1959," *Journal of Southern History*, 52 (August 1986): 403–40, notes the linkages between electoral and protest politics. Aldon D. Morris, *The Origins of the Civil Rights Movement* (Free Press, New York, 1984) offers a sociological perspective on the community structures that spawned black political protest. Doug McAdam, *Political Process and the Development of Black Insurgency* (University of Chicago Press, Chicago, 1982) also provides a sociological view, on a national as well as a regional scale, of the political resources that shaped the direction of the civil rights movement.

The impact of the *Brown* decision in shaping racial politics in the South and the nation is beautifully chronicled in Richard Kluger, *Simple Justice* (Knopf, New York, 1975). More recent works are James T. Patterson, *Brown v. Board of Education: A Civil Rights Milestone and Its Troubled Legacy* (Oxford University Press, New York, 2002) and Peter F. Lau, ed., *From the Grassroots: Brown v. Board of Education and American Democracy* (Duke University Press, Durham, NC, 2004).The hostile reactions on the part of white political, economic, and social leaders in challenging the landmark opinion are dealt with perceptively by Numan V. Bartley, *The Rise of Massive Resistance* (Louisiana State University Press, Baton Rouge, 1970) and Neil R. McMillen, *The Citizens' Council: Organized Resistance to the Second Reconstruction, 1954–1964* (University of Illinois Press, Urbana, 1971).

A number of works have examined the impact of the accelerating civil rights struggle on national politics. Robert Frederick Burk, *The Eisenhower*

Administration and Black Civil Rights (University of Tennessee Press, Knoxville, 1984) offers a well-balanced, but ultimately unfavorable portrayal of President Eisenhower's handling of civil rights matters, a view that is shared by most writers on the subject. One account that accords more credit to Eisenhower than has customarily been granted is Michael Mayer, "With Much Deliberation and Some Speed," *Journal of Southern History*, 52 (February 1986): 41–76. A sometimes fond but mostly harsh assessment of Eisenhower's role, written by one who served the administration, appears in E. Frederick Morrow, *Black Man in the White House* (Coward-McCann, New York, 1963). Roy Wilkins, with Tom Matthews, *Standing Fast* (Viking, New York, 1982) is the memoir of a prominent civil rights leader who found Eisenhower's leadership sadly lacking. A general account of the Republican party and blacks is an excellent study by Timothy N. Thurber, *Republicans and Race: The GOP's Frayed Relationship with African Americans, 1945–1974* (Lawrence, University of Kansas Press, 2013). For Lyndon John's monumental wheeling and dealing on the 1957 Civil Rights Act see Robert A. Caro, *master of the Senate: The Years of Lyndon Johnson III* (New York, Vintage, 2009).

The contrasts in style of the two most notable black politicians of this period. Adam Clayton Powell and William Dawson, are analyzed in James Q. Wilson, "Two Negro Politicians: An Interpretation," *American Journal of Political Science*, 4 (November 1960): 360–9. Gary W. Reichard, "Democrats, Civil Rights, and Electoral Strategies in the 1950s," *Congress and the Presidency*, 13 (Spring 1986): 59–81, traces Democratic Party strategies toward black voters during the 1950s. Both regional and national assessments of the impact of the black vote on partisan politics at mid-decade are contained in a special issue of the *Journal of Negro Education*, 26 (Summer 1957) and in Chandler Davidson, *Biracial Politics: Conflict and Consensus in the Metropolitan South* (Louisiana State University Press, Baton Rouge, 1972). My own *Black Ballots* (cited for Chapter 1) also covers these issues.

The story of the Macon County and Tuskegee struggle, both patient and courageous, has found a historian worthy of its merit. Robert J. Norrell, *Reaping the Whirlwind: The Civil Rights Movement in Tuskegee* (Vintage, New York, 1985) carefully and sympathetically charts racial politics on both sides of the color line in this community identified with Booker T. Washington. Three earlier studies that provide useful accounts of the *Gomillion* case and the related boycott are Harry Holloway, *The Politics of the Southern Negro: From Exclusion to Big City Organization* (Random

House, New York, 1969); Lewis Jones and Stanley Smith, *Voting Rights and Economic Pressure* (Anti-Defamation League, New York, 1958); and Bernard Taper, *Gomillion v. Lightfoot* (McGraw-Hill, New York, 1962). There is a dearth of published material on the Fayette, Tennessee struggle, but the best place to start is Robert Hamburger, *Our Portion of Hell: Fayette County, Tennessee; An Oral History of the Struggle for Civil Rights* (Links, New York, 1973). Two useful articles are Linda T. Wynn, "Toward a Perfect Community: The Struggle of African Americans in Fayette County, Tennessee to Fulfill the Unfulfilled Right of the Franchise," *Tennessee Historical Quarterly*, 55 (1996): 202–23, and Richard J. Saunders, "'Of Some Importance, But Uneven and Limited': External Support for the Local Civil Rights Action in Tennessee's Haywood and Fayette Counties, 1959–1963," *Southern Historian*, 28 (Spring 2007): 55–73.

Chapter 3

For nearly two decades after its publication, David L. Lewis, *King: A Critical Biography* (Praeger, New York, 1970), republished as *King: A Biography* (University of Illinois Press, Urbana, 1978), was the standard interpretation of the nation's best-known civil rights leader. In the late 1980s, three enormously valuable studies appeared, which draw upon manuscript records that were not available to Lewis and on extensive interviews. David Garrow has written more thoroughly about King's career than any other contemporary scholar. His early studies, *Protest at Selma: Martin Luther King and the Voting Rights Act of 1965* (Yale University Press, New Haven, 1978) and *The FBI and Martin Luther King, Jr.* (Norton, New York, 1981), paved the way for the encyclopedic *Bearing the Cross: Martin Luther King, Jr., and the Southern Christian Leadership Conference* (Morrow, New York, 1986). Adam Fairclough, *To Redeem the Soul of America: The Southern Christian Leadership Conference and Martin Luther King, Jr.* (University of Georgia Press, Athens, 1987), offers thoughtful interpretations of King, the organization he led, and the larger movement. Taylor Branch, *Parting the Waters: America in the King Years, 1954–1963* (Simon & Schuster, New York, 1988) places King within the larger black religious culture from which he emerged. See also his final volume on King, *At Canaan's Edge: America in the King Years, 1965–68* (Simon & Schuster, New York, 2006). King's rhetorical style and its connection to the black preaching tradition is best analyzed in Keith D. Miller, *Voice of Deliverance: The Language of Martin Luther King, Jr., and*

Its Sources (Free Press, New York, 1992). King's top aide, Ralph David Abernathy, adds his perspective in *And the Walls Came Tumbling Down* (Harper & Row, New York, 1989).

Very helpful in discussing the Crusade for Citizenship program is Aldon D. Morris, *The Origins of the Civil Rights Movement* (Free Press, New York, 1984). The sketch of Fred Shuttlesworth was drawn primarily from Morris. For more recent books about Shuttlesworth see Andrew Mannis, *A Fire You Can't Put Out: The Civil Rights Life of Birmingham's Reverend Fred Shuttlesworth* (University of Alabama Press, Tuscaloosa, 2001) and Diane McWhorter, *Carry Me Home: Birmingham, Alabama: The Climactic Battle of the Civil Rights Revolution* (Simon & Schuster, New York, 2001). Howell Raines, *My Soul Is Rested: Movement Days in the Deep South Remembered* (Putnam, New York, 1977) provides a revealing collection of interviews with prominent and not so well-known leaders and opponents of the civil rights movement. For additional interviews, along with a narrative of the freedom struggle that emphasizes the roles played by plain, though extraordinary, people, consult Juan Williams, *Eyes on the Prize: America's Civil Rights Years, 1954–1965* (Viking, New York, 1987).

Other major civil rights groups that engaged in direct-action protests and political organizing in southern communities have also received detailed treatments. On SNCC, see the work of Howard Zinn, a historian who participated as an adviser to the organization, *SNCC: The New Abolitionists* (Beacon Press, Boston, 1964), Clayborne Carson, *In Struggle: SNCC and the Black Awakening of the 1960s* (Harvard University Press, Cambridge, MA, 1981), which is the most judicious treatment of the subject, and Wesley C. Hogan, *Many Minds, One Heart: SNCC's Dream for a New America* (University of North Carolina Press, Chapel Hill, 2007). The camaraderie born out of the fierce battles waged by this vanguard organization is reflected in the insightful accounts offered by four former staff members: James Forman (executive secretary), *The Making of Black Revolutionaries* (Macmillan, New York, 1972); Cleveland Sellers (program director), with Robert Terrell, *The River of No Return: The Autobiography of a Black Militant and the Life and Death of SNCC* (Morrow, New York, 1973); John Lewis with Michael D'Orso, *Walking with the Wind: A Memoir of the Movement* (Simon & Schuster, New York, 1998); and Mary King (assistant communications director), *Freedom Song: A Personal Story of the 1960s Civil Rights Movement* (Morrow, New York, 1987). Joe Sinsheimer, "Never Turn Back: An Interview with Sam Block," *Southern Exposure*, 15 (Summer 1987):

37–50, furnishes a poignant firsthand account from a SNCC organizer from Mississippi.

On CORE, see Meier and Rudwick, *CORE* (cited for Chapter 1), the standard work on the subject. James Farmer, *Lay Bare the Heart: An Autobiography of the Civil Rights Movement* (Arbor House, New York, 1985) provides a moving account of the organization and its operation from the perspective of one of its founders. The NAACP still has not been the focus of a scholarly monograph for the years since World War II. However, this period is seen through the eyes of its executive director, Roy Wilkins, in his memoir *Standing Fast* (cited for Chapter 2). The legal battles of the NAACP Legal Defense Fund receive extended treatment by the group's longtime director-counsel, Jack Greenberg, in *Crusaders in the Courts* (Basic Books, New York, 1994). Denton L. Watson, *Lion in the Lobby* (Morrow, New York, 1990) records the skillful efforts of the NAACP's chief Washington lobbyist, Clarence Mitchell, Jr., to pass civil rights legislation.

The performance of the Kennedy administration is rated very highly in Carl Brauer, *John F. Kennedy and the Second Reconstruction* (Columbia University Press, New York, 1977). Another favorable study of Kennedy, by his chief civil rights adviser, can be found in Harris Wofford, *Of Kennedys and Kings: Making Sense of the Sixties* (Farrar, Straus & Giroux, New York, 1980). A sensitive portrayal, it describes the difficulties a civil rights advocate close to Martin Luther King, Jr., faced in trying to shape government policy. Much more critical of the Kennedy administration are Victor Navasky, *Kennedy Justice* (Atheneum, New York, 1971), a trenchant analysis of the Justice Department, and Pat Watters and Reese Cleghorn, *Climbing Jacob's Ladder: The Arrival of Negroes in Southern Politics* (Harcourt, Brace, & World, New York, 1967), which finds Kennedy's implementation of voting rights programs sadly lacking. A balanced and mildly critical assessment of the Kennedy administration's handling of the desegregation of interstate transportation appears in Barnes, *Journey from Jim Crow* (cited for Chapter 1). A comparison of the styles and accomplishments of Kennedy and Johnson in furnishing presidential leadership is offered by Tom Wicker, *JFK and LBJ: The Influence of Personality upon Politics* (Penguin, Baltimore, 1970). The political maneuvering behind the enactment of the 1964 civil rights law is detailed in Charles Whalen and Barbara Whalen, *The Longest Debate: A Legislative History of the 1964 Civil Rights Act* (New American Library, New York, 1986). The most recent books on the Act are Todd S. Purdum, *An Idea Whose Time Has Come: Two*

Presidents, Two Parties, and the Battle for the Civil Rights Act of 1964 (Holt, New York, 2014) and Clay Risen, *The Bill of the Century: The Epic Battle for the Civil Rights Act* (Bloomsbury, New York, 2014).

The most recent book on Johnson's relationship to the civil rights movement and Martin Luther King, Jr., in particular is Nick Kotz, *Judgment Days: Lyndon Baines Johnson, Martin Luther King, Jr., and the Laws That Changed* America (Houghton Mifflin, Boston, 2005). I have previously reviewed the literature and historiographical opportunities for research on Johnson's civil rights policies in "Civil Rights," pp. 93–125 in *Exploring the Johnson Years*, ed. Robert A. Divine (University of Texas Press, Austin, 1981), and Steven F. Lawson, "Mixing Moderation with Militancy: Lyndon Johnson and African-American Leadership," pp. 82–116 in *The Johnson Years*, vol. 3, ed. Robert A. Divine (University of Kansas Press, Lawrence, 1994).

The struggle of black Mississippians for political liberation is analyzed best by John Dittmer, "The Politics of the Mississippi Movement, 1954–1964," pp. 65–93 in *The Civil Rights Movement in America*, ed. Charles W. Eagles (University Press of Mississippi, Jackson, 1986). The same volume includes comments on Dittmer's essay by Neil McMillen as well as essays and commentaries on various aspects of the freedom struggle. Joseph Sinsheimer, "COFO and the 1963 Freedom Vote: New Strategies for Change in Mississippi," *Journal of Southern History* 55 (May 1989): 217–44, perceptively discusses community organizing and political development surrounding the conduct of symbolic mock-elections. Dittmer has successfully told the Mississippi story connecting the grassroots insurgency with the shifting politics of the federal government in his splendid *Local People: The Struggle for Civil Rights in Mississippi* (University of Illinois Press, Urbana, 1994). Several other very useful studies have also appeared. Charles M. Payne, *I've Got the Light of Freedom: The Organizing Tradition and the Mississippi Freedom Struggle* (University of California Press, Berkeley, 1995), Emilye Crosby, *A Little Taste of Freedom: The Black Freedom Struggle in Claiborne County Mississippi* (University of North Carolina Press, Chapel Hill, 2005), J. Todd Moye, *Let the People Decide: Black Freedom and White Resistance in Sunflower County Mississippi, 1945–1986* (University of North Carolina Press, Chapel Hill, 2004), and Constance Curry, *Silver Rights* (Algonquin Books, Chapel Hill, 1995), focus on the Delta, as does James C. Cobb's broader work, *The Most Southern Place on Earth: The Mississippi Delta and the Roots of Regional Identity* (Oxford University Press, New York, 1992). Fannie Lou Hamer's life is detailed in Kay Mills, *This Little*

Light of Mine (Dutton, New York, 1993) and Chana Kai Lee, *For Freedom's Sake: The Life of Fannie Lou Hamer* (University of Illinois Press, Urbana, 1999). Nicolaus Mills, *Like a Holy Crusade* (Ivan R. Dee, Chicago, 1992) argues that the Freedom Summer campaign was more successful than its organizers realized at the time. Seth Cagin and Philip Dray, *We Are Not Afraid: The Story of Goodman, Schwerner, and Chaney, and the Civil Rights Campaign for Mississippi* (Macmillan, New York, 1988) adds considerable detail to the drama of that summer.

The events of that campaign and its impact on the volunteers are analyzed from a sociological perspective in Doug McAdam, *Freedom Summer* (Oxford University Press, New York, 1988). The strains placed on black and white workers are described by Allen J. Matusow, "From Civil Rights to Black Power: The Case of SNCC, 1960–1966," pp. 494–519 in *Twentieth-Century America: Recent Interpretations*, ed. Barton J. Bernstein and Allen J. Matusow (Harcourt, Brace, Jovanovich, New York, 1972). Elizabeth Sutherland, ed., *Letters from Mississippi* (McGraw-Hill, New York, 1965) compiles the writings of the highly reflective summer participants. The challenge at the Democratic convention, which climaxed Freedom Summer, is documented and analyzed in Leslie Burl McLemore, "The Mississippi Freedom Democratic Party: A Case Study of Grass-Roots Politics" (Ph.D. diss., University of Massachusetts, 1971). For a listing of a variety of works on the same subject, see Jennifer McDowell and Milton Loventhall, eds., *Black Politics: A Study and Annotated Bibliography of the Mississippi Freedom Democratic Party* (Center for the Study of Political Science, San Jose, CA, 1971). The legal response by the Johnson administration to the widespread brutality against the summer workers, including the murder of three of them in Philadelphia, Mississippi, receives critical treatment in Michal Belknap, *Federal Law and Southern Order: Racial Violence and Constitutional Conflict in the Post-Brown South* (University of Georgia Press, Athens, 1987). The strategy of President Johnson and the Democratic Party in dealing with the black vote in 1964 appears in Mark Stern, *Calculating Visions: Kennedy, Johnson, and Civil Rights* (Rutgers University Press, New Brunswick, NJ, 1992).

The continuing story of the Tuskegee struggle appears in Norrell, *Reaping the Whirlwind* (cited for Chapter 2). Some useful data on Birmingham is furnished by Holloway, *Politics of the Southern Negro* (cited for Chapter 2). The diverse relationships between civil rights activists and southern white business leaders in 14 communities are discussed in original essays prepared for a volume edited by Elizabeth Jacoway and

David R. Colburn, *Southern Businessmen and Desegregation* (Louisiana State University Press, Baton Rouge, 1982). Colburn has also written a book-length study that ably traces the origins of a community's struggle and the impact the civil rights movement had upon it in *Racial Change and Community Crisis: St. Augustine, Florida, 1877–1980* (Columbia University Press, New York, 1985).

Chapter 4

The voting rights struggle in Selma is detailed in Garrow, *Protest at Selma*; Fairclough, *To Redeem the Soul of America*; Forman, *The Making of Black Revolutionaries*; Zinn, *SNCC*; and Clayborne Carson, *In Struggle* (all cited for Chapter 3). The local actors and politics of the Selma movement are fleshed out in Charles E. Fager, *Selma, 1965* (Scribner's, New York, 1974); J. Mills Thornton, "Municipal Politics and the Course of the Civil Rights Movement" (paper delivered at the Conference on New Directions in Civil Rights Studies, University of Virginia, May 1988); Stephen L. Longenecker, *Selma's Peacemaker: Ralph Smeltzer and Civil Rights Mediation* (Temple University Press, Philadelphia, 1987); Sheyanne Webb and Rachel West Nelson, *Selma, Lord, Selma* (University of Alabama Press, University, 1980); and from interviews contained in Williams, *Eyes on the Prize*, and Raines, *My Soul Is Rested* (cited for Chapter 3). John Lewis with Michael D'Orso, *Walking with the Wind: A Memoir of the Movement* (Simon & Schuster, New York, 1998) deals with the heroic participation by Lewis in Selma and much more.

The legal precedents leading to passage of the Voting Rights Act and the legislative battle itself are discussed in Charles V. Hamilton, *The Bench and the Ballot: Southern Federal Judges and Black Voters* (Oxford University Press, New York, 1973); Lawson, *Black Ballots* (cited for Chapter 1); and in President Lyndon B. Johnson's memoirs, *The Vantage Point: Perspectives of the Presidency, 1963–1969* (Holt Rinehart Winston, New York, 1971). For similar conclusions about the federal government's caution in implementing the 1965 law, see my *In Pursuit of Power: Southern Blacks and Electoral Politics, 1965–1982* (Columbia University Press, New York, 1985) and Howard Ball, Dale Krane, and Thomas P. Lauth, *Compromised Compliance: Implementation of the 1965 Voting Rights Act* (Greenwood Press, Westport, CT, 1982). Mary King's *Freedom Song* (cited for Chapter 3) notes the non-tangible rewards of political organizing.

The development of black power and its theoretical application to electoral strategies in the South appear in the classic work of Stokely Carmichael and Charles V. Hamilton, *Black Power: The Politics of Liberation in America* (Vintage, New York, 1967). Matusow, "From Civil Rights to Black Power" (cited for Chapter 3) places the issue in historical perspective and offers a critique of the approach. The best and most balanced biography of Carmichael is Peniel Joseph, *Stokely: A Life* (Basic Civitas Books, 2014). Carmichael co-wrote his autobiography with Ekwueme Michael Thelwell, *Ready for Revolution: The Life and Struggles of Stokely Carmichael (Kwame Ture)* (New York, Scribners. 2005). Joyce Ladner, a sociologist and SNCC veteran, offers very useful insights into different conceptions of black power in "What Black Power Means to Negroes in Mississippi," pp. 131–54 in *The Transformation of Activism*, ed. August Meier (Aldine, Chicago, 1970). For examinations into the effects of racial awareness on black voting behavior, see Sidney Verba, Norman Nie, and Jaeon Kim, *Participation and Political Equality* (Cambridge University Press, Cambridge, 1978) and Richard D. Shingles, "Black Consciousness and Political Participation: The Missing Link," *American Political Science Review*, 75 (1981): 76–91. The Meredith march, during which the slogan of black power was first publicized, is treated in Milton Viorst, *Fire in the Streets: America in the 1960s* (Simon & Schuster, New York, 1979); Sellers, with Terrell, *The River of No Return*; Carson, *In Struggle*; Garrow, *Bearing the Cross* (all cited for Chapter 3); and Lawson, *Pursuit of Power*. Martin Luther King, *Where Do We Go from Here? Community or Chaos* (Harper & Row, New York, 1967) offers a sensitive account by one of the central participants in the march about the controversy over black power.

The comment of Malcolm X on the use of the ballot is quoted in Manning Marable, *Race, Reform, and Rebellion: The Second Reconstruction in Black America, 1945–1982* (University Press of Mississippi, Jackson, 1984), which provides a provocative and informative synthesis of the larger black freedom struggle. Anyone interested in Malcolm X should start with the *Autobiography of Malcolm X* (which he coauthored with Alex Haley) (Grove Press, New York, 1966). The definitive biography of this leader is Manning Marable, *Malcolm X: A Life of Reinvention* (Viking, New York, 2010). George Breitman edited his revealing post–Nation of Islam speeches in *Malcolm X Speaks* (Grove Press, New York, 1965). Two very helpful assessments of his life and growth appear in James H. Cone, *Martin & Malcolm & America: A Dream or a Nightmare* (Orbis, Maryknoll, NY, 1991) and Peter Goldman, *The Death and Life of Malcolm X* (University of Illinois Press,

Urbana, 1979). Michael Friedly, *Malcolm X: The Assassination* (Ballantine, New York, 1992) covers the controversial events surrounding his murder. Other useful information can be found in two studies of the civil rights movement and Black Power: Robert Weisbrot, *Freedom Bound: A History of America's Civil Rights Movement* (Norton, New York, 1990) and William L. Van Deburg, *New Day in Babylon: The Black Power Movement and American Culture, 1965-1975* (University of Chicago Press, Chicago, 1992); more recent excellent studies include Peniel Joseph, *Waiting ' Till the Midnight Hour: A Narrative History of Black Power in America* (Holt, New York, 2007); Jeffrey O. G. Ogbar, *Black Power: Black Politics and African American Identity* (Johns Hopkins University Press, Baltimore, 2005); Yohuru Williams, *Black Politics/White Power: Civil Rights, Black Power, and the Black Panthers in New Haven* (Brandywine Press, St. James, NY, 2000); and Robert O. Self, *American Babylon: Race and Struggle in Postwar Oakland* (Princeton University Press, Princeton, 2005).

Case studies of black power in operation in southern politics are found in works dealing with Lowndes County, Alabama and Hancock County, Georgia. For the former see Hardy T. Frye, *Black Parties and Political Power: A Case Study* (G. K. Hall, Boston, 1980); Andrew Kopkind, "The Lair of the Black Panther," *New Republic*, 155 (June 18, 1966): 10–13, and Kopkind, "Lowndes County, Alabama: The Great Fear Is Gone," *Ramparts*, 13 (April 1975): 8–12; and John Corry, "A Visit to Lowndes County, Alabama," *New South*, 27 (Winter 1972): 28–36. The best book on Lowndes County is Hasan Jeffries, *Bloody Lowndes: Civil Rights and Black Power in Alabama's Black Belt* (New York University Press, New York, 2010). On Hancock County, see the critical account by John Rozier, *Black Boss: Political Revolution in a Georgia County* (University of Georgia Press, Athens, 1982) and the more favorable scholarly appraisal by Lawrence J. Hanks, *The Struggle for Black Political Empowerment in Three Georgia Counties* (University of Tennessee Press, Knoxville, 1987). Melissa Fay Greene, *Praying for Sheetrock* (Addison-Wesley, Reading, MA, 1991) furnishes a vivid picture of McIntosh County, Georgia's uneven struggle for black political power and the toll it took on one black leader. Firsthand accounts of the efforts of black candidates to gain office are compiled in Julian Bond, ed., *Black Candidates: Southern Campaign Experiences* (Voter Education Project, Atlanta, 1968). William M. Simpson, "The 'Loyalist' Democrats of Mississippi: Challenge to a White Majority, 1965–1972" (Ph.D. diss., Mississippi State University, 1974) describes the transformation of the insurgent movement in the Magnolia State. For case studies of successful black political organizing and campaigning in Mississippi, see Minion K. C. Morrison, *Black Political Mobilization: Leadership, Power, and Mass Behavior* (State University of New York Press, Albany, 1987). The efforts of the Democratic Party to increase minority access to its affairs are detailed in William J. Crotty, *Decision for the Democrats: Reforming the Party Structure* (Johns Hopkins University Press, Baltimore, 1979) and Byron E. Shafer, *Quiet Revolution: The Struggle for the Democratic Party and the Shaping of Post-Reform Politics* (Russell Sage Foundation, New York, 1983).

The subjects of black power, the ghetto explosions, and the white backlash are dealt with in Joe R. Feagin and Harlan Hahn, *Ghetto Revolts* (Macmillan, New York, 1973); James W. Button, *Black Violence: Political Impact of the 1960s Riots* (Princeton University Press, Princeton, 1978); and Marshall Frady, *Wallace* (New American Library, New York, 1975). Robert H. Wiebe, "White Attitudes and Black Rights from *Brown* to *Bakke*," pp. 147–71 in *Have We Overcome?*, ed. Michael V. Namorato (University Press of Mississippi, Jackson, 1979), discusses the changing shape of white public opinion during this period. The story of the Black Panther party from the perspective of its leaders is told in Huey P. Newton, with J. Herman Blake, *Revolutionary Suicide* (Harcourt Brace Jovanovich, New York, 1973); Bobby Seale, *Seize the Time* (Random House, New York, 1970); and Robert Scheer, ed., *Eldridge Cleaver: Post-Prison Writing and Speeches* (Random House, New York, 1969). Elaine Brown offers the critical perspective of the group's top female leader in *A Taste of Power: A Black Woman's Story* (Pantheon, New York, 1992).

The Ocean Hill-Brownsville controversy is detailed in Diane Ravitch, *The Great School Wars* (Basic Books, New York, 1974); Robert G. Weisbrot and Arthur Stein, *Bittersweet Encounter: The Afro-American and the Jew* (Negro Universities Press, Westport, CT, 1970); and Jonathan Kaufman, *Broken Alliance* (Scribner's, New York, 1988). Henry Hampton and Steve Fayer with Sarah Flynn, *Voices of Freedom* (Bantam, New York, 1990) contains an oral history of the school crisis. Allen Matusow, *The Unraveling of America: A History of Liberalism in the 1960s* (Harper & Row, New York, 1984), Todd Gitlin, *The Sixties: Years of Hope, Days of Rage* (Bantam, New York, 1987), and Yohuru Williams, *Black Politics/White Power* (cited above) comment on the influence of the Panthers on white radicals. Philip S. Foner, ed., *The Black Panther Speaks* (Lippincott, Philadelphia, 1970) provides a documentary collection of the organization. The complex history of the Detroit uprising is told in painstaking detail and in balanced fashion in Sidney Fine, *Violence in the Model City: Race Relations, the Cavanagh Administration, and the Detroit Race Riot of 1967* (University of Michigan Press, Ann Arbor, 1989).

On the efforts against Julian Bond and Adam Clayton Powell, see John Neary, *Julian Bond: Black Rebel* (Morrow, New York, 1971); Charles V. Hamilton, *Adam Clayton Powell, Jr.: The Political Biography of an American Dilemma* (Atheneum, New York, 1991); Andy Jacobs, *The Powell Affair, Freedom Minus One* (Bobbs-Merrill, Indianapolis, 1973); Kent M. Weeks, *Adam Clayton Powell and the Supreme Court* (Dunellen, New York, 1971); and P. Allan Dionesopoulos, *Rebellion, Racism, and Representation: The Adam Clayton Powell Case and Its Antecedents* (Northern Illinois University Press, De Kalb, 1970).

The election of 1968 is covered in Lewis Chester, Godfrey Hodgson, and Bruce Page, *An American Melodrama* (Dell, New York, 1969) and William L. O'Neill, *Coming Apart: An Informal History of America in the 1960s* (Quadrangle, New York, 1971). The changing outlines of southern politics, especially the drift toward presidential Republicanism, are portrayed in a number of impressive works by political scientists. See Earl Black and Merle Black, *Politics and Society in the South* (Harvard University Press, Cambridge, MA, 1987); Alexander P. Lamis, *The Two-Party South* (Oxford University Press, New York, 1984); and Harold W. Stanley, *Voter Mobilization and the Politics of Race: The South and Universal Suffrage, 1952–1984* (Praeger, New York, 1987). Two historians who have provided a sophisticated examination of evolving political trends in Dixie are Numan V. Bartley and Hugh D. Graham, *Southern Politics and the Second Reconstruction* (Johns Hopkins University Press, Baltimore, 1975). Each of these works owes a great debt to V. O. Key's classic, *Southern Politics in State and Nation* (Vintage, New York, 1949). Monroe Lee Billington, *The Political South in the Twentieth Century* (Scribner's, New York, 1975) is a useful text for historical background on the changes that have taken place. Jody Carlson, *George C. Wallace and the Politics of Powerlessness* (Transaction, New Brunswick, NJ, 1981) analyzes the Wallace campaigns for the presidency from 1964 to 1976. The best biography of Wallace is Dan Carter, *The Politics of Rage: George Wallace, the Origins of New Conservatism, and the Transformation of America* (Simon & Schuster, New York, 1995).

On the Nixon administration, consult the President's own account, *RN: The Memoirs of Richard Nixon* (Grosset & Dunlop, New York, 1978), as well as the work of one of his chief political aides who dealt with the South,

Harry S. Dent, *The Prodigal South Returns to Power* (John Wiley, New York, 1978). More negative assessments of Nixon's performance are found in Richard Harris, *Justice: The Crisis of Law, Order, and Freedom in America* (Dutton, New York, 1970); Leon E. Panetta and Peter Gall, *Bring Us Together: The Nixon Team and the Civil Rights Retreat* (Lippincott, Philadelphia, 1971); William E. Leuchtenburg, "The White House and Black America: From Eisenhower to Carter," pp. 121–45 in *Have We Overcome?*, ed. Namorato; and my *In Pursuit of Power* and Steven F. Lawson, "E Pluribus Unum: Civil Rights and National Unity," pp. 35–73 in *American Choices: Social Dilemmas and Public Policy since 1960*, ed. Robert H. Bremner, Gary W. Reichard, and Richard J. Hopkins (Ohio State University Press, Columbus, 1986). Gary Orfield, *Congressional Power: Congress and Social Change* (Harcourt Brace Jovanovich, New York, 1975) offers a sharp appraisal of the 1970 Voting Rights Act extension.

The efforts to form independent black political interest groups have received some treatment. Marguerite Ross Barnett, "The Congressional Black Caucus: Illusions and Realities of Power," pp. 28–55 in *The New Black Politics*, ed. Preston, Henderson, and Puryear (cited for Chapter 1), offers a useful overview of the operation of black congressional lawmakers. A wide variety of organizational attempts are described by Martin Kilson, "The New Black Political Class," pp. 81–100 in *Dilemmas of the New Black Middle Class*, ed. Joseph R. Washington (n.p., 1980). The Gary convention is discussed in Marable, *Race, Reform, and Rebellion*; Vincent Harding, *The Other American Revolution* (Center for Afro-American Studies, University of California, Los Angeles, 1981); and Ronald W. Walters, *Black Presidential Politics in America: A Strategic Approach* (State University of New York, Albany, 1988). The early years of the Joint Center for Political Studies are recounted by Alex Poinsett, "'The Joint': D.C. Center for Political Studies Backs Up Elected Officials," *Ebony*, 28 (April 1973): 124–132.

Shirley Chisholm, *Unbought and Unbossed* (Avon Books, New York, 1971) is an autobiographical account of the Brooklyn lawmaker's political career before her unsuccessful campaign for the presidency, which she writes about in *The Good Fight* (Harper & Row, New York, 1973). On that race, see Stephan Lesher, "The Short, Unhappy Life of Black Presidential Politics, 1972," *New York Times Magazine* (June 25, 1972): 12–22, and Frederick C. Harris, *The Price of the Ticket: Barack Obama and the Rise and Decline of Black Politics* (Oxford University Press, New York, 2012).

Chapter 5

Bayard Rustin's challenging analysis appears in "From Protest to Politics: The Future of the Civil Rights Movement," *Commentary*, 39 (February 1965): 25–31. On the transition of blacks from protesters to candidates, see my *In Pursuit of Power* and Bond, *Black Candidates* (both cited for Chapter 4); Ladd, *Negro Leadership* (cited for Chapter 1); Albert K. Karnig and Susan Welch, *Black Representation and Urban Policy* (University of Chicago Press, Chicago, 1980); Chuck Stone, *Black Political Power in America* (Dell, New York, 1970); Jason Berry, *Amazing Grace: With Charles Evers in Mississippi* (Saturday Review Press, New York, 1973); Leonard A. Cole, *Blacks in Power: A Comparative Study of Black and White Elected Officials* (Princeton University Press, Princeton, 1976); Lester M. Salamon, "Leadership and Modernization: The Emerging Black Political Elite in the American South," *Journal of Politics*, 35 (August 1973): 615–46; Robert C. Smith, "The Changing Shape of Urban Black Politics, 1960–1970," *Annals of the American Academy of Political and Social Science*, 439 (September 1978): 16–28; Paul Jeffrey Steckler, "Electing Black Candidates to Office in the South," *Urban Lawyer*, 17 (Summer 1985): 473–87; Jack Bass and Walter DeVries, *The Transformation of Southern Politics: Social Change and Political Consequence since 1945* (Basic Books, New York, 1976); Bette Woody, *Managing Crisis Cities: The New Black Leadership and the Politics of Resource Allocation* (Greenwood Press, Westport, CT, 1982); and Martin Kilson, "Political Change in the Negro Ghetto, 1900–1940's," pp. 167–92 in *Key Issues in the Afro-American Experience*, vol. 2, ed. Nathan I. Huggins, Martin Kilson, and Daniel Fox (Harcourt Brace Jovanovich, New York, 1971). The politics of the Community Action Program of the War on Poverty are discussed in Matusow, *The Unraveling of America* (cited for Chapter 4). For a profile of Tuskegee's Johnny Ford, see Marshall Frady, *Southerners: A Journalistic Odyssey* (New American Library, New York, 1980).

The best overview of the issue of at-large versus single-member district elections is provided by the essays contained in Chandler Davidson, ed., *Minority Vote Dilution* (Howard University Press, Washington, DC, 1984). The Washington Research Project, *The Shameful Blight: The Survival of Racial Discrimination in Voting in the South* (Washington Research Project, Washington, DC, 1972) catalogues the sundry forms of franchise abuse that persisted after passage of the Voting Rights Act. For the argument that the federal government has exceeded statutory and constitutional boundaries in seeking to maximize minority voting strength by applying affirmative action principles, see Abigail M. Thernstrom, *Whose Votes Count? Affirmative Action and Minority Voting Rights* (Harvard University Press, Cambridge, MA, 1987) and Katharine I. Butler, "Denial or Abridgement of the Right to Vote: What Does It Mean?" pp. 44–59 in *The Voting Rights Act: Consequences and Implications*, ed. Lorn S. Foster (Praeger, New York, 1985).

The performance of black elected officials is discussed and evaluated in Hanks, *Black Empowerment* (cited for Chapter 4); Margaret Edds, *Free at Last: What Really Happened When Civil Rights Came to Southern Politics* (Adler & Adler, Bethesda, MD, 1987); Peter K. Eisinger, *The Politics of Displacement: Racial and Ethnic Transition in Three American Cities* (Academic Press, New York, 1980); Rufus P. Browning, Dale Rogers Marshall, and David H. Tabb, *Protest Is Not Enough: The Struggle of Blacks and Hispanics for Equality in Urban Politics* (University of California Press, Berkeley, 1984); James W. Button, *Blacks and Social Change* (Princeton University Press, Princeton, 1989); and Paul Jeffrey Stekler, "Black Politics in the New South: An Investigation of Change at Various Levels" (Ph.D. diss., Harvard University, 1982). The black middle class has received extensive treatment in L. Bart Landry, *The New Black Middle Class* (University of California Press, Berkeley, 1987), and the underclass has been analyzed by William Julius Wilson, *The Truly Disadvantaged: The Inner City, the Underclass and Public Policy* (University of Chicago Press, Chicago, 1987).

There remains to be written a systematic study of the role of black women in the civil rights movement and electoral politics. The best place to obtain data on black female officeholders is the Joint Center for Political and Economic Studies, *The National Roster of Black Elected Officials*. The center started keeping statistics on black women officeholders in 1975. Vicki L. Crawford, Jacqueline Anne Rouse, and Barbara Woods have edited a very useful collection of essays, which should serve as a starting point for any future research, *Women in the Civil Rights Movement: Trailblazers and Torchbearers, 1941–1965* (Carlson, Brooklyn, NY, 1990). Other sources of useful information are Susan M. Hartmann, *From Margin to Mainstream: American Women and Politics since 1960* (Knopf, New York, 1989); Paula Giddings, *When and Where I Enter: The Impact of Black Women on Race and Sex in America* (Bantam, New York, 1984); and Sara Evans, *Personal Politics: The Roots of Women's Liberation in the Civil Rights Movement and the New Left* (Vintage,

New York, 1980). For a discussion and analysis of Unita Blackwell, see Morrison, *Black Political Mobilization* (cited for Chapter 4). Although not dealing with electoral politics, Christina Greene's *Our Separate Ways: Women and the Black Freedom Movement in Durham, North Carolina* (University of North Carolina Press, Chapel Hill, 2005) offers a provocative reinterpretation of the civil rights movement as a women's movement. See also Peter Ling and Sharon Monteith, eds., *Gender and the Civil Rights Movement* (Rutgers University Press, New Brunswick, NJ, 2004); Lynne Olson, *Freedom's Daughter: The Unsung Heroines of the Civil Rights Movement from 1830 to 1970* (Scribner's, New York, 2001); and Belinda Robnett, *HOW Long? How Long? African-American Women in the Struggle for Civil Rights* (Oxford University Press, New York, 1997).

Mack H. Jones, "Black Political Empowerment in Atlanta: Myth and Reality," *Annals of the American Academy of Political and Social Science*, 439 (September 1978): 90–117, offers a critical assessment of the impact of black mayors in Atlanta; and Edds, *Free at Last*, and Eisinger, *The Politics of Displacement* provide more favorable evaluations. For background on Maynard Jackson, see Fred Powledge, "Profiles: A New Politics In Atlanta," *New Yorker*, 49 (December 31, 1973): 28–40, and Peter Ross Range, "Capital of Black-Is-Beautiful," *New York Times Magazine* (April 7, 1974): 28–9, 68–78. Edds, *Free At Last*, and Norrell, *Reaping the Whirlwind* (cited for Chapter 2) offer complementary and balanced views on Tuskegee and Macon County.

The discussions of Cleveland and Gary are based largely on the thorough case study by William E. Nelson, Jr., and Philip J. Meranto, *Electing Black Mayors: Political Action in the Black Community* (Ohio State University Press, Columbus, 1977). For additional information on Cleveland, see Kenneth G. Weinberg, *Black Victory: Carl Stokes and the Winning of Cleveland* (Quadrangle, Chicago, 1968). On other victorious mayors, see Wilbur C. Rich, *Coleman Young and Detroit Politics* (Wayne State University Press, Detroit, 1989), which is a favorable if uneven treatment. It can be supplemented by Fine, *Violence in the Model City* (cited for Chapter 4); Eisinger, *The Politics of Displacement*; and Korstad and Lichtenstein, "Opportunities Found and Lost" (cited for Chapter 1). For the best treatment of liberal, biracial politics in the Motor City, see Heather Ann Thompson, *Whose Detroit? Politics, Labor, and Race in a Modern American City* (Cornell University Press, Ithaca, NY, 2001). Tom Bradley has yet to find a scholarly biographer, but background information can be compiled from the sketch in *Current Biography* (1973): 53–5. For the civil rights movement in the North see Martha Biondi, *To Stand and Fight: The Struggle for Civil Rights in Postwar New York City* (Harvard University Press, Cambridge, MA, 2006), Matthew J.Countryman, *Up South: Civil Rights and Black Power in Philadelphia* (University of Pennsylvania Press, Philadelphia, 2007), and Jeanne Theoharis and Komozi Woodard, *Freedom North: Black Freedom Struggles Outside the South, 1940–1980* (Palgrave Macmillan, New York, 2003). Jimmie Lewis Franklin, *Back to Birmingham: Richard Arrington, Jr, and His Times* (University of Alabama Press, Tuscaloosa, 1989) is a useful case study.

Chapter 6

President Ford offers his version of his efforts to work with blacks in *A Time to Heal* (Harper & Row, New York, 1979). He does not, however, explain his maneuvering on the Voting Rights Act extension. I examine the renewal of that legislation in Lawson, *In Pursuit of Power* (cited for Chapter 4). Bass and DeVries, *The Transformation of Southern Politics* (cited for Chapter 5) provides valuable data on the shift in southern Democratic support for the suffrage Act. A thorough review of various aspects of the busing controversy is furnished by Gary Orfield, *Must We Bus? Segregated Schools and National Policy* (Brookings Institution, Washington, DC, 1978). A comprehensive and eloquent treatment of the Boston struggle from the perspective of three diverse families is J. Anthony Lukas, *Common Ground* (Knopf, New York, 1985). In contrast with Boston, efforts to desegregate the schools through busing went more smoothly in Charlotte, North Carolina, and this story is chronicled in Frye Gaillard, *The Dream Long Deferred* (University of North Carolina Press, Chapel Hill, 1988).

On the 1976 presidential election and the political mood of African Americans, see Elizabeth Drew, *American Journal: The Events of 1976* (Random House, New York, 1977); Samuel DuBois Cook, "Democracy and Tyranny in America: The Radical Paradox of the Bicentennial and Blacks in the American Political System," *Journal of Politics*, 38 (August 1976): 276–294; Kandy Straud, *How Jimmy Won: The Victory Campaign from Plains to the White House* (Morrow, New York, 1977); Jules Witcover, *Marathon: The Pursuit of the Presidency, 1972–1976* (Viking, New York, 1977); and the Joint Center for Political Studies, *The Black Vote: Election '76* (Joint Center for Political Studies, Washington, DC, 1977). Barbara Jordan relates her story in her memoir coauthored with Shelby Hearon, *Barbara Jordan: A Self-Portrait* (Doubleday, Garden City, NY, 1979).

President Carter defends his policies in *Keeping the Faith: Memoirs of a President* (Bantam, New York, 1982). On his gubernatorial record, see the laudatory account of Gary Fink, *Prelude to the Presidency: The Political Character and Legislative Leadership Style of Governor Jimmy Carter* (Greenwood Press, Westport, CT, 1980). For the presidential years, Betty Glad, *Jimmy Carter; In Search of the Great White House* (Norton, New York, 1980) offers a favorable, but well-balanced, contemporary assessment. Louis Martin, the veteran black journalist, Democratic Party operative, and Carter aide offers a glowing comment in "Carter Accomplishments in Civil Rights," *Focus*, 8 (December 1980): 7–8. A highly critical portrayal of Carter's civil rights performance, especially compared to Lyndon Johnson's, from a man who served both presidents is Joseph Califano, *Governing America: An Insider's Report from the White House and the Cabinet* (Simon & Schuster, New York, 1981). The Carter administration's twists and turns on the *Bakke* case are described by Califano and in studies by J. Harvie Wilkinson, III, *From Brown to Bakke: The Supreme Court and School Integration 1954–1978* (Oxford University Press, New York, 1981) and Alan P. Sindler, *Bakke, DeFunis, and Minority Admissions: The Quest for Equal Opportunity* (Longman, New York, 1978). Relations between blacks and Jews receive historical treatment in Weisbrot and Stein, *Bittersweet Encounter* (cited for Chapter 4) and Robert Weisbrot's *Israel in the Black American Perspective* (Greenwood Press, Westport, CT, 1985). Jonathan Kaufman, *Broken Alliance* (cited for Chapter 4) is a sensitive work by a journalist focusing on the people involved in several of the episodes that heightened tensions between the two groups.

The rise of Ronald Reagan to the presidency is lucidly portrayed by the *Washington Post* columnist Lou Cannon in *Reagan* (Putnam, New York, 1982). Details of black voting in the 1980 elections are furnished in Milton Morris, "Blacks and the 1980 Presidential Election," *Focus* (October–November 1980): 3–4, 8. Critical evaluations of the Reagan administration's performance on equal opportunity and affirmative action programs are contained in Harrell R. Rodgers, Jr., "Fair Employment Laws for Minorities: An Evaluation of Federal Implementation," pp. 93–117 in *Implementation of Civil Rights Policy*, ed. Charles S. Bullock, III, and Charles M. Lamb (Brooks/Cole, Monterey, CA, 1984); Hanes Walton, *When the Marching Stopped: The Politics of Civil Rights Regulatory Agencies* (State University of New York Press, Albany, 1988); and Tinsley Yarbrough, "The Reagan

Administration, the IRS, and Discriminatory Private Schools" (paper presented at Southern Political Science Association annual meeting, Birmingham, AL, 1983). The Eddie Williams quote on the importance of the vote to counteract Reagan's budget-slashing effects on the poor appears in "Perspective," *Focus*, 9 (May 1981): 2. The Reagan administration's handling of civil rights matters is defended in Raymond Wolters, *Right Turn: William Bradford Reynolds, the Reagan Administration, and Black Civil Rights* (Transaction, Piscataway, NJ, 1996). I trace the events surrounding renewal of the Voting Rights Act in 1982 in Lawson, *In Pursuit of Power*. For different views of the Reagan administration's enforcement of the landmark suffrage law, compare Frank Parker, "Retreat on Voting Rights?" *Focus*, 14 (May 1986): 4–5, 7, and Abigail M. Thernstrom, "Voting Rights' Trap," *New Republic*, 193 (September 2, 1985): 21–3, as well as her *Whose Votes Count?* (cited for Chapter 5).

The economic crisis among blacks and the growing class distinctions are reviewed in "The State of the Union: One Nation or Two?" *Focus*, 10 (March 1982): 6; Andrew F. Brimmer, "Black Economic Progress," *Focus*, 13 (April 1985): 6, 8; and Andrew Hacker, "American Apartheid," *New York Review of Books* (December 3, 1987): 26–33. A discussion of black neoconservatives appears in Salim Muwakkil, "New Issues Reviving Dominant Arguments," *In These Times* (November 13–19, 1985): 3, 6. Thomas Sowell, *Race and Economics* (D. McKay, New York, 1975) and his *Civil Rights: Rhetoric or Reality?* (Morrow, New York, 1984) are two of the most notable works that reflect the thinking of black conservatives.

The Chicago mayoral election has already captured a good deal of scholarly investigation. For a background of black politics in Chicago, see the classic, James Q. Wilson, *Negro Politics: The Search For Leadership* (Free Press, New York, 1965). A more recent account that challenges Wilson's model of black political behavior is Dianne M. Pinderhughes, *Race and Ethnicity in Chicago Politics: A Reexamination of Pluralist Theory* (University of Illinois Press, Urbana, 1987). James R. Ralph, *Northern Protest: Martin Luther King, Jr., Chicago, and the Civil Rights Movement* (Harvard University Press, Cambridge, MA, 1993), Garrow, *Bearing the Cross* (cited for Chapter 3), and Alan B. Anderson and George W. Pickering, *Confronting the Color Line: The Broken Promise of the Civil Rights Movement in Chicago* (University of Georgia Press, Athens, 1986) offer accounts of Martin Luther King's campaigns for open housing and the grassroots struggle for racial equality in Chicago during the 1960s. William J. Grimshaw, *Black Politics in Chicago: The Quest for Leadership, 1939–1979*

(Center for Urban Policy, Loyola University, Chicago, 1980) briefly surveys black politicians and their changing relationship to the Democratic political machine. A firsthand account by an opponent of the Daley machine appears in Anna R. Langford, "How I 'Whupped' the Tar Out of the Daley Machine," pp. 3–31 in *What Black Politicians Are Saying*, ed. Nathan Wright, Jr. (Hawthorn, New York, 1972).

On the election of Harold Washington, the most reliable account is Paul Kleppner, *Chicago Divided: The Making of a Black Mayor* (Northern Illinois University Press, De Kalb, 1985). Other useful works on this subject are Abdul Alkalimat, "Mayor Washington's Bid for Reelection," *Black Scholar*, 17 (November–December 1986): 2–39; Abdul Alkalimat and Doug Gills, "Black Power vs. Racism: The Election of Harold Washington," pp. 55–179 in *The New Black Vote: A Look at Four American Cities*, ed. Rod Bush (Synthesis, San Francisco, 1984); Michael Preston, "The Election of Harold Washington: Black Voting Patterns in the 1983 Chicago Mayoral Race," *PS*, 16 (Summer 1983): 486–8; Twiley W. Barker, "Political Mobilization of Black Chicago: Drafting a Candidate," *PS*, 16 (Summer 1983): 482–5; Manning Marable, "Harold Washington and the Politics of Race in Chicago," *Black Scholar*, 17 (November–December 1986): 14–23; Thomas E. Cavanagh, "How Washington Won Chicago," *Focus*, 11 (May 1983): 3, 7–8; David Moberg, "Washington Learns that Reform Comes Slowly," *In These Times* (January 28–February 3, 1987): 12–13; and Gerald McWorter, Doug Gills, and Ron Bailey, "Black Power Politics as Social Movement: Dialectics of Leadership in the Campaign to Elect Harold Washington Mayor of Chicago" (Afro-American Studies and Research Program, University of Illinois, June 1984) and Frederick C. Harris, *The Price of the Ticket: Barack Obama and the Rise and Decline of Black Politics* (Oxford University Press, New York, 2012). A very handy compilation of newspaper clippings and other sources related to the election can be found in *Black Power in Chicago: A Documentary Survey of the 1983 Mayoral Democratic Primary* (Peoples College Press, Chicago, 1983).

On the upsurge in black voter participation in the early 1980s, see Garcia M. Hillman, "Operation Big Vote: Crusade '82 Begins," *Focus*, 12 (January 1984): 8; "Largest Increases in BEOs since 1976," *Focus*, 12 (January 1984): 8; and Adolph L. Reed, Jr., *The Jesse Jackson Phenomenon: The Crisis of Purpose in Afro-American Politics* (Yale University Press, New Haven, 1986). Harvey Gantt details his career and political philosophy in Laura Haessley, "We're Becoming the Mayors," *Southern Exposure*, 14 (March–April 1986): 44–52.

Chapter 7

The issue of legitimacy is discussed in Peter K. Eisinger, *The Politics of Displacement* (cited for Chapter 5). The importance of the presidency as a symbol of political legitimacy is noted from a critical perspective by Mack H. Jones, "A Black Presidential Candidate in 1984: More of the Same," *PS*, 16 (Summer 1983): 495–6, and from a more positive viewpoint by Lucius J. Barker, "Black Americans and the Politics of Inclusion," *PS*, 16 (Summer 1983): 500–7. We still do not have a first-rate biography of Jesse Jackson, but until one appears there are several helpful works on the subject. Unfortunately, most of these reflect the highly charged views that divide opinion about him. Barbara A. Reynolds, *Jesse Jackson: The Man, the Movement, the Myth* (Nelson-Hall, Chicago, 1975) offers much detail about Jackson's life and generally portrays the minister in an unflattering light. However, the author's negative conclusions apparently underwent modification in the wake of Jackson's bid for the presidency. Reynolds republished the book with a different title, *Jesse Jackson: America's David* (JFJ Associates, Washington, DC, 1985), and although the text remains the same, she added a new introduction much more sympathetic to her subject. Thomas H. Landess and Richard M. Quinn, *Jesse Jackson and the Politics of Race* (Jameson, Ottawa, IL, 1985) draws heavily on the Reynolds account to reach unfavorable conclusions about Jackson personally and professionally. A more scholarly but no less critical analysis of Jackson's attempt to jump from protest to electoral politics is presented by Adolph L. Reed, Jr., *The Jesse Jackson Phenomenon* (cited for Chapter 6). A more balanced account, by two reporters who covered Jackson's 1984 campaign, appears in Bob Faw and Nancy Skelton, *Thunder in America* (Texas Monthly Press, Austin, 1986). Elizabeth O. Colton, Jackson's press secretary, who resigned during the campaign, offers an inside account of the 1988 presidential bid that is critical of the candidate's personality but recognizes the importance of his cause, see *The Jackson Phenomenon: The Man, the Power, the Message* (Doubleday, New York, 1989). The most sympathetic treatments of the Jackson bid are found in the wide-ranging work of a campaign aide, Sheila D. Collins, *The Rainbow Challenge: The Jackson Campaign and the Future of U.S. Politics* (Monthly Review Press, New York, 1986), and of a scholar–Democratic convention delegate, Lucius J. Barker, *Our Time Has Come: A Delegate's Diary of Jesse Jackson's 1984 Presidential Campaign* (University of Illinois Press, Urbana, 1988).

The participation of black voters in the primaries and general elections is analyzed in a series of publications sponsored by the Joint Center for Political Studies, Washington, DC: Thomas E. Cavanagh, *The Impact of the Black Electorate* (1984); Thomas E. Cavanagh and Lorn S. Foster, *Jesse Jackson's Campaign: The Primaries and Caucuses* (1984); and Thomas E. Cavanagh, *Inside Black America: The Message of the Black Vote in the 1984 Elections* (1985). Hardy T. Frye, "Jesse Jackson and the Rainbow", *Socialist Review*, 17 (March–April, 1987): 55–80, and Marguerite Ross Barnett, "The Strategy Over a Black Presidential Candidacy," *PS*, 16 (Summer 1983): 489–91, provide an understanding of the divisions within black leadership circles on support for Jackson. The most recent collections of scholarly analyses of the Jackson campaign and its impact are Robert P. Steed, Laurence W. Moreland, and Tod A. Baker, eds., *The 1984 Presidential Election in the South: Patterns of Southern Party Politics* (Praeger, New York, 1986), in which see especially Harold W. Stanley, "The 1984 Presidential Election in the South: Race and Realignment," pp. 303–35, for a summary conclusion; Laurence W. Moreland, Robert P. Steed, and Tod A. Baker, eds., *Blacks in Southern Politics* (Praeger, New York, 1987); and Lucius J. Barker and Ronald W. Walters, eds., *Jesse Jackson's 1984 Presidential Campaign: Challenge and Change in American Politics* (University of Illinois Press, Urbana, 1989).

A substantial literature has grown around African Americans and foreign affairs. Brenda Gayle Plummer, *Rising Wind: Black Americans and U.S. Foreign Affairs, 1935–1960* (University of North Carolina Press, Chapel Hill, 1996) is the place to start. On the Cold War, see Mary Dudziak, *Cold War Civil Rights: Race and the Image of American Democracy* (Princeton University Press, Princeton, 2002); Thomas Borstelmann, *The Cold War and the Color Line* (Harvard University Press, Cambridge, MA, 2003); and Penny Von Eschen, *Race against Empire: Black Americans and Anticolonialism: 1937–1997* (Cornell University Press, Ithaca, NY, 1997). Other useful books include Kevin Gaines, *African Americans in Ghana:Black Expatriates and the Civil Rights Era* (University of North Carolina Press, Chapel Hill, 2007); Karen Stanford, *Beyond the Boundaries: Reverend Jesse Jackson in International Affairs* (State University of New York Press, Albany, 1997) and Brenda Gayle Plummer, ed., *Window on Freedom: Race, Civil Rights, and Foreign Affairs, 1945–1988.* (University of North Carolina Press, Chapel Hill, 2003).

The Reagan administration's prosecution of the voter fraud cases in the Alabama black belt is discussed in George Derek Musgrove, *Rumor, Repression, and Racial Politics: How the Harassment of Black Elected Officials*

Shaped Post-Civil Rights America (University of Georgia Press, Athens, 2012); Edds, *Free at Last* (cited for Chapter 5); Sheila D. Collins, "Justice Department Undermines Act," *In These Times* (July 10–23, 1985): 5, 22; Allen Tullos, "Voting Rights Activists Acquitted," *Nation* (August 3, 1985): 78–80; and "Vote Fraud on Trial," *Newsweek* (November 25, 1985): 10. The results of the 1986 congressional contests are analyzed in Linda Williams, "1986 Elections: Major Implications for Black Politics," *Focus*, 14 (November–December 1986): 5–7, and Bill Minor, "Congressman Espy from Mississippi," *Southern Changes*, 8 (December 1986): 1–3. The effect of the black electorate on reshaping southern white Democratic politicians is discussed in Black and Black, *Politics and Society in the South*, and Lamis, *The Two-Party South* (both cited for Chapter 4). The increasing competition between black candidates for office and the pivotal balance of power role played by whites is discussed in a paper by Monte Piliawsky and Paul J. Stekler, "The Evolution of Black Politics in New Orleans: From Protest to Powerbrokers" (in possession of author).

Of particular importance in tracking Jackson's presidential bid was *Focus*, published by the Joint Center for Political Studies, particularly the section called "Political Trendletter." In addition, from the popular press the following articles are worth noting explicitly: Doug Foster, "Interview with Jesse Jackson: He Thinks He Can Win," *Mother Jones* (October 1987): 27–45, and "Jackson's White Organizers," *Newsweek* (February 8, 1988): 26. In the *Village Voice*: "Jackson's Message" (March 21, 1988): 23–4; "Jackson's Big Takeoff" (April 11, 1988): 22; and Thulani Davis and James Ridgeway, "Jesse Jackson's New Math" (December 22, 1987): 20–5. Also, Joyce Purnick and Michael Oreskes, "Jesse Jackson Aims for the Mainstream," *New York Times Magazine* (November 29, 1987): 28–31, 34–6, 58–61; E. J. Dionne, "Black Residents of New York See a Campaign Tinged with Racism," *New York Times* (April 21, 1988): 12; Anthony Lewis, "The Jackson Reality," *New York Times* (March 31, 1988): A27; David Broder, "Jackson Becomes an Agent for Change," Raleigh *News and Observer* (May 2, 1988): 13A; Andrew Kopkind, "Is Jesse the Great White Hope?" *Nation* (December 26, 1987–January 2, 1988): 773, 790–1, and Kopkind, "Jesse's Movement," *Nation* (April 2, 1988): 448–89; "For Jesse Jackson and His Campaign," *Nation* (April 16, 1988): 517, 519–22; and "Bad," *New Republic*, 198 (April 18, 1988): 7–9. The implications of the Willie Horton issue are discussed by Michael Kinsley, "GOP Knew Symbolic Value of a Black Rapist," *Tampa Tribune* (November 5, 1988): 15A. For an academic study published before the Jackson candidacies that is pessimistic about the possibilities of a biracial coalition of the dispossessed in the South to unite politically, see Robert Emil Botsch, *We Shall Not Overcome: Populism and Southern Blue-Collar Workers* (University of North Carolina Press, Chapel Hill, 1980).

Chapter 8

On David Dinkins see Wilbur C. Rich, *David Dinkins and New York City Politics: Race, Images, and the Media* (State University of New York Press, Binghamton, 2006) and for background, Biondi, *To Stand and Fight* (cited for Chapter 5). Dinkins has written his autobiography, *A Mayor's Life: Governing New York's Gorgeous Mosaic* (Public Affairs, New York, 2013).

For an introduction to black conservatism, see the September 30, 1991 issue of *New Republic*, Fred Barnes, "The Minority," Matthew Rees, "Black and Right," and Stephen Macedo, "From Douglass to Thomas" (pp. 19–25), and Charles Lane, "Defying the Stereotypes: The New Clout of Black Conservatives," *Newsweek* (July 15, 1991): 18–19. To sample the writings of black conservatives, see Joseph Perkins, ed., *A Conservative Agenda for Black Americans* (Heritage Foundation, Washington, DC, 1987); Thomas Sowell, *The Economics and Politics of Race* (Morrow, New York, 1983); Walter E. Williams, *The State against Blacks* (New Press, New York, 1982); Glen C. Loury, *One by One from the Inside Out: Essays and Reviews on Race and Responsibility in America* (Free Press, New York, 1995); and Shelby Steele, *The Content of Our Character* (St. Martin's Press, New York, 1990). The Clarence Thomas–Anita Hill episode can be viewed from a variety of perspectives in Jane Mayer and Jill Abramson, *Strange Justice: The Selling of Clarence Thomas* (Houghton Mifflin, Boston, 1994); David Brock, *The Real Anita Hill: The Untold Story* (Free Press, New York, 1993); John A. Danforth, *Resurrection: The Confirmation of Clarence Thomas* (Viking, New York, 1994); Toni Morrison, ed., *Race-ing Justice, En-Gendering Power: Essays on Anita Hill, Clarence Thomas, and the Construction of Social Reality* (Pantheon, New York, 1992); and Geneva Smitherman, ed., *African American Women Speak Out on Anita Hill-Clarence Thomas* (Wayne State University Press, Detroit, 1995).

Useful insights into the Black Caucus appear in Peter J. Boyer, "The Rise of Kweisi Mfume," *New Yorker* (August 1, 1994): 26–35, and Howard Fineman, " 'Malcolms' and Dealmakers: The Split Personality of the Black Caucus," *Newsweek* (July 5, 1993): 26. Lani Guinier's provocative essays are collected in her *The Tyranny of the Majority: Fundamental Fairness in*

Representative Democracy (Free Press, New York, 1994). She also defends herself in "Who's Afraid of Lani Guinier?" *New York Times Magazine* (February 27, 1994): 39–44, 54–6, and in an interview with David J. Garrow, "Lani Guinier: 'I Was Nominated – and Then the Rules Were Changed,'" *The Progressive* (September 1993): 28–32. Contrast the views of one of her defenders, Patricia J. Williams, "Lani, We Hardly Knew You," *Village Voice* (June 15, 1993): 25–8, with two of her critics, Abigail Thernstrom, "A New Spin on Democracy," *Wall Street Journal* (March 24, 1994): A12 and Alan Wolfe, "Redesigning Democracy," *New York Times Book Review* (March 13, 1994): 6–7.

Kenneth O'Reilly, *Nixon's Piano: Presidents and Racial Politics from Washington to Clinton* (Free Press, New York, 1995) offers a trenchant portrait of Clinton. For a more positive analysis that focuses on Clinton's Race Initiative Commission, see the autobiography of its distinguished chairman, John Hope Franklin, *Mirror to America* (Farrar, Strauss, & Giroux, New York, 2005). The report itself is edited and published in Steven F. Lawson, *One America in the 21st Century: The Report of President Bill Clinton's Initiative on Race* (Yale University Press, New Haven, 2008). A more critical view of the committee's work appears in Patricia A. Sullivan and Steven R. Goldzwig, "Seven Lessons from President Clinton's Race Initiative: A Post-Mortem on the Politics of Desire," in *Images, Scandal, and Communication Strategies of the Clinton Presidency*, ed. Robert E. Denton, Jr., and Rachel L. Holloway (Greenwood, Westport, CT, 2003). For the AIDS epidemic and the African-American community, see Cathy Cohen, *The Boundaries of Blackness: AIDS and the Breakdown of Black Politics* (University of Chicago Press, Chicago, 1999).

A history of *Shaw v. Reno* appears in A. Leon Higginbotham, Jr., Gregory A. Clarick, and Marcella David, "*Shaw v. Reno*: A Mirage of Good Intentions with Devastating Racial Consequences," *Fordham Law Review*, 62 (April 1994): 1593–659. A critique of the ruling and a brief for race-conscious districting appears in American Civil Liberties Union, *Reaffirmation or Requiem for the Voting Rights Act? The Court Will Decide* (ACLU, New York, 1995). Chandler Davidson and Bernard Grofman have edited a collection of essays by scholars and lawyers that lend support to the argument that minority-majority districts have been critical for the expansion of black officeholding, see Davidson and Grofman, eds., *Quiet Revolution in the South: The Impact of the Voting Rights Act, 1965–1990* (Princeton University Press, Princeton, 1994). They have also edited a collection of essays by defenders and opponents of the implementation of the

Voting Rights Act in *Controversies in Minority Voting* (Brookings Institution, Washington, DC, 1992). One of its contributors, Carol M. Swain, has written critically and perceptively about the limits of race-conscious districting in *Black Faces, Black Interests: The Representation of African Americans in Congress* (Harvard University Press, Cambridge, MA, 1993). *Southern Exposure*, 23 (Spring 1995): 27–39, contains three articles assessing the political changes sweeping through the South: Ron Nixon, "Plantation Politics?"; Rickey Hill, "From Booker T. Washington to Clarence Thomas"; and D. Keith Miles, "Whatever Happened to Southern Democrats?" For a more recent appraisal of southern politics in the late twentieth century, see Robert P. Steed and Laurence W. Moreland, eds., *Writing Southern Politics: Contemporary Interpretations and Future Directions* (University of Kentucky Press, Lexington, 2006).

Chapter 9

For an overall assessment of President Bush and civil rights see Steven F. Lawson, "George W. Bush, Compassionate Conservatism, and the Limits of 'Racial Realism,'" pp. 221–60 in Kenneth Osgood and Derrick E. White, eds., *Winning While Losing: Civil Rights, the Conservative Movement, and the Presidency from Nixon to Obama* (University of Florida Press, Gainesville, 2013). The literature on the 2000 and 2004 presidential elections is already voluminous, though mostly written by journalists and participants. Donna L. Brazile, *Cooking with Grease: Stirring the Pots in American Politics* (Simon & Schuster, New York, 2004) provides insights from an African-American and women's perspective by the manager of Gore's campaign.

The voting irregularities have been well documented in books by Mark Danner, *The Road to Illegitimacy: One Reporter's Travels through the 2000 Florida Vote Recount* (Melville House, Hoboken, NJ, 2004; Douglas Kellner, *Grand Theft 2000:Media Spectacle and a Stolen Election* (Rowman & Littlefield, Lanham, MD, 2001); Martin Merzer and the Staff of the *Miami Herald*, *The Miami Herald Report: Democracy Held Hostage* (St. Martin's Press, New York, 2001); Jeffrey Toobin, *Too Close to Call: The Thirty-Six Day Battle to Decide the 2000 Election* (Random House, New York, 2001); Ronald W. Walters, *Freedom Is Not Enough: Black Voters, Black Candidates, and American Presidential Politics* (Rowman & Littlefield, Lanham, MD, 2005); Steven F. Freeman and Joel Bleifuss, *Was the 2004 Presidential Election Stolen? Exit Polls, Election Fraud, and the Official Count* (Seven

Stories Press, New York, 2006); Robert E. Denton, Jr., ed., *The 2004 Presidential Campaign: A Communication Perspective* (Rowman & Littlefield, Lanham, MD, 2005); Tracy Campbell, *Deliver the Vote: A History of Election Fraud, an American Political Tradition – 1742–2004* (Carroll & Graff, New York, 2005); Robert J. Fitrakis, Steven Rosenfeld, and Harvey Wasserman, *What Happened in Ohio? A Documentary Record of Theft and Fraud in the 2004 Election* New York (New Press, New York, 2006); Sasha Abramsky, *Conned: How Millions Went to Prison, Lost the Vote, and Helped Send George W. Bush to the White House* (New Press, New York, 2006); and Elizabeth A. Hull, *The Disenfranchisement of Ex-Felons* (Temple University Press, Philadelphia, 2006). The US Civil Rights Commission's report on the 2000 election can be accessed on the internet at http://www.usccr.gov/pubs/vote2000/report/exesum.htm (accessed April 2014). A good account of voter caging appears on the PBS show *NOW*, see http://www.pbs.org/now/shows/330/index.html (accessed April 2014). For a long-range historical account of the politics of Florida and the election of 2000, see David R. Colburn, *From Yellow Dog Democrats to Red State Republicans: Florida and Its Politics since 1940* (University Press of Florida, Gainesville, 2007).

The literature on Hurricane Katrina is growing vast. For an excellent scholarly account of pre-Katrina New Orleans, see Kent B. Germany, *New Orleans after the Promises: Poverty, Citizenship, and the Search for the Great Society* (University of Georgia Press, Athens, 2007). The most useful books on the storm and its many ramifications are Henry Giroux, *Stormy Weather: Katrina and the Politics of Disposability* (Paradigm, Boulder, CO, 2006); Chester Hartman and Gregory D. Squires, eds., *There Is No Such Thing as a Natural Disaster* (Routledge, New York, 2006); Christopher Cooper and Robert Block, *Disaster: Hurricane Katrina and the Failure of Homeland Security* (Times Books, New York, 2006); Michael Eric Dyson, *Come Hell or High Water: Hurricane Katrina and the Color of Disaster* (Basic Books, New York, 2006); and probably the most readable account, which is hardest both on President Bush and Mayor Nagin, is Douglas Brinkley, *The Great Deluge: Hurricane Katrina, New Orleans and the Mississippi Gulf Coast* (Morrow, New York, 2006). The Organization of American Historians has published a special issue containing an interesting array of essays on Katrina, see "Through the Eye of Katrina: The Past as Prologue?" *Journal of American History*, 94 (December 2007): 693–876.

For case studies of black mayors, including those in New Orleans, a good place to begin is David R. Colburn and Jeffrey Adler, eds., *African American*

Mayors: Race, Politics, and the American City (University of Illinois Press, Urbana, 2001). David Lublin's, *The Paradox of Representation: Racial Gerrymandering and Minority Interests in Congress* (Princeton University Press, Princeton, 1977) is an incisive analysis of the dilemma facing black legislative representatives. For trenchant analyses of the failure of black politicians to revamp the system, see Robert C. Smith, *We Have No Leaders: African-Americans in the Post-Civil Rights Era* (State University of New York Press, Albany, 1996) and Nikhil Pal Singh, *Black Is a Country: Race and the Unfinished Struggle for Democracy* (Harvard University Press, Cambridge, MA, 2004).

Barack Obama has told his life story in two informative books, *Dreams from My Father: A Story of Race and Inheritance* (Times Books, New York, 1995) and *The Audacity of Hope: Thoughts on Reclaiming the American Dream* (Crown, New York, 2006). In addition to these books, , the best account of Obama's pre-presidential life can be found in David Remnick, *The Bridge: The Life and Time of Barack Obama* (Vintage, New York, 2011).

Chapter 10

Not unexpectedly the literature on President Obama is expanding rapidly. For two excellent historical accounts of his ideology, see James T. Kloppenberg, *Reading Obama: Dreams, Hope, and the American Political Tradition* (Princeton University Press, Princeton, 2011) and Thomas J. Sugrue, *Not Even Past: Barack Obama and the Burden of Race* (Princeton University Press, Princeton, 2010). Randall Kennedy, *The Persistence of the Color Line: Racial Politics and the Obama Presidency* (Pantheon, New York, 2011) and Peniel Joseph, *Dark Days, Bright Nights: From Black Power to Barack Obama* (Basic Civitas, Philadelphia, 2010) offer useful insights into Obama and the myth of post-racialism. More critical of Obama's presidency are books by Frederick C. Harris, *The Price of the Ticket: Barack Obama and the Rise and Decline of Black Politics* (Oxford University Press, New York, 2012) and Robert C. Smith, *John F. Kennedy, Barack Obama and the Politics of Ethnic Incorporation and Discordance* (State University of New York Press, Albany, 2013).

Of the many books on the 2008 campaign, the most helpful are John Heilemann and Mark Halperin, *Game Change: Obama and the Clinton, McCain and Palin, and the Race of a Lifetime* (HarperCollins, New York, 2010); Richard Wolffe, *Renegade: The Making of a President* (Broadway,

New York, 2009); Michael Tesler and David O. Sears, *Obama's Race: The 2008 Election and the Dream of a Post-Racial America* (University of Chicago Press, Chicago, 2010); and Obama's campaign manager, David Plouffe, *The Audacity to Win: The Inside Story and Lessons of Barack Obama's Historic Victory* (Viking, New York, 2009). On the 2012 election and more, see Jonathan Alter, *The Center Holds: Obama and His Critics* (Simon & Schuster, New York, 2013) and Ta-Nehisi Coates, "Fear of a Black President," *The Atlantic* (September 2012), online at http://www.theatlantic.com/magazine/archive/2012/09/fear-of-a-black-president/309064 (accessed April 2014). William E. Leuchtenburg, *In the Shadow of FDR: From Harry Truman to Barack Obama* (Cornell University Press, Ithaca, NY, 2009) places Obama in the long shadow of Franklin D. Roosevelt, two presidents who confronted economic disasters.

A number of anthologies of essays appeared on various aspects of Obama's first term. The best available are Theda Skocpol et al., *Obama and America's Political Future* (Harvard University Press, Cambridge, MA, 2012); Lawrence R. Jacobs and Desmond King, eds., *Obama at the Crossroads: Politics, Markets, and the Battle for America's Future"* (Oxford University Press, New York, 2012); Robert Watson, Jack Covarrubias, Tom Lasford, and Douglas M. Brattebo, eds., *The Obama Presidency: A Preliminary Assessment* (State University of New York Press, Albany, 2012); Ama Mazama and Molefi Kete Asante, eds., *Obama: Political Frontiers and Racial Agency* (Sage, Los Angeles, 2012); Andrew J. Dowdle, Dirk C. Van Raemdonck, and Robert Maranto, eds., *The Obama Presidency: Change and Continuity* (Routledge, New York, 2011); Steven E. Schier, ed., *Transforming America: Barack Obama in the White House* (Rowman & Littlefield, Lanham, MD, 2011); and Manning Marable and Kristen Clarke, *Barack Obama and African American Empowerment: The Rise of Black America's New Leadership* (Palgrave, New York, 2009).

The most helpful monographs on Obama's first four years are Adia Harvey Wingfield and Joe R. Feagin, *Yes We Can? White Racial Framing and the Obama Presidency* (Routledge, New York, 2013; Eric Alterman, *Kabuki Democracy: The System vs. Barack Obama* (Nation Books, New York, 2011); Ruth O'Brien, *Out of Many, One: Obama and the Third American Political Tradition* (University of Chicago Press, Chicago, 2013); and Richard Wolffe, *Revival: The Struggle for Survival Inside the Obama White House* (Broadway, New York, 2010). Michael Tesler, "The Spillover of Racialization into Health Care: How President Obama Polarized Public Opinion by Racial Attitudes and Race," *American Journal of Political Science*

(July 2012): 690–704, offers important findings about Obama, racial atti-tudes, and public policy, using the Affordable Care Act as a case study. Shirley Sherrod, with Catherine Whitney, has written a powerful and honest memoir that includes her firing by the Obama administration in *The Courage of Hope: How I Stood Up to the Politics of Fear* (Atria Books, New York, 2012).

On the revival of voter suppression, see Gary May, *Bending Toward Justice: The Voting Rights Act and the Transformation of American Democracy* (Basic Books, New York, 2013) and Ari Berman, "Why Are Conservatives Trying to Destroy the Voting Rights Act?" *The Nation* (February 5, 2013), at http://www.thenation.com/article/172685/why-are-conservatives-trying-destroy-voting-rights-act?page=0,1 (accessed April 2014), and "North Carolina's Moral Mondays," *The Nation* (August 5, 2013), at http://www.thenation.com/article/175328/north-carolinas-moral-mondays (accessed April 2014). For a comprehensive account of the battles over the ballot, especially those revolving around charges of voter fraud, see Richard L. Hasen, *The Voting Wars: From Florida 2000 to the Next Election Meltdown* (Yale University Press, New Haven, 2012). Lorraine C. Minnite, *The Myth of Voter Fraud* (Cornell University Press, Ithaca, NY, 2010) argues that Republicans' charges of voter fraud are politically motivated and largely unsubstantiated. For a very different view see John Fund and Hans von Spakovsky, *Who's Counting? How Fraudsters and Bureaucrats Put Your Vote at Risk* (Encounter Books, New York, 2012).

Index

Boston (Massachusetts), 130, 190, 252
Bowers, Sam, 341
Boynton, Amelia P., 111, 112, 114, 148
Bradley, Tom, 182
Brady, Tom, 54
Branch, Taylor, 346
Branton, Wiley, 86, 87
Brauer, Carl, 81, 84
Braun, Carol Moseley, 273, 314, 315, 321
Brazile, Donna, 300, 314
Breaux, John, 241
Breitbart, Andrew, 370
Breyer, Stephen, 285n, 306
Broder, David, 253
Brooke, Edward, 146, 189, 205
Broussard, Aaron, 336
Brown v. Board of Education, 22, 33, 51, 52, 53, 54, 55, 57, 58, 60, 64, 74, 76, 79, 81, 293
Brown, Elsa Barkley, 270
Brown, Jesse, 275
Brown, Lloyd, 9
Brown, Michael, 332, 333, 334
Brown, Ronald, 255, 256, 275
Brown, Willie, 230, 233, 246
Brownell, Herbert, 59
Burk, Robert F., 54
Burwell, Dollie, 281–2
Bush, George H.W., 255, 263, 264, 266, 267, 268, 272, 274
   and Clarence Thomas, 264, 266, 267 (photo), 268, 269, 270, 271, 272, 273
Bush, George W., 307–13
   and 2000 election, 298–300, 304–6
   and 2004 election, 313
   and Africa, 338
   and Hurricane Katrina, 332, 333, 335, 336
Bush v. Gore, 306
Bush, Jeb, 299, 304
busing, 140, 142, 143, 147, 148, 186, 189, 190, 191, 192, 206, 264, 267, 353
Butts, Claudia, 263
Byrne, Jane, 212–13, 214, 215, 216
Byrnes, James F., 45

caging, 317, 324
Cain, Herman, 376
Caldwell, Arthur, 59
Califano, Joseph, 200
Campbell, William (Bill), 319
Cantor, Eric, 386
Cardin, Benjamin L., 340
Carmichael, Stokely, 120–2, 123, 125, 134, 151, 165, *see also* Student Nonviolent Coordinating Committee (SNCC)
Carswell, Harrold, 144
Carter, Jimmy, 126, 222, 223, 275(n), 281, 364, 388
   assessment of, 201
   background of, 191
   as governor, 192–3
   as president, 197–8, 199–202
   as presidential candidate (1976), 193–5
   and reelection attempt (1980), 203–4
Case of Martin Luther King, The, 83
Cavanagh, Jerome, 181
Cavanagh, Thomas, 237, 242
Celeste, Richard, 246
Chafe, William H., 48, 79
Chaney, James, 102
Charlotte (North Carolina), 219, 283
Chavis, Ben, 282
Cherry, Bobby Frank, 341
Chertoff, Michael, 332–3
Chicago (Illinois), 12, 24, 55, 58, 135, 173, 174, 205, 211–18, 235, 256, 321, 344, 345, 351, 359
Chicago Black United Communities, 214
Chicago Defender, 81
Children's Health Insurance Reauthorization Act, 366
Chisholm, Shirley, 147, 166, 222, 254
Church, Frank, 205
City of Mobile v. Bolden, 208
Civil Rights Act (1957), 59–61, 65, 68
Civil Rights Act (1960), 66
Civil Rights Act (1964), 98–9, 102(n), 244
Civil Rights Act (1968), 139
Civil Rights Division, 61, 308
Clark, James G., 110–14, 128
Clark, Robert, 154, 241